THE WAGES
OF SIN

THE WAGES OF SIN

America's Dilemma of Profit Against Humanity

JON HUER

PRAEGER

New York
Westport, Connecticut
London

Copyright Acknowledgment

The author and publisher gratefully acknowledge permission to reprint text from the cartoon *Doonesbury*.
DOONESBURY COPYRIGHT 1990 G. B. Trudeau. Reprinted with permission of Universal Press Syndicate. All rights reserved.

Library of Congress Cataloging-in-Publication Data

Huer, Jon.
    The wages of sin : America's dilemma of profit against humanity /
Jon Huer.
       p.   cm.
    Includes bibliographical references (p.   ) and index.
    ISBN 0–275–93932–4 (alk. paper)
    1. Profit—United States.   2. Economic man—United States.
3. Individualism—United States.   4. United States—Moral
conditions.   I. Title.
HC110.P7H84   1991
338.5′16′0973—dc20   91–3548

British Library Cataloguing in Publication Data is available.

Library of Congress Catalog Card Number: 91–3548
ISBN: 0–275–93932–4

First published in 1991

Praeger Publishers, One Madison Avenue, New York, NY 10010
An imprint of Greenwood Publishing Group, Inc.

Printed in the United States of America

The paper used in this book complies with the
Permanent Paper Standard issued by the National
Information Standards Organization (Z39.48–1984).

10 9 8 7 6 5 4 3 2 1

To Jonathan.
May you live in a happier world.

"How much is her gold worth in the open market?"
"Two, three million dollars."

> Two sports analysts minutes after Janet
> Evans won a gold medal at the Seoul
> Olympics, October 1, 1988

"How can we be the best dearest most generous people on earth, and at the same time so unhappy? How harsh everyone is here! How restless! How impatient! How worried! How sarcastic! How unhappy! How hateful! How pleasure-loving! How lascivious! Above all, how selfish! . . . Why do we think of nothing but our own pleasure?"

> Father Weatherbee to Will Barrett in
> Walker Percy's novel, *The Second Coming*,
> 1981

"I'm gonna make lots of money and I'm gonna be very happy!"

> A sophomore finance major, 1990

"After 5 o'clock, I close the doors of my apartment. I'm afraid to go out in the streets."

> Polla Stashevskaya, upon deciding to
> return to the Soviet Union, November 5,
> 1986

"Trust nobody—not your co-worker, not your children, and if you are president, not your chief of staff."

> William Safire, describing the vogue of
> tape-recording conversations using secret
> "body wires" December 6, 1986

Contents

Part I

Profit and Society

Chapter 1

The Profit Ethic

It may be a common tendency for each generation to think of itself as being favored by history with extraordinary events. Every generation believes its own burdens of celebration or lamentation unique and unprecedented. Observers and sages almost universally declare that their own times are "momentous," their own actions "crucial," and the consequences of their own decisions "monumental." But common sense tells us that not all generations are endowed with equal historical significance. As much as it is the privilege of every generation to think of itself as specially burdened by the troubles of its time, obviously some generations and events are more or less historically important than others.

I believe ours in American society today is one of the strangest, if not the most important, of times. Quite unprecedented in any known human experience for comparison or understanding—enough to baffle even a Charles Dickens—we face in our time the best of everything and just as surely the worst of everything. Confusion seems to reign everywhere: having so much material affluence under our control, we derive no real happiness from our abundance; surrounded by around-the-clock-entertainment at our easy disposal, we remain unfulfilled with our experience; and seeing so many smiling faces everywhere, we feel unloved and alone, unconvinced by their friendliness. With virtually everything in quantities that we cannot possibly consume or wear out, we still hunger for more of everything.

Instinctively we sense that the world we knew has now changed. Although we cannot understand or articulate this change clearly, many of us are acutely uncomfortable with it. In a nation that is so prosperous and powerful, and whose standards of living are the very envy of the world, our discontent is as profound as it is puzzling. Why do we feel this way about our lives amid the greatest possession of wealth the world has ever known? The answer to this question lies neither in the deep learning of a scholar nor in dazzling scientific research. For we can find the answer virtually everywhere we care to look in our society as well as in our private lives. But first, we must look.

Consider Sophia Collier. Eric Goode. Kent Post. Phil Akin. Brett Johnson. Bill Gates. These, like many others, are some of those who have made a million dollars before they reached the age of 30. They are justifiably the new heroes and role models of America. Their exploits are described in *Parade* magazine under the enticing title: "You Can Still Make a Million Dollars." To most Americans, they represent the thriving, prosperous, and wondrous mechanism of American entrepreneurship. They also represent the dreams of many others who toil in business and accounting classes, in computer science and management, and in countless other varieties of entrepreneurial apprenticeship. In a broader sense, these young millionaires represent America's economic ethos. "Economic consideration" as the central feature in American culture can be observed clearly in their career plans, casual conversations, daily subconscious decision-making. This economic ethos combines hard work and speculation; it is at once orderly and chaotic, rational and irrational. The outcome is an economic success story in its most spectacular form.

Then there are: Angela Helton. Stephanie Charette. Angela Spencer. Sonya Lynde. Nancee Mason. These are teenage girls unwed and pregnant. Like their counterpart millionaires, these pregnant teenagers are prodigious with their production. Each year, more than a million teenagers become pregnant, most of them unmarried. *Time* magazine, which compiled the story, described the phenomenon as the sign of "a distressing flaw in the social fabric of America." These young unwed mothers represent the many aspects of their society in which their pregnancy is merely a more visible symbol of its "distressing flaw." They represent the decline of the underlying, and in many ways pivotal, web of social network that connects one individual with another to form a human community. They also represent the vast distance between what American society *appears* to be or, rather, what we *want* it to appear to be and the way it might truly be. The incidence of teen pregnancy represents a poignant contrast against the thriving economic machine and reminds us that the absence of human community is not too far from our more prosperous surface.[1]

How can this be? What confounds the critics and observers of American society is this stark contrast—millionaires not yet 30, confident and clever and successful, existing side by side with a generation of lost souls, crushed hopes, and lonely hearts. This contradiction in American life has been observed by many, from the lighthearted comment by "Adam Smith" (not the original), "If Times Have Been So Good, Why Do We Feel So Bad?," in one of his "money books," to the more somber, scholarly observation made by David Riesman in his classic, *The Lonely Crowd*: "There is great generosity among Americans; there is also enormous meanness and mindlessness."[2] When one looks at the economic side of America, he finds plenty of consolation: thriving markets, the unbounded energies and opportunities of the entrepreneurial class, the highest standards of material consumption the world has ever known. When one looks at the cultural side of the same society, on the other hand, one finds widespread psychic emptiness, anxiety, and mistrust.

How can this be? one wonders further. How can the most prosperous nation in the world—the greatest economic triumph ever recorded—be so barren in personal happiness, so devoid of interpersonal strength that it almost verges on a silent civil war? Observers are indeed baffled by such contradictory—and irreconcilable—displays of American life. The youngster confidently planning a career in business and the pregnant teenager confronting the sorrows of life are both rather typical of America's younger population. At once hearty and heartbroken, they symbolize the strange landscape of American society so thriving and exciting, yet so empty and lonely. One is easily moved to recognize that the American economy glitters, but at the same time the human heart in it grieves.

How can this be? one continues to wonder. A society with a "distressing flaw" in its basic social fabric is also the society that produces instant millionaires and tall tales of moneymaking ventures. It is also a society whose mutual suspicion has created an astronomical consumption of locks, guard dogs, shotguns, security forces for its households. In short, it is a society of extreme contrast between economic success and personal failure, between the bulging pocketbook and broken heartstrings, and between the exciting financial calculus and the loneliness of solitary life. Nowhere in the history of mankind has a society been so strangely cast with two contrasting themes in its culture and psyche. The tension seems unbearable, its contrast incomprehensible, and its prospect unnerving even in the accustomed idioms of American optimism.

This book is an attempt to shed light on the phenomenon of contemporary American society: why Americans, being the envy of everyone else the world over, are so unhappy with themselves. But oddly, those who are unhappy with their private lives are not necessarily unhappy with their *society*. As they search for remedies to their private unhappiness, they remain largely ignorant about their society, which shapes and goads their private yearnings and moods. Hence our most urgent need here is to put American society in some sort of perspective so that our private bafflement, anxiety, and fear can find their clarification and framework. Feeling must be complemented by thinking in order to arrive at any understanding at all.

To accomplish this, we need to establish a foothold, intellectually speaking, from which an effort to comprehend our present predicament can be launched. We should begin this process by introducing two rather traditional concepts: the Profit Ethic and the Social Ethic in their more idealized forms.

The Profit Ethic as used here is not the simple ancient habit of adding as much of one's profit to a product or service as possible. Nor is it in the historically recent origin of spectacular economic ventures and profits. It is more of a "state of mind," which is rather subconsciously internalized. It is also an all-encompassing and fairly overwhelming generalization of life and thought. The Profit Ethic begins and ends with the individual's self-interest. Since it originates and ends in self-interest, it is free from obligations to be "human" and to take place in a human "community." Nor is it necessary for the self-interested parties to form human "relations" among them to make the ethic possible. Strictly speaking, profit is not—nor does it need be—"human." Money, profit's concrete medium, indeed requires no personality, no nationality, no humanity. Profit-making, if we ignore its self-serving rhetoric, can operate just as well or better by nonhuman agents. A profit created by absentee ownership is just as good as that produced by direct human toil and sweat. The Profit Ethic is impersonal in its existence, nonhuman in its character, and absolute in its command. A dollar is a dollar whether in the emperor's possession or in the beggar's or however it is accumulated. Profit, once made, becomes an object all by itself, removed and aloof from the humanity through whose hands it is first materialized.

On the opposite side of the Profit Ethic, providing the balance in the push and pull of life, stands the Social Ethic. The Social Ethic is the nemesis, and the very antithesis, of the Profit Ethic. It is the social ethos of *community*, its commanding values in unselfish cooperation, in controlled individualism, in opposition to the ever-present self-interest in every individual. While the Profit Ethic represents the individual, the Social Ethic represents the interests of society. In family obligations, in social duties, and in deference to tradition and collective images, the Social Ethic demands submission of self-interest to the larger requirements of social life.

As two antagonistic forces of life, the Profit Ethic and the Social Ethic wage an endless battle to occupy the body and soul of mankind. At different times and in different places, one or the other ethic triumphs and dominates. In the Middle Ages, the Social Ethic was preeminent, the Profit Ethic severely discouraged and often punished. In the contemporary Soviet Union, although diminishing as a model, and Amish community, it still commands sway. It was not really until the latter part of the eighteenth century, with the Industrial Revolution and other more theoretical developments, that the Profit Ethic as a philosophical system made its appearance in the human consciousness. To be sure, there had been many historical

displays of self-interest. But such displays of small greed had never transformed a society or an age into the faithfuls of self-interest until our own
times. Greed, the more crude, personalized form of self-interest, may be
partially responsible for the Profit Ethic in America today, but it is only
partially so. Other people in other historical times also had greed in their
hearts. But never did they transform greed into a society's all-pervading
ethical system. Hence the Profit Ethic is unique as a historical fact; in its
pervasiveness it is also peculiar to contemporary American society. Those
who live by the ethic may or may not be aware of greed, or even "profit,"
as a goal of their conscious daily effort. But today, at the peak of moneymaking commitment, many ordinary Americans are only vaguely aware
of their motive. The Profit Ethic is now an established fact of life in America
to such an extent that few are consciously thinking about greed as a factor.
As a habit of mind, still, it commands full control.

As the Profit Ethic dominates a society or an era, the Social Ethic declines
in corresponding ratio, and vice versa. The contest between the two has
been a historical battle of great proportions: many kings and kingdoms were
toppled in its name; many heart-rending battle cries were heard and many
battles fought over one ethic or the other; many ideas rose and declined in
the rise and decline of either ethic.

In American society, the battle was fought early and the result was fairly
decisive. John Stuart Mill, the great nineteenth-century defender of utili-
tarian capitalism, marveled at the voraciousness of American dedication to
moneymaking: "[The] whole of one sex is devoted to dollar hunting, and
of the other to breeding dollar hunters."[3] (Except now *both* sexes are devoted
to dollar hunting.) "We are living in a money culture," observed John
Dewey in the 1920s. "Its cult and rites dominate. . . . The philosophy appropriate to such a situation is that of struggle for existence and survival
of the economically fit." While vision of "personal advantage and resolute
ambition" for money is highly prized, the philosopher mused, "sentiment
and sympathy would be at the lowest discount."[4] Shepard Clough, author
of books celebrating the "American way of business," was already pron-
ouncing American society an economic triumph, if not that of the Profit
Ethic, in the 1950s:

If, as in the days of ancient Greece and Rome, it were the style to write great epics
of national accomplishments, American poets would have at their disposal a theme
which does not have its equal in all history—the achievement of unsurpassed economic well-being. Indeed there has never been a people so abundantly provided
with the material things of life as the American people of today.[5]

"In no place in western culture," he observed, "has this ideology been more
marked than in the United States." As if to bear witness to this observation,
David Pauly's review of a contemporary book titled *Greed and Glory on*

Wall Street sums up the fall of Lehman Brothers, one of the prominent brokerages on Wall Street:

In the summer of 1983 Lehman Brothers president Lewis Glucksman—greedy for power—overthrows the firm's chairman, Pete Peterson. But within nine months the other Lehman partners, worried about their personal fortunes, force Glucksman to sell the 134-year-old firm and give up control. During the struggle, everybody at Lehman seems to accuse everyone else of being greedy—and maybe they were all right. Nearly everyone ends up much richer than before—especially Glucksman and Peterson.[6]

Then, not very long after this episode, it is revealed that Drexel Burnham Lambert doled out $260 million in bonuses to its employees *less than two months before its financial collapse.* What galled observers was the fact that the bonuses were twice the size of Drexel's defaulted debt, which had precipitated its fall. More than that, "a few still unnamed Drexel hotshots got bonuses of more than $10 million each in a year when Drexel lost $40 million." These bonuses, an involved attorney argued, might have "rendered Drexel insolvent." Characteristically, Drexel officials called the uproar "much ado about nothing." It is indeed much ado about nothing. Even during its bankruptcy its caretaker executives received salaries of over $1 million a year. To say that American society's preoccupation has always been making money is really to say nothing new. Its mind-set is as much a matter of sociopolitical system as a matter of daily subconscious. As in all things, however, a reckoning of that mind-set is in order.

Thus the rise of the Profit Ethic creates new young millionaires; it creates the decline of the Social Ethic, the sorrows of unwed teenage mothers. The root of America's Profit Ethic is founded in the premise of man as a solitary being, struggling to survive in a state of nature while surrounded by his competitors, who are equally bent on their own survival. It is in the name of survival that self-interest is defined, and it is in the defense of self-interest that the Profit Ethic finds its articulation. In a "state of nature" one's survival is the prime reason for existence. One's survival determines the reason for and the extent of one's relations with others. Survival of one has nothing to do with that of another member; in its pure form it is literally every man for himself. If one can survive at the expense of another, so be it, there being neither moral nor practical rule against it. Often, in fact, one's chances for survival improve if someone else's chances for survival diminish in a competitive state of nature. The Profit Ethic is the more generalized expression of this survival theme, whether in nature or in society, which has emerged only recently.

The Social Ethic, on the other hand, defines *happiness*, not survival, as the prime reason for its existence. It derives its definition from the assumption that man left the state of nature not to survive better against one another, but to be *happy* with one another. Unlike survival, however, happiness *depends* on one's happy relations with others and relations among all with all. In society one cannot be happy unless others around him—thus forming social relations—are also happy. If one is unhappy, then the happiness of others is immediately affected. Human happiness in society cannot be ensured or strengthened by the unhappiness of others, because it is not a limited, scarce commodity like food. One cannot be happy alone in society; one is happy with others or unhappy with others. Unlike survival, the price of one's happiness is divided among all members of society. One can survive alone, but one cannot be happy alone. Society—unlike the state of nature—exists to make *everyone* happy. Human beings seek happiness, beyond survival, because they have the *means* (love, poetry, agony) by which that happiness can be experienced. Those means are unique to man in society.

They establish society as the means of pursuing that happiness, which must ensure happiness for all—not just for the select few or even the majority. The Profit Ethic results, if not as its intended goal, in the happiness of a few or the majority at best, because of the very principle of self-interest. In short, the Social Ethic assumes that society is the means of happiness and justice its end. To be human and social is to be at once happy and just. If happiness is the purpose of life, then justice is what validates that happiness as true. Happiness requires justice, and justice makes happiness possible. How is this happiness in society—as opposed to the Profit Ethic, which does not presuppose human happiness as its purpose—made possible?

The question may be rephrased as: how would the Social Ethic, if it had its way, define society to ensure happiness for all? In principle, it is simple enough to define. A society characterized by the Social Ethic would have to contain the following elements: (1) its social structure would be based on *civility*, not barbarity; (2) its social relations would reflect *community*, not self; (3) its personal moral code would prefer *spirituality*, not sensuality; and finally (4) its material management would require *rationality*, not caprice.

In these sets of contrasting concepts, the thinking piece to complement our feelings, we now have a rough intellectual tool of analysis. In order to see the two ethical systems more clearly and to comprehend our own present lives and society more clearly in the process, let us elaborate these concepts below.

CIVILITY VERSUS BARBARITY

Civility is a measure of social progress, the distance from which mankind as a whole has evolved from barbarity. Civility is the stuff of what we call civilization—conduct based on rules; the assumption of formality that things follow certain rules in society. The Social Ethic in civility makes it possible for one to deal with another person without fear of arbitrariness. It creates respect for life among those in high places as well as those in lowly social stations. Civility refines manners among individuals and establishes rules among groups and nations, making the idea of trust and peace possible in practice and theory. It represents the simple assumption that life in society is secure from sudden shifts of whims and caprice with catastrophic results in personal fortunes and happiness. To make civility possible, we create society, form human networks within a system of rules and predictability, establish permanent institutions, and legislate and live by certain principles of civilization, such as ideas of freedom, individual security, and happiness. Civility is the core of a social structure that creates the necessary framework of trust to make the Social Ethic possible as reality.

The Profit Ethic, however disguised, represents the notion of barbarity and is the antithesis of civility. Barbarity assumes that there are only rules of nature. In nature, men are pitted against one another in the primeval struggle for survival. Where rules of conduct are accepted as agreeable, such as in sport, it may be so as a simple device for winning, survival, or means to an end, which is imperative and absolute. Means and ends converge in the process, and the end result is measured in the size of power—raw, arbitrary, and self-justifiable as all power must be. Barbarity, even among those who hold the principle as dear, is not necessarily identical to evil, the inability of some to be "human" or civilized. It is simply without rules of morality outside its own rules of conduct. It is anchored primarily in the rules of survival, and its origin derives from the state of nature. What barbarity implies is fairly explicit: *there are really no rules in survival and, by extension, in the world of profit ethic.* Rules are perceived and established as expediency, a matter of convenience to achieve the ends in view. Barbaric conduct may display all the forms of social and civilized niceties, but power play can instantaneously and arbitrarily change the form and substance according to the power's very own rules.

COMMUNITY VERSUS SELF

The idea of human happiness materializes in the reality of community, which is a place of focus for individual consciousness and collective action. Community is diffused and subconscious, its existence more a matter of mind than concrete physical existence. Hence its absence is more *felt* than seen. A man who lives in a remote area, away from actual human contact, can still feel the sense of community around him, while a man who lives in a crowded urban complex may feel its keen absence. The Social Ethic of community sees "others" as the center of all human relations and human relations as the form that happiness takes as its concrete instances. It assumes that no happiness is possible outside a community of human beings. This ethic is all-encompassing for every member of the community, especially those weak, injured, and poor. Community protects the powerless from predatory powerholders and ensures a modicum of social justice. The idea of community converges on equality among all members—large and small, old and young, strong and weak. The ethic also promotes civil tolerance for those who display different views or demeanors. It is represented in what may loosely be called a "group spirit," a sense of mutual dependence, both emotional and material, as a normal state of existence. The ethic is realized in childrearing and socialization practices, in the unseen webs of mores and folkways, in role definitions and public morality. In the rules of conduct and social policy as well as in subconscious traditions and diffused values, self and ego are subordinated to the larger ethos of community.

The Profit Ethic, on the other hand, is essentially a self-generating process. It begins and ends in the self and in the self's definition of interest. There is nothing more fundamental to the Profit Ethic than the notion of self and self-interest. It has had its defenders and critics in its short history. To its defenders, self-interest is not necessarily based on evil intentions, nor does it necessarily result in evil outcomes. Adam Smith, one who first proclaimed the Profit Ethic in terms of self-interest, saw self-interest as not only good for economics, but also as essential for human happiness and collective welfare. There *must* be self-interest for any aspiring society to become happier and wealthier. Self-interest creates happiness in a round-about way. This every-man-for-himself ethic is self-generating simply because it requires no special social instruction. In other words, self-interest need not be taught. It comes naturally. It assumes that everyone in society, as in nature, owes no one but himself the burden of survival. In this assumption, the self is permanently on alert, in search of the weak, the slow, the gullible as the target of its warfare. In its pure form, the self sees the world around it as war of everyone against everyone. It is the proverbial state of nature. This main theme of self-interest—from Adam Smith, all through socialist and Marxist criticisms, the Keynesian Revolution, the Welfare State, and finally to our own Yuppies and Me Generation—has been singularly consistent. Often couched in terms like *enlightened* or *benign*, the idea is that self-interest is the source of all social progress, is balanced in the marketplace of supply and demand by an "invisible hand" (Smith's phrase), and is inspiration for vitality and creativity in individual motivation. Without self-interest fully encouraged and developed, the ethic goes, there is no personal happiness, no Western civilization, and simply no meaning of life to speak of. As such, the Profit Ethic assumes that every word uttered, every action taken, every plan contemplated by everyone is motivated by self-interest. This is one single thrust of the Western world in its modern history of industrialism, material progress, warfare, and culture.

SPIRITUALITY VERSUS SENSUALITY

If the Social Ethic's public principle is summed up in community, then its individual morality is reflected in the idea of spirituality. By spirituality

I do not mean religious dogma or following, but as an idea against the "physical," the "sensory," or, in short, the notion of sensuality as the stuff of our reality. Spirituality thus qualified is what confers upon mankind its proper distinction from other animals and from its own primeval past. Without a proper Social Ethic as elaborated and advanced in our modern world, animals and cavemen lack the spiritual quality—the quality of mind that conceives of things and meanings beyond the here-and-now, materialist terms—through which "humanity" is defined. Essential to spirituality, among others, stand the conceptions of art, perfection, heroism, faith, values, love, and many general and specific meanings of life as each individual conceives them. To that end society educates its young, promotes its cultural activity, encourages the arts, erects monuments to heroic deeds and legends, strives for perfection, ideal and real, perpetuates the family institution, and teaches the values of love and sacrifice.

If self-interest is the locomotive of society and the motive of individual action in the Profit Ethic, sensuality is the means by which self-interest is expressed. The Profit Ethic conceives everything in terms of concrete, specific values (e.g., how many, how much, how big, how heavy, how hard, how beneficial) that can be immediately determined by seeing, measuring, and processing. The ethic cannot conceive of the value of anything, much less things "spiritual," unless it is visible, measurable, and obtainable in specific terms, precisely because it cannot put something as vague and vexing as spirituality—or morality or humanity, for that matter—in terms that are not immediately and personally comprehensible. The Profit Ethic assumes comfortably, seeing no logical or empirical contradiction in the assumption, that the marketplace of supply and demand is strictly without morality. It is an amoral place where the forces of necessity—production, supply, consumption, profit, demand—come into contact with one another. As such, it is impossible for the ethic to conceive of humanity, morality, or spirituality in the market behavior of society. The difficulty of reconciling the Profit Ethic with spirituality is almost as acute as that of a businessman taking a vow of poverty. For the businessman, things must be immediate, concrete, and specific in numbers, weights, and values; it is the surface world of sensuality, the senses, and physical presence, not the aggravating uncertainty of spirituality, morality, or humanity, that counts, and count everything must in the world of profit.

RATIONALITY VERSUS CAPRICE

Rationality as a concept has had varied uses in modern social thought, many of them uncomplimentary, and rightfully so. Among the more uncomplimentary characterizations is Max Weber's famous description of rationality as a balance between "means" and "ends" that is modern man's guide to his conduct in most calculating terms. But here we shall use the concept in a more neutral sense, a sense of "doing what is right in the long run." The meaning in which we use the term becomes clearer if we contrast it with the concept of "caprice," which means that the action is without regard for long-term consideration and justification. Moreover, when the term *rationality* is applied to the management of resources, it leaves little or no ambiguity in its usage. The principle is simply that we should not leave the management of social resources—material, human, cultural, intellectual—to the whims of the immediate present. The Social Ethic conceives of the management of social resources merely as temporary custody in the long run of historical existence. It is not for one individual, one generation, or even one nation to determine the welfare of its environmental bounty. A rational management implies the uses of scientific and technological as well as psychological balance sheets—in short, rationality—in the determination of production and consumption. According to this principle in the Social Ethic, life is conceived essentially in rational terms of economic justice, of posterity beyond the present, and with the world at large in view. It strives for harmony with nature and its laws, preserving its delicate balance by avoiding overproduction and overconsumption, by restraining social "vices," and by practicing prudence in material life. To achieve these ends, the Social Ethic desires a rational economic system with a long-term—that is, rational—production and consumption policy, just and fair rewards, restraints in individual competition, and economic justice for the poor.

The Profit Ethic is by definition incapable of rational social management, for profit while rationally calculated in itself is incapable of relating to any elements *outside* it. Moneymaking is almost always a blind endeavor, as it precludes all other consideration. The ethic's inability to conceive of things in rationality and balance is most clearly demonstrated in environmental damage and imbalance it is often blamed for having created. Because profit has to be calculated on each balance sheet every moment, every day, every month, every quarter, every year, not in generations, epochs, and posterity, the logic of profit-making can take no other principle into consideration. (Its nemesis, planning for long-term consideration, is normally associated with socialism and is therefore rejected.) It is so totally devoted to its own aim of multiplication that the devotion to profit may cause its own self-destruction in the long run of economic life. Contaminating the environment for immediate cost-reduction and making risky foreign loans for immediate high interests are but two examples of caprice or irrationality. The Profit Ethic conceives of life as mortal competition of everyone against everyone; it is a strategy of chances and fortunes; it is the one-shot deal of victory and defeat, even if the consequences must lay everyone and everything waste in their wake. In its pure form, the Profit Ethic cannot compromise, seek balance, or *think* in human terms, for profit requires the most

singularly predetermined course of action: it pushes, controls, and galvanizes
the very souls of those under its spell, regardless of the consequences. Profit
must increase, increase, increase.

How strong is the Profit Ethic in American society today? Or, conversely,
how strong is the Social Ethic in American society today? To answer the
first question by way of answering the second, let us hear one of the economics teachers I interviewed: "I've been teaching economics for 25 years,
first in high school and then in college. But I have never seen anything like
this; it's money, money everywhere. There used to be a sense of balance
in the student's mind, a sense of thinking about economics in terms of some
large questions of production, consumption, and distribution, or some public policy associated with economic questions. Now, the students *assume*
self-interest as a natural thing, and that everybody is selfish. There is not
even a question about it; everybody is interested in money and just about
every freshman student in Economics 101 is interested in moneymaking
right from the start. No serious philosophical questions asked. Just teach
me all about moneymaking." The teacher's reaction might be unusual, but
the phenomenon itself is certainly not.

Not too long ago, everyone was excited about trade potential with communist China, although it would mean alienating old friend and trade partner Taiwan. The consensus, however, was: too bad, but business is business
and we have to go in the end with the bigger trade partner, which is the
People's Republic of China. No one, in this bustle of speculation and excitement, remembered that they were dealing with then deadly communists.
Did it really matter that the communist was supposedly America's sworn
enemy? Profit says it did not. Ronald Reagan, still the nation's most famous
anticommunist, decided to sell subsidized wheat to the Russian communists
while he was president. How could that be? Columnist Joe Murray is
puzzled, but on reflection offers the following answer:

I'll try to explain it to you the way it's been revealed to me over the years—wisdom
that applies not just to wheat and Ronald Reagan, but to everything that ever was
or ever will be. (Yes, folks. Ye who have sought the Universal Truth are fixing to
be filled in.)
    First off, what you have to understand is what kind of issue it isn't.
    It isn't a political issue.
    It isn't an ideological issue.
    It isn't even a global issue.
    In truth—in the Universal Truth—there are no such issues. Nor are there religious
issues, moral issues, feminist issues, racial issues—you name it, it doesn't exist, at
least not as a separate entity.
    Because there is but One Great Issue. Dare we say its name?
    Economics.

And all else—politics, religion, race, creed, or color—are but sub-categories under that One Great Issue.

Sad to say, there isn't even such a thing as great literature. There are only books that people are willing to pay money for, generation after generation.

Nor does right or wrong exist, except in the sense of profit or loss. Until you can understand the One Great Issue involved here, you are going to be making things awfully tough on yourself.[7]

Does money justify everything? It nearly does. How about patriotism? Moral decency? Right and wrong? America's culture of moneymaking says none of these things matters. Money rules. Many former lawmakers and government officials actively lobby for Japanese corporations as their highly paid employees, mostly to the detriment of American companies. An economist at the Japanese embassy in Washington explains that "it is a matter of the *American system itself.*" Could American companies hire former *Japanese* lawmakers and government officials to lobby for *American* companies in Japan? An official in Japan's Ministry of Trade and Industry replies, "It would not happen, but if it did we would pay him not the slightest heed. We would treat him courteously, but he would become a *social leper.*" When Malcolm Forbes hired former defense secretary Caspar Weinberger a magazine article only with a trace of irony referred to it as Forbes's "latest acquisition."

Take, as another example, the way heroes are rewarded in America. Only days after the 1990 Super Bowl victory, the winning quarterback, Joe Montana, appears in the newspaper: "Hero To Endorse Apparel." The article is about how L.A. Gear, an athletic shoe and apparel company, considers "using the Montana name to expand into the cleated shoe business." For that, Montana will get $3 million to $5 million. On the same day, the same newspaper has a column by Anthony Lewis about Nelson Mandela, who had just been released from a South African prison. It speaks of Mandela's "air of authority," his "commanding presence," of his having "outlasted his jailers" and "survived 27 years in prison." This is the hero who was seen mending his prison clothes not so long ago.

A "group of visionaries seeking to reconcile big-time college sports with the nobler mission of higher education" is formed to find a solution to the mess. Its chairman, Father Theodore Hesburgh, president emeritus of Notre Dame, is emphatic about the cause of the crisis: "Our institutions are being dragged down by idiots," he says, "by people with no perspective of higher education." But alas, on the same day, ABC Sports is contemplating a lawsuit against Notre Dame for having ruined its college football TV package. The reason: Notre Dame broke away from the College Football Association, which, with Notre Dame as its star, had signed a five-year contract with ABC. Notre Dame broke away in order to sign its own contract with another, higher bidder, eventually to the tune of $75 million for the next five years. "The bottom line is money, and it boils down to one word—greed," says an unhappy athletic director. "Notre Dame wants all the exposure and all the money." Other lesser schools follow suit, trying to "do" another Notre Dame, but with considerably less success, however.

In America, money reconciles nicely with all that is clean and wonderful. Greg LeMond, an American who won the Tour de France cycling race, is described as "a wholesome, family-oriented athlete, who has fought adversity to rise again." For his wholesomeness, family orientation, and surmounting adversity, LeMond, who is photographed happily holding his son, will get $5 million in endorsement money. In the profit world of Wall Street, morality does not go without its worldly reward. "At a time when heroes are few and many financial wizards have seemed obsessed by greed and ambition," a magazine describes Fidelity Magellan chief executive Peter Lynch, who announced his retirement: "Lynch was a reassuring presence, a homespun stock picker who disdained the pretensions of the experts and regularly beat them all," representing "old-fashioned virtues," "a credible and trustworthy spokesman for the entire industry," "who never succumbed to the showy excesses or the sleazy morals of the Age of Milken." This moral paragon's take prior to his retirement: $10 million a year.

Rumors of war, as well as actual war, are also good for moneymaking. When President Bush sent U.S. troops to the Persian Gulf to combat Iraq's Saddam Hussein, money fever went wild with speculative frenzy. Joseph Nocera, a finance historian writing for the *New York Times*, laments: "It's amazing that we can be obsessed about money at a time like this without even a hint of remorse. Has there ever been a time when so many people have been so unabashed about viewing the possibility of war through the prism of their own personal finances? I think not." One of the primary reasons to account for this war-stock frenzy, which numbered over 500 entries of advice in the finance literature at the time, Nocera says, is that moneymaking activity, no longer confined to the wealthy, has "become part of the daily life of the middle class." In "a remarkably candid self-portrait of a new breed of American spy," an army warrant officer who spied for the Soviet Union says, "I wasn't terribly short of money. I just decided I didn't ever want to worry where my next dollar was coming from." He added, "I'm not anti-American. I wave the flag as much as anybody else."

A 1990 survey among those selected for *Who's Who Among American High School Students* reveals their central theme of life, in the words of its publisher, who conducted the survey: "Go to college, get a good job, and make money." A professor at UCLA who has tracked the attitudes of incoming freshmen for more than twenty years finds that today's students indicate that "making more money" is a "very important factor." This attitude toward money among freshmen is a big jump from twenty years ago.

Televised religion, that odd American invention, is now unabashedly intertwined with moneymaking. "The Gospel message has what every human being is looking for," declares an aide to the Reverend Robert Schuller, one of the more successful televangelists. "The problem is that we're not *marketing it*." Also called "prosperity gospel," the profiteering Christian doctrine preaches, in the words of the Reverend Robert Tilton: "That's right! You can actually tell God what you would like his part in the covenant to be. Step One: Let God Know What You Need from Him. New Car. New Job. Fitness. House. Finances. Salvation." What every human being, even a peasant, is looking for, agrees columnist George Will in his usually passionate endorsement of capitalism, is the spoilage of materialism that only money can bring about. "Given a chance," Will declares, "the peasants say, 'Please, spoil us, as quickly as possible.'" Housing and Urban Development secretary Jack Kemp insists that the Republican party "[has] got to be the party that allows people to become rich." Ironically, Bill Bennett passes up the post of the Republican National Committee chairman, citing poor pay. "I didn't take a vow of poverty," he says. All this is soon after the 1990 elections characterized by the talk of rich-poor polarization in America.

In response to this demand, the market responds with many offers of moneymaking schemes. Take, for example, this nationally advertised "Tom Vu Method," a get-rich-quick scheme in real estate investment. The television ad aired in the midwest in early 1986, goes in part like this:

Narrator: Mr. Vu came to America from a war-torn Vietnam with no money, no credit, no job, and no real estate know-how. Despite odds that would have made most people simply give up and make excuses while their problems stopped them from doing anything, Mr. Vu started from scratch with nothing, to build a multi-million dollar fortune, the very same technique you are about to learn... You'll hear exciting money-making ideas you've never heard before.

Vu: Right now, we have it made. We have everything we have ever wanted. And I'll tell you right now, anybody can do it using the system.

Narrator: Are you saying that anybody can repeat what you have done?

Vu: Yes, anybody can do it if they have a desire to succeed. Yes, they can. Just wishing and dreaming accomplishes nothing. People can sit at home and dream all day long about these fancy things they want but unless they go out and do something about it nothing ever happens.

Tom Vu proceeds to offer a two-day seminar for a fee of $300, presumably making the "secret" of moneymaking—which has made Mr. Vu a millionaire—also available to other Americans.

"Never mind the fancy dress and pumpkin coach," pleads the poor girl in a cartoon to the fairy godmother. "Can you get me into Harvard Business

School?" Of the ten "hot" career fields for women recommended by *Working Women* magazine, eight are those occupations related to moneymaking as their *sole* purpose. The "Spencer Gifts" catalog for Christmas—blessed by no less a moral authority than Mr. Art Linkletter, who promises to "hand you the prize, one million dollars," if you are the winner—offers among its list of choices "Morning Prayer Plaque," " 'Our Daily Bread' Scriptural Verse Box," " 'Christ Is the Answer' Mug," and "Superb Standing Crucifix in Gleaming Solid Brass . . . Powerful Symbol of Christian Faith," among its more pious items. But it also offers—not too many pages down—drinking glasses with pictures of "Luscious Male or Female Models" that "undress—at the drop of an ice cube" and "Hilarious Sexual Trivia Game & Book," among its profane items. This way, both God and the Devil are covered and they share equal billing in the land of the Profit Ethic.

The contemporary scene of money grabbing—advice on how to make and manage money being one of the biggest money grabbers today—may strike some as reminiscent of the pre-Crash frenzy in 1929. The fever of money—from money market to art speculation—is certainly sweeping American society today as never before. History, including Western history itself, has never seen anything like this until now: a society totally dedicated to one single purpose in life—that is, making money. Its total resources, its total government apparatus, its total science and technology, its total arts and creative energies, its total national creed, in short, its total existence, is concentrated on that savage enterprise: making money. Does this parallel the pre-Crash fever? Is there a reasonable historical parallel between the pre-Depression era and today?

The intensity with which personal desires for profit is expressed today may find its parallel in the pre-Crash frenzy. But there the parallel ends, for the nature of the money fever today is very different from that of the pre-Crash frenzy. In large historical perspective, the pre-Crash behavior was strictly *economic*, small-time speculators trying to make a fortune in that crazily enticing adventure known as the stock market. It was a behavior aimed at and motivated by a particular, specific, one-shot speculation on fortune-making. Those who participated in the fortune hunt through the stock market had been simply gripped by the fever of the moment, like those during the Gold Rush in the West a century before. Most important, they did not necessarily subscribe to what we have called a Profit Ethic as a daily habit of mind. The phenomenon, unlike today's, was *not* a psychological or cultural one. They did not think, feel, and breathe in terms of an ethic that was subconscious and internalized in their bones. Their irrationality and stupidity, as intense as they were, concerned only their economic calculations, not their basic human assumptions. When the speculation crashed and the dream of fortunes disappeared, they merely returned to themselves and their lives continued.

Today's intensity is much more than mere individual greed. It matters little whether money comes specifically from profits, wages, absentee rents, or interests. It is in the general cultural adulation of money—an almost *theological* acceptance of money as the supreme purpose of life. It is in the definition of life for every decent young man and woman in America; it is in the curriculum of schools and colleges, where apprenticeship begins seriously and in scholarly fashion; it is also in the theoretical and intellectual assumption of human nature that self-interest is a natural part of existence, as natural as the demand for food in the stomach. It is neither a specific scheme to get rich—although true to some extent—nor a moral struggle between good and evil. For the issue has been generalized and moralized as an ethical system and established as a national commitment. There is no serious debate as to whether profit is immoral or even destructive to society. There is no debate necessary now because the issue has long since been settled. All things may be debated and argued over in America, but not profit. It is business as usual as defined by the rules of the Profit Ethic. The ethic is in the daily upbringing of children as much as in the presidential address. The parent says to the child, "The world's your oyster. Go out and get what you want." The president says to the nation: "The world's your oyster. Go out and get what you want." The fever of profit, although intense, is often imperceptible because of its very routineness, casualness, and diffusiveness as an unquestionable way of life. Throughout periodic threats of recession, war, and fashionable soul-searching, discussion on the morality of profit is taboo.

As today's profit-making culture is different from the historical experience of the pre-Crash era, it is also different from similar behavior traits in other cultures. The Japanese are often described as "economic animals" in the West because of their relentless drive to subordinate themselves—almost superhuman efforts by Western standards—to business and productive activities. But such "economic" behavior among the Japanese is rather different from American economic behavior. Certainly, the Japanese are unrelenting in their work drive, but their "obsession" is with the idea of perfection in workmanship, submission to *group* thinking and feelings, fear of "losing face" with their peers and with their community—in short, their desire to be perfect for the good of *others* and *community*, not necessarily for self-interest, although there is some of that element obviously, but not primarily. (Many of these characteristics are also true of Germany, the "Japan of Europe.") In Japan, money is still a dirty word.

So the question remains: how is the Profit Ethic made possible in society? The answer is simple: by making the Social Ethic impossible. (A similar question and answer can be given for the Social Ethic.) *Neither is possible without destroying the other*. Profit cannot exist without destroying society, and vice versa.

The contest between the two ethical systems has been a historical one involving kings, armies, and the masses, shaping the ethos of a society and the fate of posterity. Like all historical events, the contest is also felt in everyone's private moments and thoughts as a young millionaire dancing in the street or as a young unwed mother crying in distress. It fashions one's vision of the world around him, either as a gigantic oyster or as sorrows and loneliness. The victory of one ethic over the other may be a historical one, but in its wake fortunes are rearranged, a new class emerges to dominate the society, and personal happiness is drastically affected one way or another. Its consequences are at once historical and personal, enormous and intimate, for the consequences of the battle shape our history and our personal lives now and beyond. Which ethical system—Profit or Social—wins determines how we shall live now and later.

This is the subject of Chapter 2.

NOTES

About the Notes: For the benefit of easy reading and my own conscious desire to avoid academic trappings, I have kept notes to the very minimum. References not directly cited in the text, especially those attributed to specific authors, however, are found in the bibliography at the end of the book. Items that are routine and factual, in which attribution is immaterial, are cited by their titles with indications of their substance whenever the titles are not self-explanatory. All italics in this book are mine unless otherwise specified.

1. It is interesting that Kevin Phillips begins his recent book, *The Politics of Rich and Poor* (New York: Random House, 1990), pp. 3–5, with reference to the contrast between the "billionaires—and the homeless" and, a page later, to the "best of times" and "the worst of times," attributed to Charles Dickens. I began this particular section of the book in early 1986, when I was teaching at the University of Wisconsin Center, Fond du Lac, Wisconsin. I showed the rough draft to some colleagues at the time for their comments. My own date for the ideas thus established, I have decided to leave those references in the text as they are, although Mr. Phillips's use of the ideas (his billionaires and the homeless, as opposed to my millionaires and teenage mothers) certainly predates mine. This is not the first time two people have thought about the same thing independently of each other. I suppose Mr. Phillips was struck by the same incongruity of contemporary American society as I was, but on a path of inquiry different from mine, as the reader will soon recognize.

2. David Riesman, *The Lonely Crowd* (New Haven, CT: Yale University Press, 1965), 7.

3. Quoted in Joan Robinson and John Eatwell, *An Introduction to Modern Economics* (Berkshire, England: McGraw-Hill, 1973), 28.

4. John Dewey, *Individualism Old and New* (New York: Capricorn Books, 1962), 12–13.

5. Shepard Clough, *The American Way: The Economic Basis of Our Civilization* (New York: Thomas Y. Crowell, 1953), 1.

6. David Pauly, "Looking Out for No. 1," *Newsweek*, 10 February 1986.

7. Joe Murray, "Economics is Everything," *Milwaukee Journal*, 23 August 1986.

Chapter 2

Profit Without Humanity

Less than two decades after Michael Harrington's *The Other America* prompted the nation to wage a war on poverty, the government of the United States declared that poverty no longer existed in America. Harrington's second book on poverty in America, closely following the government's declaration of no more poverty, received hardly any attention.[1] With the Affluent Generation of Yuppies and their cultural experiments in lifestyles, in the now almost-deified science of investment and speculation, in the coming of a "Third Wave" high-technology industry, and, most important of all, in the increasing dominance of the American psyche by economics rather than by politics as a national issue, the Age of Profit has now been formally established as the cultural vocabulary of American society.

The United States has reached a point in its history where it can go on now as if poverty does not exist in its frame of mind, if not in reality. Even poverty can be converted into the illusions of affluence. There are billions of dollars still spent by those poor receiving welfare. In American society, all things have become matters of perception. Since no one actually starves or goes naked, reality has become "subjective." Even when materialism is pursued, as in "Material Girl" Madonna, it is less in concrete terms of material existence and more in the *appearance* of affluence and success. It is a matter of style.

When we speak of the Profit Ethic or Social Ethic, I am well aware of the inevitable objection that such analytical concepts run the risk of over-simplification. There is no such thing, one would easily argue, as a pure

Profit Ethic or pure Social Ethic, however such terms may be defined. Outside mathematical and logical categories, I am sure, there is no conceptual category in the affairs of man's social relations that can be considered foolproof. Besides, the two contrasting ethics are tools of understanding, not the snapshots of reality. Our task is to understand our own contemporary America, and anything that helps us with the task is welcome. The task immediately before us is an empirical and existential one. It must be accomplished, not for the sake of science but of reason, not of rigorous analysis but of self-satisfaction in understanding our personal as well as historical world. We must simplify the enormous complexity of modern economics; we must define our terms of analysis; we must present our argument; we must conclude, however tentatively. Such is the demand of life. We must go forward.

Whether correct or not, there is no doubt that most Americans believe in the pure form of capitalism—Adam Smith's kind—as the representation of their economic system and moneymaking as their purpose of life, adapted to today's version of capitalism. All this is preliminary to the argument that "social consideration" and "profit consideration" are inherently incompatible as a simple historical fact and personal experience. We *cannot* have both profit and community.

The dilemma between profit and society has been historically established. Where profit thrives, society suffers; where society thrives, profit suffers. The "strong" societies of the past and present—the Middle Ages, the Soviet Union until recently, and the Amish community, among others—have always existed at the expense of profit behavior. In these societies past and present, profit-making in whatever form is subject to severe penalties, both physical and psychological. Their commitment to "civility," "community," "spirituality," and "rationality"—in their various definitions and practices—precludes "barbarity," "self," "sensuality," and "caprice" as their nemeses.

Society, as opposed to profit, has thrived often in an authoritarian political environment, which is tightly controlled by either political ideology or religious theology or both. Profit, on the other hand, has thrived in an open field, in liberal and individualist environments with a competitive marketplace at the center of its focus. Historically, society has brought about community solidarity, spiritual integrity, and personal security among its positive achievements. Profit, on the other hand, has promoted egalitarianism, liberal-democratic institutions, and material progress among its positive results. But it has also been a historical fact that one set of achievements has always been at the expense of the other, for the two *cannot* exist together and prosper together. The rise and fall of one ethic is best measured, thus, by the rise and fall of the other ethic in their historical contest.

Comprehension of the rise of the Profit Ethic in American society is better served if we view profit-making in two distinct historical phases in

American psychology. For lack of more convenient terminology I would settle for *capitalism* and *commercialism* to refer to the two phases.

Capitalism is the early phase of moneymaking, mainly as a system of production. It is the "old" form of industrial profit-making personified by the captains and giants of industry, their respective movers, shakers, and dynasty makers, and demonstrated by their machines, assets, and products. It was and is to some extent today a war of few industrial warlords against other warlords, capitalists against other capitalists. It is a fierce competition with mortal consequences and enormous casualties, to be sure. But even at the peak of this capitalist war, *"society" remains relatively intact.* The masses, although affected in many economic ways by the war, are innocent by-standers, not participants. As workers and cannon fodder in the war, the masses are the mere pawns of capitalism, essentially standing outside the struggle. Their own community—the network of human bonds, ties and communication, personal feelings and beliefs, moral principles, and what-ever else forms the psychological basis of their community—remains largely intact and unaffected by the ravages of capitalist war.

When I said above that profit and society cannot coexist and prosper, I spoke a little too soon. For the two systems *can* exist together, however briefly, like two trains from opposite directions. Although the two trains move in two different directions they will briefly parallel as they pass each other, and in that frozen moment we can say they run together. History is a slow train, and its two opposite events—profit and society—move fairly slowly, as all historical events do.

The rise of capitalism itself was at the expense of society, especially at the end of the Middle Ages, which began its decline as capitalism began its ascent. Toward the peak of "material" industry, or the "smokestack" phase in our industrial history, society struggled to maintain its influence. The family was threatened by the new profit system; old habits and manners no longer held sway in the advent of urbanization and individualism; streets became a source of fear and strangeness; traditional morality was breaking down in every aspect of its existence in the rising tide of money. Society gradually lost its footing with the push and pull of capitalist development. As capitalism's material production, consumption, and profit marched on obliviously and relentlessly, community crumbled. Family life, sexual mores, neighborhoods and streets, and traditional morality finally gave way, and profit triumphed over society. It is helped by the convenient historical fact that in America "society" had always been weak even before the advent of industrial capitalism. Capitalism—the crude, ruthless form of money-making practiced largely among the industrial warlords—was now trans-formed into commercialism, and the Social Ethic gave way to the Profit Ethic.

Commercialism, in brief, can be seen as an advanced form of capitalism. It is much more psychological and cultural than real. It is a widespread but intangible practice and belief, a frame of mind, that moneymaking is the purpose of life and self-interest is the God-given nature of mankind. For ordinary Americans, every day and everywhere it is a game of cat-and-mouse, of nerve and anxiety, of perception and appearance. More than cash registers and increasing profit margins, it is a "portfolio" status, the ability to participate in the cultural sport of money-investing and money talk more than the size of one's assets. As such, what used to be a war of few against few in the capitalist era is now a game of all against all, every commercial agent against every commercial agent. Instead of being bystanders or cannon fodder, the masses now actively participate in the commercial phase of moneymaking. Which is to say that it demands their inner commitment. It is not enough to say that one likes capitalism; one must *believe* in it. Capitalism used to dominate the pocketbook; commercialism now dominates the soul.

As capitalism becomes successful in material production and consumption, it brings about its second phase of success—that is, commercialism. When commercialism replaces capitalism as a representative of the Profit Ethic, however, the destruction of society is completed. What used to be called society (civility, community, and so forth) is now but a memory as the Profit Ethic becomes the new, all-encompassing way of life. By the time capitalism successfully becomes commercialism, the profit system has replaced society by necessarily destroying it. For the Profit Ethic cannot thrive without devouring its rival, the Social Ethic and its community. Just as spectacular as the rise of the Profit Ethic, so has been the fall of the Social Ethic in America.

During Reagan's two terms as president, which to many epitomized this Profit Ethic, the so-called sleaze factor dogged his administrations. It was a charge that the Republicans, and especially the "Reaganites," were a party of the "politics of greed," to use columnist David Broder's words. This charge gathered its momentum during the "Deavergate" in 1986, in which Michael Deaver, Reagan's former deputy chief of staff and most loyal friend, was accused of influence peddling. A certain amount of influence peddling has always existed in American politics, and former politicians or government officials becoming well-paid lobbyists for private interests is nothing new. But with the Reagan Republicans in power, however, this sleaze or greed factor seemed to have become symbolic of something much larger, much more subtle and cultural, beyond the simple intersection of politics and economics in pursuit of personal profit. Broder's observation is pertinent:

What is striking now is the brazenness of the *commercialization* of contacts, the absolutely *unabashed* exploitation of government service for private gain. It is this which is different and disturbing to many of old Washington hands, Republicans as well as Democrats.[2]

This brazen and unabashed selling was becoming so rampant in the nation's capital—and thought so normal and expected—that Mr. Broder was moved to cite a former congressman (a Mr. Barber B. Conable) because he had "turned his back on huge retainers" and decided against the tradition of commercializing his influence. However unsettling, it is Mr. Deaver, not Mr. Conable, who is the quintessential American in the mold of the Profit Ethic. The Deavers are the rule; the Conables, an exception.

Let us backtrack a little to see how this has come about. First, there is the "natural self" in each individual as the source of physical existence and its limited consciousness. The self by logic cannot perceive "other" human beings, aside from its own offspring perhaps, as important, for it is totally preoccupied with its own survival. This is time before society, before consciousness, before civilization. Every natural self is on a collision course with every other natural self. It is every-man-for-himself in its most original form.

Second, society is formed to tame this wild primeval self, bent on its own survival at the cost of all else. Society creates community as the psychological substance of society. In it, "others," more than self, emerge as the focal point of social relations and happiness. Individual impulses are controlled and self-interest harmonized with social constraint. With the help of religion, the state transforms the wild man into a community man. His existence is unexciting and eventless, but is now characterized by security and predictability.

Third, somewhere along the historical development of mankind—toward the end of the Middle Ages—comes the revelation, especially after a long period of "society" over nature, that the wild "self" deserves to be the center of human existence once again. This new thought matures historically about the latter part of the eighteenth century, which goes by its historical name of the Age of the Enlightenment. The "light" in this historical drama is the idea that the individual is more important than society. Thus the struggle between society and self is now waged in earnest. Every human struggle needs a philosophy to justify the struggle and encourage the followers, so a "philosophy of the self"—known variously as capitalism in economics, freedom in art, religion, and politics—emerges. In the entire history of economic thoughts and activity, this is perhaps the most crucial time, because it was then that the idea of self-interest became a legitimate movement, slogan, and faith for the first time.

Self-interest, regulated through the free marketplace by its own balance of supply and demand, would become the "driving power to guide men to whatever work society is willing to pay for" and sustain itself for centuries as the creed of the West. To Adam Smith, one of the new economic philosophers, self-interest is a wonderful, benign, and wholly moral mechanism. The market maintains the just price through the balance of demand and supply. If demand for one product goes up, thus increasing its price, the price is immediately stabilized by other manufacturers who join in for the high profit. If too many manufacturers are involved so as to create a slump in the field, then production will be reduced until price and profit are balanced once again. In the words of Robert Heilbroner, who paraphrases Smith:

Through the mechanism of the market, society will have changed the allocation of its elements of production to fit its new desires. Yet no one has issued a dictum, and no planning authority has established schedules of output. Self-interest and competition, acting one against the other, have accomplished the transition.[3]

Fourth, for reasons that are historical, capitalism and its philosophical defense make great progress, increasing material benefits, mass-producing goods and services, raising the standard of living the likes of which the world has never seen before. In spite of the criticisms from the socialists, Marxists, and utopians, among others, and the glaring examples of industrial cruelty and poverty, the world at large is fast becoming converted to capitalism and its miracles. The United States stands at the forefront of this remarkable rise of moneymaking, adopting its philosophy earlier and more thoroughly than any other place or society. Its historical preeminence in the "New World" is apt, for it is here that capitalism is established for the first time in history as a national creed. With no feudal ghost to contend with, the creed of self-interest—"life, liberty, and the pursuit of happiness"—finds its fullest development on America's virgin soil and in America's virgin society. In short, the United States becomes a capitalist society in its *purest possible form*—only to be temporarily slowed during the Great Depression. The success of this profit-making system is overwhelming, especially during the decades following World War II, and its philosophy becomes unassailable.

Fifth, as capitalism makes its stride toward perfection, its nemesis, society (or community), deteriorates as a *necessary* condition for the other's success. As capitalism succeeds, its philosophy of Profit Ethic also succeeds in making itself the philosophy of the new age. But as the Profit Ethic rises in its acceptance at large, its counterpart in society, the Social Ethic, declines in correct proportion. For self-interest in the Profit Ethic is possible to dominate only if the restraining community influences in the Social Ethic decline or are absent. Social conditions deteriorate and community solidarity disintegrates as the economic triumph is demonstrated and lionized in every dimension. With affluent living standards in material abundance and corresponding leisure activity so visible and irrefutable, gradual increases in community deterioration and personal unhappiness are gladly overlooked.

People generally notice the rising living standards and longer stretches of their pocketbooks much more readily than the deterioration in the quality of their social and inner life. As always, human nature welcomes glad tidings and overlooks unhappy truths.

Amid this profit boom and self-congratulation, the person who points out the declining "society" is quickly labeled a cynic, a negative person who should leave it if he cannot love it. It is indeed difficult to be a critic in times of economic progress and abundant pleasures of life. In a self-satisfied society it is not easy to argue against progress with some vaguely defined notions of "happiness," "spirituality," or "humanity." These are mere words; economic progress in numbers, graphics, and VCRs is real. Politics gradually turns into economics, and the pocketbook becomes virtually the only source of national interest and debate. That "society" has been lost, that the Social Ethic has been defeated by the Profit Ethic, remains only marginally interesting if at all, especially among those who make up the parts for the grinding economic machine. Through the peak of industrial production and material consumption, with the ever-increasing means for self-agreement, capitalism becomes the undisputed god of American society and the Profit Ethic its undisputed gospel.

Finally, the Profit Ethic goes through one last phase: that is, capitalism becomes commercialism, where the human soul itself is finally converted to money. All the way through the triumph of capitalism and its Profit Ethic, the loss of society is not entirely unnoticed. There are critics of crude moneymaking. There is the memory of the "good old days" recalled by those who still remember considerable *human* elements in social life in the community. And most important, there is the residual, instinctive reaction among us to the new moneymaking culture that something is not right with the material world. But the critical voice is small and weak and is easily ignored. Often the critics either join the new ethical system or die out of attrition, the good old memory fades as the old generation succumbs to time, and the instinctive residue from community consciousness is simply outlasted and overmatched by the new tide of material progress and "life-styles." The soul may meet its reckoning, but the flesh is thoroughly in agreement with itself.

So at this stage of the Profit Ethic's progression a generation of new men and women emerges, fully internalized with the new creed of moneymaking as naturally as the medieval men and women were with the idea of salvation. With society and its ethic no longer in restraining contention, the Profit Ethic thrives almost in a vacuum or, rather, in a "favorable" environment for its prosperity. Its nemesis largely defeated and gone, the profit system now gets its unquestioned adulation from all quarters of society. The president praises it; colleges and universities eagerly seek to "serve" the business community by training its future money changers; the business of business-making thrives as a new industry; money counting (called accountancy) naturally rises to the top of occupational prestige and economic rewards; the phrase *bottom line* becomes so absolute that it shuts up any further argument about human welfare; television commercials and magazine advertisements colorfully display the new affluent generation; and everyone everywhere advises everyone how to make money and makes money doing it. Money begets money, and commercialism is the new order of the day. There are no poor people in America—only consumers with smaller expendable incomes.

The Age of Profit has begun its reign, and Everyman has become the Money Man and every soul has become commercialized. The Profit Ethic celebrates its epic triumph over the Social Ethic in America.

Not all is well with self-interest and its Profit Ethic, however. There is still the small matter of conflict between self and community. The Social Ethic is not entirely dead. However irritating, self-interest raises its head at inconvenient times, to cause minor pains and pauses. In other words, it demands analysis.

The problem of self-interest was of course the central issue in Thomas Hobbes's theory of man in the state of nature *as well as* in society. What is man like to Hobbes? He reasoned, either as psychological facts or as biological necessities, that man *had to* be in constant motion for power over others. This model of man's nature, the forerunner of the modern-day Profit Ethic, eventually resulted in the model known as the "possessive market society," where men "must be in a continual opposition to each other." If we assume any need for community in social life at all, a question is inevitable in this assumption: *Can people be nice to each other* when the Profit Ethic dominates their hearts and souls? The answer is, of course, no. In the more academic tone of Professor C. B. MacPherson, who explains the Hobbesian dilemma, the answer can be quoted more fully:

The dilemma remains. Either we reject possessive individualist assumptions, in which case our theory is unrealistic, or we retain them, in which case we cannot get a valid theory of *obligation*. It follows that we *cannot now expect a valid theory of obligation* to a liberal-democratic state in a possessive market society.[4]

The meaning becomes clearer if we just substitute "community" for "obligation." In other words, we cannot be nice to our neighbors while we continually covet their money, as they do ours. We cannot have the cake (community) and eat it (profit), too. The dilemma may be further clarified in the following two questions. First, what happens to a profit system in the long run when it has little or no community in the society in which the profit system itself must find its anchor? Put another way, can the Profit Ethic alone sustain a population of men, women, and children as a "human" group? Second, if society has indeed disappeared, crushed by profit, what is it that we now call society? We still maintain institutions; we still fall in love, marry, produce children, and have family; we still use the term *human relationships* in our relations with other human beings; we describe our experiences and feelings to others and they to us; and so on. In other words, we still have the same social forms and its institutionalized habits that we have always had. We still work and go home after work; at home we still have family life with spouses, children and dogs; we still enjoy neighbors and friends, attend and give parties on their behalf; we still smile at others and hear about their birthdays and good deeds of the day. Is it not "society"? Although the full answers to these questions must run the whole length of this book, we will attempt to give a preliminary answer to the first question in this section and the second question in the next three chapters.

What binds people in a profit society is obviously profit or its possibility. They form trade blocs, political parties, interest groups, buyers and sellers, corporations, lobbying committees, and whatnot in order to satisfy their self-interest. Thus, in a profit society, money binds persons of various backgrounds into a reasonable whole. Although there are other pressure groups organized for the purpose of pushing some topical issues or protecting some marginal interests, the absolute majority of those who unite do so for the sole purpose of profit or its equivalent. For that purpose most people spend most of their time, energy, and intelligence. But if money binds people, then money can just as easily *un*bind them. If money speaks, then more money speaks louder and less money is heard less. Without money or its promise people could not be pulled together for any purpose. Neither politics nor religion—the two traditional forces of organization—can compel people to act without some promise of money or money-related benefits. But people united by the prospect of profit can be *de*united by either a prospect of no profit or a promise of greater profit from another source. The Devil can offer them money just as well as God himself can, and the atheists as well as the true believers. Indeed, without the help from Hobbes cited above, this is a strangely amoral state in a supposedly moral community. It is obvious that we are in a bind.

In contemporary American society there is no assumption stronger than that which says that without money motives no one will do anything. Conversely, it assumes that people will do anything for money if it is big enough. Everyone has a price. Profit motives or incentives, the assumption asserts, are the ultimate machine that runs our world and pushes men and women in it to action. But, alas, only *economic actions* can be motivated by *economic incentives*. And not everything is economic. No one should attend church for money, no one should fall in love for money, no artist should create artworks for money, no statesman should enter politics for money, no parent should raise children for money, and so on. These, among other things human beings do, are noneconomic actions. No "human" actions can ever be motivated by economic incentives any more than one can *buy* love, for what can be bought is not love. The churchgoer, the lover, the artist, and the statesman would be a phony believer, a phony lover, a phony artist, and a phony statesman—although perhaps an astute businessman— if their action were taken for money. Economically motivated actions— which account for at least the majority of actions in American society today—can only be money-related actions. Money can *motivate* people only to *to make more money* and nothing else. The fear that everything might come to a standstill in America if there were no money rewards may be slightly farfetched, but I personally hate to contemplate the possibility. How "good" a churchgoer, a lover, an artist, or a statesman one might still be if there were no self-interest promised is quite another question. One can make a reasonable guess in view of the economic incentives theory prevalent in American society.

This assumption of profit incentive as the heart and soul of America's economic machine is quite enlightening in another way. The fact that profit motive must be used to compel people to do things simply shows that things social (civility, community, and so forth) no longer exist or, if they do, do not work reliably enough to be used as motives. The perspective becomes easier to grasp if one can think of American society as a gigantic economic institution or corporation where every job is assigned a specific profit value. From family relations to patriotic duties, and all other assignments of society in between, it is more instructive to think of America as a profit-sharing economic organization than as a "society." Family relations are tax exemptions, and patriotic duties are performed with financial benefits enough to offset their attendant hardships. Everywhere one turns there is the promise of money-making, there is the instruction of moneymaking, there is the reality of money-making, and above all, there is the fun of moneymaking. How easy it is to make money in America is at an all-time high in American folklore.

However, if we take the "social" as the counterpart of the "self," the fact remains that profit-making is never conceived for a social purpose, never carried out as a social process, and never designed for social benefit. It is strictly a purpose, a process, and a benefit of self-interest and nothing more. In spite of Adam Smith's magnificent defense on the benefits of self-interest, the economic history of the last two centuries has shown that relying the whole structure of human welfare on the precarious workings of self-interest is not quite rational. A society of private automobiles is not necessarily *happier* than a community of trains or buses or where people travel on foot. That there is no greater damage to humanity inflicted by self-interest and its profit-making motive only shows that humanity still retains some control over the Profit Ethic, not that it is the ethic's own virtue in self-restraint. For no self-restraint can come from self-interest or its profit-making motive. Unlike most other human desires, there is no limit to money desired and money made, for profit is not something one can have enough of. There is no such thing as a satisfied Money Man.

Donald Trump will not be satisfied until he either loses all the money he has or gets all the money *someone else* has. There is always more profit to be made sometime somewhere. Self-restraint comes from society, a human community, never from self-interest.

Of all human skills, it is only logical that the profit-making skill is perhaps the only skill that has no redeeming *social* value. The simple fact that it is our most prized skill in our profit society only demonstrates its truism. As we have seen in the two contrasting ethical systems, "skills" that are necessary for human happiness in society are already contained in the Social Ethic, not in the Profit Ethic. The profit-making skill, which is the very core of the energy and creativity that drives the ethic on its quest for profit, incessantly works to *destroy* society and humanity as a necessary condition for its own prosperity. Its energy in this task is prodigious and its creativity unlimited. Profit-making is a force with such determination that only a death of the institution itself can stop it. In its magnificent drive it is totally oblivious to its own consequences to humanity. It can do no other. It operates outside the normal assumptions of society: that there are *people* and *values*. The common epitaph about a dedicated moneymaker, "he'd even sell his own mother!" testifies to the very unstoppable power that drives the profit-making machine and its operator. Contrast this with its most extreme opposite Social Ethic: "He has a face only a mother could love!"

Not only is the profit-making skill without socially useful value, it is also the most irrational, dangerous, and predatory of all human skills, because it has only one capacity in its existence and intent: *The destruction of humanity*. To be profitable, to satisfy self-interest, it must single-mindedly destroy the web of human network that binds men and women into a community of people. It *must* pursue the relentless destruction of tradition, institutional values, feelings, mutual trust, independence of mind, the arts, and other such elements of humanity in order to have its own free hand. There is little money to be made—in the manner of predatory profit-making—where people stick together as a mutually protective cocoon of community and humanity. The usual gullibility of individual men and women is balanced by the wisdom and advice of others around them. The profit-making skill drives an invisible wedge, as it must, into this social bond that binds humanity and breaks it. And after dividing up the humanity into individual isolation, the profit-maker now offers its own substitute community— prettier and sweeter—to the now isolated and helpless individual. (More on this subject is in the next three chapters.) Now made defenseless and lonely from the loss of human network and community protection around him, the isolated individual—presently termed *consumer*—must accept the terms of the "new" humanity and community. A Substitute Society is created and offered by the profit system in place of the real society he can scarcely identify or recognize.

As we have seen, the conflict between profit and society is historical as well as logical. It is historical in the sense we have had "strong" societies in medieval Europe, the present Soviet Union, and the Amish community where self-interest is strictly forbidden. In contemporary American society we have the opposite phenomenon—that is, strong profit and vanished community. Along various points between these two extremes we have liberal social-democratic Europe, Japan, and Canada, where some semblance of a balance between profit and society is maintained. To put the conflict between the two ethical systems in a logical nutshell, we need only look at the term *capitalist society* with some care. The term is indeed a misnomer: if it is society, it cannot be capitalist; if it is capitalist, it cannot be society. If it is society, it cannot allow capitalism (or the Profit Ethic) to flourish to its own destruction; if it is capitalist, it cannot allow society (or the Social Ethic) to dominate to *its own* detriment. The term *capitalist institution* would be much more to the point.

Although the first triumphant rise of profit-making was seen in England, it has not triumphed over English "society." Although the most spectacular success of profit-making in modern times has been observed in Japan, it has not entirely overrun Japanese "society." Both in England and in Japan, society is very much in control over profit or at least in a state of stalemate. The tendency in Western Europe, especially in Germany and the newly emerging former communist societies, as well as in Japan, has been rather in the direction of enlarging the powers of society over profit, by way of increasing social security, welfare benefits, and various measures of political control over the economic machine. In the Third World nations, society's control over profit is so complete that there is no such thing as a wide-open Profit Ethic and the profit-making system enjoys virtually no open field in these societies; there the profit-maker is subject to frequent tarring-and-feathering by the irate community as well as by the government over-lords.

In the contemporary United States the triumph of profit over society has been not only complete, but also made a national sport of sorts. Can a capitalist "institution"—since we cannot speak of capitalist *society*—survive in a loose, transient structure that passes for a real society? Can profit survive its own antagonism toward society, community, and humanity in which it has traditionally maintained its "human face"? (Let's ignore, for the sake of simplicity, all the public-relations features, e.g., corporate grants to ballet companies, community orchestras, scholarships, or a number of other self-serving sponsorships; these events, noble as they may be, do not affect the fundamental facts, although we are strongly tempted to give undue credit to such displays of public charity.) In the face of constant threat and ha-rassment from its critics, the former communists included, the Profit Ethic's traditional defense has been its own economic prosperity as undisputable material evidence. You cannot argue with success. The system of the "marketplace," "free enterprise," and "supply and demand" works and works brilliantly, at least in the American context. The common notion has been that capitalism's ability to produce concrete material affluence is its own best means of survival.

But as we have seen, the success of capitalism turns out to be its own worst enemy, for its success is at the expense of its own vanished society. Its victory has been achieved at the destruction of its own community and humanity. To achieve its victory, profit sold its society to the Devil. This irony may not be as clearly evident to these who prefer to look at the millionaires under the age of 30, at the marvel and the vastness of money-making opportunities in the United States. But there is no way a person of sober sensibility can overlook the fact that capitalism's triumph has been achieved by leveling its own community and humanity to the ground. It is a Pyrrhic victory in its most extreme. So the question nags: can capitalism survive its own success?

We opened this book with two contrasting facets of American life. Whether a society can be "economically" thriving while "socially" destroyed is a disquieting yet fascinating question in itself. Can a "marriage" survive where the husband supplies all material things for his wife in lieu of his personal affection? The answer is yes. But two more questions follow: Does the wife know that she is being satisfied only on material terms? How long would the wife remain happy about the economic arrangement in an institution of supposed *happiness*? Even in a society where happiness has more or less been equated with material abundance—the size of diamond as evidence of the degree of love professed—and personal worth with the value of a paycheck, the undercurrent of unrest cannot be ignored. Although America's love for money and materialism is legendary, it is doubtful whether such love for money and materialism can indefinitely hold off the longings for the sense of "oneness," "belonging," and "community" that are inherent in human nature in society. Referring back to the woman in a loveless marriage, the analogy holds that form without substance may last much longer than one suspects, depending on the ingenuity and creativity of those who benefit from maintaining the form.

On the surface capitalism, in its most triumphant moment, is virtually unassailable. It is nearly impossible to say unkind words about capitalism, especially after the great procapitalist changes in Eastern Europe and the Soviet Union itself. Popular sentiment there is leaning heavily toward the "American model" of capitalism. According to Karl Marx, capitalism is the culmination of a historical development. Human progress takes its inevitable steps through various stages, ending in capitalism. The collapse of capitalism occurs when the system, although fulfilling its destiny in the larger picture of history, fails to satisfy its working-class masses. Misery and alienation increase, and the masses of disgruntled workers, led by intellectuals, finally overthrow the capitalist system. The collapse of capitalism is thus caused essentially by a failure of the system. But American capitalism is nothing like what Marx ever anticipated. As we have seen, the real failure of capitalism is its own *success*. The irony of capitalism's failure is that it has been only too successful: there is no one left "human" enough to feel the misery and alienation and angry enough to revolt.

It is easy enough to identify a dictator or tyrant—Somoza, Duvalier, Marcos, the Shah, communist bosses in Eastern Europe, for instance—and after identifying him as the cause of one's misery, one can gather like-minded people and revolt against him. It is not so easy, on the other hand, when the misery and alienation are the products of the very system that exalts us, that pleases us. The very canon and success of capitalism have eliminated by necessity the essential human ability to feel misery and alienation and anger. This leaves capitalism and its Profit Ethic largely on their own, stand or fall. Now it is capitalism without society. Capitalism, in order to survive, must continue to satisfy self-interest and demonstrate instances of spectacular successes like the millionaires under age 30; it is pretty much like the husband who must keep his wife happy by constantly supplying material things to keep the marriage going. It is indeed a frantic and irrational way of managing a living, either for a social system or for an individual marriage. But often the frantic and irrational picture does not emerge until the matter has already gotten out of hand and only in historical retrospect. For many in the new generation of moneymakers society is already a distant memory. One more such generation should complete the job of demolishing society even as a memory. Evidence is ample that the coming generation will be much less "human" than their predecessors.

But the assumption requires a great deal in the powers of moneymaking. There has never been a whole society before whose human association is strictly based on profit consideration. We used to form corporations, institutions, and clubs for that purpose. Although scholars talk about "economic society," meaning the emergence of profit system as a social creed, no purely economic society—where association is based purely on the profit calculus—has ever existed before. Perhaps until now and until American society, that is. It is as if American society suddenly materialized with no historical background, no tradition, no residual sentiments to form a human community—as an "orphan" of history and humanity—where strangers were attracted to other strangers for the sole purpose of making fortunes. This description of American society, although unflattering, is not far from the truth if we consider all the observations of early American behavior made by De Tocqueville and many others. But the very fact of America's economic success may demonstrate that *human beings can live as purely economic agents of profit without community or humanity*. In other words, human beings need not live among other human beings in harmony and *as* human beings with appropriate social values. Or, to put it more simply, economic human beings need not be *human* at all, as long as they can understand profit. This is indeed the ultimate horror of a moneymaking culture.

Of course, this observation exaggerates the achievements of American profit-making and down-plays the inherent vulnerabilities of human nature in society. No human being—however prodigious as a profit agent—can live alone and on the basis of the pure economic calculus. While he may be devoted to profit, he is still vulnerable to the need for social communion, community solidarity, art, affection, trust, spiritual fulfillment, and so on, which are essential to his personal happiness. But the problem—and here is the central thrust of the dilemma—is that he *cannot have both*. By his own circumstances and choice, he has made his oath of allegiance to the Profit Ethic and, as a good soldier of fortune, has destroyed all the community and social values that he himself deems essential to his own personal well-being. He cannot have *both* profit *and* society at the same time. Under his present circumstances he does not have any choice even if he wishes for one. The decision has been made historically for him in the triumph of profit over society. The issue has been settled. Now he must pick up the pieces of life as best as he can.

While observing this strange dilemma in American society we, of course, must not see the issue as settled. For the problem we have defined between profit and society is only beginning to be recognized. Capitalism thrives without society, and indeed thrive it must without society. The lures of money are fetching; the demonstrations of profit are spectacular; the saga of material conquest and its subjugation of the subconscious mind to profit is of epic proportions. Yet profit *without* society does not allow us to rest without analysis, because we simply cannot fathom *life* without society. Life cannot live by money alone. What happens to the "economic man" who recognizes no family, no friends, no neighbors, no community, who lives with his calculator, earnings, yields, dividends, interest rates, rents? What happens to his "society," which is made up of millions of economic men? In spite of the observation made earlier that human beings can live as purely economic agents, can human beings really exist as calculating, "economic" machines driven only by the insatiable force of self-interest?

American society's own story provides two paradoxical case histories. On the one hand, as in the case of millionaires under age 30 and easy displays of material success, it seems that we need not have community or humanity to live happily, however superficial or transient the concept "happily" may be. On the other hand, there is the "distressing flaw in the social fabric of America" that no amount of glitter and gold in the street can cover up; the distress is in the very experiences and sorrows of each individual biography, which cannot be dismissed by analysis. Capitalism in its development has destroyed society, and in the absence of society it thrives more vigorously. But the question of the survival of capitalism itself arises, rather ironically, because there are problems with profit without society: Can capitalism survive without society? If it does, in what form? And how long? And what kind of human beings are part of a society?

Consider the following statement:

> We have become morally ill because we are used to saying one thing and thinking another . . . The concepts of love, friendship, mercy, humility and forgiveness have lost their depths and dimension, and for many of us they represent only some sort of psychological curiosity, or they appear as long-lost wanderers from faraway times, somewhat ludicrous in the era of computers and spaceships.[5]

A harsh indictment of America today? A reminder of its spiritual decay decried by some moralist who is critical of America's mad materialism? It should be. But no, it is not. It is from the New Year's Eve message of Vaclav Havel, the newly elected president of Czechoslovakia, speaking to his fellow countrymen of their moral decline. The fact that forty years of horrifying communist dictatorship has produced something similar to what has happened in free American society should give us a startling mental doubletake and sobering pause for thought.

There has been much argument over the *economic* state of American society. Political leaders and intellectuals have argued over the national budget deficits, the failing savings and loan institutions, America's overall decline in world economic competition, and so on. Hardly a day goes by without some expert predicting dire consequences for America's living standards, Gross National Product, competitiveness in high technology, or whatever one's expertise qualifies one to speak on. However, what is deafening for its silence is the absence of a serious debate on America's *social* decline. Hardly anyone talks about it, and hardly anyone *wants* to talk about it. Or they simply assume more money will solve the problem. Obviously, the ills caused by the Profit Ethic cannot be remedied by money. But experts assume that the problem of spiritual decay is really a matter of which group, agency, or sector gets a bigger budget. The problem of teenage pregnancies is normally countered by experts with more money for counseling and the distribution of condoms.

What is on the surface is much easier to identify and remedy than what is beneath the surface (i.e., the serious absence of society and community), which defies easy comprehension. George Will, for example, is furious that a judge gave the beggars their "Constitutional right" to beg on the street. "Such behavior (panhandling, public drunkenness, prostitution, pornographic displays)," writes Will, "can destroy a community." And he calls the judge a "physically dangerous" person for the destructive consequences that his judicial action would bring about. What George Will and many other social observers like him fail to realize is simply that a "physical community" may be defaced by the low-life rabble. But a "human (or spiritual) community" is destroyed far more thoroughly and surreptitiously by the very profit values to which Will himself is favorably inclined and in which the whole community rejoices. The extent of community destruction by self-interested businessmen and their Profit Ethic—with Will's apology as defense—is many times more destructive and irreparable than the defacement of streets and neighborhoods by said lowlifes. You can keep the undesirables out of your streets. But you cannot keep the Profit Ethic out of your hearts. Policing our streets, keeping the underclasses out of our neighborhoods, will not make our souls human.

A society of greedy individuals is also a nation of warlike behavior among nations. As greed represents self-interest, imperialism represents national interest. Greedy individuals naturally make up an imperialist nation. The only way a nation made up of individual greed can prosper as a nation is by being a greedy—imperialist—nation. When individual greed is channeled nationally, it inevitably becomes a force of warmongering. A nation of individuals who prey upon each other is also a nation of imperialism that preys upon smaller nations. Without this periodic release of warlike energies, the greed-based nation simply tears itself apart within. As individuals prey upon each other within the nation, the nation itself cannot be a kind and just nation among the family of nations. That is not in its character. At will, it must attack smaller nations periodically. The Profit Ethic affects the nation in the same way it affects its individual members. It is ironic that as American society is internally disintegrating with greed, it is also externally aggressive and warlike, exploitive of smaller nations, and exporting its own decadent ways to others. It is an illusion of grand magnitude that a society made up of selfish individualists can live happily among themselves and can also be a nation of kind and just disposition toward other nations.

At this writing, there is wishful thinking that the greedy 1980s is over and the 1990s will usher in a more humane, decent society for us. Many trend watchers are hopeful as they read America's tea leaves that the perverse Me Generation and Yuppie lifestyle are over. Some political analysts predict that people will revolt against the wealthy and want to promote a "kinder and gentler" society. But, alas, it is all a pipedream. American society will not change into something like the Social Ethic, forsaking the Profit Ethic, just so that our troubled minds can rest easy. That American society is what it is today is the result of an *historical* development, and it took centuries for America to evolve into its present state. It is not going to change in a quick, easy, trendy reversal of things. The Profit Ethic will not yield to the Social Ethic without an epic battle. Who will fight the philosophy that has made America so great and our personal lives so fulfilling?

Ever since the beginning of so-called economic society in the eighteenth century, human nature has been largely described in the West in terms of self-interest and later in a more elaborate and perhaps more vulgar terms of profit motive. An economic society is formed, according to this description of human nature, to advance such various self-interests and profit motives among conflicting individuals in a more "civilized" manner, without totally destroying their fragile association. This economic theory of society and human nature—from Hobbes and Smith to our own present-day academic economists and political leaders—has held that a good society *needs* self-interest and profit motive as its lifeblood. A good society is made possible, according to the assumptions of economic society, only because of our ever-present self-interest and profit motive. "It's what has made America great!" But as we have seen, it is precisely this self-interest and profit motive summed up in the Profit Ethic that makes society impossible.

Obviously, this dilemma makes necessary an adjustment in the economic definition of society. An economic society is built on neither the foundations of "civility," "community," and so forth nor "consciousness" and "oneness" in the sense of more internalized feelings and sensibilities. The economic definition of society identifies no such *human* elements as essential ingredients for an economic existence. The assumption is analogous to that of the businessman-husband who is certain that a marriage consists of balance sheets, supply and demand, and satisfaction of material needs. The very idea of economic society implies that its own definition has to be "economic," not social, although the term *economic society*, like *capitalist society*, as it turns out, is a serious misnomer. The idea of economic society—as much as the idea of "economic man"—is possible only if we assume that a society or a person can exist purely as an economic association or as a profit agent. It is a melancholy fact that in the last two hundred years or so the Western world—especially the United States—has held this view so dear and thus described itself and its supposed human nature: man is an economic animal and will work only for money.

It may be apparent by now that the internal collapse of American society casts a grave doubt on the survival of the Profit Ethic as a purely economic form of association. But a true understanding of what's going on in our private lives now and of what looms ahead for our profit society requires that the present analysis run its full course. Until this analysis is completed and its conclusion made inevitable, we must press on with our question yet further: *what has the Profit Ethic done to destroy American society?*

Earlier, we asked how it is possible, after the destruction of the Social Ethic and society by the Profit Ethic, that we still seem to have a "society" in which we live and work. The society we have now has all the *forms* of a normal society, with all the features of a normal community. Everything seems exceedingly normal in the way we appear and act as human beings. But it is also true that our community—and our humanity in it—has been effectively destroyed by the Profit Ethic's epic triumph over the Social Ethic. But what is it that appears to be a society with all formal requirements of a community, which only *seems* to contain all the elements of normal human relations within it? Something is indeed odd.

Answer to the odd phenomenon is in what I have termed the *Substitute Society*. In short, it is an imitation society. In it, people merely *look* and *act* like real people, but they are mere shells of humanity. In it, emotion is manufactured and sold for all occasions; love, still a favorite word, is trivialized in commercial songs and banality and Hallmark cards; family life is replaced by entertainment and fast food and by television families like the Huxtables and the Simpsons; education, far from producing future citizens, grinds out degrees and future corporate workers and consumers; God is at once business and show business mass-produced and mass-consumed, and God's men are primarily entertainment entrepreneurs and social climbers; politics is a game of caprice and pocketbooks, millions of votes swayed by one event, word, or image; real life is imitated by games to death. The Substitute Society is really a Hollywood set. The creation and maintenance of this Substitute Society is perhaps one of the greatest achievements of the profit system.

The Substitute Society came into being at the same time the Profit Ethic began to dominate the Social Ethic. Historically, I would put it at the end of World War II, when the new Affluent Generation made its first appearance. Today this illusion-making enterprise is our total national commitment, its total energy and consciousness devoted to the living of a Substitute Reality—to make it ever more lifelike, intimate, and enthralling. The creative ingenuity of the Profit Ethic, as the grand overseer of this national commitment, is as efficient as it is pitiless. To keep the Profit Ethic going as a philosophy and prosperous as a moneymaking system, the Substitute Society has replaced the real society and transformed it into the most enchanting and grotesque version of the human community ever imagined. The prospect is horrifying, yet the process is fascinating, as one can be held spellbound by one's own society's spectacular self-immolation.

Let us now look more closely at the Substitute Society that we call contemporary America.

NOTES

1. Michael Harrington, *The Other America: Poverty in the United States* (Baltimore: Penguin Books, 1964).

2. David Broder, "Deaver: A New Brazenness," *Washington Post*, 30 April 1986.

3. Robert Heilbroner, *The Worldly Philosophers: The Lives, Times, and Ideas of the Great Economic Thinkers* (New York: Simon and Schuster, 1961), 41.

4. C. B. MacPherson, *The Political Theory of Possessive Individualism* (New York: Oxford University Press, 1961), 275.

5. Daniel Benjamin, "Now, the Hangover," *Time*, 15 January 1990.

Part II

The Substitute Society

Chapter 3

The Court of Jesters

_____

One of the main instruments of art and science with which the Substitute Society keeps its population happy and content is *entertainment*. To be sure, every age and every culture has had some form of entertainment. The Egyptians, the Greeks, and the Romans had their entertainers and entertaining events. ("The public . . . longs eagerly but for two things," cried the Roman poet Juvenal, "bread and circuses!") Even the austere medievals had their court jesters. What is peculiar about American entertainment today is the very *nature* of entertainment and the extent to which our total existence has become *dependent* on entertainment. Life (and living) used to be the center of existence, entertainment remaining on the fringes of life. Now life exists on the fringes of entertainment. Our daily schedule and consciousness evolve *around* those of entertainment. In short, today we live to be entertained.

The rise of an entertainment culture coincides, in a poignant way, with the decline of humanity. The Hebrews and Greeks used to think of mankind in a universal sense, different peoples and nation-states joined by the common fate of human society and civilization. This notion of universal humanity declined in size to each self-sufficient, independent community in the Christian Middle Ages. But the feudal order was held together still as a large community of man. With the development of nation-states and capitalism, the size further declined into each family unit, both as a training ground for the new capitalists and as a launching pad for profit-making enterprises. As capitalism progressed, its own progress inevitably reduced the family into each *individual unit*. The single person became the standard of reckoning in a fully developed profit society. Now it appears that no further reduction of the individual unit is possible, capitalism or no capitalism, entertainment or no entertainment. Can the individual be reduced further to fit the Profit Ethic?

Yes, of course. Now there develops a further division of each individual into different sense *organs*. Capitalism itself may have been the doings of individuals—captains of industry and movers and shakers. But in its advanced form in the Profit Ethic, the individual is further divided up into "profit units." For example, an individual American is made up of the eye, the ear, the nose, the tongue, the sex organs, and so on to serve the ever-ready entertainment industry. Obviously the eye gets the lion's share of commercial attention simply because of its high entertainment value: television, decorative packaging, commercial advertisement, and other forms of visual image-making are superb ways to isolate the eye from its owner— the person—for the purpose of heightened entertainment value. The ear gets its own share, from teenage rock music to the piped in "soft-and-easy" background music. The nose is the center of attention for the perfume-and-deodorant industry. The tongue, the centerpiece of our culinary pleasure, also gets pampering attention from the food industry. The sex organs, the last frontier to conquer in the profit society, are not far behind as a legitimate object of entertainment value.

What began some centuries ago as humanity has now been reduced to the entertainment unit of bodily parts. Thus isolated from the rest of the body and humanity, the new entertainment units of eyes, ears, noses, tongues, and sexual organs, among other parts, float around in search of more fulfilling entertainment and greater excitement. Each industry concentrates on its field of specialty. For the food industry, the tongue *is* the person; for all it knows or cares, each human being might as well be a gigantic walking tongue. The smell industry, likewise—a person might as well consist of nostrils only. Indeed, today's consumer is made up of his bodily parts, as each bodily part is a precious commodity to the entertainment entrepreneur.

As humanity has been divided up, chopped up, and isolated from each other and from the whole, its "time consciousness" has also been divided up, chopped, and isolated from each other and from the whole in the Substitute Society. Time consciousness is what connects one generation with another, one historical epoch with another. Time is history, which renders whole the temporally disjointed units of biographies. It is through the historical wholeness of time that we are connected to our unseen forebears and yet-to-come descendants. But the entertainment culture makes it impossible. One entertaining hit is unrelated to another; one best-seller is an isolated event; the excitement of one entertainment cannot be carried over into another. They are all a disjointed, unconnected, disparate series of sense experiences that cannot be put together in a meaningful whole of subconscious. One series of entertainment has to be anticipated, experienced, and immediately discarded for the next series of anticipation, experience, and discard. A repeated presentation of the same entertainment— a television "rerun," for instance—has little or no value after the initial anticipation, experience, and discard. So the now-fragmented time consciousness in entertainment society measures its own existence in terms of momentary, hourly, daily, weekly, or possibly monthly rejuvenation. It must be a "new" moment, a "new" day, a "new" week, or a "new" month, depending on whether the event is a daily, weekly, or monthly cycle. No two moments, no two hours, no two days, no two weeks, or no two months can be the same or repetitious. Entertainment must be either eternally "new" or it is no longer entertaining and must be dismissed into oblivion. It is "canceled."

What used to exist on the fringes of civilized society—cheap thrills, popular taste, dime novels, in short, trashy mass entertainment—has now become the stuff of civilization itself in the Substitute Society. Civilization has not been replaced by the new tide of entertainment; it has been *redefined*. The old civilization and taste have been simply redrawn by the new standards of entertainment. The nature and extent of our new entertainment mania are indeed extraordinary. The nation's most talented and creative individuals concentrate their dynamic energy and ingenuity for one single purpose: to entertain and to entertain better. Art, science, technology, and the vast knowledge of human nature and psychology are put together in a dazzling display at the service of entertaining people. In the images, words, and symbols that these new entertainers and entertainment scientists can conceive and master in pursuit of entertainment we see the very symbol of our new civilization and the very height of our achievement. The new court jesters will go to any length, overcome any obstacle, to entertain us and entertain us better.

An entire "Nova" program on PBS titled "The Magic of Special Effects" devoted itself to showing how extraordinary technology and human ingenuity—not to mention huge budgets—are summoned to create special effects in a scene in the film *Raiders of the Lost Ark*. And all that is *for about two seconds on your screen.*[1] Two seconds! The best of modern science and ingenuity has been summoned, for *two seconds* of fairly mindless amusement of watching some bad guys falling to their death in a "realistic" and certainly entertaining manner. (Makers of its sequel, *The Last Crusade*, spent close to $3 million for a ten-minute action sequence in which Indiana Jones fought a Nazi battle tank.)

Then there was *Captain Eo*, the seventeen-minute-long 3-D movie-commercial that cost its producer, DisneyWorld, $1 million *per minute*. If it had been a regular-length movie, it would have cost them $120 million to produce it. Even for a "phenomenal battle scene" in which "lasers and explosions burst from the screen and flight sequences" commanded by Capt. Michael Jackson, the more thoughtful among us would surely consider such a sum outrageous for a short piece of fairly mindless diversion. But in the world of entertainment value nothing is too outrageous or too insignificant. Nothing escapes the watchful eye of entertainment meters. When General Westmoreland sued CBS for defamation of character—accused of manipulating figures concerning troop strength in Vietnam, where he once commanded—CNN's entertainment program called "Show Biz Today" reported the trial as "show business news."

Indeed, it is now difficult to tell what is serious and what is entertaining. If people found out that Heaven has no substantive entertainment, certainly not the kind they are used to, I am not sure how many of them would still be so anxious to enter the premises. A lot of harp playing is just not very entertaining. How the entertainment industry struggles with one another to outentertain us is an entertaining item in itself. "Ratings Wars" themselves entertain, creating winners and losers, "cliffhangers" and "photofinishes," gloating and wound-licking, all in the process of determining who's the best court jester of them all.

But what *is* entertainment? How do we define it against those activities we enjoy—say, taking a walk in the woods, having a simple conversation with friends, or attending a symphony concert—but are not, strictly speaking, "entertainment"? There are certain characteristics peculiar to entertainment that we ought to examine with some care. Entertainment is to the Substitute Society what "high art" is to the "real society." Just so that we better understand what entertainment is, we may occasionally use high art in the following discussion as a contrasting concept against entertainment.

Among the characteristics of entertainment, foremost is the way we *choose* it. The way we choose entertainment is totally whimsical. There is neither logic nor rhyme nor reason in the choice we make in entertainment. People shift from one event to another, one channel to another, without any plausible explanation. They give no more logical reason for the shift than that "it's not interesting." When we finally find something that holds our attention we cannot explain *why* we have chosen that instead of something else. It is the most thoughtless, unconscious, trivial of all human decisions. This is in the very nature of entertainment. A child can do it; an idiot can choose it; an ignoramus can enjoy it. However inexplicable our choice, explanation is neither necessary nor possible. Entertainment producers are keenly aware of this. In the words of NBC's whiz kid of programming, Brandon Tartikoff: "All hits are flukes." Rob Friedman of Warner Brothers echoes it: "Did we know *Batman* was going to be a big movie? Yes. Did we know how big? You never know." Take 1989's top box office hits: *Batman; Lethal Weapon 2; Ghostbusters II; Dead Poets' Society; When Harry*

Met Sally; Honey, I Shrunk the Kids . . . What do these hits have in common? Absolutely nothing. Boos and cheers, heroes and villains, wins and losses, hits and flops are all by chance. Entertainment puts absolutely no burden on the entertained and reduces them to a level of children, idiots, and ignoramuses. A culture of entertainment is naturally and inevitably a culture of childishness. A caveman could just as easily be entertained by our current repertoire. Needless to say, high art, whatever its "entertainment" value may be, is normally an object of our conscious, deliberate, definite choice. One must *explain* one's choice, and normally one *can* and does. It is for adults, and involves their real choice-making.

Likewise, there is no way we can evaluate "quality" in entertainment. So-called critics vary so much in their reactions. One likes it and the other hates it—Ebert versus Siskel, Lyon versus Medev—and all in perfect conformity with logic, if there is any logic in entertainment. More often than not, the "Editor's Choice" and the best-seller list do not coincide. Many box office bonanzas meet with critical ridicule (*Rambo*, for example). "Bad entertainment" is that which fails to sell as entertainment; good entertainment is that which draws a huge crowd. A program does not get canceled because it lacks quality; it gets axed because its drawing is poor. Witness Geraldo Rivera's so-called trash TV lineup as of early 1990, fairly typical of its topics and its genre; "Lady Lifers: Bad Girls Behind Bars," "Women Who Date Married Men," "Girls Who Can't Say 'No,' " "Illicit, Illegal, Immoral: Selling of Forbidden Desires," "Parents of Slain Prostitutes," "Battered Lesbians," "Transsexual Transformations: Stages of Transition." There is no such thing as poor taste in entertainment, only poor entertainment *value*. High art may not draw any crowd at all, but high art does not depend on box office approval, nor on a large crowd; it has *history*'s approval or disapproval.[2] Entertainment, however, must sell.

With rare exceptions of coincidence, quality entertainment is indeed a contradiction in terms. If it has quality, it does not entertain many people; if it entertains many people, it has no quality. The success and failure of entertainment is measured strictly by how many copies sold, how many tickets were purchased, and how much profit it has brought to its producer, not by its quality. As such, all entertainment aims at the largest number of consumers or, what is the same thing, the "lowest common denominator" where the largest number exists. In simple logic and experience, the majority of any group is always the representative of mediocrity in taste and quality. Entertainment rightfully seeks mass audiences and profits because of it. High art brings the crowd *up* to a higher level of consciousness and enlightenment. Entertainment pushes the crowd *down* to the most basic level of banality and mundaneness; it can do no other. Art appeals to our "better" side, entertainment to our selfishness.

Entertainment may depend on whims for its selection, but it certainly depends on *transiency* for its continuing existence. It must be transient—

here today, gone tomorrow—to exist at all. Every entertainment is a one-shot event, although some items may reappear as reruns some years later. By and large, all entertainment is one-appearance only, after which it merely becomes another stop in the series of transient experiences. Once seen, once read, and once heard, entertainment value is spent from the experience and our desire demands something new. There are entertainment "classics," but even these classics—for example, *The Wizard of Oz, Gone with the Wind*—are basically old hat and become replaced by the new generation of spectacles that are bigger, better, and simply more entertaining. But few would say that Shakespeare's *Romeo and Juliet* and Beethoven's Fifth Symphony are reruns when they are performed; every performance is an event in itself, no matter how often repeated.

All entertainment must compete against itself. The next item of entertainment must simply be better than the one that preceded to survive. One best-selling writer must write another best-seller that's better-selling than the one before; one singer must sing a song that sells more records than his last one; one hit movie must be followed by another that's an even bigger hit. Every hit entertainment is doomed to be "outhitted" by the next and the next and the next, until human ingenuity and creativity are completely exhausted and no more funny bones can be tickled. (Can that happen?) An entertainment event is a novelty, and a novelty it must be. But all novelty wears off eventually. As soon as novelty wears off, it marches off to the graveyard of all those novelties that at one time or another enthralled the multitude. Our daily grind in entertainment merely piles up the forgottens and forgettables. But Shakespeares and Beethovens survive, never to be bested by another Shakespeare or Beethoven. Thus confusing art with entertainment, people expect entertainment in art and seek art in entertainment. The director of *Days of Thunder*, a typical exploitation film, indignantly declares, "I'm an artist!"

Entertainment is also different, in the final analysis, from what we might call recreation. Recreation implies that it is marginal to life, a worker relaxing after a hard day's work, for instance, reading, playing, or simply relaxing with hobbies or sports. It also implies a state of mind that is only passively aware of the energy required to enjoy the activity. Anything more strenuous than a passive consciousness would surpass the very boundary that divides recreation and work. Tired people want rest; unhappy people want entertainment. Work is where our energy is concentrated; recreation is where our energy is dissipated and regrouped. American entertainment is no longer the recreational kind that requires only passive energy consumption. It is a serious business of enormous significance. Recreation involves one's own *participation*, such as in sports, reading, walking; it produces physical satisfaction and psychic contentment. Entertainment is passive; the entertained wants everything done *for him*; passive entertainment only produces vague dissatisfaction, unhappiness, and not infrequently self-loathing. How can one derive any uplifting experience from something that requires no personal and intellectual participation?

Americans are never more serious than when they choose and pursue their entertainment. Entertainment is no longer the marginal activity that tiptoes around life; for many it *is* life itself. America's Substitute Society is in fact so hooked on its staple of entertainment—so abundant and so predictably delivered—that its producers have considerable say on the state of happiness in their society. (Witness the National Football League's withdrawal of the Super Bowl from Arizona when in 1990 the state failed to ratify Martin Luther King Day.) Big-time producers of television spectacles, sports events, political conventions—all entertainment of mass proportions—and many other such events command the status and power of warlords and masters in bygone eras. Desperately unhappy Americans must be pacified and tamed at all times. The task is at once noble and monumental. Even the Berlin Wall didn't fall down until the prime-time camera was ready to roll. All else may come to a halt in America, but entertainment must go on. Those who entertain gradually improve their status, too, becoming respectable representatives of ideals, role models, and dream-come-true folklore. They are no longer our court jesters and fools. Real life itself, largely unhappy and unexciting, is in the meantime relegated to only a marginally interesting status.

As recreation is different from entertainment, the concept of "leisure" also implies something quite different from entertainment. Leisure implies that the body is at rest, its energy output at a minimum. In the preindustrial and early industrial phases, physical rest was the best form of leisure activity than available for the masses. The simple joy of not having to work for a few hours in coal mines, at textile factories, on farms was fetching and precious enough. As industrial capitalism matured, leisure became more physical. It now involved sports, spectator or participant, traveling, social gathering, ascendancy of things sexual, and other such physical activities. With the coming of the Profit Ethic more recently, while such physical preoccupations still continue for some, the very idea of leisure has shifted to the idea of entertainment. With the shift from leisure to recreation and to entertainment also came the changes in the very nature and extent of our "play" life. Instead of being a means of rest from work, only marginally related to the business of living, play has become an end in itself. Instead of being passively physical, low-energy activity and consciousness, it has become the all-consuming purpose of life.

With physical thrills still occupying a large part of our entertainment world, a new dimension has moved into its composition: the "psychological" dimension. Play has been substituted for real life. Entertainment nowadays is no longer a simple matter of getting a few laughs, relaxing with mild bodily occupation, or tinkering with inconsequential hobbies. It must now represent the very meaning of life, feelings of security, peer acceptance, mastery over one's environment, vicarious satisfaction in acquisition and possession, search for self-actualization, and manipulation of human factors. It is an exhausting process, both for the entertainer and for the entertainee. People end up feeling more exhausted and often more frustrated from their pursuit of pleasure than before. Having fun as the purpose of entertainment is no longer acceptable; it must be psychologically fulfilling, meaningful, relevant, and satisfying. The idea of life as entertainment must be fully realized. It is a diffused cultural notion, rather than a concrete fact or act. Entertainment is no longer a specific event or place; like profit itself, it is now a state of mind. As such, life as entertainment has become an all-consuming, all-exhausting, and all-encompassing series of experiences and reactions. But in spite, and perhaps because, of such consuming, exhausting, and encompassing passions for entertainment, people naturally feel let down after each cycle. An unhappy, unfulfilled, and emotionally estranged society demands entertainment to the precise extent of its empty life.

Life as entertainment is best expressed in games. Games are as old as society. Every age and culture invented its own games to amuse the population. A game is a make-believe re-creation of real life for the sole purpose of entertainment. Its chief source of amusement is that it *imitates* life, yet it is as far removed from life as possible. While imitating life, it is never life itself. That it is never real is what makes it entertaining. Rules are artificially set up, players (athletes, bridge players) are selected and trained, and games are played with the full knowledge that they are make-believe events. Rules are designed in such a way that the outcome is in strict accordance with the rules. This means that the outcome itself—however hard-fought—cannot be taken too seriously. It is only a game. As such, other than as a moneymaking investment or as employment, in which case it is no longer a "game," no one ought to take the outcome as an ultimate. Unlike in real life, where rules cannot be changed easily to suit one's liking, rules in games can be changed any time they do not produce maximum amusement. If too many or too few points are scored so as to make the game uninteresting, we simply change the rules. Normally, therefore, only children and the psychotic confuse games with real life and take the former as seriously as they take the latter.

Yet, in the Substitute Society, imitation becomes the genuine. The imitation society takes every source of amusement with nothing less than utter seriousness. Games thus take on special meaning. Games, the silly crowd-amusing make-believe contest—or what Howard Cosell, himself a master of games, once called "children's games"—became confused with real life. Rules are confused with the "rules" of real life. Players become real heroes and real villains. And the outcome is taken with deadly obsession. For every game, nothing less than total satisfaction would do. Anticipation is built up to a fever pitch with great hype, and at a certain point the game ceases to imitate life; it becomes life itself. People cannot see games as make-believe events any longer. The anticipation, the process, and the outcome are nothing less than total frenzy—suspense, climax, and resolution. In America's Substitute Society people by and large find it impossible to distinguish life from game.

At one time in history, games used to be the stuff of leisure—that non-energy-consuming, inconsequential activity with minimum attention and seriousness, at least for the spectators. As part of play, games used to stop as soon as they ceased to be fun, being either too taxing mentally or too hard physically. In our entertainment society, however, games cannot stop at the fringes of energy and attention. Since life in America cannot now be conceived without fun and games, games must go on even *without life*. While life without games cannot be possible, games go on merrily without life. Or, in fact, games go on merrily *because* there is no real life. With every win or loss, the substitute life is profoundly affected by the outcome. Wins confirm the validity of one's life; losses, the opposite. The death of a popular entertainment hero is the death of oneself, so personal and so deeply felt. The life of the game hero enthralls the masses with every detail. An Elvis Presley's death and life become the very pulse of America's death and life. On television, in the printed media, and in the consciousness of everyday life, games take on the significance of life itself. People are no longer able to separate their reality from their make-believe world. (A popular TV show had to establish a *real* scholarship at a university mentioned in one of its *episodes* when the fictional mention caused a deluge of inquiries from the university's students and their subsequent disappointment to find out that it was just a TV show.)

In this transformation from life to games and back to life, games evoke the kind of profound reflections that used to be reserved for loftier meanings of life and death. Now every game is the messenger of God, Fate, Destiny, and Life itself. After five years of subpar records as Notre Dame's football coach, Gerry Faust gave his reflections: "You leave it to the Almighty," he said. "I think there was a purpose for me to be here." One would think—with "Almighty" and "purpose" invoked—Gerry Faust was thinking about his joining the priesthood or something equally spiritual in nature. He was simply talking about leaving the job of coaching football at Notre Dame. When things were not going very well on the sidelines, Faust was often observed praying, "Blessed Mother, haven't you tested me enough?" Notre Dame students call a campus mural with an outstretched arm "Touchdown Jesus." "*Life is [a] series of battles*," a basketball coach in Wisconsin exhorts his young men. "Life is a series of legitimate battles and there are always opponents waiting to defeat you." But this man is "not just a coach," declares the newspaper article describing the warrior-coach's philosophy. "He is a teacher." His teaching: life, like war, is hell.

The business of entertaining, which in another historical time was called court jesting, has likewise transcended its business level into the dimension of a science. Its ability to create thrills, laughs, or whatever entertains has been transformed into a respectable branch of human learning. With the exception of comedians, who still have to perfect their skills largely by innate ability and trial-and-error, the science of entertainment—or court jesting—has become a respectable *academic* pursuit. There are college degrees offered in moviemaking, in television production, in sports, in physical education, in commercial art. The university, long the citadel of serious minds for serious things, has become the biggest farm system for court jesters and for the science of court jesting. The climb of entertainment into the world of respectability comes in the form of more serious-looking literary activity. There are film "critics," sports "writers," soap-opera "analysts," television "commentators," and many such men and women of letters serving the business. Thus intellectualizing the business of entertainment gives court jesting a measure of respectability and validity. Never mind that there is really nothing to "critique" in entertainment in the sense that there is something to critique in Shakespeare, Beethoven, or even the Bible. In entertainment, either one is entertained or one is not entertained. It has nothing to do with the quality of things; it has to do with one's silly preference. But men and women of fair learning voice their opinion with all the flourish of literary criticism and tell us why we should or should not go see *Pretty Woman*. Through these "critics" of amusement, entertainment creeps into the real world of serious thoughts and then occupies a legitimately dominant place in it.

Of course, television is king among the media of entertainment. It is the most singular tool of amusement the world has ever invented. In entertainment society, with all things in economic perspective, the uses to which television can be put make the medium the most formidable instrument of entertainment ever known. In its technique of presentation its multidimensional image-making ability is unsurpassable; one can see, hear, and even feel television. In its imitation of intimate reality it creates an intimate reality that is *more* intimate and real than the real. Filling the social void for the isolated, community-less Americans, television does the marvelous job of creating substitute intimacy. As an entertainment medium, its wide-ranging yet comfortably concentrated and miniaturized presence can be surpassed, if at all, only by the sternest of God's wraths. In a Roper Organization survey taken in the early 1980s, watching television edged out friends, to place second only to family, among "the most personally satisfying things" in everyday life in America. By the beginning of the 1990s, American children will have spent 5,000 hours watching TV by the end of high school and average adults spend over 7 hours a day watching TV. Not since the Dark Ages of a relentless religious presence has a whole nation been so singularly absorbed in cultural symbolism.

Television does strange things to people. People, so accustomed to watching the world presented through television, *expect* it to be "personal" and "human" and have feelings like themselves. People become pathologically, and pathetically, attached to television and consider its "people" real, as they even prefer television to their real friends. People feel intimate about Jane Pauley's home life with her babies or Connie Chung's effort to have one. But needless to say, television exists for one thing and one thing only: as an instrument of entertainment to amuse and to make money. Everything it does—from news to sitcoms, from "60 Minutes" to political conventions—is geared to that end only. On television every moment counts. Every moment is calculated to maximize its moneymaking effect. Television, being an instrument of moneymaking, never goes astray from its path unless it is a mistake. It wants people to buy things that it advertises; it wants people to watch its programs as a way of watching its advertisements; it wants people hooked on it.

Television, like all other media of entertainment, shares the same fate of *accident*. Since it depends for its existence solely on its ability to entertain people, its existence is based on the accidental nature of people's choice. And there is neither logic nor reason in the way people choose their programs. No one knows what makes people prefer certain things in entertainment. In bread and butter, you appeal to their tongues. In household appliances, you make your case with efficiency and economy. In automobiles, you plead with comfort, mileage, style, and so on. In entertainment, there is no way of knowing. This drives all television programmers to great uncertainty. Entertainment is not something one needs regularly. Not watching television does not hurt anyone. You watch it only because it amuses you, is available, and you are hooked on it. Its existence is indeed precarious. But it is a maddening reality for many, nevertheless. No one knows what people like, why they like it, and how long they will like it. As we recall NBC's Tartikoff's comments on hits, "All hits are flukes," all television material is an accidental creature of the button, whims, caprice. All television "stars" are creatures of flukes; all things on television—however well calculated in advance—are a simple matter of a guessing game. In an age of remote control, a television analyst says, "shows that don't grab their [the potential viewers'] attention are zapped away in an instant." From the view of the programmer, the audience consists of savages and children equipped with a zapper.

This accidental nature of entertainment—monumental television hits and misses—is what gives it nerve-wrecking unpredictability. Successes as well as failures in the entertainment business are so tied to the whims of caprice and chance that it is not unlike the laboratory rat that presses the unpredictably rewarding bar. The entertainer presses on endlessly with neither a clear course nor a known destination. In a world of high technology and rational business calculation, entertainment is still in the Middle Ages of

animism and speculation—and a lot of prayer for a good omen. Hollywood—the center of such animism and speculation—is replete with stories
of how Lana Turner was discovered at a soda fountain, how so-and-so got
his or her breaks, how, after many unsuccessful attempts, they finally found
the actress for Scarlett O'Hara, and so on. But just as accidentally as they
appear on the scene, stars also disappear. Being a popular actor or singer,
for contrast, is not like being a popular orchestra conductor. An actor or
singer can become popular with big breaks, whims, and caprice, whereas
the music conductor's popularity has to do with his mastery of craftsmanship. While the actor's or singer's popularity can fade just as quickly, the
conductor's mastery is relatively immune to such ups and downs of show
business.

Because of this very unpredictability of big breaks, those who are at the
top of the entertainment world are never sure about themselves or their
accomplishments. It is always "How did your last film [or song, dance,
book, whatever] do?" Given the stable mastery of musical art, on the other
hand, one successful performance by the conductor would give a fairly
predictable clue to his next performance. But such predictable sanity is rare
in entertainment; one flop can and often does follow a very successful smash
hit (*Heaven's Gate*'s following *The Deer Hunter*, both directed by Michael
Cimino, being a legendary example). In entertainment, every film, every
play, every new season is its own popularity contest, and this fact makes
anyone who enjoys temporary popularity—all popularity by definition is
temporary—very nervous. Being at the top now is no guarantee that one
will still be there later; if one can climb up to the top by chance, so can
someone else. However spectacular an entertainment success, there is no
logic to one's success, and that makes for the peculiar wretchedness of show
business and the very nature of entertainment itself.

Television, the summary representative of our cultural artifacts, lives up
to its expectations by presenting all sorts of programs to its viewers. In any
city, no fewer than dozens of channels are now available. There are politics,
finances, classical art, popular music, rock 'n' roll, country, Nashville,
religion, nature, health, news headlines, weather, movies, sports, and so
on at one's fingertips. This variety of programs serves as the strongest
defense for our television culture—that so many varieties are offered in a
free society where people can choose what they want. But there is a serious
problem with this wonderful array of choices: all of them exist for one
single purpose—that is, to *entertain*. None of them could exist unless people
watched them. To make people watch them, they must be *entertaining*.
Politics must be entertaining; religion must be entertaining; nature must be
entertaining; news must be entertaining. *USA Today*, one of the trend-
setters in this regard, says in its own ad: "Reading a newspaper should be
fun." So politicians, from the president to local administrators, try to entertain to get votes; the preachers try to entertain to raise their ratings;

headline news tries to entertain with great items of shock, sensation, graphic scenes. With this variety of television at our own fingertips, we have lost the distinction between entertainment and serious events in life and between reality and unreality as well. Television has become the Great Unifier of thought and action, spirit and body, sacred and profane, and good and evil, with its hazy unreality and pretty pictures.

This strange twist goes one step further. What was traditionally serious—politics, religion, scholarship, for instance—now tries desperately to be more "entertaining." What were traditionally marginal matters—sex, entertainment, marketing research—now imitate the seriousness of lofty ideas. Through advertisement and entertainment, serious matters become trivial. Through the appearances of scholarship and artistic labels, trivial matters become serious. Politicians and preachers must be good crowd entertainers; sex researchers and entertainers speak with academic authority. *TV Guide*, a court jester's schedule of appearance, acquires a good bit of respectability and seriousness by adding pseudo-serious articles on social issues. Phil Donahue, the paragon of court jesting, writes a book about human nature based on his show, with the conclusion that man is weird, nasty, bad.

Television news tries to stay aloof from the rest of the more obviously entertainment-oriented programs. But the race among the major networks for ratings is no less fierce. Both on the national and local levels, news is one of the more competitive items simply because it gives the network, or the medium itself, a sense of dignity. But it is largely the dignity of the emperor who has no clothes. There is nothing in news production that is intrinsically different from other sorts of programs. The ratings of the news programs follow the same format as other regular entertainment programs. Observers have noted the trend of news increasingly becoming entertainment for some time. News must entertain. In one fairly typical segment, a station in Milwaukee, Wisconsin, gives in the first five minutes of its evening news: (1) the rape-murder of a woman; (2) the discovery of the partially decomposed body of a woman murdered previously; (3) another rapist still at large; (4) violence at a prison; and (5) five murders in another state.

But what *is* news? It is a never-ending, nerve-wrecking chase of a new answer to the question raised every day: "What's new?" One cannot give the same answer to the same question, not on television. The agony of having to come up with something truly "new" is monumental. Attractive men and women of decent education and energy are on the run every minute of the day chasing that elusive item known as news, only because they cannot give the same answer to the question, "What's new?" There *has* to be something new at all times. Thus news depends primarily on surprise, some extraordinary, sensational, or even bizarre events, or "scoops." But each surprise means that something has happened that should *not* have happened. Surprise creates suspense. Suspense creates attention. Attention is satisfied only when something extraordinary, sensational, or bizarre happens. From choosing a vice-presidential candidate for the United States to pairing NCAA basketball teams, surprise, suspense, attention-getting go through the rituals of anticipation, climax, and resolution, only to regroup for the next series of anticipation, climax, and resolution.

Surprise, the essential staple of news, means that it is basically "unknown" to us. Rivers flow steadily and this makes no news; God does his things predictably and He makes no news. Those events and persons that are newsworthy are those events and persons who do surprising things that are largely unknown to us. "Known" qualities, such as in the persons of Mother Teresa, Lincoln, or Mandela, would hardly surprise us with the extraordinary, sensational, or bizarre. They would be—like rivers and God—so predictable and so known that none of them would ever make good news stories. Certainly, none of them would commit murder or rape. The problem of news—in spite of the stately appearances of Rathers, Jenningses, and Brokaws and their backdrop stages—is that only trivial things in life change unpredictably enough to cause surprises. Aside from wars and revolutions, real changes are long in the making and are largely imperceptible to ordinary observations—certainly not newsworthy happenings. But what, if anything, makes news worth *knowing*?

What is worth knowing is worth knowing because the act of knowing is going to last at least for some time, if not permanently. The pyramids are permanent; Shakespeare is permanent; the earth is round is permanent. The act of knowing—from the most immediate reactions to the most contemplative reflections—includes the act of sifting through the mass of information that comes to one's brain. There the information is sorted into what can be immediately reacted to and what should be stored for future use. The latter then becomes part of our permanent knowledge system. But news thrives on the idea of "discarding" the information *as soon as* it is known for the next rounds of information. One cannot store all the news items as they come to one's brain capacity. In fact, the value of news is immediacy—you know something the minute it happens. But when something happens and you know it immediately, all you can do is *react* to it without being able to reflect upon it. No sooner do you know it then you must *discard* what you know. The knowledge about pyramids is permanent, as long as the pyramids are permanent. But that a pyramid climber fell off one and died is immediate and soon discarded. Yet the pyramid climber falling off to his death, a fairly negligible piece of information, makes the evening news; the pyramid itself does not.

Knowledge is important, especially the kind that lasts in our lifetime, simply because what we "know" affects the way we think and act. A person who pursues knowledge is open to changes, ideally for the better. But all reflective knowledge—as opposed to reactive information—is cumulative. One piece of knowledge becomes the foundation for the next in an unending series of cumulation and reflection. But news information is not cumulative. It exists precisely because it cannot be retained any longer than the time that it takes to give the information, be it rape, murder, or accident. There- fore, news is simply not worth knowing. Conversely, what is worth know- ing is simply not newsworthy. No one can possibly accumulate all the information on the murders, rapes, accidents, and so forth, as part of one's permanent storage of knowledge unless one wishes to become a morbid trivia expert. Nor is there any need to.

Nor does news help us understand the world around us any better. People addicted to a regular dosage of news say that they want to know what's going on in the world. But the world they want to know about then and there is the same world that they already know about *without news*. The world remains basically the same with or without news, if we can recall the times we have gone without news for some time. All the rapes, murders, and accidents that took place and what all the politicians said that day do not change our world. Nor does knowing these things make one understand the world better. I would, in fact, argue the opposite—that the less news one knows about, the better one's understanding of the world would be. The simple reason is that news makes reactions—not reflections—its natural response. People react to news; they do not reflect on it.

Those hooked on news argue that the world changes constantly. Just look at the evening news, they say, and you see another series of "new things" that has happened since the last time. But this is a superficial view of change. The changes—the "new things"—that the evening news de- scribes are really trivial changes or variations in the essentially routine life of this world. People still go on hurting each other; small and large wars go on; politicians here and abroad do what they can for themselves and their electors; those self-interested people still go on and pursue their ends. Knowing the specific instances of these and other fundamental facts does not make one *understand* them any better. Knowing that a natural gas ex- plosion took place at a certain household is important only if one lives there or has a similar natural gas setup in one's own household. That does not add anything to our understanding about natural gas; we have always known that natural gas contains certain dangers.

Knowledge about the world—gathered through the evening news—helps us understand the world better only if the world freezes or stops precisely after the news. But, alas, the world goes on, preparing for the next rounds of news. The newsmakers, the news media, and the news consumers all alike are forever engaged in this never-ending pursuit of the soon-to-be- forgottens. Because the news items change the minute they are gathered, imparted, and digested, the next set of news items must be gathered, imparted, and digested. It is transiency at its most dramatic revelation. It is like the proverbial rainbow chaser—the minute you think you caught it, it is still to be chased.

But in spite of this transiency and futility, the business of newsmaking, news gathering, and news consuming is indeed a serious *business*; the whole entertainment world looks up to it as its intellectual leader; much money and prestige of networks and personalities depend on it; and many news-addicted people "understand" their world solely from the information they get from it. As the world marches on in its relentless yet imperceptible changes of course, the evening news conveniently freezes and stops in slow motion and in instant replay these relentless and imperceptible motions of this world. By doing so, it represents the window through which many people try to see the world around them and eventually themselves and understand both.

The triviality of news is best illuminated by the curious element in the entire operation known as the "anchorman." Every major network scrambles for the most attractive anchorman. It is with the anchorman at the center of all the diverse elements and impressions in news production that the enterprise supposedly finds its continuity and stability. Normally it is the anchorman who symbolizes the network's news authority. Walter Cronkite, for instance, is still revered, although many people may not know for precisely what reason they revere him. But the problem is with *why* the anchorman is so important. For the network news ratings seem to depend largely on whose face is at the anchor desk and the networks take enormous pains to find the right man for the job. But the question is: why is the anchorman so important? The answer is found in this: simply *because the news isn't*. If the news is important, it matters little or not at all *whose* face broadcasts it. Suppose the Soviet Union declared total war upon China, does it matter *who* is at the anchor desk and tells us about it? The news itself is so earthshaking that it would matter little if a janitor was at the anchor desk. Or, more disturbingly, have we gone so far out of touch with reality that we would believe it only if our familiar anchorman's face told us the news?

The importance of anchor position rises in correct proportion to the decline of the importance of news itself. And vice versa. There is no more poignant testimony to the emptiness of our news hunger than this most useless position occupying the most visible, hence most important, element in the entire operation. ("Something at least 22 other broadcasters can do just as well," as a *Time* magazine article put it.) Of course, the most important element is the news itself. But since the news itself is not worth knowing, the messenger becomes the center of our attention. Ancients even killed the messenger for a bad message. Marshall McLuhan was right about the medium being the message. Today, in our Substitute Society, the messenger *is* the message. One slight change in the way the messenger-anchorman parts his hair, the way his mustache looks, the way he wears his sweater and in what color, his twitching face, faltering pronunciations, smooth delivery—all trivial matters—significantly affect the very newsworthiness of the news items, not the news items themselves. In the end, because of the sameness in their objective—highest entertainment value— the anchormen become interchangeable and their differences in ratings remain fairly negligible over time. "[TV] journalists are exchangeable commodities," says a former TV executive, "the highest bidder wins."

Beyond these obvious follies with news, there is something more menacing in our news culture. It has to do with our *emotional* reaction to it. News by its own nature moves from one topic to another without connection or continuity. It moves from a disaster killing thousands of people to a kitten saved by a handicapped teenager to an official in Washington resigning after a scandal, and so on. Our attention span with each topic lasts exactly as long as the item itself—perhaps ten or twenty seconds. We cannot possibly linger on the disaster with thousands dead while we are watching the missing kitten, and so on. Television demands total involvement while we are watching it, for its effect is immediate, real, and whole as much as our visual contact is immediate, real, and whole. The only way we can think about and reflect on the disaster is if we turn the television set off. The visual involvement makes it impossible for us to freeze one segment of its imagery while its imagery is continuing in variations. From utter tragedy to utter silliness, to utter seriousness to utter trivia, we are forced to shift the emotional gear rapidly without transition in which our emotion is allowed to remain authentic at least for a while. We cannot be emotional with one topic—whereas we *ought* to be emotional in view of the tragedy of the topic—when we are immediately assaulted with something quite different in substance. It is like asking a woman to maintain her emotional integrity while being alternatively loved and beaten by her lover at ten- or twenty-second intervals.

This emotional trauma is intensified further when we consider the abrupt switching of gears necessary between supposedly authentic news and obviously inauthentic *commercials*. While news items may be serious in some instances, the commercials that follow are quite the opposite in their emotional content. The tirade of a pro-lifer condemning abortion in the most damning tone as part of the evening news is immediately followed by the singsong introduction of a carpet cleaner commercial. The moving encounter between a near-death Ben Hur and a life-giving Jesus breaks for a "Summer's Eve" douche commercial. We are, by habit and tradition of the medium, required to stop thinking seriously the moment news or a program ends and switch our mind into the mindlessness of commercial substance. But this is a fairly savage disregard for the necessary integrity and authenticity of human emotion. One cannot be required to attend a loved one's wake with all sincerity and the next minute to participate in a wet T-shirt contest in all frivolity. For the integrity of life itself we *must* be assured that either both are serious or both are frivolous. We cannot switch our emotional gears between such extreme plateaus of response in rapid succession. Thus thinking about or reflecting upon news—or the way the world is—becomes impossible and our intellectual response to news becomes much the same as the way we respond to any other television pictures.

The "meaninglessness" of news can be looked at in yet another way. Meaning is possible, by definition, only if the object is not material. That is, if our reflection is *added* to the object of our reflection. If a person gives a diamond ring to another person, the meaning of the diamond ring is possible to comprehend only if the ring is put aside *out of sight* so that the meaning can be reflected on. As long as the recipient of the ring looks at the ring, the meaning is not clear. What the person *sees* is the ring, not its meaning. The meaning is even more unclear on television images as long as our senses are overwhelmed by the moving, lifelike picture itself. Whatever is graphic—shown in pictures and images before our eyes—has the advantage of grabbing our attention. But it only grabs our *sensory* attention without evoking our understanding of its meaning. The picture of a burning airplane on the screen gets only our sensory reaction to the flames and wreckage, not what it *means*. As the television medium increases its picture showing for its message, as it inevitably does for attention getting, the meaning of it all becomes less and less possible to extract from it. By the general rules of the senses, the senses cannot reflect upon the meaning of life or anything as complicated and subtle as that. Perhaps there *is* really no meaning in the burning airplane or in any other hot news item. Perhaps it is *meant* to contain no meaning. Perhaps it is merely meant to grab our sense-attention for that ten- or twenty-second span. For those who try to find some meaning in or reflect upon what they confront on television, however, it is surely an exercise in futility.

The public's "right to know" is often invoked to defend the essential frivolity and meaningless of news production. The public has the right to know, the defense simply asserts. But the right to know also contains the *obligation* to know as well. If the public's right to know X is to be upheld, then its obligation to know not only X but also Y and Z—where X, Y, and Z form an integral whole—must be upheld. If the public demands to know what the president's breakfast consists of, then the public *must* also know about other aspects of what the president does. But interestingly, not only does the public's right to know ignore what its obligation to know is, but also the right to know extends only to what it wants to know and nothing else. Only if its right to know were balanced by the obligation to know what it *ought* to know, then the matter of the right to know could be established as valid. Without this balance, however, its insistence upon the right to know is nothing but a child's demand to be satisfied without its obligation to the world. For a child it is reasonable to do so; for our world of knowledge, unreasonable and probably dangerous as well.

While we use the public's right to know as defense for trivia, we also confuse the private right to know (satisfying individual curiosity) with the public's right to know (fulfilling public obligation). As private citizens we display many curiosities; we simply want to know a lot of things for our own personal curiosity, in the fashion of the "inquiring mind." But these private curiosities are for private consumption only. The satisfaction of knowing how large a diamond Celebrity A gave to Celebrity B has no benefit beyond the individual's range of curiosity and satisfaction. While the private individual may have every right to know what he wants to know, his right has nothing to do with the public's knowledge. Public knowledge, as opposed to private knowledge, must be assumed to bring some *public good*. If we wish to know what kind of dogs the president keeps, this knowledge is assumed to add to our knowledge about state affairs, government functions, and the mind-set of the president himself, all of which are important in public benefits. If we want to have the knowledge about the president's dogs to satisfy our private curiosity—say, we have a parent his age and we want to compare their pets—then the right to know cannot be a *public* right to know. The news producer's insistence on the public's right to know for its trivia has no defense on public airwaves.

News is justified only if it has something to do with the welfare of the whole community. The result of knowing something has to have some beneficial consequences for the public in a truly "public" sense, such as storm warnings or other such advisory functions. Knowing that certain accidents took place or that someone murdered someone or that a child is missing or that a car-bomb exploded in Beirut or that Princess Diana has a new dress, and so forth—essentially one-shot topics with no *public consequences*—has absolutely no benefit for the public. The public's right to know about them would simply be the waste of a significant principle. All important items must be "discussed" at length, not just a minute or two allocated to typically opposing personalities to state the issue. The British style of public discourse has academic experts address the issue directly with the public on the medium and at some length. This way, the gap between academia and public is narrowed and the public's right to know is truly well served. It is interesting that in American society it is not normally the academic professors but columnists and journalist "personalities" who get to state the issues and discuss them. In the British way, the public is challenged to elevate itself; in the American way, the speaker is challenged to demean himself. And in the former, everyone benefits from this exercise; in the latter, everyone loses.

In the final analysis, news is also addictive and habit-forming because of its very regularity. We expect something spectacular, sensational, unusual, bizarre happening between six o'clock and ten o'clock and between ten o'clock and morning news. As anything fundamental rarely changes, the news producer obliges only by furnishing sensationalism with the result that sensationalism begets more sensationalism by our regular expectation-and-satisfaction routine. The end result of this rather strange twist of news habit is that we are perfectly content with the *artificial* manufacture and presentation of the world as if it were true and with the *substitute* knowledge of our lives as if it were real.

Naturally and inevitably, the Substitute Society is also a "thirty-second" society. All things large and small—from job interviews to lovemaking— must be conducted in thirty seconds. All good impressions must be made in the first thirty seconds. Monumental decisions—including presidential elections—are based on a series of thirty-second commercials. Issues are articulated and debated, and conclusions drawn, all in thirty seconds. Columnist Sandy Grady describes the World Series in Cincinnati. "On the chest of each Cincinnati Reds player in the World Series is patched a small American flag. The woman who owns the Reds bellows over the microphone, 'This game is dedicated to our men and women in the Persian Gulf.' The crowd cheers. *Patriotism has been given its thirty seconds.*" In fact, even as a symbolic attention span, thirty seconds may be too charitable because, in all likelihood, the crowd instantly forgot about the Persian Gulf.

Dan Duko, one of the influential congressional lobbyists pushing our lawmakers for his clients, established what he calls a "five-second rule." His rule stipulates that "all background documents must be simple enough to be absorbed by Congressmen at the rate of five seconds per page." Bryant Gumbel, the cohost on one of the morning shows on television, asks his student guests whether they think there will be a nuclear war between the United States and the Soviet Union. "Quickly, yes or no," he demanded. To their credit, the high school students managed to answer the weighty question with some intelligent comments of their own. A *New Yorker* magazine cartoon shows a church advertising itself as the "First NO SERMON Church." As everyone knows, a popular preacher is, among other things, one who knows when to quit; it is only a short step from short sermons to no sermons. NBC's braintrust Brandon Tartikoff's Ten-Second Commandment goes like this: "View skeptically any show whose concept takes longer than ten seconds to explain." The Madison Avenue executives, the political experts, the media consultants, and other specialists who determine the substance of our society may be called audacious for their assumption that they can persuade the nation with thirty-second spots of images, words, and slogans. But time and again, their assumption proves correct and their undertaking succeeds. They indeed do persuade a nation of oversaturated sensory experiences with still more sensory reactions.

In those thirty seconds, life and death, success and failure, and, for that matter, the future of American society may be decided. As such, every second counts, and it counts in the sense that the impression each second creates is the ultimate substance of that impression. Facial expressions become supremely important. One must smile at all times, as smiling has become the fixed motif of every American. We notice that the American presidents, especially since the graphic era of television began, smile more excessively with each succeeding generation, culminating with the most smiling of all presidents: Ronald Reagan. It is not exaggerating to say that Ronald Reagan, say, as opposed to Abraham Lincoln, was all smiles. Not only does each American president smile more than the preceding one; the American president also smiles much more than his counterparts in other societies. In spite of the heavy burden of statecraft, the American president smiles everywhere while his opposite numbers in other countries display a demeanor that is a good deal more somber. That includes both capitalist heads of state and the more customarily dour-faced former socialist bosses. Smiling is an essential function of the American president, and the American public *expects* their president to smile at all times. The president is merely a symbolic representation of a hugely smiling republic, for every American is also supposed to smile and be happy at all times.

Since no one knows and no one has the time to find out what is beneath the smiling face, what passes for real substance in American society remains on the surface. What *appears* to be on the surface is taken as the substance of what *is*. People loved Walter Cronkite because he *appeared* to be sincere; people trusted John Houseman in his varying roles, including commercials, because he *appeared* to be a man of utter integrity, which he perfected. With appearance has come the importance of pictures. Pictures on television, pictures in newspapers and magazines, are the stuff of understanding and reflection. We say a picture is worth a thousand words, but it is so only if we know the words already. We say a picture tells the whole story, but it is so only if we know the whole story already. But never mind. Visual imagery—what we can grasp in one quick glance or comprehend within thirty seconds—is what makes life and history in America.

A "visual" (what can be seen) may be contrasted with an "image" (in the sense of "a mental picture or conception"). A visual is the work of our senses, an image, of our mind. A visual is represented in film, television, photography, and other graphic forms of representation. An image is the substance that our mind gives to written or oral representations. While the visual puts the burden of representation on the visual object, the image puts the burden of comprehension on *both* the narrator and the audience. For the latter, there is the mutual communication, reflection, and dialogue. For the former, there is only the active presentation by the producer and the passive reception by the consumer. A visual is a one-way process; an image is a shared experience. But in a thirty-second society the visual takes precedence. The reasons are obvious.

The visual is selective with the choice of its material. It can select any visual scene it wants and freeze it in visual graphics. It selects life's most agreeable moments and present them as generally representative. The material is always selective in that the dreadful repetition and boredom of sameness is sharply focused in one graphic, one story, or one personality as if that were the case at all times. A smiling face, a swimming duck in the pond, a wonderful one-hour segment, and any such chosen moment can be preserved in an infinite variety of presentations.

The properties that make up the actual components of a visual command technical virtuosity that is state-of-the-art. The quality of progress toward a perfect visual—be it a commercial, a television episode, a photographic display, or a movie—has been such that it can now present anything as almost as real as (or often more real than) life itself. Commercials emerge as lifelike, sincere, and authentic, with all the wrinkles of human emotion; television, photography, and motion pictures can be just as heartrending as anything in real life. The superb technical quality, in both the material and human components, easily overwhelms what little analytic ability one might still control. The art of presenting these visuals becomes a subject in its own right. It is not merely a commercial or a television episode. One is speaking of the very stuff of visual media with all their authority, authenticity, and persuasion in thirty seconds flat.

Since the visual is only for the senses and senses cannot imagine, it does not allow the creative connections of imaginary narratives. What the eye can see cannot be connected to the mind for further understanding and reflection. What the eye can see begins and ends with the eye. The senses begin and end with reaction. The senses cannot remember; they merely react to the same visual object without locking it into their permanent remembrance. What memory the visual creates is likely to remain within the narrowest sphere of one's personal experience as well as within the narrowest span of one's time consciousness. Memories of old physical pains no longer endured are rarely painful.

A visual—the frozen amount of life, technically re-created—is infinitely more attractive than any slice of real life. Because of its superb technical ability to enhance the quality of graphics and because of the requirement that it must appeal to the viewer immediately, a visual is obligated to look and act more attractive than its counterpart in reality. The sky is bluer than the real sky, a vegetable greener than the real vegetable. Ben Kingsley is more attractive to look at than the real Gandhi he portrayed in the film, Peter O'Toole more attractive than T. E. Lawrence, Alec Guiness more than George Smiley in "Tinker, Tailor, Soldier, Spy," George C. Scott more than George S. Patton. Because a visual re-creation is always more attractive than the reality it portrays, the viewer almost always prefers the re-created visual than its reality. We enjoy the pictures of the Grand Canyon more than the real Grand Canyon. The visual can emphasize the more attractive aspects and ignore the undesirable. Like our selective memory but with greater force of persuasion because of its graphic quality, a visual emerges like the retouched face of a dead hero or saint forever etched in indestructible remembrance. In a society where a patient reflection is not part of its cultural and psychological habits, an attractive visual sways millions of voters, persuades reluctant consumers, and determines the measure of personal intimacy.

Everyone in America values "highly visibility." All heroes and saints must be visual heroes and saints. They must remain *visible* at all times to exist. Yesterday's hero or saint, if not seen today, is but a distant memory. Reality cannot exist unless it is visible. Responding to the question of why the savings-and-loan debacle has not received greater coverage on television, Maureen Bunyan, a reporter for a Washington station, comments, "TV is a visual medium. S & L has *no visuals*. No blood, no fire, so there is no story." Similarly, 64 percent of Americans agreed in 1989 that drugs were America's "No. 1 priority" when it was so pushed on television; once it was replaced by other topical issues on TV a year later, the percent who so agreed dropped to 10. We can solve any social problem and dissolve any political conflict just by keeping the topic off television.

The most important function of a visual in entertainment society is its ability to dramatize. Where there is little or no drama in real life, the visual creates a series of dramatic tension, suspense, and climax. Simple issues are dramatized into complex issues, complex issues are dramatized into simple issues, all through the magic of visuals. Anything can be condensed into a few pictures or stretched into a miniseries. Bed-wetting is dramatized; AIDS is dramatized; World War III is dramatized. Without seeing it dramatized as visuals on television we do not seem to grasp the meaning of any issue at all. Television is the most dominant medium to convey any serious message—war, famine, violence—but ironically, because it is through *television* that the serious message must dilute its serious purpose. Television conveys issues but stupefies people. A visual can make people see things clearly, yet without any serious purpose in that clarity. It dramatizes events but trivializes their significance.

Dramatization is a high form of entertainment in an otherwise humdrum life of repetition and boredom. The Substitute Society loves to dramatize everything into a high drama of great emotion and solemnity. Since there is not much high drama in real life, the producers of entertainment must *manufacture* dramas out of trivia. A college football team wins a game dramatically with a last-second field goal, there is a dramatic announcement as to where the committee recommends that the sports stadium be built, a child is dramatically rescued from a pond, the stock market makes its dramatic recovery, and so on. Every race must have a dramatic photo-finish to satisfy the crowd. American society's calendar is in reality a schedule of dramatic events and dates nicely paced for the routine of buildup, anticipation, suspense, climax, and resolution that is central to American life. There may be some real-life dramas in terrorist acts and natural disasters, but much of America's dramatic tension comes from games and visual creations. In our entertainment society we cannot simply enjoy a day of uneventful bliss. We must torture ourselves with artificial tension to feel fulfilled and significant.

Thus all things American must now be measured in visuals. The uncanny guru of modern trends in mass media and one of its moguls, Rupert Murdoch, is right on the mark in his prognosis: "Certainly in the medium future," he predicts, "it appears there will be more growth in TV than in global print. We are focusing our expansion in electronics until we've got a better balance in our portfolio." Undoubtedly Americans will watch much more than read in the future.

The problems of a Substitute Reality are thus resolved by the solutions of a substitute kind. We simply look for solutions within our make-believe world of entertainment and thrills. Whatever malaise we suffer, the solution is only a telephone call away; whatever loneliness we may feel, it is only a channel away from being dissolved; the most intimate of all personal problems in love, family relations, questions of life and living can be solved by the most impersonal means of commercialism, for example, by how-to-find-yourself-and-be-happy best-sellers. However serious our problems, solutions must be easy, quick, and even entertaining.

Ultimately, in our all-consuming desire for entertainment we also confuse entertainment with art. Art inspires and entertainment seduces. To inspire, art appeals to the very best in everyone. To seduce, entertainment must appeal to our worst instinct. Inspired, we excel; seduced, we regress. In our confusion, we expect to be enlightened by entertainment when we are actually dulled by it. We expect to be inspired by entertainment when we are actually reduced to moral inertia by it. "The process exacts a spiritual cost," commented Carl Bernstein in a related context. How good is our entertainment? "No country does better than the United States," observed film director Milos Forman.[3] Indeed, in a society of crisscrossing yellow brick roads that lead to perpetual excitement, no less will be acceptable.

NOTES

1. "The Magic of Special Effects," "Nova," Public Broadcasting Service, 5 November 1985.

2. I have dealt with the subject of art and American society in *Art, Beauty, and Pornography: A Journey Through American Society* (Buffalo, NY: Prometheus Books, 1987).

3. Carl Bernstein, "The Leisure Empire," *Time*, December 24, 1990.

Chapter 4

The Trivial Heart

On November 10, 1989, NBC Radio began its regular news broadcast with a report on the East Germans pouring through the Berlin Wall and ended the program only moments later with the news of Oprah Winfrey having (re)gained twelve pounds. From the sublime subject of a collapse of communism to the most trivial, two wholly unrelated topics on the same news program were smoothly and unconsciously presented to the world. But why did the listener *not* detect the incongruity, the stupidity, and the absurdity in this otherwise entirely "normal" program? When and how have the world of reality (the Berlin Wall) and the world of trivia (Winfrey's weight) converged to make up our perfectly familiar reality—to our comfort, enjoyment, and enlightenment?

What is truly noteworthy is *not* that this phenomenon exists in our midst, but that we now thoroughly *like* it and *demand* it as our normal reality and entitlement. In an extraordinary coincidence of interests among the Profit Ethic, the Substitute Society with Substitute Reality, and people clamoring to be fulfilled and happy, American society has crossed that fine line that divides sanity and insanity, serious and trivial, and real and unreal. It is not that American society has forsaken the sane, the serious, the real; it has simply made them meaningless. With no history to define them as a whole, with no personal moral precepts to guide them as individuals, to give their existence meaning or coherence, Americans lurch along for the moment. In our "subliterate TV culture . . . each new day begins afresh," observes historian Dan T. Carter, "without past, without future." Hence that peculiar appeal of thirty-second messages.

The New World has created a still newer world that does not really exist, but exists in the minds of those who live in their own illusion. Let me conjure up a hypothetical advertisement that appears in the local newspaper:

Are you hungry for real family life? Family life you no longer have? Family life you wish you had but never did? Are you lonely without the warmth, support, and love of a family that you once had, you wish you had, or you would like to have?

We have the answer. Come to us and spend a week, a month, or even a few days with a family that you can call your own, a family that is exactly like the one in your dream. We have many professionally trained personnel who would be glad to be your father, mother, aunt, grandparents, brothers, sisters—all to your specification. Just write in the attached form what you want. What kind of parents, brothers, sisters, or grandparents. Their religious preferences, if any. What kind of pets. Send photographs if you have them, which would help us give you a more lifelike family, thanks to our highly professional makeup specialists.

Many who have tried our service were so satisfied that they return time and time again to reexperience their family life. We believe that life can be richer and more fulfilling with family experience, especially those who have never had one in the way it should be. We are a large family waiting eagerly to serve lonely hearts like you—with warmth, support, and love. Call or write us. We are open 24 hours. Visa and MasterCard accepted.

A similar hypothetical ad appears on television. It is more graphically illustrated on the screen, the staff lining up in front of a house greeting the lonely heart customer in a variety of roles—father, mother, sister, brother—specified by the customer and playing the roles in slow-motion cuts. Fantasy? Too farfetched? Not really. We are much closer to it in reality than many of us realize. (I wouldn't be surprised if some enterprising person has already started this fantasy-family-on-order business.) This fictional illustration is used to demonstrate how far we have gone in destroying our reality and substituting illusion—without even realizing the switch. The fact that this "commercial" family seems reasonably "normal," with some mental adjustment, suggests the subtle way in which our reality has been replaced by illusion.

There have always been two aspects to our social reality. In one reality we display our spontaneous, uncalculated emotional responses to persons and events that we consider dear. We might call this our Primary Reality. The other consists of our *public* behaviors and relations. We might call this our Secondary Reality. When a person dies, his family may experience primary emotional responses to the event, with all the attendant varieties of spontaneous, deeply felt, and unpremeditated results. The consequences of primary emotion are not calculated and do not normally include anything but an understanding nod in the close circle of relatives and friends. But the same primary members may display their "secondary" or "public" reactions to the event—for example, at public funerals. There may be an appropriate statement made by the family, mixing grief with politeness, and such. There may be eulogies spoken by the associates, friends, and acquaintances of the deceased. There may even be a display of deep emotion by those secondary members at the funeral. But all those demonstrations of feelings at the funeral, both by the primary and secondary members, must follow certain rituals that are premeditated according to the rules of Secondary Reality. Never mind that Secondary Reality is not as real or not as spontaneous as Primary Reality. Secondary Reality is a public necessity. A nice hug, a kiss, a handshake, an expression, although social rituals of no real substance *are* created and accepted simply as gestures of formality, sometimes uncomplimentarily called "public posturing" in some instances. A mayor, a governor, or the president of the United States may display a nice gesture or give words of condolence in public on an occasion like the one above. But tradition has it that one does not take it seriously. It is just a nice gesture required by our Secondary Reality.

All commercially related gestures make up the most extreme form of Secondary Reality. What is sold and bought at an agreed-upon price has no primary meaning. One sells what one can and buys what one must. It is an exchange of equal values between two consenting agents of commerce. In it there is no private sentiment. One always hunts for bargains. Only a fool will deliberately pay a higher price for the same product. That the seller smiles and makes the buyer feel good is entirely irrelevant; the buyer still must *pay* for the goods and services. Nothing personal, either for the seller or for the buyer. It's just business.

Primary Reality—in which we live, feel, and express joys and sorrows—has been effectively destroyed with the destruction of the Social Ethic by the Profit Ethic. In its place we have erected a Substitute Society and its own Substitute Reality as well. How thoroughly this substitution has been wrought parallels how *natural* our substitute reality or Secondary Reality seems to us in our routine day-to-day life. Secondary displays of emotion on public occasions—by media reporters, politicians, celebrities, spokesmen for organizations and personalities, lawyers for their clients, in public memoirs and biographies, during and after a game by athletes, who "break down" and show emotion—have become such a natural part of our emotional landscape in America that few would think of challenging the authenticity of such displays. Tears and emotional outbursts on television are taken as authentic. What the television camera catches is the stuff of real life, because the picture does not lie. Few would think that these are calculated and premeditated gestures appropriate for the occasion, not spontaneous or real.

The seeming wholeness of television makes the distinction between the two realities all the more difficult to draw. Only the most discriminating observer—one who is almost wholly alienated from the daily goings-on of American culture—would notice instinctively that television makes all primary human emotions expressed through it seem patently artificial and superficial. Once put on television, all human emotions, either in words or in gesture, would seem false and contrived. The discriminating observer simply realizes that the television set is not a natural environment and the television picture not a spontaneous snapshot. Because of the enormity of the expense and profit considerations, it is only natural that everything on television must be carefully premeditated and the effects minutely calculated. We must assume that human emotions on television, while undoubtedly genuine in some cases, are also part of that premeditation and calculation. The president consoling a victim, people reacting to disasters, family members expressing sorrow for their beloved, and many other such scenes may be authentic. Yet the very presence of television makes them seem utterly prestaged and insincere.

To most Americans television represents a strange crossroads of cultural schizophrenia: on the one hand television is the mirror of reality, and on the other it is also the artificially created world of beautiful color, sound, and visuals. But appearing so convincingly sincere and authentic on television requires a mastery of the art of deception and illusion-making of the highest order. It is almost safe nowadays to assume, whenever someone or a program on television refers to something like "love," "compassion," being "sad," "moved," and "touched," and "concern," "care," or other such emotion-laden themes and words that it is well-staged, prerehearsed fakery. But the power of television in creating the illusion of reality has become so potent that now people habitually measure the authenticity of an event in terms of television, by saying, "It's just like a TV drama," or, "It was just like what you see on TV," and so on. It must be on TV to be real as an event and authentic as experience.

Ronald Reagan is not only the most successful master of illusion-making but also the one who gave television-created reality its aura of seriousness and ring of authenticity. When Barbara Walters proposed to interview the president and the First Lady—to be broadcast just before the celebration of the most illusion-making of all events, the Academy Award night—the national ad for the interview had the Reagans sitting in a movie house with the caption: "BARBARA VISITS THE WHITE HOUSE. AND YOU'RE ALL INVITED."
The rest of the ad went like this:

What were the Reagans' favorite movies of the year? Did Nancy Reagan *really* date Clark Gable? Will Ronald Reagan ever return to acting? For answers to these questions and much, much more about the Reagans' family life and political life, join Barbara Walters for an intimate, behind-the-scenes visit with the President and the First Lady . . . and some Hollywood friends, on "The Barbara Walters Special."[1]

The program was "Brought to you by Stouffer's frozen foods."

What was more instructive than the simple fact that no serious issues of national or international magnitude were discussed was the complete lack of any critical response to the sinking of the presidential authority to such a low level of frivolity and unreality. The interview simply confirmed the complete convergence of reality with illusion. Presidency and Hollywood mixed perfectly and naturally. In the hands of skillful experts television is a lethal weapon of image manipulation. To most Americans it is the only window through which thought is made possible and the world made intelligible. They are fair game for those who create reality out of illusion for the purpose of selling Secondary Reality.

A society built on illusion—finely crafted, well advertised, ubiquitously present—also affects its more serious matters, including the military mind-set. Soldiers are recruited by TV ads created by those who create the Pepsi-generation ads. Those who join the military are basically those of the Pepsi generation who watch too much TV and have too little to do. Private Benjamin in a hit movie tried to persuade her sergeant that she joined the army for "the condos and the private rooms." It is not just a job, the ad says, it's an adventure. The army promises that you can "be all you can be." Recruiting letters sent to high school seniors tell them of an enlistee who has bought a new car, has a new stereo set in his room, and has thousands of dollars saved up, in only his first two years in the army. What happens when they are asked to do the real job of killing and being killed? They complain, as they did to a conscientious-objector counselor: "I signed up to go to college; I didn't sign up to go to Saudi Arabia." An army National Guard sergeant actually filed a suit against President Bush during the 1990 Gulf buildup when ordered to go to the desert to fight Saddam Hussein. Although actual lawsuits against the commander in chief may be rare, the following "Doonesbury" strip is perhaps more accurate a measure of the Pepsi generation's confused mind-set. In this one, a soldier stationed in the Gulf muses to his comrade:

I sure didn't bargain for this crap when I upped! I was gonna to be all I could be, understand? I was gonna get a free education, see the world, learn how to program computers! It was today's army! Nobody said anything about actually having to *fight*!
    Sigh . . .
Damn, I feel betrayed![2]

People lost in unreality confuse their self-image, magnifying their importance and ignoring their reality. It is not unlike a credit card holder who only thinks about the power it gives him, not his debt-ridden powerlessness. This false sense of reality affects the whole of American society, young and old, black and white. About to retire, writer David Bouchier observes that the world of retirement, at least in the way it is portrayed by its chief magazine, *Modern Maturity*, has "no sense of continuity" with reality. "Youth, children and families are almost entirely absent from the sunny pages of *Modern Maturity*. Unlike any previous generation of elderly, the new affluent seniors have abandoned this link to the future. These elders live like a separate nation, as if old age itself were a state of grace. They are connected to society only by the umbilical cords of money and medicine."

A standardized mathematics test was given to 13-year-olds in six countries—the United States, Spain, Britain, Ireland, Canada, and Korea. American kids scored the lowest on the test, Koreans scored the highest. But when asked what they *thought* of their own math skill, Americans scored the *highest* in self-image (60 percent saying they were "good in math") and Koreans the *lowest* (23 percent). "Feeling good" while "doing bad" is a national "fixation," says a magazine essay reflecting on the incident. "American students may not know their math," it further observes, "but they have evidently absorbed the lessons of the newly fashionable self-esteem curriculum wherein kids are taught to feel good about themselves." A Junior Achievement–Gallup International Youth Survey in 1990 again confirms this strange denial of reality. "By most standards, Japanese students are doing better than American students," the survey reports. But the results showed that U.S. students are more "optimistic about their schools and themselves compared with their Japanese counterparts." Nine out of ten American students rated their high schools as "do[ing] a good job teaching math," while only 70 percent of Japanese students felt that way about their schools.[3]

In the world of unreality, fun, and games, adults are like children. Explaining the popularity of Nintendo games among *adults*, a report quotes an "expert": "Now, a lot of the executives in their 30s and 40s . . . have computers, their kids are familiar with the computers and there's big crossover when the kids go to bed or when the video game system isn't being used, that you might find Mom and Dad playing the games as well." What does an adult find in the games? "You literally go into this trance," a man describes it, "that is, like, time goes by and, like, you don't know where it went." Incidentally, a TV ad for "Tetris," one of the more popular electronic games, runs like this: "Competitive Spirit! Heart Beats Pumping! It Gets Me to Take on the World!" It is no wonder that math-poor American students think so highly of themselves in math skill. Extended to a serious national issue, say, the federal deficit, public opinion becomes childish, unreasonable, and therefore impossible to take seriously. They want the deficit reduced, but they refuse to do anything about it. "All the people are against the deficit," an exasperated congressman complains, "but they're also against doing anything about the deficit that affects them." Not surprisingly, political observer Paul Taylor's conclusion on the 1988 presidential campaign in his book *See How They Run* is that the election was basically a choice "between the illusion of Bush and the unvarnished reality of Dukakis."[4] Of course, illusion won.

The difficulty of distinguishing Primary Reality from Secondary Reality goes one step further: American society now *demands* that Secondary Reality have all the requisites of Primary Reality. It demands that illusion replace reality with all its authenticity intact. Of the seemingly ageless presence of celebrities like Joan Collins and Elizabeth Taylor, both in their fifties, a psychologist observed: "Joan Collins and Elizabeth Taylor represent a marvelous fantasy of eternal youth. People now very much *want* to believe in their indestructibility." A 1985 issue of the *New England Journal of Medicine*, and picked up by newspapers later, introduced a strange topic: whether physicians should be *required* to attend the funerals of their former patients. As usual, pros and cons on the issue were aired. Among the cons, "one physician's wife lamented that adding funerals to doctors' duties would further cut into the time they spent with their own families." A Dr. Patrick Irvine, whose original essay on the subject touched off the debate, wrote, according to a newspaper rephrasing, that "going to patients' wakes and funerals gives families a chance to talk about their own experiences during the death." Further, Irvine wrote: "My feelings need resolution just as the family's feelings do, and society's rituals help me with that as well." Not unlike the fictional commercial family quoted before, physicians' being *required* to attend the funerals of their deceased patients to share their mutual feelings and experiences doesn't seem as strange as it first appears. "Have you hugged your kid today?" a familiar bumper sticker asks. It might be required one day that all physicians attend their patients' funerals and shed at least two ounces of tears or that all parents must hug their children three times a day. Notice that the reality of emotion ("my feelings") is appeased through the force of illusion (*required* funeral appearances).

Notice below another classic example of mixing, or rather confusing, make-believe reality (the Super Bowl) with traditional reality ("fellowship," "love," "God") in Mike Ditka's speech to his Chicago Bears just before the team went on the field:

We're in this together as a football team and we are going to play it for each other and we're going to win this game for 49, 50, or whatever number we have in this room. We are going to win it for each other. We are going to play it for each other and we're going to pick each other up. That's what it's all about. This is out of love for each other, this is your game. Any other intentions won't be accepted. But you are going to win this game for each other.

Let's have the Lord's Prayer. Heavenly Father, we are grateful for this opportunity and we thank you for. . . . We pray as always in the name of Jesus Christ your Son, our Lord, Amen. Let's go.[5]

This blithely pious and love-thy-brothers approach to perhaps one of the most mindlessly phony events in America by one of its best-selling hustlers is a far cry from the era of Vince Lombardi, whose no-nonsense roar was: "Winning is not everything. It is the *only* thing!" He might have flinched to hear "play it for each other," "love for each other," "Heavenly Father," and so on. Years later, Ditka advised a fellow coach whose team had been on the skids, "It's no crime to shed a tear in the sincerity of the moment. I think that's the humanness of this whole thing, that we get passed over as humans." Or, in another sports affair, notice the similar mixing of vicious corporate fighting with appeal to God in the speech of a lawyer representing the now-defunct United States Football League suing the established National Football League for multimillion-dollar damages, as described by a reporter. Notice the infusion of "God" and "bless" into the reality of money: " 'Nail them!' he said. . . . Then, at the end, he sat down in his chair and said, 'Without minimum damages, this league is dead. Please God, find for us. God bless you.' "

Their reference to God and love, or whatever other emotional triggers to which they appeal, may be deliberately false or truly authentic. But what is significant is that all participants seem to *believe* in their ringing authenticity.

In a society of Substitute Reality, it is common to see the deep fusion of the phony secondary event with profound primary emotion. Even Oprah Winfrey, whose talk shows routinely deal with the lurid and sordid and whose struggle with her diet is of some public curiosity, "genuinely believes she has a spiritual purpose and that she is guided by '*divine direction.*' " Listen to the serious tone of David Burke at CBS announcing the reinstatement of a previously laid-off employee: "Painful though these events have been, we have all learned a great deal about how sensitive and fragile our society is . . . how deeply people and groups can be hurt if great care is not taken in conducting public discourse." A grievous academic injustice? A grave constitutional matter? What prompted such a serious reflection in a network executive? A "public discourse" of national importance? No, no such thing. The reinstated employee was none other than Andy Rooney, whose insensitive remarks about homosexuals had touched off a controversy resulting in his forced layoff. But *what* was his job at CBS that caused a careless remark to teach everyone such a painful lesson? Here is his job description, according to *Time*: "Weekly musings on *trivia* like junk mail and vacuum cleaners." But, why is a commentator on trivia taken so utterly seriously? In so grave a manner?

The comico-serioso fusion is endless in our confused society. *Time* magazine ran a summary-of-the-decade special in January 1990. Who were the "Faces of the Decade"? They were (among others), according to its selection: Bruce Springsteen. Cher. Madonna. Nancy Reagan. Eddie Murphy. Mother Teresa. Mother Teresa? What is Mother Teresa, the Nobel laureate who is described by the same magazine as "the saint of the gutter," doing with the likes of show-biz celebrities? Why is there no gut reaction that something is terribly odd in the lineup that mixes the most sublime with the most ridiculous, the purest with the trashiest? Would it be clearer if we substituted Jesus Christ for Mother Teresa? Would we *then* know anything different? Or would Jesus be another "SuperStar," as an Oral Roberts show called Him? The world in which Mother Teresa lives is so different from the world in which these celebrities exist that putting them together as the "Faces of the Decade" would, under normally sane circumstances, be supremely insulting to the sublime and incongruous to the sane.

Our popular culture—the main staple of Substitute Society—stoutly refuses to believe that there is a fine line between sublime and ridiculous. The American culture of massive circulation is a great equalizer, large and deep enough to drown any previously established contradictions and typologies into a groggy harmony. *Parade*, one such massive outlet, regularly presents its smooth version of incongruence. Questions about American-made X-rated movies, Irene Dunn, Tom Cruise, and Nicholas Cage appear on the same "Q & A" page with questions about President Bush's thoughts on Dan Quayle, Jewish justices on the U.S. Supreme Court, the historical place of Dwight Eisenhower, and soldiers killed in Vietnam. *U.S. News & World Report*, a weekly magazine almost exclusively devoted to moneymaking and the defense of moneymaking, runs a special cover story on the last days of Jesus. In it, the writers blithely describe the scene in which Jesus drives the money changers out of the temple. Does it ever occur to them that should it be today, *they* would be the ones to receive His first blows? But, of course, among the more devout churchgoers are the modern-day money changers, and there seems to be no irony in it, either observed or felt.

America's hunger for signs that everything is what it seems to be is voracious. Things must be personalized, intimate, trustworthy. What is objective reality and what is subjective reaction mesh into a hazy conception of reality. In an age of intimate television, there is an "increased blurring of the entertainment and information function," reports a media expert. For weeks preceding the showing of a drama based on the California earthquake, NBC issued releases on "quake history and projections, as if this movie were a public service instead of just the latest dunderheaded soap-opera disaster epic." Why is the gossip business about celebrities so prosperous in American society? A magazine article answers: "TV personalities become surrogate friends or family members, and faces glimpsed in the news or on talk shows become significant presences in the lives of many viewers. Their private lives thus seem a genuine public concern." How durable are celebrities, the creation of illusion in a society of unreality? "Celebrity is the perishable commodity," declares George Will, "that renewable resource of a throwaway culture."

To enforce the false blurring of the line between public and private, there is an organization called Emotions Anonymous in which people discuss emotional problems "with a group of strangers." For children and their agreeable parents in pursuit of authentic feeling the Cabbage Patch doll was personalized, with every model different from the others, with its own adoption paper. "Show Biz Pizza," the new mecca of high-tech amusement for children and the home of Chuck E. Cheese, its mascot, tells its customers: "You can even write Chuck E. Cheese and tell him how your summer turned out." Never mind that Chuck E. Cheese is a total fabrication of the entrepreneur. McDonald's, not just a fast food place, is a home away from home, a substitute mom where you have your birthdays.

Most people who have ever had the need for psychiatrists, psychologists, counselors, or other "support" personnel expect to feel intimate with their helpers in the same way they do with their family, relatives, and friends and perhaps expect them to come to their funeral, too. A number of female patients fall in love with their male therapists, as few patients can resist their seduction, especially from a position of trouble and vexation. Reacting to rumors of discord in his team, former New England Patriots coach Ray Berry indignantly declared, "We are a *family!*" Not to be outdone, Dexter Manley, disappointed that his former team, the Washington Redskins, waived him upon his return from a drug-related suspension, was more emphatic about his love for his former team: "If I died right now," he said, "I told my wife I would want my ashes scattered over RFK Stadium." That's love of the most intimate kind, symbolized by a football and a multimillion-dollar contract.

When a group of rock singers staged a "Rock and Roll Caravan for Human Rights," with the purpose of introducing "young people to Amnesty International's work," the *Milwaukee Journal* lamented: "[I]t's regrettable that . . . the arousal of social conscience among the masses of young people seemingly must depend upon the social consciences of rock stars."

In the absence of Primary Reality people must now identify themselves with many *pseudo*-primary groups: professional helpers, politicians, celebrities in entertainment and sports, radio talk show hosts, news anchormen, television characters in shows and soap operas, communal "families," cult leaders, unorthodox religious sects, encounter groups, commercial characters like "Mrs. Olsen" who sell coffee ("she reminds me of my aunt"), and any number and variety of commercial and professional agents who specialize in creating a sense of intimacy, happiness, and moral right. Most European and Japanese commercials tend to be exaggerated, wildly colored, cartoonlike. Many American commercials are much more subtle and real-life–like, or "realistic," using all the real life reference points—grandpa, grandma, mom, dad, brother, sister, love, birthday, success, career, happiness. Van Gordon Sauter, former president of CBS News, wanted "stories that reach out and touch people. Moments." He said more on the illusion of television intimacy:

The kind of thing we're looking for is something that evokes an emotional response. When I go back to the [control room], I tell them, goddamn it, *we've got to touch people.* They've *got to feel a relationship* with us. A lot of stories have an inherent drama, but others have to be done in a way that will *bring out an emotional response.*[6]

Don Hewitt, who hatched the popular "60 Minutes" program on CBS, attributes the success of the show to its approach to "personalize" so that the reporter "takes the viewer along with him on the story" as a way of dealing with "the viewer's short attention span."

The personalized approach works. People cannot tell Secondary Reality from Primary Reality, make-believe from true life, public images of celebrities from real human beings. They emerge as one confusing but largely authentic picture of reality. Bill Cosby, who is having a tough time with his own children, emerges as the perfect father on television. Someone writes a national magazine article nominating rock singer Bruce Springsteen for "man of the year" because Springsteen is a man "with no gimmicks, only talent and sincerity." ("Strictly blue collar," says *Time*'s description of him. But why is that man so fabulously wealthy selling his "blue collar" image?) Dolly Parton talks about her "humble" social origin and "sincere" human values. (Never mind her artificially enlarged bust, which is her trademark, not her "humble" and "sincere" self.) Springsteen may be sincere, and Parton humble in person, but both are in the entertainment business where personal sincerity or humbleness has no vital, much less causal, function. A Times Mirror survey shows that 81 percent of Americans believe Dan Rather (*as if* they *know* him enough to trust him) as opposed to 67 percent of those who trust their president (about whom they *do* know a great deal). When Joe Theisman, the former quarterback of the Washington Redskins, was badly injured, a Virginia preacher said, "When he went down on the field, I felt as though there had been a death in the family." (Perhaps Ray Berry *was* authentic.)

What accounts for the phenomenal success of Ed McMahon, Johnny Carson's sidekick? "People think they know me very well," McMahon explains. "I'm part of the family. Ed. Big Ed. Just like a next-door neighbor, a pal, a guy they could sit and have a beer with." Except the pal and guy next-door lives in a $3 million mansion in Beverly Hills and spends weekends on a fifty-foot yacht, just appearing to be a guy who looks real and friendly. Leo Buscaglia, that fabulously successful writer of love best-sellers, is said to "really love people" and is rather sincere about it. "Dr. Ruth," the ubiquitous diminutive sex adviser whose valor is no discretion was selected one of the "10 Outstanding Mothers of the Year" by the National

Mother's Day Committee. When ABC's news with Peter Jennings at anchor overtook NBC's news with Tom Brokaw, Jennings gave credit to the "measure of spontaneity" that he perfected through interviews. Even local news anchors and reporters are prone to banter with each other (spontaneously) after a survey shows that people *want* them to act spontaneous and banter with each other. A bank commercial says it is "genuinely interested in your business," not just your money, and banks that are only interested in your money are shortchanging you because this bank's interest in you is "genuine" beyond money, the key word emphasized over and over being "genuine."

When hunger in America was staged as a show, "Hands Across America," a participant was personally moved, as were many others: "What we gave, we got back in so many ways—new friends and a good feeling inside. It's been such a wonderful day, I don't want it to end." Never mind that it began as a reminder of the hungry people in America. The serious issue became secondary to the alleged 7 million participants. "Most everyone exchanged telephone numbers. Several made plans for a reunion party." CBS Radio, reporting on the event, called it "a spectacular day." As soon as the event was over, out of sight, and off television, scarcely anyone mentioned or remembered it. By late 1989 it was a distant memory. "Famine lost its luster once the strains of *We Are the World* faded and the television light went off," a magazine report dryly noted. "There is little money or prestige in hunger."

This inability to separate the public world from the private feelings and domain eventually trivializes life. Issues are ritualized into something to do for those whose lives are leisurely and affluent enough to display civic consciousness. People are insistently told to find "meaning," "a favorite charity," and "rewarding hobbies," such as gardening or advocating political issues, trivializing the significant and signifying the trivial. Miss America contestants *must* choose an issue among the array of "issues" safe enough to make its advocacy inconsequential: care for the elderly, stamping out drug abuse, physical fitness, the environment, arts in education, volunteerism, cancer education, and motivating youth. The U.S. Supreme Court has nowadays become the ultimate arbiter of insignificance. The justices are asked to rule on whether women should fight in combat, whether school prayer should be allowed, whether drugs should be legalized, whether abortion should be allowed. Only in a Substitute Society where reality must be artificially made up would we expect such weighty issues to invade the nation's highest court. In a nation threatened with extinction, the question of women's combat role would not even be raised; in a society with genuine fear of God, school prayer would not become an issue; in a community of real life and living, drugs would be a luxury, much less a problem; in a world of overpopulation, abortion is an obligation, not a right.

The ultimate trivialization of America, ironically, is in the glut of "freedom of choice." Average Americans must face for their daily choice at least 25,000 items at their average supermarket, as many as 55 television stations, 11,100 magazines and periodicals, and an untold number of solicitations from a great variety of organizations and special interest groups that make up the vast freedom of choice in their society. At one store in Los Angeles, customers face over two hundred different types of breakfast cereals. Columnist Pat Truly calls this sort of freedom of choice "the right to indulge in the meaningless." Why are we trivializing our lives and indulging in the meaningless? Columnist David Broder answers: "Because we are floundering. No American leader in 25 years has discovered or articulated a popular goal to focus the nation's energy and attention." Americans cannot bear any bad news from their leaders unless it is somebody else's bad news. They prefer flattery, illusion, and trivia, and the politicians know it. No one has been elected for telling the truth.

The personalized approach to public issues and commercial relations—for example, the shopkeeper remembering the customer personally—has always been part of the business culture in America. On the surface of it, there is nothing unusual about today's approach; commercial agents still try to be friendly with their customers to make them feel good. With one crucial difference, however. Traditionally, there was a certain measure of true spontaneity and friendliness in the way shopkeepers and receptionists dealt with their customers and the customers responded in kind both in manners and feelings. Today it is a masterfully calculated creation of gimmicks—like a grocery store that posts a sign: "If the cashier forgets to say hello, you get a free bagful of groceries." There is neither the true spontaneity that gives such gestures their credibility nor the informal structure for friendliness that accounts for the mutual trust that existed in such exchanges. What is worse, the customer himself *believes* and *wants* to believe that such gestures of artificial spontaneity and friendliness are genuine. Even service stations, automobile repair shops, and used car salesmen, among others, engage in this "feel-good-like-real-family" policy by sending letters and greeting cards on holidays to their former customers. A church in North Carolina advertises itself as "a friendly church that loves people." The church's motto might as well be a bank's, a grocery store's, a pizza restaurant's, or even a massage parlor's, for that matter. Everyone speaks of "friendliness" and "love." A trade paper advertises a service for "Problem Solving Therapy" for "individuals, couples, families. First session free," and the ad is placed between "3 Piece Bedroom suite" and "Waterbed, quality constructed queen size frame." A hospital in Chicago promises: "We treat our patients with understanding and concern," but not with respect and competence. A congressman informs his constituents to contact him to get "presidential greetings sent on birthdays and anniversaries." A local television station shows an ad for itself in which the anchor staff banter with one another and the anchorman says to the camera, "We enjoy the relationship, it's *real*." Even a Campbell soup commercial says that their soup is the thing to offer "if you love someone."

The unreality of Secondary Reality is easily accomplished in America by the perverse influence of mass media, especially television, which in many ways is a tradition destroyer. Before the media era, goods and services, and their reputations, took generations to be established. It was basically a word-of-mouth means of living or dying in business. A good or service could not possibly be established overnight, as it can be today thanks to the mass media. Calvin Klein jeans, blockbuster movies and videos, electronic games, or what have you is established as "hot stuff" overnight by the simple fact that it is advertised in the media. Traditions are thus made overnight: the Linda Carter "Classic" is held every year in professional tennis; goods and services that took over a century to be recognized simply vanish overnight; celebrities, heroes, greatnesses are born with one hit, one act, one best-seller, and vanish just as quickly.

Because of its ability to slice, freeze, and create any segment of reality, the mass media can overcome history and reality and effortlessly merge with timelessness and unreality. With the passing of time and tradition, media characters are then established as true-life characters replacing time and tradition. Moving pictures on television—with stories that are tailored to be real—create the impression of reality and real characters. People feel the pangs of pain, sorrow, joy, sadness in the whole range of emotion with the television stories, events, and characters *as if* they are real.

Even before television, of course, there were movie "stars" created by Hollywood studios. Clara Bow, Clark Gable, Humphrey Bogart, Alan Ladd, Lionel Barrymore, Gary Cooper, and Marilyn Monroe, among many others, were "stars." Everything about them was fantasy and larger than life. Ordinary people admired and fancied them, as young Judy Garland did Clark Gable. But such admiration and fancy were just that: admiration and fancy in a wholly fairy tale–like creation of one's mind and of celluloid in the way the moving pictures were supposed to have been. They had—and everyone knew it—*nothing* to do with reality. The actors were like real stars in the heavens, shining brightly, to be admired and fancied, but never reachable in real life. Their celebration still took place in the fan's fanta-syland, never to be real and never to be taken seriously. To their dying days, many of the stars tried to preserve their star image that they and their studios had cultivated. They held, and tried to hold, the places in the world of fantasy from which they had come and in which they lived. It was their very aloofness that made our admiration and fancy for them so sweet and crazy. In those days, Primary Reality and Secondary Reality lived in two separate worlds. Ordinary mortals like us rarely crossed the boundary, and fewer of us ever expected to.

It is interesting to note that even the actors of the Substitute Society tend to confuse reality with illusion. The old-line actors (Henry Fonda, William Holden, James Stewart, Gregory Peck, Charlton Heston, and others like them) were first stars and then actors. Their own personalities merely wore different roles in different films, but they were almost always themselves, rarely playing anything else but themselves. "I can recollect only one good expression from Gary Cooper," Hollywood's legendary director George Stevens used to say, "but I've seen great pictures built around it." The new generation of actors, on the other hand, have been strongly drawn to an acting science known as "Method Acting." In it, the actor immerses himself in the role he plays to a point where the actor and his role become one and indistinguishable. This Method Acting became the trademark of many young actors, from Marlon Brando to Dustin Hoffman, Al Pacino, Robert DeNiro, and many other lesser knowns. Even Sylvester Stallone tried it in playing Rambo. The old actors knew precisely that they were merely playing out a role, according to the script provided, and there was nothing more to it: it was all a day's work for a day's pay. There was no confusion with what was real and what was make-believe. (One pathetic exception was fictionalized by Gloria Swanson in Billy Wilder's *Sunset Boulevard*.) In today's Method Acting, the point is to create a reality, to cross that fine line between reality and illusion that the old-timers would find absolutely intolerable. Theirs was a world of simple craftmanship; ours, illusion meshing with reality.

The intimacy of television in everyone's living room—all roads of illusion seem to lead to television—has much to do with all that. We now know all about the abortions, miscarriages, drug problems, intimate details of love life among the celebrated, as if such knowledge could bind us as intimate friends. The aloof, larger-than-life stars have become the next-door-guy Ed McMahons. Pernell Roberts, very much looking like the Dr. Trapper John he played on television, pitches for the National Kidney Foundation. Robert Young, cashing in on his image as Dr. Marcus Welby, gives advice on his brand of decaffeinated coffee. Raymond Burr, who played lawyer Perry Mason, stages his insurance commercial in a courtroom, properly attired like a lawyer. Richard Dysart, who likewise plays a lawyer in a TV series called "L.A. Law," is seen in a speech and hearing ad holding a child, but the place is a *law office* and the background props *lawbooks* on the shelves. When pro basketball players Larry Bird and Julius Erving had a real fight on the floor during a game, two color commentators were wondering whether that would hurt the commercial in which they appear as two friends kidding each other. One commentator didn't think so. Why? He said, "Because people would believe the commercial as real, not the real fight."

People who used to name their parents, grandparents, or even some real historical figures like Abraham Lincoln now name television and sports personalities as the "most influential" persons in their lives. What used to be the reference points in Primary Reality—excellence, essence, brilliance—are now used in the secondary context altogether. Corporate moneymaking is the "Pursuit of Excellence," so described in a book of the same title. There is the "Essence of Shaving," "of Batting," and "of Bobsledding." Then a football color commentator is called the "Most Brilliant Mind" in the business. Whenever President Reagan needed support, the usual battle cry was "Win one for the gipper," which was one of his movie roles he played decades ago. Nancy Reagan (a professional practitioner of illusion) receives a "humanitarian award" for her fight against drugs (a problem of social illusion) from the American Sportscasters Association (salesmen of illusion), which is presented by baseball commissioner Peter Ueberroth (the master salesman of illusion in the travel business, then the Olympics, then baseball, then onto presumably bigger and better things). The personalities and organizations and events that personify America's grand illusion are also those that personify America's public virtue as well. As actor Morgan Freeman said in an explanation of why he enjoys sailing, "When you live in the world of make-believe, you need something real. I go sailing. I'm in the real world." He is, of course, referring to Hollywood as make-believe. We are, however, referring to the whole of America as make-believe.

Sports, one of the more popular items of illusion for mass consumption, can build and destroy a community. Modern athletes—unlike those in yesteryear—are mostly multimillion-dollar businessmen, more conscious of their commercial and professional images to sell than their teams or team spirits and certainly less virtuous than those of old. Yet they become the human symbol of "community," "brotherhood," "fellowship," and "charity" around which people's hunger for Secondary Reality rallies. What is essentially a product of a managed competition and manufactured excitement, a dramatized heroism in injuries, victories, and defeats, and the "human story" in phony intimacy becomes the stuff that makes or breaks the community spirit. When the Baltimore Colts left Baltimore for Indianapolis, the former cried and the latter rejoiced. When the owner of the Philadelphia Eagles threatened to leave the city of brotherly love, the city capitulated to the team's demand with public monies.

The struggle for an expansion sports franchise is fiercely fought among major cities. Each hopeful believes that the city's "community spirit" can be revived and maintained with the closeness that only a sports team can bring. A franchise can solve all the social problems of community. When it was announced that the Los Angeles Raiders might return to Oakland, "fans whooped it up in a city suffering from a high crime rate, troubled schools and the earthquake that caused billions in damage and killed 44 people." "It's beautiful," a customer bubbled as "The Boys Are Back in Town" played on the jukebox. Often the community's *image* hangs in balance with the team, the team becomes the *symbol* of the city, the players become the *role model* for its citizens, and the team's win-lose fortunes touch the very heart and soul of the community. A winning team makes everyone a brother and sister of everyone, and the whole community becomes one happy family. Never mind that the sense of intimacy is entirely artificial, the feeling of euphoria short-lived, and the allegiance of fans only "overnight," as sportswriter Tom Sorensen observes with irony.

Sport in America has become America's "secular religion," as many observers have noted. Some of its events, such as the Super Bowl, are the nation's secular holidays, and the Halls of Fame are meccas of sorts. Political discourse also adopts sports metaphor as naturally and comfortably as traditional proverbs and aphorisms. During the 1988 presidential campaign, "Democrats found inspiration Sunday in the Los Angeles Dodgers' win in the first game of the World Series," saying that "Dukakis can still pull off a come-from-behind victory over Republican George Bush." This sentiment was echoed by Dukakis: "It looked like they were down and out, and all of sudden they hit a home run and won it. I think we can do that in the next 24 days." Bush responded in kind: "All I know is to just drive down to the wire." Senator Albert Gore, pushing Dukakis, said, "You are going to see Mike Dukakis come on like Kirk Gibson in the bottom of the ninth inning last night in that game with two outs . . . he could barely walk around the base path, but he knocked a home run to win the game." After a series of accidents that killed and injured many, the navy ordered a two-day safety stand-down to "review the game plan and get back to the basics." A naval spokesman said, "A timeout also can be called to halt the momentum of the opponent . . . in this case, the string of mishaps." Even the Reverend Jesse Jackson is good at it as a way of making a point for his black community:

When a basketball team keeps missing free throws, they don't blame conditions or the rules of the game or unfair officiating. They work on analysis: timing, technique, trajectory. Well, when our team keeps making babies out of wedlock, keeps having crack-addicted babies, keeps on killing each other, it's time for analysis.[7]

Lest we suddenly realize the essential emptiness of meaning and unreality, the best and the brightest of the Substitute Society are hard at work to keep our lives authentic and fulfilled at all times. No one is immune from this drowsy unreality. Some manufacture and sell it; many consume it.

The world in which Secondary Reality has replaced Primary Reality is a world gone upside down. Yet the prestaged and re-created Secondary Reality is so infinitely more pleasant and attractive as images, acts, and promises that many people gladly accept that as their true reality. The destination of Hell may be unpleasant and Hell itself unattractive, but the journey to Hell is surely made pleasant and beautiful in the world of Secondary Reality in a Substitute Society. The pains or unpleasantries of Primary Reality have been nicely re-created and touched up to be as trivial and attractive as our creativity and ingenuity can manage them. Many people in fact would swear that Secondary Reality is much preferable to Primary Reality and might prefer to call it "progress," "affluence," or "fulfillment." Whatever its philosophy, whatever its current status of acceptance in American society, Secondary Reality has brought some peculiar and even bizarre anomalies to America's cultural scenes. Let us survey some of them.

So-called entertainers have become entertainees. The public, which is the object of their entertaining acts, has become their entertainers with adulation, wealth, and fame. The entertainer is showered with everything that the public can spare, because the public cannot live without entertainment. Like the proverbial opium addict, the public would do *anything* to keep the supply of entertainment coming uninterrupted. If only the entertainers of America (all of them) could be unionized, they would have the world under their thumb. The court jester has become the lord.

The reporter has become the reported. Those who interview other people have become the interviewed. While they report the news that other people make, reporters themselves make news by virtue of their media status. Play-by-play is just as fiercely contested as the game itself, and game commentators demand greater authority than the players themselves. In many cases, the play-by-play man becomes bigger than the game he broadcasts. It is the case of the tail wagging the dog, but in American society of unreality it is commonplace. When Brent Musburger was "fired" from CBS in early 1990, a sportswriter observed: "[Musburger] had become bigger than the players, bigger than the game in his own mind. . . . CBS Sports said explicitly over the last 15 years that it wasn't a big event if Musburger wasn't there." It was the tail that wagged the dog. (Incidentally, Musburger was making $2 million a year at the time.)

When Diane Sawyer became the newest member of the "60 Minutes" crew, this move itself became the subject of many reports and articles. More than a humble, anonymous reporter of events, Sawyer was shown in one article with the aura of a superstar of yesteryear. The process has become substance. In its cover story titled "Star Power," *Time* magazine asks in exasperation: "Are celebrity anchors like her upstaging the news?" But ironically, while questioning the trend, the article also helped the trend by giving her such prominence. Why are reporters like Sawyer so important? The article answers: "They have influence that betokens great wisdom and judgment. They are the people America listens to, relies on, trusts. The major events of the day are filtered through their eyes and ears. News becomes bigger news simply because they are present. . . . They are overwhelming the news they purport to report." Does her success betoken "great wisdom and judgment?" Leading women journalists on a panel describe her as "indisputably terrific" and "extremely intelligent." How? A member on the panel lets out Sawyer's secret of success: "Sawyer [is] *packaging herself* very well." Another panel member was puzzled, but her puzzle is instructive: "She's the biggest star in the world. But no one knows why."

We have solutions for everything, every social problem in Secondary Reality. We have a telephone number for every problem, large or small, family or individual. "Help is only a phone call away," says a newspaper article about a Crisis Intervention Center. All one has to do to solve alcoholism, missing children, drunk driving, teenage suicide, divorce, family violence, drug addiction, abortion, you name it, is call a telephone number usually available in the Yellow Pages. The Substitute Society does not tolerate problems. It wants everyone to be totally problem-free and worry-free, so that everyone can live happily every after. No one should suffer in Secondary Reality. To prove it, call any of the following "helping" numbers—all real numbers in Madison, Wisconsin:

Advocates for Battered Women	251–4445
Al-Anon family group	241–6644
Alcohol, drug information	251–4558
All-Gays Crisis Line	255–4297
Alliance for Mentally Ill	255–1695
Alzheimer's Information Service	258–3358
Arson Tip Line	1–800–362–3005
Arthritis Information	1–800–242–9945
Assoc. Pregnancy Counseling	233–3211
Briarpatch, teen/family counseling	608–251–1126
Campus Assistance Center	263–2400
Cancer Info. Service	1–800–422–6237
Coast Guard Auxiliary	221–9711
Childbirth & Parent Education	274–3736
Cocaine Helpline	222–0100
Crisis Intervention	251–2345
Dane County Sheriff	266–4920
Dane County veterans	266–4158
Dane County medical assistance, child abuse and neglect, financial and family counseling	249–5351
First Call for Help	246–4357
Madison Air Quality	275–3270

Madison Fire Dept.	255–7272
Madison Fire-Ambulance	255–7272
Madison Police Dept.	266–7422
Parental Stress Line	251–2266
Planned Parenthood	256–7257
Pregnancy Helpline	249–5370
Poison Center	262–3702
Rape Crisis Center	251–7273
Red Cross Disaster Services	233–9300

And Madison is only a medium-sized city.

We used to stay healthy to live longer. Now we just live to stay healthy. Fitness used to be a means to the end of healthy living. Now it is the purpose of life for many, as if we live every day just to be healthy and fit. With diets, vitamin supplements, exercises, and many other gadgets, advice, and activities to keep ourselves fit, we have forgotten why we are trying so hard to stay fit. Like conscientious sinners who cannot wait to go to their confessions after sinning, many of us cannot wait until we can hit the jogging trail, exercise our muscles, or stand on the scale to check our progress toward perfect fitness. There is no burden quite like having to live healthy and long, but not knowing why.

Leisure has become work and is no longer enjoyable. The so-called leisure or recreational professionals have taken all the joy of simple fooling around from our lives. Everything now has to be planned and followed through according to the "science" of leisure. Hitting a softball or golf ball is no simple matter; there are instructions, methods, variations, principles, and the "right way," which are all scientifically measured and practiced. Dagwood Bumstead's leisure activity of curling up on his couch for an afternoon snooze is positively un-American.

Television preachers no longer preach the Gospels; they preach themselves. Like the reporter who becomes reported, the preachers make themselves the subject of preaching. When Oral Roberts stages a show called "Super Star," the superstar he is referring to is not Jesus Christ; it is Oral Roberts himself, as he puts his own picture under the heading of "Super Star." One does not hear or watch the words of God from these preachers; one hears and watches the preachers themselves. That they preach a particular brand of religion and not another is entirely irrelevant.

What we lose in reality we can regain in illusion. The latter is much less painful and less expensive and certainly easier. We lose the war in Vietnam, but "Rambo" wins it in the film. The missing men in Vietnam are easily rescued by Chuck Norris in *Missing in Action*. Rambo, as Rocky IV, simply knocks down our real-life nemesis the Soviet Union single-handedly, and the crowd cheers wildly for Rambo-Rocky. The reds, who audaciously invade the United States, are repelled by a handful of American teenagers in *Red Dawn* armed only with their bravery and patriotism. The Gulf "war" has only reinforced this manufactured invincibility. All of which proves that illusion is more palatable than reality. So who needs reality?

Best-*selling* has become best *quality*. With it, we have replaced quality with quantity. Judging the quality of anything—scholarship, art, philosophy—takes the best of human minds and often many generations. Yet we can bypass all that by simply counting the sales slips and bottom lines. People ask, when confronting the question of quality, "If it is *so* good, why doesn't it *sell*?" Because best-selling means that a large number of people have approved it, there is no greater assurance than the simple numbers. Accountants can now replace mind and history for the judgment of quality, and the bankbook is the repository of human treasures.

All in all, we have replaced substance with image. Packaging is the secret of success. Michael Jordan's face on the package sells the cornflakes. The way we dress determines our success. One must impress people in the first ten or twenty seconds. The size of the Hallmark card one gets is the measure of the sender's sincerity. We prefer self-congratulations—the president always calls the *winning* team—to painful reality or a true understanding of that reality. Walter Polovchak's parents—to be followed by many more Soviet expatriates years later—wanted to return to the Soviet Union after a year or so in the United States, and their 13-year-old Walter wanted to stay in America for "a big car and house." We celebrated Walter's freedom fight and ignored why his parents and the others wanted to leave this paradise. When Vitaly Yuchenko, who had supposedly defected to the West from the Soviet Union, only to "defect" back to Russia for not so obviously known reasons, President Reagan was "genuinely confounded." He said, "I think it's awfully easy for any American to be perplexed by anyone who could live in the United States and would prefer to live in Russia." Walter's parents, Yuchenko, and the other returning Russians deflate our self-image, our belief in the wonderful world of Secondary Reality in a Substitute Society. We simply put the burden on those incomprehensible Russians.

The case of image replacing substance manufactures what we commonly call personality. What is personality? Personality used to mean a constellation of unique individual traits, forged through time and trial, that served as the identity of an individual and as the character of his conduct. One had a personality if he showed consistent beliefs and principles or what we would call the force of personality. Today we say Person X has or is a "personality" if he has none and is nothing as a person. For he is a constantly smiling face, afraid of offending anybody and trying to please everybody. Possessing neither beliefs nor self-identity, dedicated to neither achievement nor self-growth, he is liked by everyone for no other reason than there is nothing dislikable about him. He has a "personality" as his greatest weapon of success; no one can find anything to hate him for, and he survives by simple defensive tactics. He is persona non grata par excellence in Secondary Reality and the Substitute Society. At once puzzling for the absence of individual traits and for the abundance of resources for survival, Person X with personality to sell is a representative citizen of our world gone upside down.

The celebrities ("personalities") in entertainment and sports are increasingly becoming mixed in politics—some call it "celebritics"—representing a variety of pet "causes." Increasingly also, there is a convergence among politicians, celebrities, and preachers in which politics, entertainment, and religion blur all their traditional divisions. Politics and religion—traditionally serious subjects—become confused with entertainment. Interestingly enough, entertainment itself acquires the appearance of seriousness through celebritics. This is done by the celebrities who represent causes—for example, John Denver protesting whaling. We tend to take this celebrity-cause convergence as an expression of civic rights displayed by the celebrities. But this is a wrong conception. The celebrities have become famous, hence publicly effective, *not* through causes but through their entertaining acts, which are fairly trivial and insignificant. Take away their entertaining act; then they instantly become themselves—inconsequential and meaningless. Aspiring journalists confess their admiration for Ed Asner, who once played a newspaperman in a television series, as their "role model." But Asner, the once fictitional newspaperman, is an effective spokesman for many *real* left-of-center causes, which, without his fictional character on television, would have been difficult, if not impossible, to do so effectively.

Those who become famous for largely trivial reasons—Asner's role in "Lou Grant," Ronald Reagan's role as the Gipper, Clint Eastwood's role as Dirty Harry, and so on—have now partaken, on the basis of their celebrated status, in serious "real world" businesses: Asner, not Lou Grant, advocating political causes; Ronald Reagan pleading for support *as* the Gipper; Clint Eastwood getting elected mayor in a California town because people thought he was still Dirty Harry. Asner's causes, Reagan's policies, Eastwood's mayoralty are all *real things*, and their consequences are also real; they are not roles from television or movie scripts. But these celebrities as well as the public seem to have forgotten the origins of the celebration, thus transforming illusion into reality.

The confusion is profound and unconscious. Not only can we not tell them apart, but we also forget that there are two separate presentations of reality, one real and the other not. Unreality takes on the appearance of reality and smoothly substitutes itself for the latter. When a clever Marriage and the Family course instructor tried a "simulation marriage" approach—students actually going through the motions of a marriage, including bridal registry, finding an apartment, planning menus, shopping for groceries—the effect of this simulation was electrifying. The students going through the "motions" of a wedding forgot it was merely a game. They believed it to be real. An observer commented, "They went through the bridal registry, picked out furniture, planned a budget and *acted out real life problems of a marriage.*" The very assumption that real life marriage problems can be learned through a game itself may not be so astonishing, but the confusion of the two as one reality indeed *is* astonishing.

When a research center wanted to experiment with a "growth hormone" on the cattle in Wisconsin there was a protest against animal cruelty. A spokesman from the research center, appearing on the radio, tried to assuage the concern: "Our cows," he pleaded, "enjoy all the rights and privileges of other dairy cows in the state of Wisconsin. . . . " The rights and privileges of *cows*, indeed! Terms reserved exclusively for human beings are now applied to animals as well, where love of animals takes on the level and seriousness of love for humanity. Where unreality cannot be separated from reality, animals and humans are the subject of our equal confusion. Expensive research tells us that chimpanzees can talk like us and we can learn a great deal about ourselves by observing their behavior. But why should human beings learn from *animals* and *not from human beings*? Don't we have the greatest teachers, the best minds, the most excellent books the world has ever created? Some people love their animals *not* as animals but as *human beings*. Bingo, a Texas mutt, inherited $50,000 from his keeper-family, affording him "air conditioning, telephone, television and piped-in music." At the same time, it is not unusual for human beings to be treated like animals if their market values go below those of the animals. Cows having their rights and privileges and a dog's life more decadent than many of our own are but two of the examples of our strange unreality.

The profound confusion of reality with unreality seems to have drained the emotional authenticity from the middle-class ranks of American society. Truly genuine human emotion is now rarely expected from a white middle-class person, who is thought to have lost, through habit, much of his ability to feel and reflect. The reason for the power of authenticity, emotion, and sincerity in "ethnic" movies (*El Norte*, about a Chicano couple who travel to Los Angeles from Central America, *My Beautiful Laundrette*, about a Pakistani family in London, *The Color Purple*, about black women, among others)—aside from their excellent craftsmanship—is essentially because we see the Chicanos, Pakistanis, and blacks as still capable of "human" qualities. These qualities of emotion are seen as trivialized and made meaningless in mainstream America's phony reality. Although resembling real life in many respects, America's reality no longer commands the authentic ring of pain, suffering, and truth, which can now be found only among the ethnics and perhaps foreigners.

This turn of events is extraordinary in itself, for up to now it was almost always the foreigners—or at least non-WASPs—who were thought unworthy of emotional authenticity. It is now almost impossible to trust the authenticity of American emotions. Life in America perhaps is just too beautiful, too entertaining, too trivial to be real. We can almost imagine the contrast between the surface congeniality at a show-biz award occasion—everyone smiling, everyone recognizing debts to everyone, everyone loving everyone—and the vulturelike backstage back-stabbing treacheries of these make-believe personalities. The greatest show of intimacy normally hides the coldest reality of cutthroat competition and meat-market bloodbaths.

This excessive effort toward intimacy, however phony, is in especially stark contrast with America's phobia for "real intimacy"—for instance, in touching. In elevator cars, in public transportation like buses, trains, and airplanes, people are extremely cautious about coming into physical contact with one another. Even in crowded bars, at stores, at ball games, and in restaurants people incessantly apologize for even the slightest brushes with one another and feel easily offended if others accidentally touch them. No wonder a superb salesman of intimacy, in the person of Leo Buscaglia, makes a fortune writing a book about hugging. In a perennial hugging society like France that could never happen. The facade of intimacy swiftly collapses, as if to prove its essential phoniness, if something unexpected hits it. The AIDS phenomenon is a case in point. In a classic demonstration of American paranoia, the absence of reality or of the ability to grasp reality, people panic and refuse to shake hands with each other. Some even insist on quarantining those suspected of having AIDS, including children, in spite of repeated assurances by the authorities that it is unnecessary.

The reality for most Americans is made up of a series of make-believe, happy smiles, which can collapse at the smallest tremor. It is a fragile world indeed.

NOTES

1. This advertisement for ABC appeared in many nationally circulated magazines.
2. Garry Trudeau, "Doonesbury," 27 September 1990.
3. Compiled from an Associated Press report, "U.S. Students More Confident in School Than Are Japanese," 22 September 1990, and Charles Krauthammer's *Time* essay, "Education: Doing Bad and Feeling Good," 5 February 1990.
4. Paul Taylor, *See How They Run* (New York: Alfred A. Knopf, 1990), 18.
5. A series of excerpts from *Ditka: An Autobiography* appeared in the *Chicago Tribune*, 19–24 July 1986. This particular quotation is from the 24 July excerpt.
6. George Will, "Reporting Means More than a 'Moment,' " *Chicago Tribune*, 3 November 1982.
7. Quoted in William Raspberry, "Jackson's Right: Blacks Must Save Themselves," *Star-News*, Wilmington, N.C., 3 February 1990.

Chapter 5

The House of Cards

One of the more curious and peculiarly American phenomena is the tendency toward first-name informality in America's cultural life. Our penchant for informality is well known, and its explanations are largely historical. The frontier origin, physical spaciousness, the egalitarian principle of the Enlightenment, the absence of a feudal past with all its trappings of aristocracy and entitlement, the first genuine free-market system that presupposes a flux of social status, and other large factors all contributed to the image of an easygoing Yankee society. But like all things in a Substitute Society, the appearances are highly deceiving. The first-name informality and its casual carryings-on conceal beneath them serious individual neurosis and collective conflict that belies its seemingly formless manifestations. Thus informality and psychological-structural schism reveal another dimension of illusion in this smooth society of first names and casualness.

After years of sojourn in wintry and formal settings of Paris, an expatriate was welcomed into the warm first-name fuzzies of Los Angeles. This is what he found:

One of the most reassuring things was the rediscovery of a boundless first-name friendliness. In Los Angeles now his banker is Judy, his mortgage-loan officer Adam, and his used-auto dealer Gary. Restaurant tables are held under his first name, as are pizza orders. A TV skit conveys more documentary accuracy than comedy when it shows a couple sitting down in a restaurant and telling the waiter, "I'm Sheila, this is Bill. We're your customers this evening." Try that in Paris on that ornery waiter one is careful to call "Monsieur."[1]

This is not peculiar to Southern California, where the modern trend of first-name informality might have originated. It is everywhere in middle-class America and for everyone, from the president to the domestic. But its incongruence may be more dramatically demonstrated in Los Angeles with its "daily drive-by shootings," as the same writer observes, to go with its first-name informality in the sunny filmland, not to mention with a survey reporting that 17 percent of irate freeway drivers state that they would actually shoot the offending motorists "if they had a gun." By contrast, it is reported that one of the most difficult things to teach workers at the newly established McDonald's in Moscow was for them to "look each customer in the eye and smile." A McDonald's American executive complains, "Smiling and looking people in the eye are not things they do *naturally*." But it is such a "natural" thing for an American. Foreign visitors are always impressed with informality in American life, then puzzled as they become more knowledgeable about the incongruence between its informality of illusion and its savagery of real life.

Beneath the easygoing, first-name casual atmosphere of American society lies the tension of a formally rigid society. But because of the very insistence on the casual appearances of its illusion, the real society must stretch to its breaking point to accommodate the conflict. It is a curious phenomenon because its contribution to tension and stress in life seems so incongruent with America's tradition that prizes its democratic ability to be so casual, so informal, and so equal for everybody regardless of one's station in life. But like many things in American society, this simple fact of American pride is also an elaborate illusion, a Substitute Reality. The smiling informality is breaking America's inner back.

Let us look at some more instances to begin our analysis. A Milwaukee car dealer advertises on television that customers should choose his lot because (1) they offer the lowest prices; (2) their service is the best; and (3) they are "*first-name friendly*." A plumbing commercial promises a "friendly atmosphere and casual conversation." A bank advertises its motto on the billboard: "Friendly. Helpful. Personal. That's What I Want." We are not to question the sincerity of the car dealer or the plumber or the bank, which cannot be proved. But should we question the assumption that we should feel friendly in reality *because* of that very manufactured symbolism of friendliness?

Former president Reagan, the commander-in-chief of friendly illusion, writes Italian premier Bettino Craxi a letter after the *Achille Lauro* affair, which begins "Dear Bettino" and ends "Sincerely, Ron." I don't know how heads of state address each other in their correspondence, but I cannot imagine Craxi writing Reagan with "Dear Ron." The weight of the matter in the letter—concerning disposition of the terrorists under Italian custody—makes it all the more curious that Reagan would be so casual and informal in his salutation. In his 1990 memoirs, Reagan recalls his first meeting ever with Soviet leader Gorbachev: "I had considered suggesting to him that we go on a first-name basis. But our experts had told me he wasn't likely to appreciate such informality at our first meeting, so I addressed him as Mr. General Secretary." Naturally as an American, it had never occurred to Reagan that the seriousness of the event—meetings between representatives of two world-leading antagonists with over 10,000 missiles aimed at each other at the time—would have been absolutely incongruent with first names between the leaders. (Imagine Hitler and Churchill meeting during the Battle of Britain calling each other "Winnie" and "Adolf" or whatever Hitler was called for endearment. Or imagine Gen. George Patton and the soldier he slapped having a meeting at which they call each other "George" and "John," or whatever was the soldier's first name. However, good material for comedy lurks in the situation.) As he left the presidency, Ronald Reagan delivered his last radio talk. Notice the ringing tone of intimacy and informality: "Over the years I've greatly enjoyed this opportunity to *get together with you.* . . . We go with full hearts, with best wishes for George and Barbara." "George," and "Barbara" are, of course, not the White House chef and his wife, but the next president of the United States and his First Lady. Incongruity aside, the speech seems *so* natural and so *American.* Never mind that there is really no intimacy over the radio waves and Reagan and Bush had not really developed any chumminess over the years. But America is ready to accept the illusion anytime. Years later, upon the publication of excerpts from Reagan's memoirs, a reader wrote to *Time*: "It was like meeting a good friend I hadn't seen in a long time. I truly miss having *Ron and Nancy* in the White House." In a slightly different way, this personalization of the formal world is also expressed by Bush himself. Exasperated by Saddam Hussein's intransigence during the Gulf crises, Bush confused the public with the private when he blurted out, "I've had it . . . [Comparing Hussein with Hitler] I don't think I'm overstating it. I know I'm not overstating the feelings I have about it." Gathering from the president's reaction, one would think that the disagreement had to do with a sandlot baseball score, not a potential war. Mulling over the statement, George Will concludes that Bush "confuses autobiography with foreign policy."

I once received a "Dear John" letter from Congressman Jim Leach when I had asked for a list of Political Action Committees (PACs) actively lobbying in Washington. Congressman Leach's cover letter began with "Dear Jon," but the rest of the letter was strictly formal, contrary to what one would expect with a salutation like "Dear Jon." In fact, one would expect a handwritten note from the congressman the way he addressed me. Now AT&T appreciates your business patronage whenever you use their lines. The operator says, "Thank you, Bob, for using AT&T." When Jerry Glanville was hired as the Houston Oilers' head coach, his employer held a press conference to announce it: "We felt," he said, "Jerry was the person who could get the maximum potential from our football talent in the shortest possible time." Finally, consider the following Merrill Lynch ad in a mag-azine:

He heads the largest municipal finance organization in the world, but he's a local hero to hundreds of cities and towns across the country. He's Jean Rousseau, head of our municipal market professionals.

This year alone, Jean and his group have helped raise nearly $70 billion for schools, hospitals, highways and other local projects in every state, the District of Columbia and Puerto Rico.

Using the vast resources of Merrill Lynch, they have created more municipal investment opportunities than any other securities firm. And they did it with in-novative financing that made these public projects cost less. Cost less? Now that's the stuff heroes are made of.[2]

The man is a "professional," raised $70 billion, and is a "hero," but you can call him "Jean."

Informality, such as using first names, *as* informality is nothing to talk about in itself. Members in a group of equal status and familiarity adopt it as a matter of convenience and necessity. The problem is that such infor-mality is used as a tool of creating a *false* reality, which finds its acceptance in society as real. All the examples cited above are no casual over-the-tea encounters. They are all serious—even deadly serious—matters ranging from the future of the world, commercial profits, terrorism, PAC lobbying, and bureaucratic policies to winning and losing in sports and a $70 billion business enterprise. Yet all of them are presented with the false impression of first-name casualness and informality. Under that false impression is the reality of some of today's most hard-boiled affairs of individuals and society. David Broder, a columnist, noted these peculiarities during a recent election, perhaps, along with business, the hardest-fought arena in American life.

To Tip O'Neill's reminder that "all politics is local," you can add that most of it is also highly personal. In Oregon, the last stop on this swing, the rivals in the gubernatorial race are almost universally known as "Neil and Norma," Goldschmidt and Paulus respectively. Voters discuss their histories, accomplishments and short-comings *as if they were relatives or co-workers*.

"Kit" (Bond) and "Harriet" (Woods) enjoy the same kind of instant identification in Missouri, and at least one candidate has gained similar *first-name familiarity* in other states from Massachusetts to Washington. Even in the states where challengers have had to use ad dollars to teach the pronunciation of such unfamiliar names as Wyche Fowler Jr., or Arliss Sturgulewski, *first-naming by the voters is far from rare.*[3]

Bank tellers, receptionists, cashiers at grocery stores, and anyone who deals with customers as well as political candidates are actively encouraged to call their customers or voters by their first names as if doing that alone is sufficient evidence of their intimacy. Customers by and large *like* the idea of being called by their first names, although such acts have absolutely no substantive basis. Both customers and business employees know next to nothing about each other and certainly are not meeting for friendly chitchats, not any more than Reagan would call Craxi or Gorbachev for a tea. Normally the first-name calling is accompanied by a smile. Just like the first-name basis, what used to be a display of extreme personal satisfaction or friendliness—that is, smiling—has become a meaningless permanent mask on our faces. Worse, it is often taken as *genuine* along with first-name calling.

One immediate consequence of this phony casualness is our inability to see serious matters as serious matters. We trivialize our life, at least on the surface level, by "casualizing" the serious purposes, questions, and analyses intrinsic to it. Even in the nineteenth century, when America was far less formally organized than today, much formality prevailed. In the halls of government, in casual neighborhood encounters, in academic and business meetings, a certain formality existed and was respected in exchanges of opinion and oration. Although American society's informality is legend, its real existence in its historical past has been highly exaggerated. In its historical past people were casual and informal with each other *only when* such casualness and informality were warranted by the fact of actual friendship and intimate biographical knowledge.

Today, in an age of information and formlessness, we know far less about each other and our society is far more complex than warrants a casual bridging of this forbidding gap among individual Americans. Yet the psychological—more than historical—demand for casual informality, or at least its appearance, is as overwhelming as it is disturbing. It is an overwhelming and disturbing desire to trivialize life and reduce it down to a level of meaningless first-name calling. Casual informality has its value in society, especially in American society, only if it does not replace the rigid reality of society, is not used as an escape hatch from the hard facts of economic life, and is based on true equality in power and intimacy among the casual and informal.

Observe the following description, written by an admiring reporter, of the casual and informal atmosphere at the California Institute of Technology, one of the most pressurized, competitive, and take-no-prisoners institutions in American higher education:

Formality is taboo. The president is not Dr. Goldberger but "Murph" to faculty and students alike. Professors lecture in jeans and open-collared shirts, shorts and sandals. They encourage questions and expect challenges. Gray has been known to wear a horse's head while lecturing. Feyman, who played a bongo-banging tribal chieftain in a student production of *South Pacific*, mixes serious physics with stand-up comedy. And Murph marked the centennial of Einstein's birth by donning pith helmet and chaps and riding an elephant across campus.[4]

The description on the face of it is of an idyllic campus where true learning and unpretentiousness prevail. But what kind of school *is* Cal Tech? Is the Cal Tech Ph.D. in nuclear physics pursued and given out so informally and casually in the manner of "jeans and open-collared shirts, shorts and sandals"? Are the Cal Tech students like students partying in Daytona Beach during their spring break? Obviously not. The appearance of casualness, while taken seriously, merely masks the tautness of the interior that is anything but casual and nothing short of man-killing. The secret is for one not to take this confession of informality too seriously. But in a society that craves and perfects illusion it is difficult not to.

The irony is obvious. The facade of smiling, first-name-calling casualness in Secondary Reality makes the harshness and rigidness of Primary Reality all the more *necessary*. This seemingly most casual society in the world is also the most rigidly bureaucratic, formalistic, and rule-bound society that has ever existed. Social scientists are unanimous in declaring the United States as having the most complex and "bureaucratized" administration in the world today. America's laws, statutes, rules, policies, guidelines, and so on are perhaps more numerous than the rest of the world's put together. America's mountaneous paperwork makes the Soviet bureaucracy pale by comparison. Pre-Gorbachev Soviets loved to do things by fiat, Americans by memos and committees—that's more formality and paperwork. Those who interpret them, namely, lawyers, in one major American city often outnumber those of the whole country in other parts of the world. Contrary to our first impression, the former and present communist countries have relatively few rules. They govern by informality and assumed power structure.

Under the smiling, first-name-calling casual encounters, Americans suffer from chronic formal committee hearings, swearing-ins, rules, procedures, votes, and so on more than anyone ever imagined possible. An average Japanese business contract consists of three paragraphs. An average American business contract calls for at least a dozen pages and a similar number of witnesses and their signatures. Even a lowly trailer-park contract brandishes pages and pages of contractual policies and rules for residents. If casual informality assumes the existence of "gentlemen" and "honor," we seem to have an abundance of the former without the latter. For hardly anyone trusts anyone nowadays without some forms of contract, witness, or legal interpretation. Everyone must read the fine print or pay the price. There is no such thing as "word of honor" or "upon my word" that is taken seriously by anyone—perhaps with the exception among those in the Mafia and other such secret brotherhoods. The most informal and smiling society is also the most mistrusting society.

The irony goes further. Along with the notion of informality exists also the notion of "openness." Open democratic society is something any decent

American is proud of having in his own country. Impressionable foreigners are quick to notice the openness in American society—in government businesses, in human relations, and in life in general—that has been a traditional hallmark of American character. But this impression and the self-image of an open society go along with the fact that America is the most secrecy-shrouded nation on earth. Outside totalitarian regimes and the former Eastern Bloc, where information about anything was generally scarce, American society hides more things in official secrecy than anywhere else. Over 1 million pieces of government documents a year—many of them trivial and bureaucratic—are classified as "Top Secret." While America may be one of the easier places to steal government secrets, it is certainly the most difficult place to get any information if it is not readily available. But unlike in the Soviet Union, most Americans are terrified of breaking rules by divulging company secrets. Most secretaries, businessmen, and government employees have a stock reply: "I am not at liberty to give out that information." Never mind that the questioner only asked for insignificant information.

Everyone is scared to death about giving out information, opening his operation to the outside. The smiling, first-name-calling face freezes instantly as soon as someone wants some information that has to do with the inner operations. There are numerous official acts guarding secrecy and privacy. A parent cannot get his son's college records without going through an elaborate bureaucratic labyrinth of rules and procedures safeguarding information. Alongside or perhaps ahead of the present totalitarian regimes and formerly communist societies, American society is perhaps the most closed society since the Middle Ages. Evidence is not hard to find. No other society suffers so many elaborate "conspiracy" theories. The most open, casual, informal society is also the most paranoid. In just about every major event people suspect that the CIA, the FBI, and Mafia, or whatever they know little about has been involved. Years and numerous formal investigations have failed to satisfactorily answer the question of who killed John F. Kennedy. In America, secrets real or imagined are easily kept and forbiddingly inaccessible if someone wants it that way.

Since there is little or no "informal" network that naturally exists in other societies to make up for their lack of formal procedures, much private, corporate, and government information can be accessible only to those who keep records for their institutions. Hospitals, government agencies, corporations, schools and colleges, and other institutional record keepers attract enormous envy from other Americans. But their envy is without foundation, because there is little the record keepers can do about what they know to benefit from it. They are sworn to secrecy. The battle for information in an "open" society is often the most fiercely contested fact of life in America. Where open knowledge about each other is thus lacking, Americans are resigned to living with false intimacy and illusive informality.

The reason secrets are easy to keep in America is also instructive. It lacks an underground network that informally gathers, sifts, and circulates information outside the open channel. America is one society where "rumor" (not gossip) is so scarce. There is no underground information network, no neighborhood rumor mill, no workplace exchanges of hushed information. There may be a good deal of gossip exchanged, but no hard information on affairs of the state or on personalities in high places. There has not been one single "underground" piece of gossip mongering about persons of some prominence—political or business leaders—unlike the Soviet counterparts, about whom abundant rumor, much of it surprisingly accurate, used to circulate in Russian society. (Gorbachev's *perestroika* partially ruined this favorite Russian pastime.) Every average Russian can cite a joke or two about the Soviet leaders or some "secrets" about their private lives, but such is a rarity in America.

That, of course, does not mean that everything about high personalities and places in America is openly known. Quite the contrary, information in America is released only through official acts, manufactured press releases, deliberate leaks, wild speculation on the market, and topical media exposés like those on "60 Minutes" and "20/20." Anything that is not obtainable through these sources remains secret. Millions of pieces of state and corporate information are guarded so effortlessly because of the absence of informal networks in neighborhoods, in workplaces, or through old-fashioned underground channels. The illusion of an "open" society pays its price. We mislead ourselves believing that what we get on the evening news and in the newspaper headlines is all there is to get. Why, we tell ourselves, we live in an open society!

Americans are woefully ignorant about the huge gap between what is openly known—which is manufactured or fragmented and trivial—and what is publicly unknown—which is often vital to a truly open and free society. They take for real the saturation of their senses by largely media-relayed information. A documentary filmmaker's three-year quest to interview a corporate chief executive—Roger Smith of General Motors, now retired—even became a popular hit because of his very *futility*. Was Roger Smith unseen and inaccessible all that time, like some former premier in the Soviet Union? No. Smith was seen fairly abundantly in newsreels and at stockholders' meetings. But all such appearances were strictly controlled by him. There was absolutely no off-chance exposure about Roger Smith. There was nothing casual or informal about this smiling man with awesome power to keep himself closed.

The price we have to pay for this illusion is enormous. It is like the chickens living in the same coop with foxes, vultures, hound dogs, and cobras, *all with smiling faces*. The chickens, confusing the appearance of casual friendliness with the reality of deadly threats, eventually develop the familiar malady of modern life that we all experience: neurosis. The smiling face is also the face that could pronounce you fired; all your pleas with him for the long-standing friendship with him and loyal service to the organization would be to no avail. The idea is that no one should take the smiling face *for real*. But the temptation to take it seriously as real life, as a real friend, as real human nature is so strong that we succumb time and time again— only to our great regret and sorrow. The lesson that what seems real in a Substitute Society is never what it seems to be is taught over and over. Yet is is so often lost in the overwhelming but unreal friendliness and casualness that our society stages so well for us.

Few have been better at this technique of combining idyllic casualness with deadly business hardness beneath the surface than the indisputable symbol of America's Profit Man, Mr. Peter Ueberroth. He is the whiz kid formerly of the travel agency business and the 1984 Olympics, who then proceeded to occupy the hall of greatness in America by becoming the baseball commissioner. In his word-processed autobiography appropriately titled *Made in America*, Ueberroth says that "authority is 20 percent given— 80 percent taken. When you're in charge, you assume complete and total authority, and your decisions reduce everything else to mere record-keeping and back-up functions." Cruel words from a smiling man. How can a man whose philosophy is nothing short of dictatorship also manage the image of an idyllic leader who is so casual and friendly? Nicholas von Hoffman, reviewing the book for the *New Republic*, comments:

We have here the informal American executive, decked out in "complete and total authority," grinding his subordinates down to "mere record-keeping and back-up functions." But he does it without clicks of the heel in the loose, first-name-basis, outdoor California style. Peter is true to the title of his autobiography, a Made in America man taking and using power in a Made in America way . . . Peter likes the little people when they do what they're told, quickly. Subordinates who anticipate their orders make it easier for the boss to seem easygoing and collegial, the laid-back martinet.[5]

No society or institution can survive without formal rules. That it may *appear* to be without formal rules is reason enough to alert us to the deadly structure beneath, as in the case of Mr. Ueberroth. Even in Great Britain, where there is no constitution, everything follows tradition with great precision and predictability. There is nothing casual about the British social system. If there were truly no formal structure and true informality prevailed, the stress placed on each individual member would be unbearable. One has to do everything right all on his own determination of what is right and wrong without any formal guidance. Aside from the proverbial "community of saints," which has never existed in reality, there is no such thing as an informal society or institution. Most human beings cannot tolerate informality as the real structure and rule of their life. With the exception of saints and artists, everyone requires rules of life and every society is built upon elaborate obligations to this requirement.

For historical and ideological reasons of profit and illusion-making, however, American society has been most successful in *hiding* this fact of life and convincing its population with it. There can be no more formally prepared occasion than a presidential press conference in America, yet between the shouts of "Mr. President!" and equally formal questions and answers are the strangely American habits of the president calling the questioners "Tom," "Dick," and "Jane" as if part of the whole happy occasion. The extremely formal character of the occasion is contradicted by the extremely informal episodes in first-name calling, and no one seems to notice the ludicrousness. Why practice informality, which only creates a sense of false intimacy?

The price we must pay follows these patterns of informality. Informality inevitably creates uncertainty. The natural progression from informality to uncertainty is a *necessary* development in human affairs. Informality negates a clear line of authority and responsibility, without which no institution or society can exist. The seeming lack of formal structure both blurs and intensifies the fierce power struggle beneath it. Nowhere is this power struggle more fiercely waged than in American society. There is too much vacuum unfilled in this informality and its consequent uncertainty. "Rank pulling" is a familiar tactic that Americans use over other Americans since their more formalized relations are lacking. When all else may be smiles and casualness, rank is always certain. It was reported that Neil Armstrong, the first man on the moon, often "pulled rank" over Buzz Aldrin and Michael Collins, his juniors in command during the mission. But all we remember is how wonderfully informal and casual the three were.

No American can tell by sight or tradition how he stands with another American. The only way to know is by comparing ranks and the powers inherent in them. In this sense, Americans are more rank-and-title conscious than their more formalized fellowmen abroad. At a meeting of colleagues, for instance, the chairman and members may call each other by their first names. But since informality is expected to prevail, everyone is constantly alerted to the fact that their ranks are differentiated. It is an often agonizing exercise in informality; one must act "cool" and "casual," not openly recognizing the superiority of his colleague-chairman, yet he must not exceed his bounds and offend the colleague-chairman. If the whole meeting started with a clear line of authority and responsibility—everyone being aware of it and acting according to the rules—there would be much less stress in the situation. In the military and economic institutions, where they mean serious business, this playing with informality is correspondingly rare.

Along with rank pulling is the nasty, mean abuse of personal power. Everyone may be famous for fifteen minutes in America, but every American may also enjoy a fifteen-minute *aristocracy* while exercising his power in office. Since everyone is equal to everyone and supposedly friendly and casual with everyone, the only difference that exists is in the actual exercise of power one has under his command. Everyone in America has some official power at his disposal, however minor, that can be used against someone he dislikes for some reason. These powers are petty, to be sure, but in a casual society nothing is too petty to be used for personal vindictiveness. Even a lowly secretary can put her power to some vindictive use against her boss. From lowly secretaries to high-ranking government officials, the abuse of personal power can be nasty and mean and petty in scale. In a society where such pettiness seems least necessary or possible because of its excessive emphasis on casual, informal friendliness, the extent of petty abuse of power is often startling. Everyone has a turf to guard, a personal domain of power and symbolism, and its assertive presence can replace the smiling face almost in a schizophrenically instantaneous metamorphosis. The one with an angel's face—calling you by your first name, no less—has the Devil hiding inside ready to spring out. It is downright scary for many innocent Americans who still believe in smiling faces.

It is tough to live in a society where everyone is a smiling friend and at the same time everyone can be a deadly enemy. When a person was summoned by an official in the bygone Soviet Union, he could face either a bullet or a medal. The best way he could guess which fate awaited him was by judging the way the collectors treated him on the way. If they were rough, a bullet was presumed; if they were nice and respectable, a medal might be tentatively assumed. In American society, however, the smiling face of your boss gives absolutely no clue as to what is your true fate when he summons you into his office. Even the most dreaded pronouncement— say, that you are fired—can be made with the most friendly and smiling gestures; you are assured that you can still rely on his friendship with you, and if there is anything he can do, don't hesitate to call on him. Those who saw the movie *Kramer vs. Kramer* can recall the scene in which Kramer begs his friend-boss for reconsideration of his dismissal, which his friend-boss just announced at their lunch together. This conflicting picture can be simply visualized if we can imagine the Spanish Inquisition, perhaps the most feared instrument of torture in history, conducting its business of torturing heretics, witches, and maniacs on a stretcher while smiling and calling them by their first names. It would be comical only if the consequences weren't so devastating. The friendliest society in the world is also the one that locks up after dark, where strangers are feared, and no one walks at night.

In a seemingly casual society it is difficult to uphold one's status. Hence the difficulty of leadership in America. Albert Einstein received high public esteem and enormous respect from people in America, but it is doubtful they would have voted for him for any high office. American leadership consists largely of smiling, baby kissing, and glad-handing a great deal. In other words, it is a popularity contest. But popularity by definition is based on triviality. One need not have achieved something immortal or great or demonstrated superior character. The term *leadership* in America is still really a misnomer, for a good leader is one who follows. Authority is impossible in America unless one pulls rank. Every bit of authority in America is either rank pulling or demonstrating popularity. Little or nothing is assumed by simple deference to authority or tradition. Everything in the exercise of authority is a wretched series of I-am-the-boss-and-you're-fired indignities. This is true from the highest offices to the more intimate parent-child relationships. Little or nothing is ever conceded to anyone by anyone. An American observer of the Japanese industrial scene, whose name escapes me, was impressed by how little demonstration of power by the executives was necessary to get things done in Japanese companies. On the other hand, the Japanese executives seemed more secure about their societal rank, freely mingling with their inferiors to a greater extent than their more rank-conscious but superficially egalitarian American counterparts. The American demonstration of authority has to be loud, articulated in so many words and references, legally right, and often crude. An exclusive parking space or dining room is an important symbolic appendage. There is neither subtlety nor gentility in it. It is counting votes or money to claim power, following guidelines to exercise it, and bullying subordinates to make it all worthwhile.

The reason for this excessive reliance on formal structure in American society in spite of its casual appearance is its lack of a common goal as a community or as a people. American society was neither born as a community of common history and background nor established by a people with common purpose and psychology. It was, and is, a voluntary social club where membership is determined solely by whether it is a benefit to join it. As such there is neither a sense of community among the members nor a psychological bond that binds its members. Without history, nothing is assumed and nothing is taken for granted in America. Every rule has to be argued and debated, since there is nothing else to direct their action. In the end a vote must be taken. Because of this excessive formalization, there are always winners and losers in every issue and the conflict goes on. With no clear sense of community or purpose, every issue is a fresh battle to be argued, to be fought for, and to be voted on. Unlike other societies where a vote may merely be a matter of routine formality, counting the vote in America is where the final body count is. It is the end of one battle and the beginning of the next. The winner gloats with it, and the loser plots a comeback. The confusion between the appearance of informality and the reality—and necessity—of formality runs deep in America. The confusion naturally generates animosity, fear, tension, and neurotic stress in virtually every dimension of its life, just beneath the surface of first names and smiling faces.

In formal societies—I would name Great Britain, the pre-Gorbachev Soviet Union, and Japan as common examples—where the appearance and reality are fairly close, there is little or no conflict of confusion. What you see is what you get. Their social structure is at least subconsciously and historically formalized; so is their daily expectation with each other's behavior. Unlike American society, where most issues are formally decided by rules and votes, not by tradition or subconscious, these formal societies carry on their tasks largely by *informal* means of deference to authority, tradition, and not uncommonly their collective goal. Whereas American society is informal only *in appearance*, these formal societies are informal *in reality*. This distinction alleviates much of life's uncertainty and stress otherwise unbearable in these rigidly structured societies.

In many ways, an average person in England, in the Soviet Union, and in Japan—in spite of their horrendously ritualized social expectation—suffers much less than an average American in his seemingly free, informal, casual society. The citizens of these formal states know where each of them stands, where everyone's place is, where the line of authority lies, who their enemy is, and where he is and what power he possesses. In these societies what seems to be real is *indeed* real, at least in most cases. What seems to be a rather brutal fact of life in these highly structured societies is really a safety valve through which much of life's unhappiness can escape. There is far less pretended casualness and informality in these places, either as cultural necessities or as personal traits. Since their line of authority is clearly established and respected there is no need to be demonstrative about who is boss and who has more power. There is really no authority more powerful than one that is *assumed* to exist.

The danger of our familiar casual informality is that it is entirely contrived as a game and that it is accepted as real in a world where it cannot possibly be both, in logic or as experience. Formality in behavior establishes a clear line of responsibility, expectation, and mutual respect. The president of the United States who calls reporters "Mr. Smith" or "Miss Jones" is showing the seriousness of their business and his respect for those who are there for serious business, not as intimate friends. The dean who calls his faculty members by their correct titles or functions—"Dr." or "Professor" so-and-so—and is also called by his own proper function merely recognizes their mutual functions, lines of responsibility, and therefore their mutual respect. Calling by their first names and showing other gestures of informality, while their tasks remain fairly serious—involving war, peace, economic survival, no less—would only create confusion and stress and eventually neurotic fear and uncertainty. This is not a suggestion to return to the more elitist stuffiness of a bygone era, but a recognition of the *reality* and *necessity* of formality in society and institutions. There is much misery in being misled by the appearance of friendliness, in confusing Secondary Reality with Primary Reality, and in taking the Substitute Society as the real one we have destroyed while pursuing the Profit Ethic.

Yet how sweet is our phony intimacy, our make-believe reality, our smiling friends, and our fantasy life. Not that Americans have lost touch with their reality. They simply found one more to their liking. In view of all the wonderful fantasy the new reality has given them, one can hardly blame them for liking it. But it is largely a House of Cards, ready to collapse any moment. In the meantime, machineries of the Profit Ethic grind on relentlessly and unconsciously upon the unsuspecting and happy Americans.

NOTES

1. Jordan Bonfante, "A Long Way from the Rue de la Paix," *Time*, 19 June 1989.
2. One of the common ads for Merrill Lynch appearing nationwide in 1986.
3. David Broder, "It's Local—and Personal," *Washington Post*, 12 October 1986.
4. Peter Stoler, "Formality Is Taboo," *Time*, 16 June 1986.
5. Nicholas von Hoffman, "Move Over, Sammy Glick," *New Republic*, 14 April 1986.

Part III

The Profit System

Chapter 6

The Marketplace

The Substitute Society has given the rootless, restless Americans in search of illusion a place where they can all converge. It is called *the marketplace*. It is at the marketplace that all the diversities and conflicts in American life—political, religious, academic, cultural—find their harmony, peace, and logic. It is America's secular place of worship, at once a church, a synagogue, a temple, an altar for the Olympian gods where people pay tribute and ask for oracles and guidance. It is one place that all Americans—young and old, white and black, men and women, rich and poor—call their home.

The marketplace is not really a place. It used to be a real place where sellers and buyers gathered to exchange goods for a price. When Adam Smith wrote about the marketplace as the center of individual happiness, material affluence, and national wealth, it was indeed a market *place*, a physical location set aside for that purpose. Today the marketplace is an *idea*, a place only in our mind. In our mind, the marketplace is a political philosophy that says free enterprise is what has made America great; it is a dream in which one makes a bundle with his ingenuity, luck, and hard work; it is also a state of being that perceives moneymaking as the central issue in life and death and all things in between. The marketplace, both as an idea and as a reality, is at once the heart of America's economic machine and the soul in America's moral bearing. The marketplace is everywhere in America, yet it is nowhere as a concrete place of reference. One can find it everywhere, yet one cannot go there as a destination. It is with us in our intimate awareness, yet it is far removed from our daily existence.

Whatever it is, the marketplace is a mean place. At the turn of the century, when America's economic machine was gaining its great momentum for the century ahead, marketplace was described by Robert Heilbroner as "an unbridled energy which knew no barriers of conscience and nice usage." Impressed by the primitive forces that locked horns with one another at the marketplace over economic advantages, Thorstein Veblen was convinced that "by heredity human nature still is, and most indefinitely continues to be, savage human nature."

In the history of mankind since it first began the process of civilization many years ago there has never been anything quite like the idea of the marketplace as an explanation of human savagery. Neither in emperor Nero's tyranny, nor in the cruelty of the Roman circus, nor in the terror of the Spanish Inquisition, nor in any philosophy or massacre ever recorded has so much human misery and unhappiness been defended and explained away by so many scholars and ordinary individuals alike as has been by the single idea of the marketplace. Not even Christianity in the Western world can match the total and absolute grip that the marketplace has on the social system and individual mind; nor could even once-absolutely-totalitarian communism stand up to the perversity of the marketplace's demand for submission. The marketplace is where all the arguments, all the doubts, and all the searches end. It gives no quarters for qualms; it takes no prisoners in its logic and proof one needs for scientific conviction; its close ties with mathematics—after all, money has to be counted—give it the magical charm of accuracy. Its long shadow is cast across every race, both sexes, and every class with absolute command.

The marketplace, savage as it is, has become a ritual, a spiritual homage without whose blessings the meaning of life remains unfulfilled. A decent American can go without religion or whatever his spirit may hunger for, but he cannot go without the marketplace. It is America's home on the range, a beacon on the hill, a city of our millennium, where we can forget all about our own home, community, humanity, and whatever else that can restrain us from the savagery of the Profit Ethic. It is at least the place of our ancestors way back when they roamed the jungle with spears and stone chips; it was their real marketplace then.

In our reality today the marketplace accepts nothing but its own logic and reason, however illogical or absurd. As long as one accepts the logic and reason of the marketplace, all conflict is resolved within its rules. What makes no sense at all in our lucid moments makes perfect sense in the marketplace within its own rules. Anything goes and anything is sane as long as it takes place in the marketplace. It would be a place of high comedy if its consequences were not so tragic, its grip not so absolute, and its lure not so pernicious. Among the devout and clean-living all sins may be shunned or condemned in America except the biggest one of them all—money.

This doesn't seem at all strange to anyone who has grown up in America with the marketplace on his mind. "Should Arabs cut back production to check oil prices from sliding further?" the vice president of the United States was asked. "Our answer is *market, market,*" Vice President George Bush answered. "Let the market forces work!" The vice president then became president. Asked about his dealings with Soviet leader Gorbachev, the president answered the nation, "I am not going to mishandle the Soviet *account.*" This belief in the market was central to Mr. Bush's idea of a perfect society. A strategist for Bush's presidential campaign told reporters about the campaign's progress: "Over the last three months," he said, "George Bush has *made the sale*; he has convinced the American public [or should it be "American customers"?] that he has the strength and the ability to lead this country." Columnist Anna Quindlen, in an otherwise-thoughtful piece titled "Mr. Bush Needs to Listen to His Consumers," advises that Bush must get "to know the consumers of his foreign policy" while he "tries to be consumer-responsive... [but] misreads the consumer" and "cannot overlook how smart and experienced the consumers are."

Along with sports metaphor, market talk is also popular among preachers and ministers. A Dr. Smith, a minister in North Carolina, calls on his flock to become a *"shareholder* of His Gospel." Why are "mainline" churches losing members? An observer of religion in America answers: "[Because] too many mainline churches are sorely lacking in the *marketing and communications savvy* that the Evangelicals employ to win new members." Many colleges have turned to marketing strategies to bolster sagging enrollments, never mind the fact that there just aren't enough bodies to go around. Daytona Beach Community College, one such campus, has a "director of *marketing*" whose job is selling the college to prospective students. Combining market appeal and drug culture, Penn State University advertises its business program: "Winning is Addictive."

We tell our students to choose a "marketable" skill or subject area. Counselors in college tell their students that they must go out and "sell themselves," as one such example of counseling literature exhorts the graduates. Parents who discover that their children are "gifted" in some ways immediately map out a career for them, very likely in "marketable" subjects like medicine, law, nursing, business, computer science, and such. Their market considerations are so natural that thinking any other way would be an astonishing discovery in American society. The market justifies anything and everything in the name of moneymaking. It is impossible for anyone to argue against the theology of the marketplace. There is nothing in known logic that can outargue the money argument that is at least as all-compelling as the marketplace. The world has never seen anything quite like this that has such a fantastic grip on the whole society and its human soul.

The marketplace corrupts everyone, but corrupts the talented more thoroughly while making less use of their talent, for example, with Olympic medal winners. Few of the more successful among them ever become coaches in their respective fields. All American heroes are market heroes sooner or later. Alan Shepard sells "Top Flite" golf balls, capitalizing on the fact that he played golf on the moon; test pilot hero Chuck Yeager sells "Delco" batteries, which must somehow be related to his flying exploits. "How much would key players in the gulf war fetch on the lecture circuit?" *Newsweek* asked (March 18, 1991). Talent Network speculated at the close of the war: General Norman Schwarzkopf: $20,000 to $30,000; General Colin Powell: $17,000 to $28,000; Peter Arnett: $15,000 to $20,000; Arthur Kent: $15,000 to $20,000; Bob Simon: $12,000 to $17,500; Lieutenant General Thomas Kelly: $10,000 to $15,000. When football player Herschell Walker quit college in his junior year and signed a multimillion-dollar deal with the now-defunct U.S. Football League, which he lied about and then recanted later, apologizing for his lies, *USA Today* ran front-page coverage of Walker, calling it a "fairy tale."

This all-pervasive corruption of the marketplace also affects one group that should be immune to such pressure: the so-called electronic evangelists. For the likes of Jerry Falwell, Oral Roberts, Robert Tilton, and others their enterprise is a perpetual economic machine. Whatever religious messages they may represent, theirs is but one form of entertainment among many available channels on television. Their moral crusade is at once business and entertainment, and they think like businessmen and perform like entertainers. Their rise and fall are measured by the usual standards of business and entertainment: the amount of money they raise and the size of their audiences. They rise and fall in fortunes and ratings just like any other businessmen-entertainers. Some are superstars and others has-beens. Impressed by their energetic presence on television, a magazine intoned: "They have changed the face of television." Indeed, they have added a new dimension in television entertainment. Their histronics often approach high, if not divine, comedy in a way these evangelists do not intend. The medium of television demands good looks, flashy performances and settings, sleek promotions, and other such gimmicks intrinsic to electronic medium entertainers. The Jimmy and Tammy Bakker team, with their lurid lifestyle and astonishing income before their spectacular fall for something almost entirely unrelated to their lifestyles or income, was adored by the viewers who described them as "cute."

Can we characterize televangelism as "Christian" at all? America's best-known social critic disagrees. Decades ago, C. Wright Mills made an observation that is still stinging: "I do not believe," he stated, "that anything recognizably Christian can be conveyed in this way." Further,

This religious malarkey diseducates the congregation exposed to it; it kills off any real influence religious leaders might have. Even if the crowds come, they come only for the show; and if it is the nature of crowds to come, it is also their nature soon to go away. And in all truth, are not the television Christians in reality armchair atheists?[1]

In the great tradition of the American marketplace, all of these electronic moral crusaders live well. They command housing that would be fit for corporate executives and the extremely wealthy; they control a mode of transportation that would stand up to that of the oil sheiks of Arabia. None of the preachers make any bones about their "good life" and economic success. In fact, some preachers preach as well as live economic prosperity as one of God's commandments. They see no virtue in material self-denial or in religious asceticism. Their empires are an American success story, a story that makes for front-page headlines and high school commencement speeches. Their success story is no different from any rags-to-riches saga that is as American as apple pie. In business and entertainment, using religion as a product, these preachers are some of those American entrepreneurs who have made it. They appear on the most American medium of all: television. They command the most American commodity of all: money. They cherish the most American value of all: audience popularity. As electronic performers, they stand alongside politicians, movie and television stars, sports personalities, and athletes—in short, those from the entertainment world in whose claim of moral virtues we take little stock or credence. Although these electronic ministers claim to represent moral virtues, they would hardly be fit to be in the company of saints and artists. They belong in the great tradition of American hustling, from politics to entertainment, from door-to-door selling to corporate takeover. They are all too typical creatures of the market society in the Age of Television.

The marketplace is amoral or claims to be without morality. The fine balance of demand and supply is so logical and ultimate that imputing any morality to its mechanism seems positively absurd. Both academic economists, at least a majority of them, and the general public take this infallibility for granted. Of course it is impossible to have an amoral living philosophy in society that is by necessity morally constituted. Every society, even one with a market philosophy as its creed, has its rights and wrongs. Even in American society, where the entrepreneurial sky is unlimited, we still hold certain things off-limits. The American marketplace does not sell babies, although many are demanded; does not sell drugs, at least legally, although much is demanded and supplied; does not approve of selling sex, although much of it is sold and bought illegally.

Prostitution, selling of one's body, so to speak, however lucrative a business proposition in the marketplace, is absolutely abhorred by most Americans. While most Americans value the integrity of the body somewhat, as shown in their rejection of legalized prostitution, however, they fail to show any corresponding degree of respect for the mind or soul. While selling the body in the form of sex business is condemned, selling the mind is not only immune from condemnation but also is encouraged everywhere. Mind may be a terrible thing to waste, but it is more terrible if it is unsold. Parents encourage the sale of the mind; counselors on campuses encourage it; everyone urges everyone else to go out and sell himself to some buyer, preferably a corporation; to sell oneself better, one goes to college. Dale Carnegie, one of the most venerable American institutions of selling techniques, promises to teach you how to "sell yourself," among other things. A Miss Donna Edminston from North Carolina made the November centerfold for *Playboy* and proudly hoped that "the exposure will help her real-estate career," giving salesmanship a strange twist.

Can America's "mind" or "soul" be up for sale, as its body is? Well, why not? It is only a matter of price negotiation. Consequently, Americans are the easiest ones to "buy." The Soviet Union's KGB, its secret police, knew this better than anyone. Among the agency's instructions for its American resident agents was the observation that "any American can be bought." All they have to do is get down to the right price. For the right price any American and any secret are fair game. (Could *all* of Americans have been *bought if the KGB had enough money*? An audacious and expensive undertaking, to be sure. But not theoretically farfetched.) If Americans can be bought for a price, so can others, for we expect that principle to work on others as well. When Honduras, a Central American nation of extreme poverty, heavily dependent on American aid, refused to cooperate with the Unites States in training the contras against Nicaragua, the refusal was "greeted in Washington with contempt," columnist Tom Wicker reported. "Honduras could be *persuaded*," an anonymous official said, "with a new package of military and economic aid."

It is indeed difficult to preach the ethics of the marketplace on the one hand and expect the practice of chastity in the name of patriotism or love on the other. When spy scandals erupted one after another in the 1980s, all the trails inevitably led to one common denominator of the American soul: money. One disgusted intelligence official called the sold-out spies "tawdry little people who sell their soul for a few thousand bucks." He might as well have called them good soldiers and practitioners of the marketplace. The FBI director, sharing a similar disdain for the spies, said that in all cases "money is the common denominator." What he did not say was that money is the common denominator of virtually *all* Americans, spies or no spies. One who lives by the sword dies by the sword; a society that lives by money may yet die by money. No one, even during the height of soul-searching after the spy scandal, mentioned the dilemma of an amoral marketplace and morality in society. Can a market society have any morality at all? Perhaps because of the enormity of the question and its disturbing answer, no one bothered to raise that question. Few still do. Talking profit is a national pastime; talking Profit *Ethic* is taboo.

In spite of its venerable place in American consciousness, the marketplace is basically a vulgar system of social relations. It is vulgar because its logic excludes humanity and community from its economic calculus. The logic is as powerful as it is impeccable. But its ingenuity is pure evil at its most persuasive. What is demanded is supplied for a price; the consumer is happy because he got what he wanted; the supplier is happy for his profit. Everyone is happy in a market society. The rise and fall in price are determined by the size of demand and the costs of supply. It is a system of eternal movement and logic, as natural as the movement and logic of heavenly bodies. The significance of God, man, society, world, love, whatever, pales by comparison, and none can stand up to the powers of the marketplace. Its very vulgarity is what gives it its childlike simplicity and primeval force. Profit, demand, supply, price, costs, preference, and other such elements of a market system are as elementary and primeval as one's self-interest, so that even a child can understand the principles of the marketplace.

The complexities of economics as a scientific specialty come from the simple fact that so many people want the same thing from each other's pocketbook. This fact creates an enormous traffic of often unmanageable proportions. What they all want is simple, and how they want to get it is also simple. The only trouble is that what can be gotten is limited in quantity and not everyone who wants it can get it in the quantity he wants it. Hence the necessity of studying it as a "science" of enormous complexity. Miss America from God's country wants it; spies sell for it; one goes to college for it; some kill for it; others lie and steal for it. It is no wonder that it had to become a science that requires the best of human minds to sort it all out. Business schools, often with the cleverest minds enrolled, teach the science of economics full-time.

In a market society of amorality, there is nothing inherently "good" or "bad" in anything. If Florida oranges freeze, it is a boon for California orange growers. And vice versa. If recession is bad for employees, it is good for employers, who can slash wages. Full employment, great for employees, is a nightmare for employers. Sicknesses and injuries hurt people; doctors thrive in them. Stockmarket crashes are bad for stockholders, but they are good for those who have just sold their stocks. Is war good? It all depends. War creates new opportunities and enhances old values. "Wall Street Sees Good News in War," heralds an article in the "Money" section of *USA Today* during the Persian Gulf buildup, which goes on to say "the cold-hearted consensus on Wall Street is that, like past wars, this one would *push stock prices higher.*" Is smoking bad? It depends on which side your money is on. Smoking kills 400,000 people every year and costs taxpayers over $52 billion in expenses and productivity. *Who* benefits from the $52 billion? But if your money is on the other side, the tobacco industry is responsible for more than 1 million jobs and over $10 billion in tax revenues. Is death good? It all depends whose death it is. Is God good? It all depends on . . .

Since the idea of morality is at best ambiguous in America's market society, often one is unclear as to what is right and wrong. Hence the most accurate way of gauging one's moral place may be on which side of the marketplace one is placed. Baby selling, pornography, drugs, and prostitution are on the wrong side of the marketplace, but junk food, smoking, alcohol, television, and firearms are on the right side of the marketplace. The former are condemned, the latter glorified on every billboard. If the idea of a moral place is ambiguous, so is the idea of a vice. It all depends on whether one gains or loses from it.

Many states are legalizing gambling, as long as the state government can cash in on the profit. In some states, official gambling is a thriving, revenue-producing business; in other states, gambling is a crime. The governor of Illinois even gets on the radio urging the new generation, who have been staying away from horseraces in increasing numbers, to come back to the horse track so that the sport can "survive." The state of Illinois, not known for its moral qualms, promotes its state gambling in radio commercials like this one: "[friend to friend] What would you do with a million dollars?" (Gasp, choke, speechlessness. The question is repeated. Still no coherent response.) "With a million dollars you can do anything you want—so play the Illinois State Lottery Game." States make money off public stupidity. Chances of winning a lottery are about as remote as chances of being hijacked to Cuba while flying. Can we imagine the governor of the state urging people *not* to fly? Why is the governor urging people to play the lottery game when the chances are about the same? Why does logic work in one instance (flying despite hijack odds) and not in another (playing lottery despite odds)? The marketplace requires cunning and savvy in the beneficiary; it requires an equal amount of stupidity in the victim.

Not surprisingly, the marketplace recognizes neither national boundaries nor patriotic duties. In a market society everyone sells what one can and buys what one must. Selling dear and buying cheap is its law of life. In the end nothing else matters. God, country, mother, or whatever else may be deemed important must fade into insignificance. It is the very nature of the market society and its Profit Ethic. It can do no other.

When Pat Choate wrote a book about Washington's Japanese lobbyists—former high officials, political insiders, and Japan experts doing lobbying for Japan, thus undercutting America's interest and raising questions about their "patriotism"—*Time* magazine complained that Choate failed "to develop a compelling theory of causation." A compelling theory of causation? What theory is indeed necessary to explain this sellout other than the theory of the marketplace? What is more compelling than the compulsion of the

Profit Ethic? From Ronald Reagan, with his $2 million for a speaking tour in Japan just weeks after the end of his presidency, to lesser government officials who "ingratiate themselves with Japanese companies in hopes of future reward," every American who has anything to sell plays the marketplace. What do we make of all this? "The *moral* answer is," says the article, and I italicize the word for irony, "that patriotism does matter." Morality has always been comfortably mixed with the Profit Ethic, as has churchgoing piety with hard-boiled business. But morality or religion has never stopped anyone in America from making a profit. Profit has always been America's business. America's God has always found Himself in the winner's circle. The article cautions that America should not "tolerate a laissez-faire ethical climate in which all of Washington is available to the highest bidder." Indeed, *moral* and *ethical* are wonderful terms to soothe the savage soul of the Market Man, but cannot and will not change his nature.

It is not necessary for a man who sells chastity belts to believe in chastity; he has only to believe in selling. His moral and ethical belief may be in chastity, but he still has to sell the belts in the marketplace. America may still adore saints and scholars, but it instructs its young to become worldly achievers. We may profess to believe in equality and justice for all Americans, yet the marketplace creates privileges for the wealthy unavailable to the not-so-wealthy. Entertainment celebrities and athletes become "role models" for our children simply because they make a lot of money. To be sure, some of them are personally virtuous and visit sick children at hospitals. But Mother Teresa is more virtuous and *lives* among the sick and poor. Yet most parents would not want *her* to be the role model for their children. She has no money and is not successful in the "American Way." We may still admire virtuous people. But we admire people *with money* more, pure and simple. In fact, it is not even those who *have* money we admire. It is *money itself* that we admire.

Are we discomforted by that fact? Yes, but we are willing to live with the discomfort. Chrysler chairman Lee Iacocca, who made millions of dollars on the job, faced the question of having made too much money—if you can believe the gall of the questioner. As usual, Chairman Lee is unfazed by the moral implications. "That's the free enterprise system," he says in self-defense. "What do you want me to do? I made the stock go up." Indeed, what was there for Iacocca to do, other than make Chrysler profitable, help the stockholders make money, and collect his own money in the process? If hospital beds go unoccupied, what does a good hospital administrator do? The market naturally dictates the answer: create new illnesses and patients and *hospitalize them.* So-called mental illness is always fair game. A University of Michigan study shows that psychiatric hospitalization for youths under the age of 18 has increased dramatically in "private hospitals." In fact, increased psychiatric hospitalization was precisely what a commission studying the problem of underoccupancy had suggested as a solution: *create* the mentally ill and hospitalize them. Martha Anna Tudor, reporting for the *New York Times*, naturally observes that "within the past decade, the medical community . . . has joined the business world wholesale." Can we blame the medical community? A senior vice president of a company that sells toys for the New Kids on the Block, a teenage singing group, says, "We continue to *search for new ways to get the 'tween' market*: a little too old for Ronald McDonald and a little too young for the car keys." A heartless scheming to exploit our "tweens"? Yes. Immoral and unethical? No. It is the market strategy in a market society.

The savings-and-loan institutions of Charles Keating, accused of having influenced five senators with large campaign contributions, instructed their salesmen to "always remember [that] the weak, meek and ignorant are always good targets." Keating himself, among other things for which he was investigated, during the heyday of his reign paid his young son one year a salary of $34 million in wages, bonuses, and stock. Was Keating a hopelessly immoral man? No. He was, reports Walter Goodman for the *New York Times*, "a stern moralist known for his preachments against the debilitating effects of pornography and abortion." What we learn from the Keating case is simple: morality and moneymaking are unrelated. The marketplace paralyzes even the moral man. The normal standards of moral principle do not apply in the marketplace. Even Mother Teresa is enlisted on behalf of establishing Keating's moral character, as relayed by one of the Keating Five. "When I met Mother Teresa," the senator says, "the first thing she said was, 'How is Charles Keating?' " And there is no contradiction in that.

The marketplace in America represents at once sane insanity and insane sanity, illogical logic and logical illogic, which is to say anything goes. Even Michael Milken, the junk-bond king who got ten years for fraud, is a moralist. In a letter to the judge prior to sentencing, he insisted on his goodwill: "I went to Wall Street with the desire to help change society for the *better*," he wrote, "not to find a fortune." But in spite of his good intentions, the fortune found *him*, to the tune of $1.1 *billion* in salaries between 1983 and 1987, $550 million in 1987 alone; he also held junk-bond conferences known among the insiders as "the predator's ball."

Consider vice in America. It is peculiar to America's market society that vices are—at least those that stand on the right side of the marketplace— not only blessed, but also pushed with all the ingenuity and vigor of the marketplace. If it is unnecessary to suppress certain vices people enjoy, there would seem to be no need to *promote* them and much less for a state governor to help promote them. But in the American marketplace such incongruities should by now be commonplace. In an open, voluntary, and free society each citizen should be able to enjoy certain vices of life, such as alcohol, tobacco, gambling, and so forth, as long as objective appraisals of such vices are allowed and no concerted encouragement of these vices is made. Certain vices, like alcohol and tobacco, would be subject to scientific inquiries, their harmful effects, if any, becoming public knowledge. This public knowledge, which is made possible by the natural process of human consumption, should then result in a reduction in the consumption rate of such vices. If it is clear that certain objects of human passions have harmful effects on the individual and on the community as a whole, that clear knowledge should be produced and distributed undisturbed to the public. Strangely, in a market society, however, while such knowledge may be produced and distributed (for example, drinking and smoking studies), their effects are immediately counterbalanced and consequently obliterated by the very glorification of such objects. While smoking seems to produce harmful effects, as many studies show, the effect of such knowledge is substantially countered by the billions spent by the cigarette companies to promote smoking. The contradiction between listening to scientific studies showing smoking is harmful and watching the Marlboro man on the billboard seems to escape everyone's attention, no one feeling this contradiction at all. The marketplace does many strange things, and making illogic seem logical and perfectly normal is certainly one of them.

It is no accident, then, that many of us prefer to call the market society by more familiar expressions of everyday variety: "cutthroat" or "dog-eat-dog" is often heard. Of the two, the latter is more often heard, meaning that we are right back in nature's jungle. But this analogous reference to the behavior of dogs has undergone some changes in the last two hundred years or so in the development of the marketplace. In the early phase of industrial capitalism, dog-eat-dog life was ferocious. It was a clash of determined individuals bent on survival and profit. But the game was played somewhat differently then: everyone knew where the dog was, how strong it was, how sharp its teeth were, what to do to protect oneself when attacked, and so on. Although the contest was hard, the rules were clearly established and understood. The stakes were of course smaller, and the knowledge of market warfare was fairly limited. They did not have all the scientific apparatus and its scientists in a variety of disciplines with appropriate knowledge at their disposal. Each man was the warrior and the general, the winner and the victim, the spoils and the loot.

Today the nature of the game has changed. Not much is known about the dogs on the prowl, the stakes are enormous, there are more of them, enemies and friends are not clearly divided, and each attack can be fatal. This fact puts intelligence—or information or knowledge, not brute strength or size—among the highest prized items in the modern warfare of the marketplace. Knowledge-gathering, whether as science or as commercial commodity, is in great demand. Hence the popularity of "studying" people.

The marketplace as a whole finds it immensely necessary to study people: the way they feel, think, desire, fear, act. It is certainly not because knowing how people feel, think, desire, fear, act, is important in themselves to know. But such knowledge can be collected to pinpoint human weaknesses, to be channeled into market research and advertising strategies. This is to say, to be used for the marketeers. Knowledge about the target population is incalculably valuable for commercial advantages in all varieties of production, promotion, and consumption. Needs for consumer information are endless. As the marketplace wants to know everything about its consumers, the discipline most closely related to this endeavor—psychology generically defined—is highly prized. Every facet of human behavior can be observed, recorded, and analyzed for those who seek the information. *U.S. News & World Report* declared psychology the "in profession of the '80s" because experts in human behavior find a "rising market for their advice." It promises to continue in the 1990s as a strong field of choice among college students.

The brain drain into the marketplace likewise is a tidal wave. The best talents from the nation's universities and colleges join the marketplace as its brain trust in a variety of ways: They join "entertainment science" as review critics, scriptwriters, special effects specialists; they join "money-making science" as best-seller makers, marketing experts, profit strategists, economic forecasters, research specialists, and accountants; they join "manipulative science" as psychologists, human engineering experts, counselors, lawyers, professional helpers and advisers, product testers, advertisers, poll takers; they join "killing science" as computer scientists, weapons engineers, game theorists, strategic experts. In all of these and others, they represent the very best of America's intelligentsia. One by one the best of the lot go to the market to be sold.

The corrupting magnetism of the marketplace is as overwhelming as it is inevitable. Its sphere of influence has been so wide and deep, in fact, that now it requires a conscious effort just to recognize its corrupting magnetism in our day-to-day businesslike decisions. Money corrupts us all and it corrupts even the purest of the heart, the bravest of the soul, and the most zealous of believers. Idealists, utopians, revolutionaries, dreamers, artists, spiritualists, and any other who may struggle to maintain his integrity are constantly threatened by the all-encompassing power of money. American society has always been uncomfortable with those pure at heart, the dedicated and the incorruptible, for they defy the logic and reason of the marketplace for the strangest of all commodities: principle. A society where everyone has a price naturally punishes those who refuse to be bought for a price.

The American marketplace has always believed and acted as if everyone has a price—a price derived from the market mechanism of supply and demand. If anyone defies this market creed, he is thought to be a fanatic or a lunatic or both. As such, America's market society does not see anything wrong with mixing patriotism with commercialism in Pat Boone and the

Olympics winners; mixing religion and money, as in modern evangelism; mixing personal wealth with public poverty; mixing half-naked cheerleaders with antipornography tirade; mixing business crookery with Boy Scout leadership; mixing desires for cheap oil with lofty moral rhetoric. In fact, even the traditionally nonmarket institutions—colleges and universities, hospitals, charity organizations—operate more and more like market-oriented business enterprises. Their chief executive officers are like any corporate executives in their backgrounds and salaries; they share the belief in the "bottom-line philosophy" of operation; they increasingly see themselves as "serving" the "public-consumer" with a "product" and striving for "consumer satisfaction."

Naturally and invariably in our marketplace, then, everyone is on the predatory lookout. As a man cannot be nice to his neighbors while he schemes to steal their money, a man on the lookout cannot *trust* his neighbors. The marketplace is where suspicion—not trust—is the instinctive reaction. One of the more fantastic episodes of a market society running its course of absurdity and corruption came to light when then president Reagan, irritated by the numerous leaks and spies, signed a bill in early 1986 subjugating all federal civil servants to a lie-detector test. This order was rescinded only after secretary of state George Schultz threatened to resign if *he* also had to take the test. While this episode was a fairly good topic of attention in Washington and nationwide, no one ever brought up the deplorable state of distrust in which the marketplace has put American society. Closer to home and on a more local level, the city of Chicago was considering a mandatory fingerprinting of all schoolteachers as a measure of preventing sexual molestations of children and child pornography by teachers. The outcry was triggered by a number of teachers' being accused of child sexual abuse. In addition to fingerprinting, psychological profiles and background checks of all teachers were also under consideration. A police state is not necessarily a fascist monopoly. Where everyone is money-mad, suspicion is naturally rampant.

It is not necessarily that one becomes morally corrupt, but that one—whether a small-time hustler or a corporate raider—does what any decent American would do: he goes for the money, which is the rule of the game in a market society. Eventually, as it is now, the marketplace ethic—or the Profit Ethic—creates a social atmosphere appropriate to that ethics system: everyone fears everyone, everyone mistrusts everyone, everyone betrays everyone, and the president of the United States orders every federal employee to take a lie-detector test, test for drug use, and schoolteachers get their fingerprints and psychological analysis on file. There may still be honesty left and integrity valued, but the forces of the marketplace—dishonesty, corruption, suspicion, betrayal—inevitably march on and devour everything, both human and material, in their path.

As the market ethic reaches its fever pitch, so does distrust among individuals in a market society. As their forebears fought against each other first with spears and clubs in the jungle and later with guns on the frontier, contemporary Americans go after one another with laws and lawyers. As distrust mounts, the intensity and frequency with which the war of distrust is fought also increase. In the end, everyone ends up suing everyone, individuals against groups, groups against corporations, corporations against other corporations. Over 20 million civil suits are filed every year in America, and the reasons are as varied as the ingenuity of the half-million or so lawyers can manage. There are many theories offered to explain the phenomenon: too many lawyers, too many large damage awards, and so on. Former chief justice of the U.S. Supreme Court Warren Burger, himself a lawyer, declared the lawyers to be a "public menace." Putting all the blame on the lawyers—however greedy and self-interested, for sure—is unfair. The lawyers, as numerous as they are, are merely a market response to the demand, at least in the initial stage. They are only a part of the simple truth in America: people who are becoming extremely distrustful of one another take advantage of their mutual distrust. In a market society everyone is your competitor and prey as much as you are someone else's competitor and prey. Either you take advantage of his weakness or he takes advantage of your weakness. There is neither sentiment ("nothing personal") nor community ("looking out for number one") in the hearts of a market society. Everyone is fair game. With the ingenuity and eagerness available and reward promised, one can simply hire the mercenary lawyers. Together they go after their victims on their search-and-sue missions.

Physicians on the cutting edge of predatory lawyers are extremely leery of malpractice suits, often prompted by the eager lawyers. The physicians' agony is so typical of our social dilemma. What if we called off all malpractice suits so that doctors could do their job of healing in peace? While doctors may work in peace if malpractice is out of the way, their *patients* are not necessarily at peace. Why? Because we cannot *trust* the doctors. Who is going to watch the doctors so that they do their job conscientiously? Without malpractice threats, doctors would have an open field. As of this writing, the Associated Press reports that "doctors take four times as many X-rays when they own X-ray machines and make money on them . . . [because] doctors make a profit on every picture they take with their own equipment." The article adds that these doctors also charge 40 percent *more* for their own X rays. Is this surprising? Not really. In a market society, where healing has to be paid for, you cannot trust the healing professionals any more than you can trust the money printers at the Treasury Department. They will steal you blind if you don't watch them. We may know some merciful and conscientious doctors, as we may still have some money printers who would not steal the money they print. But these are exceptions, not rules. The moneymaking instinct may be in their person, but like anything else we are innately capable of, it must be nurtured by our society. In our market society, it is so well nurtured that it is everywhere: in good citizenship and civics lessons, as well as countless other ways to be good Market Men for Profit.

So, agonizingly, we must rely on the foxes to protect us from the wolves. Thus the solution to malpractice is the search-and-sue lawyers who are our antidotes to malevolent doctors. Either way, it is an unhappy consequence. As clients and patients, we are robbed by both. In a market society you cannot do otherwise. Opportunity makes a thief, and in a land of opportunities all are thieves. The best defense is to assume this as a fact of life in America. Everyone must watch everyone. We call it checks and balances. The Congress, the executive branch, and the judiciary all watch each other.

Is justice possible in a market society at all, however the term may be defined? If it is, what *kind* of justice? In America's market society the primary assumptions about human motives is that people are selfish, stupid, and predatory. Given a chance, the assumption goes, everyone can turn savage against one another. Under this assumption, justice is not designed to be achieved. It is justice of procedures, not substance. As procedures, we may have the best justice system in the world. But the best justice *system* is not the same as the best *justice*. We certainly have the most elaborate checks and balances and most thorough going grievance procedures available in every aspect of our organized life. But such are not the same as justice, for our social system is not meant to achieve justice. What we call justice is a nice procedural battleground on which two adversaries can fight it out. Every case in court is a battle of two gladiators or what were once called champions, and when the smoke of battle clears the survivor is declared the winner and justice served. For lack of a better term we call it justice, but the very conception of justice in a market society must follow the principles of the marketplace itself. In it, justice is identified with winning and injustice with losing. After the smoke clears, we move on to the next instance of justice and do battle with our next adversaries. The best and the smartest—blessed by the marketplace—almost always win their so-called battle of justice. Market justice is no justice; it has to do with winning or losing "cases," not justice.

There is a phrase relating to the marketplace that is quite dear to those who are old-fashioned enough to remember it: the *marketplace of ideas*. The expression simply represents our wishes and hopes for the best in defense of the market system. According to such wishes and hopes, the open, competitive nature of the market system would allow anything—not just ideas—to come out in the open so that honest debates can be carried out. The ideas that emerge after such debates, held without prejudice or traditional bias, would ultimately represent the very best in human progress. In this sense the term *marketplace of ideas* does not really mean any specific physical location; it is the essence of democratic faith and longing that if honest, open debates were held on all ideas proposed, the best would emerge victorious from this process. But the actual dominance of the marketplace in society itself has transformed the "marketplace of ideas" from ideas *at* the marketplace to ideas *by* the marketplace.

The producers of ideas—like everyone else in a market society—come under intense pressure to conform to the rules of the marketplace, that is, to make their ideas *marketable*. As professors, journalists, writers, scientists, and men and women of letters in general, they cannot possibly avoid the pressures of the marketplace: their books have to be published by the marketplace; their products have to be consumed through the marketplace; their research grants must be obtained at the marketplace; best-sellers and hits have to be produced. Ideas are no longer debated *at* the marketplace, but dictated *by* it. The ideas that *do* require debating—such as the question of public morality and private virtues in a market society—have traditionally been a poor market venture. And no one can borrow money using one's morality as collateral.

The sentiment for the marketplace runs deep and dies hard, however. Many of us still believe in the old maxim that is is through market competition that the best in mankind can be assured. Just look around—many are convinced—how can the progress that has made our lives more comfortable be possible were it not for competition at the marketplace? But to answer this view we may raise some other questions: What is the *purpose* of competition? What *is* competition? Competition for what? There are three main types of competition. A brief discussion of them helps us answer these questions.

First, there is war, the most serious of all competitive human enterprises. But war is justified on grounds that, like an individual in self-defense, a society is permanently in a posture of self-defense against other societies in a state of nature. In short, every "society" exists only because it exists at all. But old societies die out and new ones are born. War is a constant threat to all existing societies. So is their extinction. As long as war is fought for social survival, the rhetoric of competition need not be invoked to justify it. Survival itself requires no such justification; the need for social survival takes care of itself. In a state of nature, which is the usual state of being among societies, survival needs no justification or explanation.

Second, there is athletic competition. But all athletic competition is a *game*, a set of make-believe imitations of life in which we go through certain preconceived motions for the purpose of entertainment. Whether or not the best comes out through athletic competition, the *best* in athletics is still nothing. The fastest human being, the highest jumper, the strongest man in the world, and the rest of the best mankind can offer have absolutely no value for mankind. As long as one is placed in a competitive situation one might as well do one's best; there can be no objection to this. But competition in this situation is merely a make-believe imitation of life to enhance its pleasure value, not a *representation* of life itself. It is neither art nor life itself. Competition may bring out one's best in athletic competition. But the best itself that comes out of this contest has no value whatsoever, in the same sense that the best fighting army in the world has no value outside that very context of self-defense.

That leaves the last of the three areas of competition: that is, *competition for life* in a market society. This is the familiar landscape in which most Americans have been born, live, and die. It is the traditional characterization of competition as the "natural" condition of man, destined to fight the battle to the finish against other men. It is the conception of man as a solitary figure whose life is constantly threatened by his mortal enemies. Its image is now transposed as the all-against-all philosophy in a market society. This self-perception both *explains* human behavior as nasty and competitive and *justifies* its nasty and competitive practices. It is essentially a circulatory reasoning: human nature is mean, so go and outmean the others; look how mean they are to you; and therefore, human nature is mean and competition is our purpose of existence.

All this meanness takes place in the marketplace, and the marketplace's meanness justifies and defends competition. Of course, it is inconceivable to have a market system without its competition. The former is impossible without the latter and the latter unnecessary without the former. But how fundamental is the idea of competition to human nature? It is essential, of course, if one is to think of human survival in the raw sense of survival in nature's jungle, surrounded by enemies, as all societies are by definition, or if one is in a state of nature. But in a human community, where all men and women in the modern world are placed today, only market societies as a continuation of nature may justify competition as a condition natural to human survival. In a market society, however, we tend to justify one by referring to the others. War is justified by the inherent competitiveness of the marketplace, athletic competition by the morals of war, the marketplace by the analogy of all-against-all war and athletic competition, and so on.

This can be further enlightened if we consider the fact that the best in society that mankind can produce—namely, the arts, mercy, salvation, justice, truth—does not necessarily emerge from the marketplace, nor through its competitive weeding-out process. The *best of mankind*, in fact, has nothing to do with the market. A man or woman cannot buy salvation or find true love at the marketplace. There is something terribly atavistic and primitive about a society and its self-image whose sole concern evolves around the central idea of survival. None of the products of true human progress—the arts, mercy, and so on—is an outcome of the competitive marketplace. The historical process itself is competitive but not market-competitive, from which certain artworks, for instance, may emerge victorious. Nothing would be more repugnant to those who have endeavored to produce the best for mankind—artists, saints, philosophers, revolutionaries—than the very idea of marketplace competition. Neither the marketplace nor its competition has produced what is *historically best* in mankind.

Even as we may concede competition as the dynamic force that forged the early phase of American capitalism, there is no need to be so competitive about it now, at least among ourselves. All indicators of history—standards of living, material limitations to growth, north-south disparity in wealth, and so on—support the idea of a point in history where *enough* progress has been made. This point of view takes the inevitable fact that all human needs begin and end in specific material terms of survival and comfort. And, at least collectively, life in American society, as in many other industrial societies, has been assured of both. Beyond this state of adequate survival for society and comfort for life, competition does not produce any better society or any more improved social life. Survival and comfort may improve materially through competition as long as they are the central issue in human evolution. But after the point of reasonable material satisfaction, neither is the main issue any longer, at least in American society in the 1990s and beyond. But in America's marketplace, enough is never enough.

Nature requires survival first, then comfort. A human community requires happiness. Neither survival nor comfort leads to happiness by its own progression. In an advanced market society of computers and videos, the aim of survival and comfort has largely been replaced by the pursuit of *pleasure*. Pleasure, however, is a *natural* definition of existence. Through its pursuit, we please our senses and enlarge our power of control over our environment. Since it is through money that we pursue pleasure, it inevitably leads to the subjugation of *people* among the subjects of our control. A wealthy person—to the extent of his wealth—controls everything in his environment and bends the will of others to his. But unlike this natural definition of a market society, *human existence* aims at happiness, not pleasure. For happiness is a *social* definition of existence. It is not like wealth or material things that can be accumulated and enlarged. It involves the concept of people *as* people (not as objects), justice, and truth. These are all intangible qualities. There is no true love where there is no justice or truth in the relationship. Hence happiness has to be *felt*, not demonstrated or counted. It is impossible to obtain happiness through the mechanism of the marketplace. One goes to the marketplace to get rich or get things one needs, not in search of happiness. If and when one *does* search for happiness in the marketplace, one is likely to be disappointed. But the lures of the marketplace are fetching and shiny—that is to say, deceptively attractive to the unwary.

Human happiness takes place often in adverse material circumstances—that is, the circumstances of bitter hardships for survival and of scanty comfort. Many in American society fondly recall the atmosphere of mutual trust and fellowship that seemed to flourish even during its darkest days, the days of the Great Depression. Bitter hardships and near-death catastrophes almost always tend to pull people together into a community. In fact, we may say with some assurance that American history has also proven that *material progress has an inverse relationship to the level of human happiness in society.* Of course, happiness is a difficult thing to measure. Material progress is easy to define by Gross National Product and average income and other quantitative indexes. For the sake of simplicity, people tend to equate happiness with material progress and say that greater material progress ought to bring about greater happiness: just make the cars larger and faster, television more entertaining, and the paycheck bigger. (Children are always seduced with candy bars, not with moral virtues.) Yet material possession and happiness are unrelated. Material possession is a public fact; happiness is a private feeling. Fact does not necessarily translate to feeling. A man who has everything and is the envy of everyone for his material possessions does not necessarily *feel* that he is happy.

Life in America for those whose existence is slightly above the bread-and-butter struggle is one continuous what-if-I-were-wealthy imitation and daydreaming. One could say that the American Dream itself has now become largely an imitation of the rich and the famous to the extent that fame also brings wealth, facilitated by the intimacy of gossip television. Why this imitation? Because imitating is *all* that we can do about the fact that there *is* a great deal of difference between the wealthy and the not-so-wealthy. The way the wealthy live is beyond the *imagination* of most Americans. What is available to the wealthy in America is simply *un*available to ordinary American citizens. Democracy is in votes, not in dollars, and the twins usually do not meet. The simple realization begs a tantalizing question: should we *dispossess* the wealthy as the East Germans overthrew Erich Honecker and the Romanians executed Ceauşescu? What *were* their crimes? Among other things, they enjoyed the luxuries denied their more humble citizens. In applauding the Europeans for demolishing the privileged class, how are *we* to take the late Malcolm Forbes's $2 million birthday bash in Morocco, Bill Cosby's $75 million income, Sam Walton's $7 billion ownership, or Donald Trump's gaudy lifestyle in *our* midst?

Those quick to defend the marketplace will say that the Americans' fortunes are "legally" made and the way they choose to spend them is *their* business. But here we are not interested in the question of legality, which is for the lawyers to argue. Rather, we are interested in the question of *morality*, in the sense that it takes place *in society.* Besides, we did not applaud the irate Europeans in their revolution because the dictators' actions were *illegal.* Powerful and wealthy people always *make* their power and wealth legal. No government or class has ever been condemned in revolution because it was constituted *illegally.* Legality is a game; moral judgment is a real life event. Are the wealthy in America worried that their fate might be like Honecker's and Ceauşescu's? No. Definitely not. But why are the wealthy in America—with their unprecedented luxuries denied other Americans—so *secure* with their place in American society?

The answer is deceptively simple, yet deceptively difficult to comprehend. In a money society—that is, an advanced market society—all things are *defined in terms of money*. Morality, justice, right and wrong, and whatever else are defined on money's terms. Money not only dictates the body (as workers and laborers), but money also buys the soul (justice, law, moral ideas). In America, wealth is always right and wealthy people are almost always right. The not-so-wealthy must rely on the merit of their case and hard work, which is to say that there is no special privilege in being not-so-wealthy. Money confers upon its owner the right to *buy* whatever it wants that belongs to other people. That naturally includes their *minds* as well. Not surprisingly, money wants people to think highly of money; and it has all the tools to make people think so. It can write its own constitution; it can install politicians sympathetic to its cause; it can interpret gospels the way it wants them interpreted; it can raise its own army and pay the police; it can determine the way people think, speak, and relate with one another; it can teach children's rhymes and fairy tales to suit its purpose; it can install its own judges and magistrates. In the end, it can *do anything* it wants to do in a market society where money means everything. This is done, mind you, all legally and voluntarily. Money need not force anyone. The "marketplace"—perhaps the greatest single invention ever made for money, by money, and of money—takes care of it. In it, not one Market Man *feels* that he is forced against his will. That's why the wealthy in America are never worried.

Human evolution in material technology is justified as long as it contributes to the matter of survival and comfort so that life can be made more livable. But the essence of evolution for mankind is that it is a *means* to an end, not an end in itself. It must serve mankind, not the other way around. Animals live to survive, while human beings live to be happy, after the problem of survival has been resolved. Survival comes from good material progress; happiness comes from good human relations, for happiness is created by the presence of others in one's life. A 1986 survey showed that most women in executive positions identified their success or failure less in terms of their economic position and more in terms of their "personal relationships." We may say that what makes one happy is not a more sophisticated, more spectacular special effect produced by our science and technology to tantalize our senses, but the little things we do or do not do for one another in our daily lives.

Survival may demand solitary endurance. Happiness demands community and communion, in which men and women no longer see other men and women as their mortal enemies. It is a strange landscape indeed: a world of most marvelous scientific and technological development existing side by side with the most "primitive" savagery of the marketplace, which even our cave ancestors might find too bloody for their liking. Living with this contradiction is an exhausting one. For one must constantly struggle within oneself wedged between two conflicting forces—savagery against civilization, freedom against dependency, and community against the self. The most nerve-wracking struggle to make it in the marketplace and the most sensuous enticement of the wonderful life collide constantly, and the collision hurts our sensibility beyond human endurance. We long to escape from this pain by believing in the fantasy world of our own creation, which futher increases our pain. The market society can do no other.

It is the world of advertisement to which we now turn.

NOTE

1. C. Wright Mills, *The Causes of World War III* (New York: Simon and Schuster, 1958), 151.

Chapter 7

The Targeting of America

Let's imagine a fairly commonplace TV commercial for McDonald's. The commercial "shows a young boy, obviously depressed, as he walks around an empty apartment that his parents plan to rent. The boy looks out the window, however, and observes that a McDonald's occupies the opposite corner. Immediately his depression vanishes. The ad ends with the boy happily wolfing down some food in the restaurant." Let's suppose that the court, upon the urgings of a complaining citizen, rules that "the advertisement could not be telecast because it might convey the wrong impression—that eating in McDonald's or buying its takeout products can banish loneliness or serve as a substitute for friends." Let's further suppose that McDonald's argues that "all the ad meant to show was that eating at McDonald's—especially with children—made for a happy family outing." The court rules in favor of the plaintiff and threatens to fine McDonald's $50,000 if it "employed a child's loneliness to promote its business."

This is from a real case, not in the United States, but in Finland, where McDonald's has its outlets, as reported by *Parade* magazine in July 1990. Of course, Finland is not the kind of market society that American society has been. Their sensibility in the matter of advertising is quite different from ours. In America, we consider the business of advertising protected under the First Amendment, covering freedom of speech. In fact, the *Parade* article titled the story "Censorship in Finland," not "Finland Declares McDonald's' Ad Fraudulent." Under the Finnish principle of truth, of course, no advertising would be possible in America. Granted that Finland is no America and Finnish sensibility to advertisement is quite different from ours, this episode illuminates something about advertising *in America* as if we see ourselves in the mirror in a dramatic highlight. Several questions come to mind immediately. Why does Finland *see* this ad as fraudulent, as a grave and dangerous distortion of reality, which it is? By the same token, why in America do we see nothing wrong in this distortion as a matter of daily occurrence? How does this particular episode show the way Finland defines its social reality and the way American society defines *its* social reality? But perhaps more important, how does advertising in America in general—which is nothing short of a total distortion of reality, if not outright fraud—*affect* our minds and behavior and our social reality? Advertising in America does not simply let the consumer know about a product; it shapes the very way the consumer thinks about himself and perceives his needs. In short, the whole notion is that his reality must bend to the world of advertisement.

If competition is the engine that powers a market society, then the advertisement is the fuel that fires the engine. Even spending on beer advertising on TV exceeds $1 billion a year. Magazine advertising alone costs over $5 billion a year, which is many times the total annual budget of many nations of the world. American society is simply the most advertising nation in the world.

As human history up to now has never seen anything like America's material consumption, the likes of its advertising methods and varieties have never existed before. Advertisement comes in a variety of shapes and contents: they are shocking, colorful, pretty, emotional, or whatever that will grab the audience's attention for a few seconds. Selling everything from toothpaste to God, from toys to the president of the United States, the advertising machinery hums and churns out ideas and images for the target audience everywhere. Ever since we entered the era of an Inverted Economy—to be dealt with in the next chapter—where we no longer seek goods and services out of necessity, we are now adroitly and scientifically courted by the new genius of American advertising. From morning till night, from night till morning, the machine never rests. Everyone has something to sell, and the simple fact of advertising elevates the product quickly to a level of respectability. The claim of "nationally advertised" itself is proof positive that it has gained its place of legitimacy. The new motto in our inverted society is: when in doubt, *advertise*!

Modern advertising in America strives to get *inside* the consumer. It is not enough to tell people what kind of product is available. It must make the consumer *believe* in the perception that the advertisement is designed to create in the consumer's mind. In prompting the business owner to appear in his own ads, an expert gives this reason for its effectiveness: "It almost gives the *feeling* when I go into the place that I've already met the owners and know something about them." To achieve this effect, "the message

[must] appear *sincere.*" What if the owner does not quite manage to be "photogenic" or "pleasing" or "sincere"-enough-looking on TV or in printed ads? The expert advises "paying a few extra dollars to hire a professional." In stressing the "importance of being sincere," another expert says, "If you don't believe what you're saying, you better be a tremendous actor, because people will know." Notice that the expert didn't say, If you don't believe what you're saying, don't sell the product. He simply said, *Either be a convincing liar or hire somebody who can lie convincingly.* Never mind that there is a world of difference between *being* sincere and *appearing* sincere. But why is this sincerity so important? Another expert explains: "The public is not stupid. They can see through someone who is not sincere." The public is *not* stupid, while all these experts are talking about how to fool them with their *manufactured sincerity*? If the American public is smart, the advertising expert is even *smarter.*

In American society, advertisement is no longer an appendage to the product that it advertises. The ad *itself* becomes the event almost as eventful as the product it is designed to advertise. The fact that Pepsi signs a multimillion-dollar advertising contract with Michael Jackson is an event itself; the public eagerly waits to *watch* the ad. Madonna's $5 million two-minute Pepsi ad to appear during "The Cosby Show" itself is a special news event. According to *USA Today,* consider the following previewed description of the advertisement as event:

The spot makes *Like a Prayer,* the title tune from Madonna's album out March 21, the first song to go public in a TV ad rather than on radio or music video. It begins with Madonna at home watching movies of her eighth birthday party. It unfolds as Madonna swaps places with the little girl on the screen, then revisits her Catholic girls' school, sings with a gospel choir and dances in the street—as the little girl roams Madonna's house.

The ad ends after the two have switched back. The Material Girl, again watching the movie, raises a Pepsi in toast as the little girl is set to blow out the candles on her cake.

"Go ahead," Madonna whispers to the girl on the screen, "make a wish."[1]

Either way, it works. On the one hand, the adman uses sincerity to lure the consumer to believe in the *product.* On the other hand, the adman uses the elaborateness of the ad itself to lure the consumer to believe in the *advertisement.* In one way, sincerity works. In another, outright fraud works. The "Joe Isuzu" case was classic. Is "negative" publicity bad? Is there such a thing as negative publicity in the world of advertising? No, apparently not. The maxim is that *any* publicity, even bad publicity, is better than *no* publicity. This is based on the audacious assumption that the American public *cannot* tell the difference. In late 1990, a voter referendum in Arizona turned down a proposition for a Martin Luther King holiday. In fear of anticipated criticism, the National Football League pulls out of Arizona its scheduled 1993 Super Bowl. However, the Fiesta Bowl, another Arizona-bound event, is stuck with its schedule. Is this negative publicity going to hurt the bowl game also? Not necessarily. A Fiesta Bowl official is optimistic: "There will be an enormous amount of interest in the game because of this [rejection of the King holiday]," he says. "In some perverse way, one might benefit from this [negative publicity]." When Donald Trump's name was splashed in the media for his marital trouble, was it bad for his business, as some marketing experts predicted? Not for Trump, who told a reporter that "the splashing of his name throughout the media since the breakup was announced has *boosted* his businesses." How about the scorned woman, Mrs. Ivana Trump, who suddenly became a household name and an object of considerable public sympathy? There is advertisement value in her sorry predicament, too. Advertising executives were saying that "the outpouring of sympathy for Mrs. Trump makes her an *ideal celebrity endorser.*" The assumption, again, is that the American public cannot tell the difference. They can only tell a recognizable name or face. Even a Hitler could endorse something in America sometime in the future. His is one of the most recognizable faces in history, yet the new generation may not remember for what.

The ads in America are wide-ranging and creative. Sometimes the ad contains nothing, as in the case of the ad for Infiniti luxury cars, which showed no automobile, just rocks, surf, lightning, clouds. A famous advertisement can save a falling corporation, as in the case of L.A. Gear, which sought help from Michael Jackson, who "would lift the company out of the financial doldrums and challenge Nike and Reebok." Even churches advertise, as in Victory Alliance Church in North Carolina, which shows a cartoon of people falling asleep, with a caption: "Does Church Have To Be Boring? It's Not, At Victory Alliance!!! A SPIRIT FILLED PEOPLE! A WORSHIPPING CHURCH! AN EXCITING PLACE TO BE!" Like Victory Alliance, other good causes must advertise, too. Blood donation ads show a father on the street desperately asking for blood for his daughter; antismoking ads show cigarette company executives heartlessly conspiring to increase smoking in America. Whether on the good side or bad, the tactic is still the same. It appeals to the audience's gullibility to believe the distortion as true.

Advertisement shows up everywhere, not necessarily in places where we normally expect it. This unexpected advertisement is called ambush advertising. Reporter Jeffry Scott describes the advertising's new frontier thusly:

When cigarette ads were banned from television in 1971 America thought it had seen the last of them. So how is it Marlboro got almost $5.5 million worth of advertising on TV last year? It snuck on the air—at about 200 miles an hour.

Much the way Jim Beam bourbon, another banned product, slipped into America's living rooms uninvited and unannounced.

Marlboro made its way onto TV via on-camera shots of the cigarette's logo during telecasts of Indy-car races on NBC, ABC and ESPN. In the hit movie *Bull Durham*, featured recently on pay cable, Jim Beam was "placed" in the poolroom scene with sex symbol Kevin Costner.

Both are examples of "ambush advertising," Madison Avenue's evolving strategy to catch consumers—already bombarded with some 255 television, radio, newspaper and magazine ads a day—unaware in moments of what used to be commercial peace.[2]

"About all that's left that hasn't been advertised on is caskets," the reporter relates an adman's comment.

Why is advertising so successful in American society? Advertisement is effective in a society with certain conditions, and American society fits these conditions perfectly. They involve history, community, and gullibility.

First, the society must lack certain historical bases of knowledge about reality. Unlike most other societies, America's knowledge about its reality does not derive from its past history, either human or chronological. Its contemporary self-conception and personalities are generally forged here and now, and there is little or no subconscious reference to the past. Unlike other societies of the Old World, where their reality is largely a construction of the collective wisdom of bygone generations, American society suffers no such burden. Every generation in America must cope with its own present conditions without either the blessings of the past or the deadweight of the bygone generations. The brief burst of "back-to-roots" itself shows the pathetic absence of those very roots that in other parts of the world are inevitably the subconscious stuff of the present. But every society, every present, is and must be history, a history of collective wisdoms and a chronology of collective deeds. A society without history is like a ship without anchorage, floating forever in the sea at the whims of the wind. And advertisement is the seduction of a siren, luring and devouring the unaware orphans of history.

Second, the society where advertisement thrives is one in which there is little evidence of community. As American society learns nothing from its past because there is no past, its population also learns nothing from one another because there is no community. A community, as noted, is as much a state of mind as a physical presence. It is a network of human conscious-nesses in which many bits of relevant and often irrelevant information about life are exchanged and forged for the individual and the group. More than a formal network of information, it is a word-of-mouth transmission of life's secrets to which only the insiders are privy. It is the uniqueness of community life, the privilege of social roots, that forms the inner core of human social consciousness. It is in this self-contained cocoon of life and its protective shell that one's security and self-image are forged and pre-served. Without community no one can be human in the true sense of the term. One may have an immense array of material or physical power under his control, but he may not command the security and self-image that only others in the same community can give, and give only voluntarily. In American society close to 30 percent of people move from one community to another every year, uprooting their neighborhoods, realigning their friendships, and nullifying their schools and peers. It is a wretched form of social rebirth, destroying and rebuilding the cocoon that is the essence of humanity. Material technology enthralls the body, but the mind cannot rest unless it rests within a human community. Without this community and its secret network that protects them, Americans remain vulnerable and alone. Into this vulnerability and aloneness, which is so peculiarly American, the advertising machine creeps, whispering and promising a lot of sweet nothings. There is little most Americans can do but surrender.

And third, there must be a pool of reasonably gullible individuals in society for advertising campaigns to succeed. Reasonable affluence makes people careless about how they spend their "expendable" income. In India every dollar summons the utmost economy in everyone; in America affluence makes people vulnerable to suggestion. It makes them easy marks for advertisers. Whatever might have given P. T. Barnum his confidence in American "suckers" who are born one every minute, there is much to speculate on concerning American innocence, which produces its brand of historical gullibility. In spite of its blunders in diplomacy and political decisions, Americans have always been known for their shrewd Yankee horse sense in trade ingenuity and pragmatism. Essentially free from historical biases and regionalism, Americans have always been free to bargain, rationalize, and hunt for the best deal. But this image was largely formed when America was relatively poor and everyone had to economize. Contrary to this Yankee shrewdness, advertisement's extensive existence today itself proves the considerable extent of American gullibility. The very success of modern advertising in American society has amply rendered irrelevant the time-honored notion that one cannot fool all of the people all of the time. Now one obviously *can*. With the massive reaches of advertising arms, one now can easily fool all of the people all of the time. Given time and ingenuity, Madison Avenue has nothing it cannot sell. One of the sure chuckle-getters in Europe when a winemaker is on the verge of a business failure is advice from a friend: "Why don't you try sell it in America?" As products and services have become less clear in their purpose of existence, the advertising campaign becomes more and more subtle, confusing, and bewitching. One can bargain-hunt for a used automobile much more sensibly than for a VCR or a stockbroker. The very nature of what we consume has changed the very nature of the process in which we make up our minds. Hence the increasing gullibility among American consumers. Next only to entertainment, advertisement has become the most illuminating index of

America's state of mind. Advertising as a commercial art form has never found a more fertile place for its prosperity.

The essence of advertisement is in graphic display, a total assault on the senses. Beginning with photography and illustrations, then with moving pictures, and finally with television, a fantastically lifelike reality has been created not only to spice up our otherwise boring reality, but also to replace our otherwise boring reality. Advertisement selects, re-creates, and manipulates the display of a new reality or an event that has nothing to do with reality. Display in our economic life is both cultural and commercial. Culturally, "conspicuous consumption" is a form of display confirming our conformity to the prevailing styles of life. Commercially, graphic display is what gets one's attention, and America's life consists largely of a series of wandering attention. But display—from wealth to beauty, from spiritual salvation to commercial commodities—lacks substance. It is a weapon of lure, an appeal to the senses, an exploitation of the vulnerable and weak, and a trap for the unsuspecting. Graphic display, if presented continuously, renders the distinction between appearance and substance extremely difficult. What we see is the end result, not the process. Even the Phil Donahue show is advertised as "Spontaneous, Emotional, and Real." But all its spontaneity, emotion, and realness is nicely packaged and rehearsed precisely for a certain hour of the afternoon, broken regularly for commercial messages. One ad magazine (*Advertising Age*) advertises the "believable sources" it employs as its major asset. Note that it says "believable," not "trustworthy." One toy manufacturer claims in its ad: "WE REALLY DO CARE! We make each toy with tender loving care." In the world of advertising, the line between what is real and what is realistic simply is irrelevant. As Andre Agassi says in a TV ad (I can't recall for what product), "Image—is everything." If image is everything, one supposes, substance is nothing or close to nothing. But the problem is that life cannot be lived in image. One has to work, love, bring up children, and die in reality, not in image. Hard as we may try, image does not change reality—it merely helps us escape it for a few precious, expensive, not to say confusing moments.

Economist John Kenneth Galbraith says that "a man who is hungry need never be told of his need for food." Since our economic system is no longer concerned with food, anything sold through advertisement only has zero utility or urgency. It is safe to assume that any advertisement-created utility or urgency is either erroneous, unnecessary, or irrelevant. But such erroneous, unnecessary, and irrelevant consumption is what gives our economic system its greatest defense: that is, "freedom of choice" or what economists call preference. We in America value such freedom of choice and ability to prefer one product over its other varieties. From presidential candidates to breakfast cereals, choices are duly announced and exercised.

But what is this thing called freedom of choice or preference? In an economic and cultural system where behavior is governed by a reasonable standard of expectation in production and consumption, such freedom of choice or preference is largely irrelevant. People everywhere have a universal set of requirements for bodily functions and survival. We all have similar physical wants and limitations, which tend to produce similar consumptive wants and desires. When we are hungry, we require food; when we want to go from one place to another, we require transportation; when we sleep, we want to sleep on a comfortable bed; and so on. There might be regional or cultural exceptions—for instance, someone preferring a hard floor to a soft mattress. But the uniformity in human nature brings about uniformity in production and consumption in a fairly predictable manner. Goods and services produced in one country can be safely consumed with but minor modifications in another country. Certain objective criteria can be expected based on universal human needs and wants.

When such goods and services are no longer of the basic and predictable kinds that the world has known in the last two hundred years—automobiles, bathtubs, refrigerators—this tried-and-true assumption goes out the window. Now in an Inverted Economy of surplus consumption no one knows which color, shape, size, character, story ending the consumers actually prefer. Packaging, which used to be largely peripheral and ceremonial, takes on an exceedingly important role in this new exercise of freedom of choice or preference. Freedom thus ends up being the most unpredictable and whimsical human caprice, not a choice based on substantive reasoning. There are of course certain things in life in which individual freedom of choice is essential. In the arts, religion, personal decor, color preferences, and so on, individual freedom to choose cannot be questioned. But such freedoms are not and have rarely been the issue in the past. Even in the era of standardized productions and consumptions such freedom was always respected and exercised. In an era of an Inverted Economy, however, this exercise of personal freedom and preference that is so dear to consumers has little or nothing to do with such fundamental choices.

The freedom to choose in America is no longer between to consume and not to consume, but what color, shape, flavor, fads, fashion, and so forth, to consume. An average American has no choice between having and not having an automobile. He *must* have one. His *society* has committed itself to automobiles: highways, parking spaces, maintaining bridges and freeways, readily available gasoline, and a monthly payment on the car loan as inevitable as payment on a mortgage or rent. One's freedom now consists simply of what kind of car at what kind of payment. It is a reality of dictatorship in an illusion of freedom. When there is no real choice in culture or in the political arena in a dictatorial society, for instance, such trivial choices can have immensely important consequences for the general mood of society. People under hard conditions of life who cannot change their conditions may cling to certain given choices of life *in place* of real choices. A condemned man may prefer the easiest method of execution or the last meal of his choice, since life is not available, and make a big deal of his "freedom of choice." The kind of freedom of choice and preference that is so dear to American consumers today serves that sort of function. It is essentially a pacifying one, in view of the fact that economically and culturally we really have no choice but to consume. *Not* to consume—like the condemned man's life—is not in the cards. In that sense, what kind of breakfast we choose, what color, shape, size we pick for our amusement— which are really trivial choices—tend to have enormously significant psychological functions. Because of this psychological, rather than real, significance we attach to freedom of choice, we tend to exaggerate our moral commitment to such choices, so that, for instance, choosing the "right" meal from a menu, picking the "right" toy, selecting the "right" television program, and so on, is attended to with all the solemnity of commitment and ritualism. Most people may refer to the Constitution for theoretical freedom. But for practical freedom they refer mostly to trivial exercises. Whenever we hear the "constitutional right" mentioned, we can almost expect trivia defended by it.

Few things advertised indeed are of the functional, basic variety. Even food is no longer advertised with the selling point of good nutrition or appeal to palatability. Human food advertisement is replete with sexual undertones and cultural connotations, while to no one's surprise, animal food—dog food, cat food—is advertised only with the emphasis on nutrition. It is implicitly assumed that animals have better sense than human beings in seeing their food strictly from the nutritional point of view. A good example of human food advertisement, a Campbell soup commercial, on the other hand, shows a wife telling her husband (with a sexually beguiling expression on her face) that her husband's exercise "*is working*," presumably making him a better lover and presumably with the help of Campbell's tomato soup. Either on regular networks or on cable television, advertisements appeal to the most unsavory human instinct almost without exception; they rely in one form or another on sensory pleasure, selfish motives, deceptive practices, trickery, sex, color, irrationality, and exploitation of the vulnerable, the unsuspecting, the insecure, the lonely, the weak. Likewise, since most ads must create an impact in less than thirty seconds, they must call upon the most savage kind of raw appeals that human ingenuity is capable of—fear, anxiety, greed, envy, neurosis, ignorance, prejudice, loneliness.

The fact that heavily advertised goods and services are not of the bread-and-butter variety does not mean that the business of consuming them is attended to light heartedly. In an Inverted Economy where goods and services tend to be unrelated to our vital needs, people tend to spend *much more*, not less, time on decision-making. They demand perfection from and concentrate a great deal more on seemingly insignificant decisions of life— for example, on the choice of restaurants and dinners, of TV programs, of movies, of birthday and holiday gifts—until they are *completely* satisfied. Hell knows no fury like an irate and unsatisfied customer, who on the other hand may be quite willing to ignore congressional or presidential misbe- having on a national scale. On urgent matters of life, however, the de- manding and perfectionist Americans are fairly fatalistic and undemanding. Perhaps in their bones they *know* that in matters of real importance—like job, money, power—they are basically powerless. In the meantime, their trivial choice increases in the number of TV channels, in available credit cards, in the variety of Hallmark cards to express one's incidental feelings. As this trivial power increases, the consumer's determination to demand perfect satisfaction also increases. Nothing less than perfection will do for the American consumer.

This sense of increasing power among consumers begets a serious but hidden consequence. As their sense of freedom of choice—a false sense of power—has increased through the image-pleasing workings of advertise- ment and consumption, their *real* power of choice has declined. This is a serious consequence, because its process is subtle and undetectable, while its effect is personally felt. Through the increased range of choice in con- sumer goods, people feel their increasing sense of individual autonomy, of the range of self-expression, and of political power. All of these are totally induced by advertised illusion and are therefore false. But as this false sense of individual power has increased through consumption, so has the *control* of the individual consumer by the increasingly sophisticated *manipulative means* of the commercial institution. Through this manipulative means— largely wrought through advertising—people feel *freer* when they ought to feel more controlled and feel more *loved* when they ought to feel more used.

Naturally and inevitably, advertisement in a surplus society not only lets people know that there is a product available; it also propagates the *idea* that consuming this product is the proper thing to do. In that sense, all advertisement today is a form of propaganda, if propaganda is understood as an advertisement of ideas. Du Pont ads not only sell its chemical products; they also promote Du Pont as an *idea*, as a company dedicated to saving human lives, concerned about the environment, and otherwise dedicated to humanity. When Upjohn discovered that one of its drugs had something to do with hair growth, its ads immediately worked on creating the *idea* that more hair is a more desirable thing than less hair on men's heads. John Houseman's ad for a brokerage that includes the line about a child being "tomorrow's tycoon" promotes the *idea* of moneymaking as a noble as- piration. Likewise, "The Lifestyles of the Rich and Famous" subtly idealizes overindulgent lifestyles. Mobil Oil Company's magazine series on free enterprise has as much to do with pitching the *idea* of market society as selling its oil product. In these and other ads, ideas about "happiness," "justice," "fulfillment," and "propriety" are defined and propagated through the seemingly neutral commercialism. If one recalls the masterful propaganda classic of Hitler's Third Reich *The Triumph of the Will*, one is struck by the uncanny similarity between our contemporary ads and Hitler's propaganda. Both are absolutely beautiful, sincere, and effective. But much more brilliant than Hitler's version, modern advertisement is one wonderful series of seduction.

Contrary to what Advertisement 101 says, there is a difference between advertisement and information. The basic function of advertisement is to create a message in words and images and implant it in the audience's passive subconscious mind. Information, on the other hand, is sifted through and debated by the active mind. As to their channels of communication, messages come through advertisement; information comes through announcement. Aside from the simplistic, quick messages in words and images, advertisement necessarily assumes the *worst* about mankind, of which stupidity is indeed dominant; announcement for information necessarily assumes that the audience is intelligent. The two varieties of communication of course have to do with their respective purposes of communication: advertisement to sell, announcement to inform. Indeed, no advertisement, as an economic concept and in actual practice, would be possible without a large dosage of stupidity on the part of the intended audience. (I would define stupidity as different from ignorance. Ignorance is a simple lack of knowledge; stupidity, the product of refusing to acknowledge that fact. Gullibility is the psychological end result of stupidity. Ignorance can be cured by knowledge, but by and large, stupidity cannot be cured, because it consists of one's inability to recognize one's own stupidity. More on this later.)

Most products advertised, such as beers or ball games, are really no different from one another within the same stock and often across different stocks. All advertisements therefore tend to emerge as about the same—the same scenery, human interactions, background music. One advertisement could be replaced easily by another. "KNOWLEDGE IS POWER," a newspaper ad proclaims in bold letters. What is the product? A night course in college or business school? A computer program? Encouragement for senior citizens to go back to school? A warning for high school dropouts? A vocabulary-lesson cassette tape? A political campaign strategy? The answer is: none of the above. It turns out to be an ad for a law office offering its services for driving-while-intoxicated charges, divorces, wills, and so on. But who'd have guessed it? One can sell any product with just about any commercial on television or in the newspaper; any pretty face or pleasing scene or suggestive phrase will do. All college campuses shown during

NCAA games are almost identical, making one campus look exactly like another. Since all advertisements tend to be similar, because they are produced by similarly standardized professional ad agencies, they tend to compete against each other. This competition cancels each other's immediate effect. This canceling-each-other effect is about the only protection there is for the audience against the immediate effect. We have no antidote, however, to fight commercial advertisement or the phony reality it creates in our minds. Commercials do not tell on the others as phonies. Neither tradition, nor community, nor our native intelligence can protect us from advertisement's rather one-way assault on our senses. No advertisement is followed by a disclaimer saying: "This is only a commercial" or something to that effect. Thus while advertisements cancel each other out, their *total* effect remains upon the subconscious. Collectively and individually, every advertisement message evolves around a particular presentation of reality that is absolutely false. While an AT&T advertisement may cancel out an MCI commercial, their combined effect remains uncanceled; one must reach out and touch someone or do business with someone by long-distance.

No advertisement intends to change one's view of life permanently and absolutely. The very format of ten-, twenty-, and thirty-second spots on television and radio or graphic displays in magazines and newspapers makes it impossible to do so. Permanent change requires an absolute reevaluation of one's way of life, and even in American society thirty-second spots are not long enough for that sort of persuasion. But since most advertised messages have a one-issue purpose, a simple, quick message is deemed adequate in most cases. You do not advertise a way of life; you sell a specific product with advertisement. If the idea is complex, it must be reduced to a simple, often stupefying, image. Even a concept as controversial and complex as "Star Wars," or "Strategic Defense Initiative," can be put on the air as thirty-second spots explaining away the whole concept. Both sides of the SDI issue actually launched thirty-second commercials to reduce the complexity to a simple yes or no.

Along with the simplicity of the messages in advertisement is the assault on the psychic vulnerability of American loneliness. There is a good deal of reference to God, patriotism, love, family, and friendship as added measures to generate good feelings. No one is more keenly in tune with America's psychic undercurrents than the adman, and his knowledge of America is reflected in the way he designs his commercials. In other words, he knows where it hurts in American life. Mental health centers are usually advertised late, close to midnight, when many of the lonely souls stay up and watch a program during which many of life's vexing problems commonly crop up. These commercials claim to love and care in their messages. Hospitals advertise themselves with love and care: "Nobody cares for you the way we do" or simply "We care for you." We may not actually believe a prostitute's self-admitted business motto: "I *love* my customers." But this reference to love and care is powerful to the lonely and unfulfilled.

Hence our vulnerability about life in general is a good source of advertising assault. An Avon lady says, "[Being an Avon lady] gives me confidence," and that it makes her "happier." In a storybook ad aimed at parents, the message offers to print the child's name in the book. It is important for the children's "self-confidence," the ad says, and hearing their names in the storybook apparently gives them that self-confidence. "It is important," the ad says, "that they feel good about themselves . . . Your child will be thrilled to hear his or her own name." To feel good about oneself, all one has to do is buy the product. In these and many other instances, it matters little or not at all *what* they are selling. Their message is the same: "care," "love," "self-confidence," "happiness," although the products they are promoting are hospital services, cosmetics and jewelry, and tape-recorded storybooks, which have nothing to do with these emotions. Some of the nation's best and brightest engage in the game of advertising, reducing complexity to simplicity, reality to illusion. It is a display of consumer gullibility—and the sophistication of persuasion skill—on a scale the likes of which the world has never seen before. In a commercial pushing for a perfume called "8 O'clock Mint," two women talk about the kind of men they dream about and one says to the other, "Tall, handsome, and lots of money." It is not with the charm and innocence of a Doris Day that the comments are made. Rather, they are devised with the most ruthless and sophisticated series of testing and scientific research our modern technique can muster. That these ads do not always work has to do more with competition and caprice than with consumer intelligence.

No one in America likes to be called stupid or think of himself as stupid. Our own instinctive belief in liberal egalitarianism gives everyone the benefit of the doubt, often against a mountain of evidence to the contrary. But the very fact, if nothing else, of such advertising proves something terribly uncomplimentary about the American public's collective wisdom and intelligence. Incongruently, we are supposed to be the best-educated people human history has ever known. Our total college population today outnumbers all the college students outside the United States put together in history. Nowhere is this display of public stupidity more evident than in the political arena. Politics has become essentially one of those surplus, unimportant aspects of life in America. Its continuing survival is in the production of headline grabbers usually by political idiocy, not by statesmanship. It is not too farfetched that Walter Mondale's 1984 Democratic nomination was rescued from the jaws of defeat only by his clever use of a commercial line: "Where's the beef?" referring to his rival Gary Hart's supposedly unsubstantiated "ideas." If Mondale had defeated Ronald Reagan and gone to the White House, which could have happened, he might very well have been the first president certifiably elected *commercially*.

America's penchant for commercially tailored messages—simple, quick imagery and sloganeering—finds receptive users in foreign lands, who love to give us good dosages of our own medicine in the great mechanism of American commercialism. In Richard Lamm and Arnold Grossman's novel *1988*, it is asserted that "given a large enough budget and enough creative genius, Colonel Qaddafi could get himself elected president." Or, for that matter, so could Saddam Hussein. Perhaps not quite. Not yet, but our gullibility is uncomfortably close to that fiction. Even the revolutionaries and saints, communists and atheists, those from the left and those from the right, friends and foes, everybody from a crackpot dictator to a pope uses this image-making device known as advertisement. It is always safe to assume nowadays—whenever the package of a product changes, a politician plans his campaign strategy, or someone is trying to improve his image through public relations—that there is a singular assumption about the target of their brainstorm: *people are stupid*.

As one of its most telling characteristics, advertisement harmonizes a diverse set of circumstances, events, and personalities into a thematically simplified, culturally homogeneous, and intellectually unobjectionable quality of presentation. After all, images on television can create any impression their creators wish to create. Even going to Hell can be presented with such comfort, fun, and amiability that viewers would *want* to go to Hell with full enthusiasm. God and the Devil, good and evil, right and wrong, friends and foes, complexity and simplicity, or whatever else we think is irreconcilable can be reduced to the thirty-second spot so effortlessly, so wonderfully, fitted with nice background music from Bach or Mozart, narrated by one of the celebrities for hire. Arabs can look next-door all-American; Eskimo life can look positively idyllic; a black family can look WASPish. With one shot of the camera, with one flick of the scissors, we can create any image and any effect we want to produce and preserve on the screen. All contradictions dissolve; all human conflicts disappear; all social problems evaporate—all with simple images and words.

Can anything survive the onslaught of advertisement at all? Is there anything immune from advertisement? Religion? Love? Patriotism? What of patriotism, the love of one's country? Can patriotism be advertised like all other commercial products we advertise to the gullible souls? Consider the following letter, the standard one sent to high school seniors by recruiting sergeants.

Dear so-and-so:

Let me show you how the average person who joined the Army two years ago is doing today.

After two years the average Army enlistee has been promoted three times and is an E-4; that means he earns $____ per month, and that's spending money. His food, housing, clothing and medical expenses are taken care of by the Army, so he can buy a new car or stereo or start a savings account that'll grow each month. If you're married, your monthly paycheck will include $____ in salary, $____ for renting an apartment and $____ to buy groceries, and you still get all of the other benefits. . . . Do you want a job in electronics or law enforcement? Or maybe a job in heavy construction is what you're looking for. I can guarantee in writing training in these or 300 other exciting job areas. . . .[3]

Notice that there is no reference to country or flag. It is strictly a business proposition, like all other advertised messages: "Come on, we've got something exciting for you. Lots of money and the easy life."

The television commercials put out by the military have the same appeal to the reluctant heart, trying to lure the unsuspecting soul with all sorts of promises, images, and musical background. The souls that the army is trying to recruit are not one bit different from the souls any other selling ad is trying to reach. One commercial publicizes the need to register on the eighteenth birthday by showing three typical youths with their boomboxes rocking and skipping to the Selective Services Board. The utter lack of seriousness for a reasonably serious business of national defense is thus made tantamount to a school principal trying to discipline a naughty pupil while breakdancing. But like all other commercials, military commercials for the purpose of boosting patriotism *cannot* act serious, simply because they are commercials. Military or not, patriotism or not, all commercials have to look, sound, feel like commercials—quick, simple, and pleasant—ideally compelling one to action.

The U.S. military is perhaps the only military institution whose members are recruited into the system by the same method—that is, advertisement—as is used to sell Pepsi, special effects, and other such products that require selling. It is an appeal to the weak and vulnerable, using much color and sound to lure the unsuspecting victims, presenting images and words quite unrelated to reality. It promises fun and games and money, while hard work and sacrifice should be the norm. All commercials assume that the buyers are generally precarious, whimsical, flipping-minded, sensation-seeking, unintelligent if not outright stupid, and unpredictable. It is impossible to think otherwise in view of the commercials. The requirements of commercials are such that they cannot be any more intelligent than the very minimum level of comprehension. David Robinson, formerly an ensign in the U.S. Navy and a graduate of the Naval Academy, a man of dignity and intelligence, is suitably reduced to a fairly idiotic hustler in his Nike commercials. The military commercials—based on the same principles of advertisement, because they are produced by professional ad-makers, not military men—appeal to the same sort of crowd that, by chance, might be lured to the military in search of excitement, careers, easy money. Simply

notice the fact that air force recruitment soared when a movie about pilots—
Top Gun—became a hit. One can imagine the bitter disappointment of
those would-be Tom Cruises realizing that nothing in reality was like that
suggested in the movie. (A similar overflow of recruitment took place
during the Gulf War.)

Adding insult to injury, the advertisers on Madison Avenue make no
bones about exactly what they intend to do to fool the buyers just by changing the ad tactics without changing substance at all. When Alka-Seltzer
needed a boost, its advertising agency changed the image of Alka-Seltzer
from a stomach-soothing antacid tablet, mainly used for overeating, to a
price paid for the stressful success of "a senior Vice-Presidency by age 39."
They also changed Sara Lee's commercials by adding a bit of French accent,
all to positive commercial results. Through all these changes, the agencies
responsible for gauging human responses openly brag about the changes
they contemplate, directly challenging or even daring the public. "This is
what we are going to do with our ad," the ad agency is in effect saying, "because that's what the public likes. Now, watch how they respond. See, I told
you they would respond positively." The antacid substance of Alka-Seltzer
did not change at all. Yet its changes in image, so publicly discussed and analyzed, resulted in changes in consumer responses exactly as anticipated by
the ad makers. For his celebrated antidrug speech in 1986 President Reagan,
joined by Mrs. Reagan, told the viewers in the beginning of the speech he
had changed the set from his usual Oval Office to his more informal living
room set, because he wanted the American people to take his message as one
concerning an urgent family problem. The Americans presumably did, and
the set change was effective. During the 1990 election, President Bush took
the advice to look "more presidential" and acted or tried to act presidential
to oust his "wimp" image. Virtually everyone in America *knew* that he was
trying to look presidential. But the point is that there is really no difference
between "looking" and "being" presidential in America.

After its image had been severely tarnished following criminal convic-
tions, E. F. Hutton hired Bill Cosby—"TV's most persuasive celebrity"—
to clean up its *image* without, presumably, changing one bit in its substance.
They trusted Cosby because of his outstanding selling job with Jell-O Pud-
ding Pops and on "The Cosby Show." A magazine article predicted only
in half-jest that the outcome of Cosby's pitching for Hutton would be
successful: "If Hutton can regain America's trust, it will show that when
Bill Cosby talks, people listen." Never mind that, with or without Cosby,
it is the same E. F. Hutton once convicted of 2,000 wrongdoings in its
financial dealings. Again, everyone in America knew it was a "commercial,"
done by an actor for money. But how did the ad men expect it to work?
The thinking is simple: people are stupid enough to believe Cosby, whose
pitching reward is "at least $1 million annually for three years." Upon
learning that singer Michael Jackson signed a multimillion-dollar deal with

Pepsi, which, incidentally, Jackson doesn't drink, the normally conventional *Milwaukee Journal* was incensed that the deal "symbolized such distorted values":

But if these are the facts of life in the marketplace of 20th century culture, let us at least lament the profoundly cynical messages that Pepsi, Michael Jackson and Co. are beaming to young people: (1) Packaging is everything, and (2) *The world is full of suckers*; take their money and "Beat It."[4]

If ad makers bank on consumer stupidity, most of the time they are not disappointed with the results.

Most unsettling of all is that both—advertisement and stupidity—are vital to the continuing prosperity of the current economic system in America. The Inverted Economy in American society makes selling imperative, for without it high standards of living cannot be maintained. Anthropologist Jules Henry saw this dilemma decades ago.

In order for our economy to continue in its present form people must learn to be fuzzy-minded and impulsive, for if they were clear-headed and deliberate they would rarely put their hands in their pockets; or, if they did, they would leave them there. If we were all logicians the economy could not survive, and herein lies a terrifying paradox, for in order to exist economically as we are we must try by might and main to *remain stupid*.[5]

This imperative selling makes advertisement, the tool of selling, absolutely necessary, and advertisement makes public stupidity, the response to advertisement, as necessary as selling is for the economy. This is a roundabout way of saying that without stupidity abundant on a large scale, advertisement would be impossible; without advertisement, selling goods and services would be impossible, for few things are really needed anymore; without selling, America's economic system could no longer maintain the standards of living to which its population is accustomed. In short, it is our stupidity that sustains the economy and our enviable living standards, not to mention the supplying of soldiers to fight for the country's interest. The consequences of a highly intelligent public, totally oblivious to commercial influences, are too catastrophic to contemplate, both economically and militarily. Our consumption would drop considerably; unemployment would rise; our living standards would decline; the military would be unable to fill its quota with recruits.

From this point of view, a view that asserts stupidity as the essential ingredient in America's continuing prosperity, the inversion of the American economy is seen most clearly. Instead of intelligence, we must now reward ignorance; instead of information, we must now encourage stupidity, or else the American economy as we know it would collapse. We have painted ourselves into a corner of stupidity, and there is no way out of it.

Greater emphases on education, consumer information, Ralph Naderism, and so on would only make matters worse by creating a generation of intelligent beings, smarter than they have the right to be, who could not be manipulated by advertisement. While many believe in education as the solution to many of our social problems, education itself could be the most serious of all problems. For ignorance is indeed bliss in our market society where education is its most deadly folly. There are periodic cries of poor education in America on all levels. But we do not really *want* and cannot *afford* a well-*educated* public. We just want engineers and mathematicians who can compete with the Japanese and Germans in inventing new things. But there is a world of difference between a well-educated public and well-*trained* scientists. We want the latter, not the former.

Gradually we begin to believe in the powers of advertisement even for things that have nothing to do with selling products. We begin to believe in advertisement as a *substitute* for everything else in social life. Advertisement—those magical ten-, twenty-, thirty-second images—becomes the predominant mode of communication and socialization. Under the headline of "MEDIA PLAN BLITZ AGAINST DRUGS," UPI reports that "the nation's media and advertising agencies this fall will launch the largest volunteer advertising campaign in history—a three year, $1.5 billion war on drugs, officials announced." Parents no longer need to break their backs to raise their children right day in, day out, year after year; if anything goes wrong with them—drug addiction, teenage pregnancy, alcoholism, what have you—*we simply advertise and tell them not to do it. Just say no* has become a catchphrase in fighting drugs among teenagers in America, as it is widely advertised. It is not necessary any longer for the parents to raise their children day in, day out, year after year not to take drugs; we just advertise it on television.

Children may eventually learn to say no because of the effectiveness of advertising, but we are not sure if *that* advertisement can fight the effectiveness of *the other* advertisement—that is, the pleasure of *taking* drugs. Our advertisement urges to say no; the other, yes. It is all a matter of advertisement, not upbringing, morality, right and wrong, or whatever else a child is supposed to learn through his socialization. Right upbringing takes too long and is too hard on the parent; advertisement takes only a few seconds and breaks no one's back. Perhaps advertisement works in raising the moral level of our young, but even if it does, it is a strange way of going about it. But the parent cannot be blamed; poor child behavior has to be called something other than poor socialization or inadequate parenting. "Does your child have any of the following behavior traits?" one help-is-only-a-phone-call-away organization asks:

1. Scores average or better on intelligence tests, but has poor grades.
2. Doesn't apply himself.

3. Spends too much time watching TV or doing nothing constructive.

4. Is not a self-starter.

5. Spends too little time doing homework or preparing for classes and may even claim he has no homework.

6. Is immature in relationships with grownups and views any criticism as being picked on.

7. Often fails to complete projects.

8. Does worst in important subjects like math and English.

9. Is a procrastinator and regularly responds "later" or "in a minute" to parental requests.

10. Rarely accepts responsibility for personal failure. Blames it on bad luck or others.

11. Reported by teachers to be almost always behind in his work and lacking self-discipline.

12. Excuses his bad performance in school with "the teacher is boring," "the class is irrelevant," "I had a bad day."

13. Seems to have a short attention span.

14. Spends more time getting out of work than completing it.

15. Refuses to make any realistic plans about his future.

16. Does well only when he feels like it.

17. Becomes angry when things don't go the way he wants.

18. Cannot save money.

19. Lacks self-confidence, particularly around kids his own age.

20. Can work only with one-on-one attention.[6]

The Institute for Motivational Development, the seller of this service, calls a child with such traits "an underachiever," for which there is a remedy, just one phone call away. What they are proposing to cure is indeed audacious; it covers virtually the whole range of behavior and personality. There are no more bad boys or girls, just underachievers. Who is to be blamed for underachievers? In American society we let paid caretakers and experts raise our children and let sports build their character. This way, of course, no American parent can fail. How do we instill honesty in our children? By advertising, of course.

It is no longer necessary to bring up our children teaching them honesty and other lifelong values. We simply advertise "to be honest." In a television commercial sponsored by the Church of Jesus Christ of Latter-day Saints (Mormons), a girl steals a necklace from another girl, denies it, then later returns it. All in thirty seconds. The voiceover says, "If you want to be someone special, be honest." The idea of honesty is thus delivered through a medium—television commercial—crowded with the messages of dishonesty, greed, heartlessness, selfishness, mindlessness, stupidity, vanity, ab-

surdity, obscenity, sexuality. It is indeed an audacious expectation to teach
our children the value of honesty by simply advertising it. It is a shortcut
of Substitute Society perhaps at its most bizarre.

For nearly two centuries, since the first roar of the Industrial Revolution
was heard around the world, the size of the middle class has been used as
one of the best indicators of a society's evolutionary progress. The larger
the middle class, the greater a society's claim to modern nationhood. Even
before the Industrial Revolution, American society was largely populated
by the "old" middle class of farmers, merchants, free professionals, and
others who had never experienced European feudalism and its rigid upper-
and-lower scheme of social class. American society began almost from the
beginning of its history as a middle-class nation. Today, in an age of total
communication and consumptive economy, American society has another
reason to call itself a nation of the middle class both in image and in reality.
As a "target" of the vast network of advertising efforts Americans have
become one large varied but homogeneous group of message receivers.
What works on the middle-class person thus applies easily to all other
middle-class persons. To be sure, there are different strategies and levels of
messages to reach different socioeconomic subgroups. But there is so much
overlapping in this scheme of things and messages are so abstract and universally applicable that any commercial message could be relevant to any
group in the socioeconomic categories.

   As a massive target class of consumers, middle- and lower-class have
become irrelevant as categories. Together, they form the mass of consumers
crisscrossing the different social, racial, economic, political, and cultural
boundaries that used to be fairly visible even in America. Since the sources
of income are no longer as relevant as they used to be in determining social
status, it is how much one can *consume* that is the yardstick of class distinction. Together, the target class is visible in every consumptive sector
of society; they attend ball games, they eat out at family restaurants, they
shop at department stores, they buy groceries at chain supermarkets, and
they vote either Republican or Democratic. With unionism largely on the
wane, with the decline of old industrialism, lifestyles are no longer bound
by the blue- and white-collar socioeconomic differences that used to give
rise to distinct lifestyles. Even in the welfare class, billions of dollars are
available for daily consumption of common goods and services.

   With this change in the meaning of the term *middle class*, the very notion
of exploitation has also changed. The crude early capitalist exploitation of
workers, either in the socialist or in the Marxist terms of exploitation, has
been replaced by an entirely different sort. While the basis of an exploitive
economy has remained intact, its mode of practice has changed so much
so that to say that the target class is being exploited requires a bit of mental
double-taking. The earlier forms of exploitation were more obvious and

cruel: control of wages, monopoly of production and distribution, child labor, price fixing, frauds, economic-political collusion. Today such practices still form an important element in the new economy, but their significance has been in decline on a historical scale. Largely because the basic composition of what is produced and consumed has changed, the physical and material forms of exploitation have also changed. The way the new target class is "exploited" with special effects and new video games is quite different from the way children were tied to their machines or from the way labor wages were kept down to increase the capitalist's profit. Wanting our labor at the cheapest cost possible has been replaced by wanting our money however it can be lured out of our pockets. We are no longer driven hard at work by profit-crazed capitalists; instead, we see a pretty face smiling on us from television screens and billboards asking us to buy their goods and services, talking about love, happiness, and fulfillment. Even for the traditional "worker," the greater part of his life consists of being a "consumer," a distinction he himself perhaps prefers. He may work like a slave to earn his wages, but he surely consumes like a king.

In the scheme of selling and consuming, what might be a rather sinister implication is the word *target* is fast disappearing. Targeting specific socio-economic groups has become more and more respectable as science in marketing and advertising. One ad agency advertises its services thus: "Your message should be running in the prestigious national magazines that reach this fast-moving target audience." Another says: "Our free Target Media evaluation will help you select the best magazine mix for pinpoint accuracy . . . " Still another one has the picture of a bomber dropping tons of goods on earth with a caption: "HOW TO SCORE A DIRECT HIT ON A MILITARY TARGET." A magazine runs an editorial in which it simply calls the public "The Target," as if no further explanation is necessary. Right at this moment, they are being classified into appropriate target groups; their habits and wishes are being studied scientifically; their weaknesses and yearnings are being examined under the psychological microscope; their reactions and responses are being tested and retested to determine what makes them want to buy certain things and what does not.

Money used to be made when a product or service, be it a washing machine or plumbing, performed a particular function in satisfying our needs. In a culture where we have virtually no need unsatisfied, the new economy must create new needs and new means to service the new needs. It is a war on a scale and in intensity the world has never seen before to capture the attention of the now increasingly restless and demanding population. It is a war of competing illusions about our fears, fulfillment, entertainment, security, self-awareness, meaning of life, loneliness, love,and friendship. Salesmen no longer knock on our doors and demonstrate their latest models for housecleaning or mouse trapping. Instead, they now use the state-of-the-art technique of illusion-making, specially designed for each target population, in order to create a climate of need, a vague sense of urgency that we cannot resist.

The illusion-making function of advertising in America reveals its more hideous underbelly. People so conditioned by the advertised world cannot see themselves as they *truly* are. Our Horatio Alger may become a corporate executive and company president by dint of hard work, ingenuity, and luck. But the rest of those also-rans remain exactly where they have always been: at the bottom of the social pyramid. They must endure daily humiliation and gut-wrenching agonies for their paychecks; they must beg for mercy for their continuing survival in a merciless wage system; they must think and act like animals in a competitive market society where every other human being is at least a potential predator to take the bread away from them and their children's mouths; for most Americans, with the exception of the Horatio Algers, life in the suburb and life on unemployment compensation are only one pink slip apart.

By all factual accounts, if we didn't believe the advertisements, most Americans represent the classic underclass—those who must toil at the mercy of their most merciless economic overlords. In spite of the images that advertisements create and many Americans would like to believe in, they have more in common with the traditional underclasses of the world— peasants, servants, slaves, serfs, paupers, pimps and prostitutes, petty criminals, mercenaries and bodyguards, footmen—than with the wonderful inhabitants of television fantasies, billboard commercials, and the Horatio Alger stories. A recent research project found that an average Soviet woman spends five hundred hours a year standing in line to purchase the necessities of life. This news evoked considerable pity for the Soviets and much self-congratulation for our material affluence in America. But one wonders what the Soviets are thinking about the poor American woman who spends almost two thousand hours a year in television's fantasyland and with its unending stream of advertisements. The Soviets have their problems— namely, a shortage of *things*. Our problems are very different from theirs.

In a dictatorial society or a society of extreme poverty, we may blame the dictator or poverty for our misery. In an affluent open-market society we have no one but ourselves to blame if things are not the way they should be. In a "free" society where every man is for himself, so much responsibility of avoiding and identifying deception—from the presidential campaigns to common advertisement—is placed on the shoulders of each individual citizen. In view of the best and brightest who engage in the deceptive process, the citizen stands a slim chance of recognizing the consequences of his gullibility and stupidity. All modern deceptions and frauds come with a smiling face. Yet all things pretty have one purpose in mind: to seduce the brains of their target audiences.

The marketplace is also good at keeping us busy: they run twenty-four-hour-a-day television; one sports season follows another without a break;

one innovation in entertainment follows another before we get bored with it. The marketplace is unrelenting. It corrupts our soul with such art and science that we have never enjoyed our soul corruption so much. And what's worse, we can never have enough of it.

NOTES

1. "Pepsi's Madonna Ad Premieres Tonight," *USA Today*, 2 March 1989.

2. Jeffry Scott, "No Place Seems Safe from 'Ambush' Ads," *Star News*, Wilmington, NC, 31 December 1989.

3. This form letter was standard among recruiters in the 1980s, who practiced the "seven-rejection" rule: namely, the recruiter gave up on a prospect only after receiving a minimum of seven rejections.

4. Editorial, *Milwaukee Journal*, 12 May 1986.

5. Jules Henry, *Culture Against Man* (New York: Random House, 1963), 48.

6. Advertisement for the Institute for Motivational Development, with the main office in Lombard, Illinois, 1986, distributed to teachers.

Chapter 8

The Inverted Economy

America's industrial development no longer produces things that people wish they could own; it now produces things that people wish they never knew about. Even with an automobile, a vacuum cleaner, a refrigerator, and a television set in every household, the residual economic resources, energies, and dynamics of American society are so enormous that they must somehow be dissipated through the marketplace. The marketplace and its advertising machine must now perform perhaps their most daunting task: to persuade a society to consume products it neither wants nor needs. The task of producing and pushing products no one needs or wants requires an economic ingenuity and cultural convulsion on a scale the world has never imagined. It is America's Inverted Economy in its most brazen moment. Just witness the gradual decline of references to economizing. Nowadays we hardly ever hear anyone referred to as a "miser," "tightwad," "penny pincher," "skinflint," or other such designations of frugality. Economizing is no longer culturally acceptable.

Consider the items listed in a fairly typical "gift catalog" easily available to average members of the American middle class: Marquee Clock; Growling King Kong; Satin Marquee Jacket; Cart'N Case; Minirecorder; Stereo Receiver with Speakers; Compumate; Answering Machine; Electronic Organizer; Electronic Dictionary/Thesaurus; Levitating World Globe; Iron/Hair Dryer Combo; Alarm Clock/Radio; Pocket Translator; Executive Organizer; Expanding Bag; Versatile Soviet Courier's Case; Ankle Wallet; Phrase Translator; Digital Diary; Leather Lappack; Dual Time Zone Watch;

Hair Dryer; Towel Warmer; Shower Mirror; Hair Removal Kit; Revolving
Bookcase; Personalized Carton Straps; Thermometer and Clock; Mother-
of-Pearl Watch; Solar Auto Vent; Vacuum Cover Maid; Kitchen Whiz; Golf
Programs Led by the Pros; Football Follies Video; Basketball Bloopers;
John Madden on Football; Self-Discipline Program; Stereo Sound Feeder;
Portable Locker Bag; Remote Control Airplane; Sound Sleeper Clock; Ul-
tra-Small FM Stereo Radio; Personalized Baseball Bat; Time Pyramid;
Cordless Videophone; Copykit; Your Own Street Sign; Propeller Letter
Opener; Personalized Passport Case; Tie Shade; Electronic Dictionary; Col-
lapsible Luggage With Wheels.[1]

If the reader has been patient or curious enough to have glanced at the
list, it is obvious that only those who have extra money to spend—on their
own or at company expense—would find the items attractive enough to
purchase them. Of course, one can find some usefulness in all of them, but
not useful enough to forsake more urgent needs of life. In a bygone era of
different economic lifestyles, virtually all of them would have been thought
of as the exclusive purview of the idle rich with money to burn. Today
they are for the conspicuously consuming American middle class with
money to burn. Much of their savage struggle at the marketplace consists
of earning the money so that their conspicuous consumption becomes not
so conspicuous. One who has made it in America is the one who feels no
guilt at wasting his money. America's retailers make close to one-half of
their annual profit during the Christmas holiday. By the time New Year's
Day arrives, most of the products purchased during the season will have
lost their meaningful existence—totally wasted.

America's economic system itself has become a "paper economy," as
David T. Bazelon called it in his book *The Paper Economy*.[2] As much of the
nation's wealth consists of paper assets borrowed or inflated, much of what
Americans consume has become *nonmaterial* goods and services. The paper
economy, in other words, evolves largely around phantom goods and services. By arriving at a paper economy, American society has, for the first
time in human history, actually made economics *obsolete*. If economics is
understood—as we have always understood it—as the system of production
(supply) and needs (demand), our paper economy is neither about production nor about needs. It is an inverted, surplus economy where production
and consumption have no significant relation to what economics is supposed
to solve—that is, producing goods and services to meet human needs. In
an inverted paper economy, moneymaking, not producing goods and services, becomes its central activity. Its consumption, likewise, has nothing
to do with meeting human needs. It is this surplus nature of America's
economic system that gives our whole notion of economics its hollow and
surreal texture. As workers and consumers, we are also strangely dissociated
in our very economic activity. As our social life is no longer about reality,
our economic life is no longer about the real bread-and-butter stuff. As

workers, we toil as we have always toiled. As consumers, we consume like never before. The two central activities of society and human beings, perhaps for the first time in history, have no connection in American society and life.

Consider the inverted way some people make money. At this writing, Donald Trump is on the brink of bankruptcy. Why? It is simply because he owes more than he owns or earns. His total assets and their earnings are smaller than his debts and their interests. But why is he perceived as one of the wealthiest men in America, with all the attendant envy and publicity? Bazelon would explain that it is because he can *borrow* a lot of money that we ordinary people cannot. In a paper economy, your ability to borrow almost equals your wealth. It is very possible that Trump could still come out on top, depending on the turns of his economic fortune. Since Trump, like many other modern entrepreneurs in America, produces nothing of any real usefulness, how does he increase his assets above his debts? He cannot. He has to depend on the moods and perceptions of society in general. In other words, his—and America's—economic fortunes stand or fall on phantom factors that have nothing to do with production and needs. "More than we'd like to think," money writer Andrew Tobias observes, "economic and financial swings are creatures of fuzzy, nonquantitative things like *psychology, confidence, and the national mood.*" The prosperity of the 1980s, political economist Kevin Phillips says in his book *The Politics of Rich and Poor*, epitomized American society "consuming, rearranging and borrowing more than it built." The economically untrained, including myself, will have to take the experts' word for it. Yes, I agree that in an inverted, surplus, unreal paper economy like ours, our mood swings determine the nation's economic health and borrowing and rearranging constitute its wealth. The science of "economics," it is now certain, has given way to the science of mood swings.

Borrowing is true on all levels of economic balance sheets—federal, corporate, and individual. As economization and frugality have gone out of style in the American economic idioms, our standard for economic virtue has also been radically redefined. We no longer have debtors' prison. Instead, *being in debt* is taken as a sign that a person has come of age. As borrowing is the main form of business prosperity and government strategy, it is also a necessity for social status in the individual consumer. Without borrowing, thus establishing a "credit history," a person is persona non grata in America. There is no record of him or, now increasingly, of her. "We call them invisible [men and women]," an American Express executive comments on those who have had no history of being in debt. "No credit is not good credit," says a finance professor. "It's considered *a sign of immaturity or irresponsibility.*" Now one's whole social standing depends on how much one has been *in* debt, not clear of it. According to this new, inverted standard, Americans as a whole are doing well. By the end of the 1980s,

America's credit card transactions, the main form of individual debt economy, stood close to an impressive half-trillion dollars. Of this, close to $5 billion became delinquent. No wonder there are no debtors' prisons anymore; we cannot accommodate all the debtors.

It is difficult to get a comprehensive picture of this strange inverted economic system. It is not the case of the tail wagging the dog, but *becoming* the dog. Of the thirty top-earning athletes in their 1990 estimates, as an example of our upside-down economy, fifteen of them earn more from their *fame* than from their actual competitive winnings. It is not unlike debtors transforming their debts into assets. Just for our amusement I list them here (amounts are in millions):

	Winnings	Fame earnings
Jack Nicklaus (golf)	0.6	8.0
Greg Norman (golf)	1.5	7.0
Michael Jordan (basketball)	2.1	6.0
Arnold Palmer (golf)	0.1	8.0
Boris Becker (tennis)	1.2	6.0
Steffi Graf (tennis)	1.1	5.0
Andre Agassi (tennis)	1.0	4.5
Stefan Edberg (tennis)	1.5	4.0
Ivan Lendl (tennis)	1.3	4.0
Diego Maradona (soccer)	2.0	3.0
Bo Jackson (baseball/football)	2.0	2.5
Gabriela Sabatini (tennis)	0.5	4.0
Joe Montana (football)	1.4	3.0
Greg LeMond (cycling)	1.7	2.5
Curtis Strange (golf)	0.8	3.0

Source: Adapted from "Intelligence Report," *Parade*, 30 September 1990.

It is nothing short of a magnificent twist on our surplus society. These athletes earn more from their *surplus* income, which is greater than their real income, which is itself a *surplus* activity in society. They make millions from make-believe "work" and much more from the "fame" of their make-believe work. But few Americans will see any irony in it. After earning millions as a football player, Steve Largent retired from playing for the NFL's Seahawks. "My mom always asked when I'd get a *real job*," Largent said the day after his retirement, "and I think that time has come." Sports on television are wholly phantom events. What is advertised, often using sports personalities, is also mostly phantom products whose urgency must

be artificially promoted: shaving gear, shampoo, hair loss remedies, automobiles, beer, financial magazines, moneymaking tips.

Also consider some of the more popular electronic items: answering
machines, video cameras, compact disk players, home computers, prerecorded videos, projection TVs, satellite dishes, telephones, VCRs. The
electronic items that are the hallmark of modern living standards are striking
because of their essentially toylike "plaything" nature. They represent an
overripe economy trying to regain its vitality and dynamics with new fron-
tiers of ingenuity and creativity. But beyond these obvious points, they also
indicate what kind of economic system we now have and what kind of
products we produce and consume and why.

In American society we naturally believe that it is good to have many
Good Things and better to have many more Good Things. Our national
moods move up and down according to the barometer of our national
wealth going up and down. But what are those Good Things more of which
are Better? Of all the items mentioned above, one can take or leave any of
them, with the possible exception of the telephone. None of them has the
functional usefulness of bread and butter. This very mention of "usefulness"—or what economists call utility—immediately invokes a protest. The
consumer, and nobody else, in cooperation with the market mechanism of
supply and demand, determines the usefulness of anything or lack thereof,
the protest says. The consumer will not buy anything in which he sees no
usefulness. But since the issue of usefulness is real and it has been one of
the major issues of modern economic thought, we should tackle it here.
Indeed, *how* do consumers choose certain items, such as those listed above,
among the objects of their consumption? The manner in which people
choose them tells something about the seriousness of their consumptive
intention and therefore some measure of usefulness as well. And how do
they do it?

In buying bread, as an illustration, one takes all sorts of factors into
consideration: nutritional value, freshness, ingredients, taste, testimonials
from reliable sources, price, general reputation, and not the least simple
habits, some factors more or less prominently considered than others. Not
all consumers practice this much care when they buy bread, for they tend
to rely on repetition and habit. But the principle of certain "predetermined"
ideas—what-I-want-in-my-bread—that governs one's initial selection behavior remains true, if only subconsciously. In other words, there is no
other serious consideration *unrelated* to bread that is used in buying bread.
We normally do not buy a loaf because the package looks good or there is
a space in the refrigerator that needs filling. Bread must be of a certain kind
that is also needed.

But with certain other goods, such as the electronic items listed above,
all of which one can take or leave based on many factors, most people tend

to be less than judicious. A decision to buy or not buy a VCR may be a serious one for the consumer. But *why he wants* to buy it does not have the same predetermined seriousness as buying bread. One does not buy bread unless one absolutely *needs* it. But whether one needs a *VCR* cannot be so easily determined. The decision depends on a lot of factors, the least of which is *whether one NEEDS a VCR*. The reason for that is simple: there is no such thing as need for a VCR. Unlike the need for bread, one is *persuaded* that one *needs* a VCR. The way we are persuaded in an Inverted Economy—to own a VCR, to support a sports team, to go see a movie, to consult a psychiatrist, to invest in a stock—tells much about that controversial issue of how "useful" they really are. How *are* we persuaded? Let us change the subject slightly so that we arrive at a better understanding of the problem.

No better example can serve us than the manner in which we become the ardent followers of a surplus, nonvital product. We call the ardent follower, the enthusiastic consumer of a cultural phenomenon, a "fan," short for "fanatic." A fan is one who prefers certain events or products with great enthusiasm. One is a fan of the Chicago Bears, a fan of Michael Jackson, a fan of Sidney Sheldon. Although these followers are called fans, notice that we do not assign the same designation to the followers of Beethoven, Shakespeare, or Van Gogh—they do not have fans; they have devotees. Nor does Holsum bread have fans, just satisfied customers. The difference is not just in the name. It is in the manner in which one becomes either a fan or a devotee or a customer. The fan *does not* know or *cannot* tell with reasonable certainty *why* he is a fan of the Bears, of Michael Jackson, or of Sidney Sheldon. If pressed, he will say things that are totally unrelated to the principles of rational decision-making: that he was born in Chicago, that he likes Michael Jackson's footwork, that Sidney Sheldon's books are interesting to read. All in all, the decision-making process is so chance-ridden and whimsical as to be useless as an explanation of why a fan is a fan. "Fandom" is, really, best understood as something about which one does not ask questions. For there are no answers. Questions may be raised and answers attempted only if the issue is reasonable enough to discuss rationally. One can explain one's choice in Shakespeare, Van Gogh, or Holsum bread. But this is impossible in a fan. Fans become fans for no other reason than they already are. There is absolutely nothing to discuss.

Another thing about a fan is that he can change the object of his ardor as quickly and as unpredictably as he became its fan in the first place. Perhaps he doesn't like the team's new uniform, new coach, or new stadium, he is simply tired of their losing record, or whatever. Anything and everything will do. Becoming a fan of something requires no logical explanations; neither does changing one's object of fanaticism. Fans come; fans go. But the same attitude could not be applied to the devotee of Beethoven, Shakespeare, or Van Gogh. Because the reason for having become a devotee of this or that has been clearly articulated in the first place, at least in one's own mind, the reason for changing that devotion must also have clear reasons. Nor would a Holsum bread customer change to another bread without some reason (e.g., price, quality). One does not become a devotee or customer of anything without giving the matter due consideration. Becoming a fan, on the other hand, requires nothing that even remotely resembles logic or reason. That one likes it or that one hates it is all that one needs to be a fan. Being or becoming a fan is the easiest and often the dumbest thing one can do in a free society.

A fan is one who has been persuaded to find the "need" of this, that, or the other in the endless stream of production, promotion, and consumption in our society. The need or usefulness of the object to which he is so attached requires no serious consideration as to its merit or demerit. Nor does his attachment—or finding the "need"—require that such serious consideration be given to the decision. The decision can be made for any reason or even no reason, and changing that decision can be made for the same reason. Here reenters our original subject, a VCR. *Why* does one need and buy a VCR? Now we know that this question is as irrelevant as the question of why one is a fan of this, that, or the other. There is no point. No matter what reason one gives to buy a VCR, it will *not* be considered irrational, stupid, illegitimate. One can even say that he wants it to fill a space in his living room, and no one will strenuously argue the matter. For the very object itself has no rationality, intelligence, or legitimacy for its own usefulness and existence. One can live with or without a VCR. On the other hand, it would be considered fairly irrational, stupid, and illegitimate if one bought a loaf of bread because the color appealed to him or because the shape reminded him of his best friend's head when there was no need for bread at all. One cannot create a need for bread that does not exist. In the case of a VCR or fandom, one need not create any reason; a VCR or fandom requires no such need or reason. All things deemed desirable in an oversupplied Inverted Economy are like the VCRs purchased by their fans. While we call it an economic system governed by supply and demand in the marketplace, it has nothing to do with the "economic," if the term is used to mean *some* intelligent "economic thinking" exercised by the consumer. Like being a fan, any reason will do, and that's no "economic" behavior.

It is in a "surplus" economy that we have More Good Things than we need. We are of the habit to think that if we have More Good Things, it is better than just having Good Things. It is part of that American commitment to strive for a bigger, better, and faster development in everything. But what we now have is not more of Good Things, because Good Things do not become better if there are more of them. The things we have *more* of are vastly different in nature from the things we have *enough* of. Surplus means more of the same thing; the Inverted Economy, which I prefer to call it, means our economic behavior in production and consumption has been turned upside down. The More-Is-Better school of thought rejoices in the development of surplus, from more bread and butter to more entertaining events, sports, film and television, video games, best-sellers, fashion and fad consumption on a daily, weekly, monthly, seasonal basis of change and variation. It is merely a natural progression in the creation of affluence and its consumption, the surplus view asserts. But this is, of course, a fallacy.

Consider the way bread is produced, to illustrate the point. Although the technology of bread-making has come a long way, with the introduction of machines and management, the basic method of bread-making remains pretty much the same as it has always been. The grains have to be ground and mixed with other ingredients, baked at an appropriate temperature, sealed, and delivered to a store fresh for consumption. *The technology of production* and *the manner of consumption* (the way we eat it) have not changed that much.

By way of contrast, consider video games. A video game is a sophisticated achievement made possible with the highest levels of modern technology coming together. No video game is possible without all the ingredients of modern technology. A video game today is more advanced than that of yesterday, yesterday's more advanced than the day before yesterday's, and so on. Today's video game represents the cumulative technology of at least 10,000 years—taking 10,000 years as an arbitrary point of our technological beginning. All of this contributes to its production. The efforts of mankind in technological evolution to make our present-day video games—and most other forms of inverted consumption—possible are stupendous in their dimension and cost. It could easily have been a million years of evolution to make our video games, television, films, special effects, what have you, possible.

But more stupendous than the technological miracle in producing the video game is the manner in which we consume it. The manner of its consumption—unlike the technology of its production—is so primitive, so infantile, so simplistic, so juvenile that any child or any caveman from 10,000 years ago could play it and enjoy it to the hilt. In fact, it is geared to that age group's intelligence. It is as if we have *never made* that long march of mankind's progress and evolution; it is as if we are *still* in the cave. For all the "usefulness" and the "need" of the technological miracle, it is not one step more advanced than the intelligence of a caveman. For all that it signifies, for all the intellectual and moral advancement it represents, we might as well have *stayed* in the cave. The level of the technology of production has not translated into the level of the manner of its consumption. The greatest achievement in technological marvel is, as it turns out, merely a juvenile caveman's toy, nothing more, nothing less. The waste of human progress and evolution—as represented in the gap between technology and consumption—is another yardstick by which we measure what is useful and what is necessary in our production and consumption. Need for bread does not evolve into need for video games. We can now see that our economic system has been taking a gigantic step backward in history, while strangely, it appears to be moving forward. This is one illustration of why what we have today are not More Good Things.

Entertainment in general, for reasons of its more obvious surplus character in an Inverted Society, reveals the greatest discrepancy between technological capacity and consumption value. In filmmaking, television programming, devising advertisement, and many other areas of persuasion, the gap stands out greater than in any "material" products such as automobiles or vacuum cleaners. The rise and fall of these entertainment products are prodigious. They rise and fall in popularity for the strangest and most trivial of reasons, loved one minute and rejected the next by their fans. They may be the hottest thing, the best-seller, the toast of the town, the media darling one day, but they may hit the cold trail the next. Their "usefulness" to their followers and the "need" for them perceived by their consumers rise and fall without a pattern of predictability. Monumental rises and falls on the economic front are the consequences of the most trivial of events. The Trumps and Ted Turners win or lose on the basis of no apparent reason. Presidential elections are won or lost, million-dollar contracts made or blown, best-sellerdom created or missed—all by some minor trivia of human whims and caprice.

Until recently, all human industry was concentrated in one single purpose: to make the biologically defined existence of mankind as comfortable as possible. Technology, industry, and science formed the main components of that process. With a success story unmatched in human history, many of the Western nations, notably the United States, essentially accomplished that purpose. Physical survival is no longer a matter of serious concern, comfort in living has been achieved to an extent unimaginable even by aristocratic standards, and poverty, however defined, has been declared, at least by the American government, no longer existent. Most American households now contain at least one car in the garage (soon to be one person, one car), one television set, one refrigerator, internal plumbing, hot water, one vacuum cleaner. The wildest dream of the Industrial Revolution is deemed realized. Many journalists and observers have declared the Industrial Era over and a new age of high technology begun. With manufacturing automobiles and bathtubs no longer the prime objective of industrial energies, however, the gigantic productive machinery of the Industrial Era has turned to the new commercial frontier with the same characteristic ingenuity, creativity, and determination with which it created the Industrial Era a hundred years earlier. New products have to be designed, new markets have to be explored, and a whole new notion of "needs" and "usefulness" has to be devised. America, more than any other Western nation, has embarked on its course toward the Inverted Economy with its accustomed energy and speed.

In entertainment, in spectator sports, in financial speculation, in health and fitness, in counseling the troubled and uncertain, loving the unloved, and fulfilling the unfulfilled, and in countless other ways, the new era has been producing, promoting, and consuming its products. There are many ways of defining the New Product, as a means of understanding how it finds its way into our consciousness and into the new notion of needs and usefulness. *Affluence, surplus, high technology, Third Wave*, among others, are some of the more familiar ways of describing the new phenomenon and its new products. How are the new products different from the old products? Several contrasting points stand out.

ADVERTISEMENT VERSUS INFORMATION

Not always mutually exclusive as a way of telling us about the product, however, the *public* was informed and the *product* was advertised in the past. The emphasis of information was on the public, while that of advertisement was on the product. Even though advertisement often tended to overwhelm the fragile defenses of information, the tension between information and advertisement was always maintained. In individual consciousness as well as in public issues, the balance between advertisement and information was as important as it was natural in the Industrial Era. The public needed and sought information for its decisions.

With the coming of our new economic era, however, the "public" has subtly changed to "consumers," and with that change has come the overwhelming importance of advertisement overshadowing the traditional role of information. The "public" is assumed to be intelligent; the "consumer," to be stupid. The product is presented to the consumer in ten-, twenty-, or thirty-second spots, primarily with flashing pictures and smiling faces. We know no more about AT&T after its massive media advertisement, other than that Cliff Robertson does the commercials for AT&T, than before. We really know no more about the company as a result of the advertisement beyond what we already know or don't know. We only know they are a telephone company. Beyond that, nothing. If one wished to know more about AT&T or anything else advertised, one would have to go to a source considered reasonably objective and informative, not the self-serving, prefabricated flashes of images put out by AT&T itself. Even the idea of "public information" has been incorporated into what is essentially an advertising campaign in "consumer relations." Little information is now sought and given and made available; all seems to be one form or another of advertisement. Hence the perception of the New Product—its needs and usefulness—is now largely determined by advertisement, not information, in this new era.

MATERIAL VERSUS PSYCHOLOGICAL PRODUCT

For lack of a better dichotomy, the term *material* would apply to the old products (automobiles, bread) and *psychological* to the new products (video games, marketing advice). The contrast between "things" and "ideas" has always existed, but now the New Product is more and more characterized by ideas or images. It is no longer having *actual* fun with a thing that is the issue. It is the very idea or the image of being part of a "fun generation" or "fun lifestyle" as a more subconscious habit of mind that counts. The old product could actually be seen, fixed, and used to its old-age wear and tear. The New Product has no such definite qualities. It is not how healthy one has to be in concrete pursuit of a long life, but the image of health pursuit and its psychological necessity—the necessity of peer approval, of the "highs" of fitness exercise, of doing things in conformity with neighbors, of being in the fashionable crowd—that is far more significant. The computer, for instance, may have all the characteristics of a material thing, but a closer examination reveals it essentially as an idea, an image. It is the "computer generation" that appeals to the consumer, not the actual utility of the machine. In many ways, possessing a computer, being able to say that one has it, like many others of one's generation, is far more important as a measure of one's self-image than how the machine may fulfill certain specific functions.

SATIABILITY VERSUS INSATIABILITY

Following the above conception of the New Product, the idea of satiability logically emerges. The old product used to help one accomplish the need-satisfaction cycles in life. If one had to go somewhere, the automobile was there to perform that function. Once that function was performed, the need for the automobile was essentially satisfied. With the completion of each need-satisfaction cycle, a sense of satisfaction—a state of temporary fulfillment—always followed. The need was definite and so was its satisfaction. The need-satisfaction cycle had a definite point of beginning and an equally clear point of termination. The need recognized by the public and the satisfaction met by the product always assumed a finite, specific range of human necessity and capacity. One could not demand more cars, more food, more of everything indefinitely, for with each demand a definite state of satisfaction had to be assumed. The classic notion of "progress" also assumed this material point of departure (needs) and that of destination (satisfaction).

In our new era, however, this point of satisfaction has become not only difficult to define, but also impossible to reach. Since all new products begin and end with no particular points of need or satisfaction, possessing and consuming them brings their possessor and consumer no definite satisfaction. After each entertainment and amusement, after each encounter with a new gadget, one still remains vaguely dissatisfied with the outcome. It is difficult and often impossible to reach a point of clear-cut satisfaction, even temporarily, with the new variety of goods and services. One has to go back for more, and going back for more creates a greater urgency to go back for still more. The producers obliging with new models and variations, the demand remains insatiable. Exhausting but giving no happiness, the New Product is at once the creator and the beneficiary of this human insatiability.

THEME VERSUS VARIATION

Since the very existence of the New Product is based on no definite notion of needs and usefulness, one cannot remain fulfilled with the same model until its natural old-age wear and tear. The old product used to be purchased with the idea of a definite need and was kept until it exhausted its functions. A replacement, whether an automobile or a loaf of bread, was purchased only because the old one was worn out or used up. A "new" model was acquired because it was truly an "improved" version of the old. This still continues, for a very large part of our lives still runs on the old premise of needs-and-satisfaction cycles.

But with our increasing purchasing power, the saturation of our basic necessities in life, and the increasingly clever way our senses are stimulated, coupled with the vague changes in our cultural-psychological climate in human relations, we now occupy a considerable and increasing portion of our consciousness with "new" things to do and consume. We now demand that life, work, marriage, leisure—previously taken almost as routine facts of existence—and all other aspects of day-to-day experiences be constant variations with exciting freshness. We expect the evening news to bring us new events from around the world; we expect to be tickled with new, fanciful gadgets; we expect the new "fall lineup" on television to surpass the previous season in sensational and entertaining value; we expect our marriages to be forever romantic and satisfying and never to go stale; we expect our work to be personally stimulating and creative in a never-ending series of new challenges. In short, we want and expect the world around us to be the same and different and the New Product always a newer version of the old. The old product had its established and predictable quality, which demanded loyalty and consistency from its public. The New Product responds by changing its packaging and cosmetic arrangement in unending variations.

DEMANDED VERSUS SUPPLIED

To the chagrin of professional economists I am going to give the traditional concept of demand and supply a slight twist here, to add to our current discussion one more intellectual means of understanding. In the old economy goods and services were supplied because they were *demanded*, and the goods and services were demanded because they were *necessary*. It has been a familiar criticism of capitalism since Marx that the suppliers create demand itself, rather than letting demand arise naturally from its own necessity. This criticism cannot be more pertinent than in the new economy with its new products. To put it in a nutshell, certain goods and services exist because they are *demanded*; certain other goods and services exist because they are *supplied*. The goods and services that are demanded, arising out of life's necessities, *must* be supplied. The goods and services that are supplied without being demanded are consumed only with artificial and tortuous processes of persuasion. The old product used to persuade the customer with price and quality, which were often the same thing. The New Product persuades the consumer with a totally new means of persuasion, since the old yardstick of price and quality is no longer central to the consumptive cycle. Neither price nor quality can be reasonably computed from the New Product, because its production and consumption do not follow the usual economic fact of costs and utility. How much should one pay for tickets to a Michael Jackson concert, a football game, or a celebrity's appearance? As much as fans and fandom follow no particular course of economic logic, the supplied product reveals no inherent reason for its existence. The struggle for profit in the old economy was fierce enough, but at least the struggle followed a certain line of predictable economic rationality in its homage to price and quality. The struggle in the new Inverted Economy has no such rational explanation, and the intensity with which goods and services are produced and promoted today has all the makings of a great and ominous social transformation.

Since no one knows of recognized needs for the New Product, much of the economic energy is concentrated on selling the product as much as on producing it. One can always sell a bar of soap to a man who needs cleaning. But one needs good persuasion to sell VCRs. There are two main ways in which this selling effort is made: one is *before* it is produced, commonly called market research, which consists of exploring the potential market for a particular product under consideration; the other is advertisement, which takes place *after* the product has been created. Often the two go hand in hand, because advertisement also determines market potential. Along with advertisement, market research is the lifeblood of inverted production. But what is really market research?

Corporations and individuals spend much money, effort, and ingenuity in market research, a thoroughgoing survey of the consumer market for the anticipated introduction of a product. The "prelaunch" market survey itself is not new, but the scientific way it is carried out is. The method in which it is carried out may be scientific, yet the purpose of it is definitely not; the purpose of conducting market research is to create demand for a product *that has never existed before*. The market research expert often speaks of "consumer needs," but the consumer needs he speaks of do not exist, or he would not be searching so hard to find them. Simply stated, *needs* cannot be hidden very long. Since demand arises out of needs, it cannot be suppressed even in a most methodically dictatorial society at least not very long. Demand based on human needs is the most powerful force in the history of mankind, not necessarily in the economic sphere alone. It has toppled kingdoms, it has executed emperors, it has reversed the tides of history, and no man of power has ever overcome this tidal wave known as demand. The Soviet and Eastern European bosses have recently learned this lesson the hard way.

Consumer demand in American society, the most open and voluntaristic system the world has ever seen, is always out there for all to see. There is no demand in America that is hidden from even the most cursory inspection. But market research is still devoted to finding more demand, as if there is some more out there hidden that has to be explored. If there *were* "consumer needs" yet unfulfilled, however, the existing mechanism would already be satisfying them. If there were a need for a product in our affluent society, the product would have been produced instantaneously to meet the need. Market research merely wants to see if the public would accept a new product it has never demanded and whose need it has never recognized before. The market researcher says to the consumer, "According to our research, you need a new video game." The consumer, surprised, says, "I do?" After some persuasion, the consumer recognizes the need for a video game. He says, "Yes, I do need a new video game." And, if all goes as planned, the consumer isn't happy until he gets the new video game.

One cannot persuade a person to consume more bread than he can possibly eat for his bodily needs and capacity. But with products that have no definite necessity, usefulness, or satiability, there is no telling how much the same person can consume with the New Product. A successful corporation or individual is one that best anticipates or stretches this unique human capacity to enlarge one's satiation point. This human capacity is unique indeed in the entire animal kingdom. Other animals either store surplus, if there is surplus food, or stop working for survival to enjoy leisure or rest. Humans have the almost-infinite capacity to stretch their satiation point, especially with nonmaterial goods and services where satiation cannot be clearly determined. If a man can enjoy $1 million, he can certainly enjoy $1 *billion*, for there is no definite point at which one can feel one has "enough" of it. A child with abundant toys can always play with more toys. Whether or not one really "needs" more money or more toys, the capacity is infinite. In fact, it is so infinitely stretchable that supply becomes the key to the whole chain of economic activity in an affluent society. The consumer—to the extent of his money and time—will consume anything he desires.

We cannot consume more bread than our bodily capacity, because bread applies to our need-satisfaction aspects of life. Our capacity to enjoy any amount of money or any number of toys, on the other hand, has to do with their sensory quality. Having a lot of money or having a lot of toys merely relates to our senses—as most New Products do—which has nothing to do with the definite need-satisfaction cycle. The "need" for money or toys has little or nothing to do with our physical, biological demand for nutrition or comfort. It has to do with the tantalizing sense of pleasure of a kind that has the capacity for an infinite variety of needs and satisfactions. Our new economic system is a sensory economy, so to speak, for it is concerned with "consumer satisfaction" that can never reach a point of real satisfaction. With this infinite capacity for enjoyment available, all that the producer of a new product has to contend with is his competition. Barring competition that might offer a more sense-pleasing alternative, there is really no limit to the consumption for the new product. Purchasing power can also be created with credit. Market research thus has as much to do with consumer needs as with competition.

A successful product not only defeats its competition but also creates a new need that never existed before. A good example is the telephone company. It urges people to "reach out and touch someone." Translation: use the telephone and call somebody, of course, on the telephone, but not by face-to-face contact or writing letters. If people use the telephone more, not only more often than before but also more of it than other forms of communication, then the product has succeeded in both. What is peculiar about this is that if people *needed* to communicate with someone, if they had a message to convey to someone, they *would have done so* without the telephone company's urging. The need to communicate is one of life's real necessities, and that need would be met, or would have to be met, as long as it was physically possible. But we have an inverted situation where the telephone no longer serves *our* needs to communicate; we instead serve the *telephone company's need* to be used and increase its profit. Market research has determined that people can use the telephone infinitely more often than they do now. All that the company has to do is push the new need. In a similar example, a Midwest newspaper is suitably impressed with the increasing use of male cosmetics, a new need.

How to account for this wave of male vanity? Experts offer all sorts of tortured explanations, from the fitness boom and the culture of narcissism to the decline of rural life and the rise of decadent urbanity and two-earner families. We suspect the simpler truth lies in *the apparently limitless capacity of capitalism to reinvent itself. If there is money to be made from ministering to masculine insecurities, someone will find a way.*[3]

Aside from the competition factor, about 80 to 90 percent of new products fail to sustain their market consumption enough to justify production. But why would a trial consumer product fail, if its pretrial market research had established its consumer need? One might blame faulty research techniques, the caprice of the marketplace, or any number of factors. But the most obvious point in all this is that there never was a need for the new product. All necessary products have already been demanded and supplied before. However, the main part of our economic energy is now concentrated in discovering that elusive new need, a product that would appeal to consumers who did not have the faintest idea that they ever needed it. In the bygone era the main concern was to meet demand adequately, for demand was real and the need to satisfy that demand was also real. It caused many revolutions, international wars, and class revolts, because the demand had to be met one way or another.

Our new economy is in a jam for an entirely different reason: what used to be a problem of supply (not enough of it) is now a problem of demand (not enough of it). Supply cannot be created out of thin air, because of its specific production costs and material realities. But demand has no such specific perimeters within which it has to run its predetermined course. While not anything can be supplied at will, *anything can be demanded at will*. This very thought drives any entrepreneur crazy with possibilities. All one has to do with the new economy is, like the need for male cosmetics, persuade people what to demand. Thus the solution to the new Inverted Economy is difficult as a task because of competition but strikingly simple as a concept: let them make new demands.

How far our new economic system is removed from a semblance of logic and rationality can simply be glimpsed in the way the new product is promoted. One best indicator is in measuring the gap between the promoter and the promoted product. Advertisement is set apart from information by the fact that the advertiser has little or nothing to do with what is advertised. Pretty women, not engineers, pitch for automobiles (the connection?); gymnasts, not nutritionists, sell breakfast cereals; good-looking men, not chemists, promote colognes and deodorants. If one really tried, one might after all find a connection between promoter and promoted. But the very fact that some effort is required to find logic and rationality in them is proof enough that there is no logic or rationality in them, and none there could be. The very idea of advertisement is to create a need where there is none. The fact of need is based on the logic and rationality of life's necessity, which naturally entails its demand. Advertisement follows the opposite road by using illogic and irrationality to create what is essentially logical and rational demand.

All advertisement is illogical and irrational by definition, not only in its specific instances, but also in its basic premises. The size of advertisement in any economic system is in many ways inversely related to its efficiency, logic, or rationality. Every energy expenditure associated with advertisement is therefore inversely related to the economic health of society. Whenever a product is advertised, we must assume that a proportional amount of our economic energy and resource is being wasted and that human stupidity is expanded to the necessary extent.

But there is more than simple waste and stupidity in advertisement, of course. It has to do with the arousal of feelings. Every human being has the capacity to be aroused by some awareness. He may be aroused by moral indignation, by sexual desires, by avaricious impulses, by artistic awakening, by the pleasure of inflicting pain on other people, and so on. But there is a hierarchy of arousal; some are easier to arouse in us than others. For instance, sexual arousal is easier to accomplish in general than arousal by moral indignation. By its own rules of profit-making, the new product has to follow the rules of greatest profits. That is, it must accomplish the task of arousal through advertisement with the smallest amount of effort for the strongest effect. In an economy in which arousal—creating a new awareness where none existed before—plays a central role in its consumption, the *easiest* arousal is always its first preference. The widespread existence of pornography, for example, is often blamed on the unscrupulous pornography producer, who is bent on creating a state of sexual arousal in the impressionable and unsavory. But this blame is unfair, not to say hypocritical, in view of the fact that our general economic system could not possibly sustain its market mechanism without cheap arousals in all aspects of its production, promotion, and consumption. To make the point more clearly: it would be economically suicidal to try to produce, promote, and arouse *virtues* as a new product. No market society has ever successfully marketed moral virtues other than in times of dire disasters like war, depression, or natural catastrophes, where the market mind-set must be at least temporarily suspended. Even the "Christian stores" must operate on the principle of balance sheets. Not surprisingly, then, the cheapest of all arousals—namely, sex—has always done well in the marketplace. Sexual arousal is always cheap and effective. Angels may not dare to tread in a society where arousing people from their slumber to the new need of consumption is the norm of its economic and cultural way of life. But American society is for business, not for angelic virtues.

Still, in an economic system in which advertisement and market research testify to its wastefulness—simply because both are means of finding new sources of "undemanded" consumption—the traditional notion of capitalist *efficiency* has to be reconsidered, too. The market system is defended by its supporters for its most "efficient" uses of resources in society, by virtue of its operation based on demand and supply. In this model of efficiency, demand and supply must always equal each other. But the very idea of efficiency is based on some finite notion of a material nature. To be efficient, and to be able to measure the notion of efficiency, there has to be something that *can* be identified clearly in finite material terms. There are efficient and inefficient ways of feeding, clothing, and housing 1,000 people; the results of efficiency can be clearly identified by measuring how well or poorly the people are fed, clothed, and housed. But when the measurement of efficiency involves a different sort altogether in an "inverted" economic system, the idea of efficiency is impossible to uphold as defense of the market economy. Suppose the 1,000 people must be "entertained" efficiently, must be made to feel "happy" and "fulfilled" and "secure" efficiently, how are we going to make the operation efficient?

We have now come to a point in our discourse where we have to put all this together into some theoretical and historical perspective. In short, what are we to make of this enormous misdirection of human and material energy in our society to produce goods and services that nobody demands and to raise the "standards of living" that no longer need to be raised? Two cars do not make a man twice as happy or comfortable or efficient as one car. A video game does not represent a more advanced form of recreation than reading an old book. What is the actual usefulness of all this abundance that we go through much convulsion to dispose of? Below I will try to answer the question raised above, in the form of a Theory of Utility.

Utility—the usefulness of a product—has been much debated in economic history, first in the form of "value," as in "What is the value of Product X?" There have been all sorts of answers. The classical economists gave the "objective" factors of costs and the market mechanism of price as their basic consideration. Later economic theorists sought the answer in the "subjective" definition of utility—often synonymous with "desire" or "want"— as perceived by the consumer. For our purpose of discussion and of the need to transcend the objective-subjective quagmire of economic argument, we must assume that value and utility are united in making up the whole of Product X. We must assume that cost and utility—or the product's objective value and its subjective desirability—are in good measure the same thing as they change together. As the objective cost of Product X goes up, so does our subjective pleasure in having wanted and purchased it, and vice versa.

Up to our recent economic era the rule of demand and supply, and its price mechanism, seems to have justified this assumption. It is especially so in view of the predominantly "material" and "physical" nature of the products produced and consumed. But in our present Inverted Economy with its New Products, however, the cost-and-utility concept must be reexamined and redefined from a different perspective altogether by inserting what I would call the historical factor. Although the discussion that follows may appear quite novel at first glance, alert readers will soon recognize that they have often thought about it themselves or have heard before something that resembles it. I merely use this space to simplify the idea.

Let me, then, state the conclusion first: *As civilization represented in tech-*

nology rises, utility declines. The more technologically advanced a society is, the more useless its production system becomes, creating greater and greater waste of resources for smaller and smaller utility value. For those readers who are either impatient with intellectual theories or already persuaded by the main points of discussion in this chapter so far, I am going to first state the main argument in the paragraphs below.

The correct measure of utility in Product X is defined by how much of the energy and resource required in producing Product X is actually recovered from the consumption or use of Product X. Neither the price (how much it costs to produce) nor the preference (why people want to consume it) alone helps. Neither is a very accurately measurable quantity to determine the "usefulness" of a product. In our Inverted Economy, all traditional concepts of productive activity—price, value, wages, profit, cost, and so on—have become more or less obsolete. We need to think in a new way to come up with a true measure of a product's usefulness or wastefulness. In other words, we need a new concept of some precision to measure how much of our energy and resource is used up in production and recovered in consumption. The measure of utility in a product is then defined as *the difference between production cost and value recovered from consumption.* Obviously, the closer the two values, the greater the utility or, conversely, the less the waste. By measuring the difference in each instance of our economic activity and summing it all up in one unit, if this can be done at all, we have the most accurate estimate of utility and waste in society. In the preceding paragraph I have already tied the measure of utility to evolution and civilization. Historically conceived, the question now is: how does history figure into the calculation of utility?

When the level of technology is zero or close to it, say, at the dawn of human civilization, every energy consumed is geared to produce near-perfect utility. For example, a caveman would not kill a rabbit unless he meant to use all of it: the meat to eat, the fur for clothing, bones for tools, and so on. So every bit of energy and resource he uses produces a full utility value in the object of his economic action. If killing the rabbit consumes the value of 100, what he recovers from killing the rabbit, in the form of meat, fur, and so on, is also 100. There is no waste of his energy and resources as long as the utility value produced equals energy and resource used to produce it. In this way, we can see that at the most primitive level of zero technology or zero civilization utility value is almost perfect. This is so even when he sometimes misses the rabbit. The idea is to total his effort as well as his catch.

As the level of technology increases with the introduction of tools, weapons, and knowledge, however, the total amount of human effort to produce the same effect, such as catching a rabbit, becomes smaller and smaller for the accomplishment. As the task becomes easier to accomplish, it is only natural that human beings would be inclined to do *more* of it, given a

modicum of reason for doing it. But as we do more of it because it is easier
to do, we tend to get less value out of what we accomplish. For example,
we may shoot a rabbit with a rifle when we have no use for it, just for the
fun of it. To use another example, a society might stockpile weapons when
either the enemy does not exist or there is enough weaponry already in
stock, but the fact that technological development makes it much easier to
do it makes people do it. The telephone encourages more talking among
us only because it is there and makes it easier for us to talk—often for no
apparent reason. So that *while zero technology produces perfect utility, the utility
value declines in direct proportion to the rise of technology. Theoretically, therefore,
perfect technology produces zero utility*. We have never achieved perfect technology, so the latter part of this conclusion cannot be demonstrated. Zero
utility—using human agents, namely slaves and servants, not technology—
however, has been attempted by some past aristocracies in human history
and is not exactly an abstract theory.

Let us now proceed step by step with our Theory of Utility for a more
complete explanation. Everyone will agree that the calculation of utility has
to do with costs. If no cost is involved, then the question of utility does
not arise. If costs become larger for the same result, then utility obviously
becomes smaller in direct proportion. If it takes one man to catch a rabbit,
utility is much larger than if it takes five men to catch the same rabbit.
Determining utility with any precision has been problematic, because there
are so many different and even conflicting reasons for catching a rabbit.
Some would say catching it for meat and fur is higher in utility than catching
it for sport, such as fox hunting in England's high society, or vice versa;
others would argue that no one can tell that one is higher in utility than
another. Based on what has been said above, let's switch our attention to
costs for an explanation. The difficulty may be less prohibitive if we tackled
the problem from the side of costs, not psychology.

Let me therefore introduce a pair of cost concepts that are not part of the
standard economic terminology: direct costs and indirect costs. Direct costs
consist of the specific human, material, technological, and organizational
resources required to produce Product X. These costs can be fairly easily
calculated on the basis of Product X's requirements and have been used
commonly in our conventional economics to calculate costs. Indirect costs
are defined by the extent to which direct costs rely on all *cumulative* technology available to mankind. The higher the reliance of direct costs on
cumulative technology, then the higher the indirect costs for producing
Product X. The conception of indirect costs added to the specific (direct)
costs of production is called for to give costs their historical accounting
whenever that is necessary. This historical accounting is necessary to get
the most accurate costs possible for production and therefore for the value
of utility in the product as well.

Two examples may be used to illustrate costs: making a pair of wooden shoes versus creating special effects for a movie. The first task would have fairly large direct costs, consisting of wood, tools, time and energy to produce the shoes, and small indirect costs: cumulative human knowledge required to produce the shoes. The ratio between the two types of costs may be arbitrarily put at 95 to 5.

But the task of creating special effects for a movie like *Star Wars* or *Indiana Jones* involves an entirely different ratio of the two types of costs. The direct costs themselves are miniscule (although they may run into the millions in actual expenses) compared to indirect costs. In computing direct costs for the task we simply ask the producer who produces it or the banker who bankrolls it how much it has cost the company. But indirect costs consist of all human endeavors, since the dawn of civilization, that are the results of cumulative historical knowledge that is necessary for the product. Together, direct and indirect costs make up what we might call "true" costs. This way we can see that the special effects would be enormously indebted to the vast amount of knowledge that mankind as a whole has accumulated without which the special effects making is impossible. All of human technology accumulated to make the current special effects possible or the push-button telephone possible, if it can be calculated, constitutes the real value of indirect costs. For the sake of simplicity, let's call the ratio of direct to indirect costs in special effects making a 5 to 95, a reverse of the wooden shoemaking.

Now we have arrived at specific, though arbitrary, numbers that can be used to define the value of utility itself: *The ratio of direct costs to indirect costs determines the utility value of Product X, where utility increases with higher direct costs and decreases with higher indirect costs.* According to this formula, a ratio of 95 to 5 has much larger utility than a ratio of 5 to 95. This is one way of saying that as more technology is involved for the same product, the less utility value we can recover from using the product. The example of rabbit killing serves us well here. We can simply compare two ways of rabbit killing: bare hand versus rifle. The direct costs of the bare-hand method give the ratio of almost 100 to 0, whereas the rifle method would obviously affect the ratio in favor of indirect costs. Still more so if it involves a laser gun.

As indirect costs increase in proportion to direct costs, utility declines accordingly. While primitive technology would favor larger direct costs, gradual increases in technology would favor the rise of indirect costs in the ratio. With this change in the ratio, utility changes in value also. So the highest level of utility—most useful—would be possible with the highest direct costs in relation to indirect costs, meaning the lowest level of technology. Conversely, the lowest level of utility—most useless—would come from the highest level of technology, which increases the proportion of indirect costs in the production. Put this way, we can easily see that rabbit killing has a prohibitively higher utility value than special effects making.

By the same token, higher utility is found in less developed societies, where there is less technology to be used. As the level of technology increases and things become easier and more convenient to do (e.g., in push-buttons), utility must decline proportionally.

The idea is simple. As technology increases in society, things become easier to do. As things become easier to do, we tend to do more of them even when there are no clear needs for them. As we do things without clear purposes, we waste more of our resources relative to needs and purposes. The introduction of photocopying machines tends to produce many times more copies—"Xerox this, Xerox that"—than we have needs and purposes for the copies. The introduction of word-processing mechanisms tends to produce many times more words in the proliferation of books, memos, paperwork—not to mention their generally low literary quality—than we have needs or purposes for them. The same analysis can also be extended to television, telephone, electronic games, mass-spectator sports, and whatever else our modern technology provides for our consumption. As these items become readily accessible—thanks to technology—we tend to use them more often, simply because they are so easily accessible, than either our needs or their functions would warrant. Any time the uses exceed needs or purposes, we have high waste of resources or low utility value recovered in our consumption.

To further simplify the idea, we can use the "portion" of direct costs in the ratio as a sort of "Utility Index" of goods. A ratio in favor of direct costs would have a higher Utility Index, which would gradually decline as the proportion of indirect costs increases in the ratio. Thus bare-hand rabbit killing would have a Utility Index close to 100, as opposed to laser-gun rabbit killing, which would have a Utility Index of something close to zero or thereabout.

However, maintaining a high level of utility as a measure of how efficiently we use our economic resources is not, of course, the purpose of life. The purpose of life is to create and enjoy civilization. This makes it imperative to increase the level of technology and consequently decrease utility value. Not only is material production part of the costs of civilization, but civilization also costs in human terms as well. Rules of behavior become elaborate in human relations; institutions have to be established to ensure the many functions of social life; generations have to be educated in the proper ways of a civil society. It is inevitable that civilization costs and technology, which is the substance of civilization, further erode utility value. In a civilized society we must do everything according to the institutional rules and the material means that are available. As civilization develops further, the role of technology becomes increasingly important and utility declines accordingly. So the ratio of 100 to 0 at the dawn of civilization between direct and indirect costs gradually changes in favor of indirect costs as civilization increases in the procession of 90 to 10, 80 to 20, 70 to 30, and so on.

A utility value of 100—perfect use of energy and resource—is produced by the most primitive level of human existence. Animals and human beings in harsh climate maintain that level or close to that level at all times. On the other hand, a utility value of close to zero—little or no value recovered from consumption—is produced by the highest level of technology. Thus technology inevitably forces a loss of energy and resource as it raises its level of complexity. But because a high level of civilization, not a high level of utility, is the purpose of life, a certain amount of sacrifice in utility becomes necessary to improve that very civilization. In fact, according to our thesis, the level of civilization and the level of wasted utility are directly related—that is, the more we waste, the higher our civilization. This is natural to human evolution. But a question can be formulated to solve this dilemma: at what level of civilization and utility or, to put it another way, at what ratio of direct to indirect costs in production should we consider our life in *optimum balance*? This question can be pondered from each in-dividual's daily life as well the society's existence as a whole. But either way the balance between utility and civilization should come out the same.

The question of balance also points to the irony of modern technological civilization. On the one hand, a society like the United States with high technology must go through convulsive market research and advertisement to exhaust its energy and resource in search of *utility*, while the wretchedly underdeveloped societies are frantically in search of *technology*. On the other hand, while we are looking for ways to *increase* our utility because of the higher level of our technology, the poor societies are trying desperately to *decrease* their utility by increasing the level of technology. The reasons for the two equally unhappy circumstances are as enormous in their differences as they are ironic in their human meaning. We have too much technology; they, too little. The secret is to *balance* the two. How shall we balance the two so that efficiency and happiness—or utility and civilization—may be best achieved?

The traditional division between "necessary" and "luxury" products serves us somewhat better in our quest to solve the problem of balance. As technology and indirect costs rise and utility declines, the proportion of luxury goods (aesthetic and sense-pleasing things in life) rises as that of necessary goods (basic necessities of life) decline. But this rise and decline of luxury and necessity respectively is only in *proportion*, not in absolute terms. So while luxury items may occupy a 90 to 10 ratio in their favor, it does not necessarily mean that the production of necessary items has shrunk in absolute terms. Even with a ratio of 90 to 10 in its disfavor, the production of necessary items may still be huge in absolute terms so that all life's necessities can be satisfied.

At a certain point in the society's technological evolution, all the necessary basic items of life may be produced in abundance. At this point, as we have seen, there is a considerable rise in indirect costs already in existence. To put it simply, the rise of technology is historically accompanied by the rise of luxury goods in proportion to necessary goods and by the rise of indirect costs in proportion to direct costs. As these two sets of rise and fall continue there is a place in the society's development where the two sets meet each other exactly in the middle, where the ratio would be 50:50. This is the point where a perfect balance is achieved between direct costs and indirect costs as well as between necessary goods and luxury goods. This is what I would call the Point of Inversion after which the era of an Inverted Economy begins, if the ratio shifts in favor of indirect costs and luxury items.

As the ratio shifts in the latter's favor, greater and greater waste is required by the simple fact that greater indirect costs have to be added to production. A correspondingly smaller utility value can be recovered from consumption. The economic system at the Point of Inversion represents the perfect balance that can be achieved between economic efficiency and human happiness and between necessary goods and civilized pleasures. But the economic system, especially one with an abundance of energy and resource to move on, does not stop at the Point of Inversion. It moves on, pushing the scale in favor of greater indirect costs and greater luxuries of civilization even at the cost of greater cultural dissonance and economic irrationality. Thus the system would insist on producing a product at enormous (indirect) costs and push it on the market at still greater costs for research and promotion. From it all only a tiny value in utility may be recovered. Consider "Super Mario Brothers" and its enormous technological backup to make the few minutes of pleasure possible. There is neither human reason nor economic logic for this "progress" to have occurred beyond the Point of Inversion. For at that point in historical evolution we have reached a level of perfect balance in everything. Going any further would serve no good purpose for mankind. Only waste and irrationality await. Is there any point in American history where we can say that this Point of Inversion was reached?

I would venture to say that this point was reached perhaps in the 1950s. Many of our high-tech ideas and items and much of the basic research necessary for the high-tech economy made their appearance in the 1950s. Television as a purely commercial instrument, the computer as an actual working tool, among other items, made their entries into American society at the time when its economy was about to enter the Age of Affluence. The economy, previously on a war footing, was now switched to a consumer economy, and the Good Life was beginning to become a reality for most middle-class Americans.

Some may disagree with my placing of the Point of Inversion in that decade. Nevertheless, many critical thoughts on the affluent generation—assuming affluence as a given fact in American life—notably those of C.

Wright Mills in *White Collar*, David Riesman in *The Lonely Crowd*, William H. Whyte in *The Organization Man*, John Kenneth Galbraith in *The Affluent Society*, David M. Potter in *People of Plenty*, among others, crystallized during that decade. Among the culturally sentimental as well as in the general population who remember the decade personally, the tendency to think of the 1950s as a "perfect decade" in American life, a time of balance in life for some reason, seems to have become a mythical nostalgia. The United States would still see many more spectacular technological and cultural feats in the coming decades—in space adventures, in entertainment, in sports, in cultural diversities—yet the feeling of contentment has never exceeded that which is associated with the 1950s. Perhaps unknowingly, the United States had reached the Point of Inversion, a dream of mankind, the end of all human evolution, a state of perfect balance, in the 1950s.

Historian Eric Goldman in his book, *The Crucial Decade—and After: America 1945–60*, characterizes the mid-1950s as the balance between tradition and progress, a point of suspension between past and future, or what he called the "Eisenhower Equilibrium." It was the crossroads between things past (tradition, mother, country, babies, growing standards of living, basic industry) and things to come (high-tech industry, corporate economy, civil rights, dominant amusement business, the Me Generation). It was almost a miraculous suspension in time where the weight of past and the forces of future met in perfect neutrality. Neither the past nor the future dominated that era, however precarious and transient, for it was at once past and future. The two slow-moving trains of Profit Ethic and Social Ethic, however briefly, paralleled. Content with the past yet unafraid of the future, America was looking backward and forward at the same time. The past produced stability; the future promised excitement. American society wanted to have both, the stability of things familiar and the excitement of things unknown. Economically, culturally, and politically, the 1950s was a decade of balance and equilibrium. Goldman thus describes it:

As the Crucial Decade closed in the summer of 1955, the American people could face the onrushing years and the onrushing crises with one solid fact to buttress them. Whatever their addiction to chrome, comic books, and comic-book politics, whatever their yearning for the prepackaged, one-minute solution to everything, they had not, however sorely tempted, committed the supreme foolishness of trying to defy history.[4]

Within three decades, by 1990, however, this history would become irrelevant. By 1990, American society would be a society without history. America's attention span could not possibly encompass anything beyond the thirty-second spot, much less history. By 1990, Americans could not remember the past or if they had any past at all; human values would be discarded as easily and unceremoniously as an outdated model or yesterday's newspaper. All would be here and now, and no history or past would stop or slow the relentless march of a new economic order. The Inverted Economy, which was only glimpsed in the 1950s, would be the order of the day by 1990.

NOTES

1. These items are from USAir's in-flight magazine, *USAir Gift Catalog*, available in 1990.

2. David T. Bazelon, *The Paper Economy* (New York: Vintage Books, 1962).

3. Editorial, *Milwaukee Journal*, 26 April 1986.

4. Eric Goldman, *The Crucial Decade—and After: America 1945–60* (New York: Vintage Books, 1962). There is an interesting piece by journalist David Schoenbrum, who compares the Eisenhower 1950s with the Reagan 1980s, under the title "Would You Trade Today for Life in the 50's?" (*Parade*, 6 December 1986). His conclusion is that the 1980s are better off in material terms but not in "human" terms. Again, it is a bitter trade-off: destroying our community for materialism.

Part IV

Wealth and Power

Chapter 9

Economics and Politics

A strange thing happened on our way to the modern world: we took power away from the Political King and gave it to the Economic King. The modern world took the king's political power and gave it to everyone in the form of one man, one vote, so that never again would political power be concentrated in one dictatorial person. But the same modern world did a strange thing with the king's economic power: it was made up for grabs, so that some men ended up with a lot of it, others with very little or none of it. While destroying the old world of political power, we created a new world of economic power in its place. And we called it "democracy," "free enterprise," "supply and demand," "open market." What was once concentrated in politics has now been transferred to economic concentration. Those who held power in politics now hold the same power in economics. The rules of the game have changed, but the score remains the same.

How did it happen? This is how Robert Heilbroner described the transition:

Before capitalism came into being wealth followed power, and power was an adjunct of social and ecclesiastical or political prestige. . . . But after the economic revolution the old order changed. Now power followed wealth, and wealth accrued to the winners of the game of the market place. . . . Individuals would still rise above the mass to impose their will on others, but for society as a whole, it was the process of money-making which gave it its elan, its movement, and its direction.[1]

Both economics and politics are two means of power. (The third means, sheer physical strength over others, though absolute in nature, is not counted as serious in society.) But economics is superior to politics as a means of power, especially in an economic society where wealth enjoys its unequal preeminence. Wealth is measured in precise, absolute terms. Power relations are defined by those precise, absolute terms of relations. For instance, 10 has twice the power of 5, 20 twice that of 10, and so on. Politics, especially in the United States, on the other hand, follows a predetermined structure in its rules and procedures. Whatever is gained by the political process is carefully circumscribed for its expression, and every political act is counterbalanced by its opposite in a democratic society.

For a clear illustration, consider the following examples. The first invo. s Donald Regan, secretary of the treasury for former president Reagan, and former Republican senator Charles Percy from Illinois. Regan had served as the chief executive of Merrill Lynch, a corporate organization whose main business is investment brokerage, before he joined the Reagan administration. As chief executive of Merrill Lynch, Regan's power was absolute and unquestioned; as secretary of the treasury, his power was made relative and impotent by the countervailing forces within the political system. This is how he expressed his frustration through an interview:

"When I was chief executive," [Regan] explains, "and I said, 'Jump,' people said, 'How high?' As Secretary of the Treasury, I say, 'Jump,' and people say, 'Well, do you have an environmental impact statement? What do you mean, jump?' "[2]

Similarly, Charles Percy, also a transfer from business to government, felt the difference between the world of money and the world of politics: "It's a terrible plunge into an icy bath to jump from business, which is essentially an *autocracy*, into government, which is a *democracy*." Money's rule is absolute; democracy's rule, relative.

The second example involves the 1990 federal budget fiasco. Congress and the White House could not agree on the following year's national budget. This resulted in the temporary closing of many nonvital government functions, such as national museums, zoos, and parks. Reactions from the irate public were swift and unforgiving. "The other zoo was closed," a Chicagoan explained why he decided to come to the Capitol to watch the lawmakers in session, "so I came to see the trained baboons." Another man from St. Paul said, "I wouldn't let these wimps mow my lawn." A man from Alabama who had gone to the National Zoo only to see the animal houses closed to visitors came to see Congress in action. "I was in the Senate Gallery for an hour and a half last night, watching them do caucuses and roll calls and talk about the budget," he said. "And I saw more monkeys there than I could ever see at [the] zoo." His wife promised that she was going to call her senator: "I don't know what he's doing there, except running off and talking in groups of three with other senators and going in and out of doors and not getting anything done." Then she added, "Even if I knew exactly what these government officials were doing, I'd probably want to hang them anyway." A disillusioned woman who was turned away from a closed museum vowed, "We will remember this when we go to the polls."

These are strong, contemptuous, unforgiving words from the electorate. Would these irate voters be as strong, as contemptuous, and as unforgiving toward their *economic bosses*, say, when they come to announce that their plants or offices must close temporarily?

The elected politicians were as contrite as their constituents were merciless. "Face it, we are the laughingstocks of the world," a representative from New Mexico said. "We're a national joke," said a senator from Wyoming. "Our countrymen are sick and tired of our farce," agreed a senator from Tennessee. "If there were a vote tonight," a senator from Pennsylvania said, to applause from the gallery, "535 of us and the president would be out of work."

The president here referred to is George Bush. Until the Persian Gulf deployment, his popularity maintained what *Time* magazine called "resounding job approval" in opinion polls, although his actual achievement was decidedly low-keyed. "How does a President stay up while going down?" asks the article. The answer is that politics has become irrelevant to most Americans. "American people have much less need for Washington," says a political observer and former aide to Lyndon Johnson, "than Washington wants to believe." As he can be popular for no reason, he can also be put down for no reason. During the Gulf crisis, Bush was asked by a reporter what he thought of the comment made by Saddam Hussein of Iraq, who compared Bush with Hitler. (Hitler has become so infamous that almost anyone can be found to have something in common with him.) One eyewitness said, "Bush bit his lip but stayed silent." Then another reporter gave him the ultimate personal put-down: "Oh, I see we're getting the cold shoulder today." The tone here is nothing short of total disrespect for the president of the United States.

Again, would company presidents and corporate chief executives, facing a downturn in their firms, be *this* penitent or humble about their mismanagement? Absolutely not. There would be neither outraged workers, openly expressing their disgust and anger, nor hang-me-down responses from the management. Would the employees believe that what the management decides has no serious consequences for their welfare? Would they ever consider the managerial comings and goings irrelevant? Could an employee refer to his president's silence as "the cold shoulder"? It happens in politics, not in economics. Why?

These simple episodes not only illustrate the absolute superiority of economics over politics as a way to power, but also illuminate the disturbing ascendancy of wealth over political power. It is money now that wields power, not politics. In many ways, the coming of the modern economic system has erected a new form of absolutism in place of old political tyranny. Politics has become more or less ritualistic and ceremonious.

Both forms of power—political and economic—have the same result: that is, control of human action. In "political" societies and eras—such as the Middle Ages and the pre-Gorbachev Soviet Union—a form of political absolutism and even dictatorship prevails. This political absolutism has been historically opposed in the West by the new theory of democracy, freedom, and equality. With the exceptions of dictatorial societies and remnants of feudalism—such as Saudi Arabia and Kuwait—political power has been tamed and even crippled by the coming of the new world order. But the new Western world order of democracy, freedom, and equality has created a new form of absolutism under the marketplace, free enterprise, and economic freedom of the individual. Unlike the old political tyranny in which people were ruled often by brute shows of force, in a free economic society people are controlled by the impersonal, "anonymous" forces of the marketplace and the power of wealth it creates and concentrates. Whereas the world of politics was ruled by the iron hand of power, the new world of economics is ruled by the almighty dollar of the marketplace. The powerholder has changed, but not the power itself. In a strange twist of history, the freedom gained by destroying the old tyranny of political power holders—kings, warlords, popes, landlords, guild masters—has been lost through the new *free system of economics*.

The economic form of tyranny has become many times more pernicious than the old form for several important reasons. First, in the old form of political tyranny people could feel the repression personally, directly, and physically. The repression was visible and commonly recognizable as the source of common misery and unhappiness in many. Today in the new form of economic tyranny, a "friendly fascism," as Bertram Gross called it, few feel the burden of repression, much less as a personalized experience of misery and unhappiness. It is always a vague, diffused sensation that something is wrong, but not quite clearly recognizable. The old form may have led to physical tortures; the new form leads to mental tortures and eventually to vicarious forms of remedy as well in drugs, alcohol, gratuitous violence, suicide, psychic disorders, and many other such manifestations of uncertainty and anxiety. There is nothing like the irony of freedom to feel unfree as a measure of freedom.

Second, the old tyrant was always clearly identified in a persona—such as kings, popes, warlords—whose power and its symbolism left no doubt as to who was to blame. The presence and range of power were fairly brutal and its exercise always direct. One knew exactly where the responsible person existed; in this political tyranny, one was simply outpowered by someone who had more brute power. God, though often called upon, was an after-the-fact device. There was little subtlety either in the possession or in the exercise of power; all was out in the open and physically visible. Today in the new form of power, one is never physically outpowered by another whose power is clearly superior; instead, one is simply outsmarted by another. There is no such thing as an economic tyrant in the sense that there was a political tyrant. In our modern world of economics, all possession and exercise of power are through the impersonal means of wealth. It is the money that represents power, not the powerholder. As opposed to the old way of acquiring power through heredity or brute force, the modern form allows everyone, at least in theory, to have an equal chance at it. That gets the Economic King off the hook. In this sense, it is difficult for one to conceive of power through wealth as personal, unjust, or permanent. Everything is understood only in terms of outsmarting one's opponents and failing to do so, one comes under the economic domination of another. Given time and luck, however, the pendulum of power will swing in one's favor. There is no reason to think of the temporary, transient holder of wealth with anything more than envy, certainly not anger. People today do not perceive a Jackie Onassis's extravagance in the same way the French did Marie Antoinette's. Those who are wealthy and therefore powerful are merely the recipients of good fortunes in a freewheeling society where everyone is entitled to his share of fortunes sooner or later. Nothing personal. One could bitterly condemn the old political tyrant and try to redress one's grievances. But today one can't complain about his own misfortune and stupidity after being outsmarted by his equals.

Third, the old form of political tyranny often led to the formation of countervailing forces, either publicly or underground. The brute, open form of tyranny necessitated whenever possible the formation of groups, clans, regions, and sects in opposition. Revolutions were fomented; loud protests were made; grievances were articulated as declarations; specific individuals were accused of wrongdoing and injustice. In short, people banded together with others under similar circumstances and formed an organized resistance to the supposed tyranny. Even in the pre-*perestroika* Soviet Union, where political control was fairly complete, underground opposition was lively and became almost a tradition among dissidents and unhappy citizens. Even during the era of the dreaded Spanish Inquisition the channel of opposition was active and extensive.

But none of this is possible in the tyranny of the marketplace. The market society divides up the individuals into isolated competitors and consumers so that it is both impossible and unnecessary for them to see each other as a group with common grievances. The very philosophy of liberal economics—"each to his own"—assumes the individual as a sovereignty in himself. He is the king unto himself. His relations with others, where necessary, are formed only voluntarily and therefore on the basis of a mutual satisfaction of self-interests. Organizing opposition against a tyrant requires a greater sense of commitment and urgency than this rational calculus of individual benefits. Hence organized opposition, thereby the strengthening of awareness by mutual support, becomes impossible to materialize under economic tyranny. The "free economy" makes it irrelevant. Only on second thought does it rule by dividing and conquering the individual will.

Finally, but perhaps most important, the new form of tyranny is also different from the old in the way power comes to one's possession. Access to power in the old world was severely limited by the very rules of heredity and the difficulty of physical conquest over other individuals. Political power was largely limited to a few secular and ecclesiastic rulers, and the masses by and large remained outside the circle of real political power. Those who held power lived extravagantly in a style quite distinct from the day-to-day lives of the powerless. Politically, socially, culturally, intellectually, and in many other ways, the world of power was quite different from the world of the powerless. Today, in the new world of economic power, there is no such barrier to power. The process and the contest of power are so open, governed by rules that are arrived at only by voluntary agreement. In a democracy, everyone participates in the making of rules. People no longer see tyrants with exclusive power. They do not see the world divided between justice and injustice, but merely between chance and lack of it. One's own poverty and lack of good fortune are the result of a perfectly just and fair system, fought out and contested in the open, free arena of the marketplace. The visible increase in the standard of living and the diffusion of focus through entertainment help redirect national energies in strictly private, economic pursuits. In an economically open, free society there is no such thing as injustice, only ill fortune and missed opportunities. It is the gambler's luck or ill luck, the individual's own fault, not the society's. Today's economic tyranny therefore is a case of perfectly just injustice.

For the first time in the last century of economic development, politics in the traditional sense has become irrelevant in American society. With the irrelevance of politics, the *society* itself in the determination of individual welfare and happiness has also become largely irrelevant in America. Politics and economics have become so thoroughly infused with each other, all as a singular exercise in the free contest of the marketplace, that it is now almost impossible to tell what is politics and what is economics. For all *is* economics. One joins government to increase one's earnings later in the marketplace; one leaves the government to join the corporation that he regulates while in government; one writes memoirs and sells one's knowledge gained while in government to the highest buyer in the market world. What is significant is not that such infusion of politics and economics exists, but that it seems so perfectly *natural* and *normal* in the idioms of American life. When one resigns or retires from a government position, people *expect* almost logically that he will come out in a stronger economic position because of his government experience. Everyone does it regardless of what position one has occupied in politics. Presidents do it; cabinet members do it; members of Congress do it; other lesser members of government do it on a lesser scale.

The spectacle of rise and fall from grace in the case of Geraldine Ferraro—rising to the vice-presidential candidacy and falling to the multimillion-dollar Pepsi commercial and book writing and to calling the press "vultures" and finally disappearing from the marketplace to enjoy her spoils of politics—is a sad but illuminating reminder. In this game of politics as economics and vice versa, no one has been more astute than Henry Kissinger, formerly the president's adviser and secretary of state. His "economic" success to surpass his political mastery is in many ways reminiscent of the grandeur of the old aristocracy.

Nine years out of office, Kissinger has maintained a luster rarely matched by any former Secretary of State since Martin Van Buren made the leap to the White House in 1837. Even without his Air Force jet, Kissinger travels with the aura of power. He alerts the embassies. Bodyguards watch over him. The maid at London's posh Claridge's covers the floor with towels because Kissinger, she says, does not like to walk barefoot on hotel carpets. Arriving in Paris, Kissinger is invited to the Elysée Palace for a chat with President Francois Mitterand; in Peking, Deng Xiaoping suggests a talk over tea. Back in New York City, the famous face and graveled accent cause a stir even at the Four Seasons, Manhattan's power-lunch emporium.

The expertise and access gained in years of power are carefully nurtured, valuable commodities, to be marketed now through Kissinger Associates, his international consulting firm. . . . Kissinger is sole owner of the firm, which grosses an estimated $5 million a year.[3]

Kissinger, and now Ronald Reagan, may be among the more prodigious, but we also have the Jeane Kirkpatricks, Geraldine Ferraros, David Stockmans, and others of lesser distinction, with General Schwarzkopf and other Gulf heroes waiting for their turns.

One glaring irony in all this is that wealth gained from politics *must* transpire *at* the marketplace and according to the *rules* of the marketplace. It *cannot* be done politically as a political process and according to political rules. The selling of one's political knowledge must be an *economic* process. That is the crucial catch in the game of politics and economics in America. In other words, one can sell one's government experience and influence, à la Kissinger, to anyone who can afford the price, but *not* as a spy or an influence peddler while in office. In the arena of free-for-all economic war in America this is a crucial distinction, albeit a tenuous one. Why? Because the distinction preserves its fragile moral justification among its more prominent officials. If done according to this rule of the game, one can be as successful as Kissinger. If not done according to this rule of the game, one can go on trial for corruption like Louisiana's former governor Edwin Edwards or the South Carolina legislators accused of selling political influence for money.

This is the moral distinction we make in American society so that some politicians go on trial and the Kissingers go on to riches auctioning off their largely government-supported experience and knowledge. Never mind that while in office they are paid a salary many times the average American's. The true corruption in American officialdom is not that there are characters like Edwin Edwards and wayward state lawmakers, but that we have such fabulously wealthy former officials as Henry Kissinger and Ronald Reagan. The marketplace creates strange bedfellows in corruption and wealth, all with the perfect blessings of American morality. It is the miracle of the American way. Moving from political riches to economic riches, they cash in on fame, government secrets, or whatever else with market value. No one has ever accused Henry Kissinger—or Ronald Reagan—of selling national secrets or American interests. Whatever he is selling at the tune of $5 million a year, it's all his own business. It is perfectly legal and therefore moral as well.

While our modern liberal market economy has set the economic machines free, it has effectively constrained politics to the extent of meaninglessness. To be sure, politics is not totally absent from view. There are elections at every level of government; the exercise of power in office is carefully regulated; officials are watched over by various watchdogs of democracy, from the press to neighborhood and grassroot organizations; few ever escape publicity if wrongdoings are committed while in office. Just recall the sorry spectacle of Mayor Marion Barry of Washington, D.C. In sharp contrast, however, there is virtually no restraint placed on the economic sphere of American life. There are no electoral checks and balances on the *economic* front. No corporate executives—for all their social implications in corporate comings and goings—are subjected to public scrutiny in the way political officials are. Within the loosely stipulated rules of commerce, which are mostly written by the monied, money matters are free to run their courses in a free-market society. The "state of nature" thus translates easily into modern economics. In a modern society where political power is severely regulated and controlled so as to have become meaningless and impotent, the economic front has set free all its constraints—public, private, moral, whatever—to the extent of virtual dictatorship. Hitler, if he had been an equally ruthless "economic man," dominating the whole continent *economically*, would be greatly admired by the marketplace for his ambition, efficiency, and accumulation of wealth.

There is a serious gap, as a result, between our practice of *political democracy* and that of *economic democracy*. In political democracy we believe in checks and balances, equality in possession, and exercise of political power, no one having the right to be more powerful than others. In economic democracy, however, our belief is totally the opposite: we believe in and practice the worst form of brute nature and tyranny. In politics, we believe in control; in economics, we believe in freedom. We believe on the one hand that political justice is achieved only when power is constrained by society and its rules. On the other, we believe that economic justice is achieved only when all social constraints are removed from the marketplace. We vehemently support the idea of one man, one vote in politics, but we just as vehemently oppose the idea of one man, one dollar in economics. We want no one to have more than one vote, yet we want no limits placed on how much wealth one can have in society. We absolutely abhor the idea of hereditary nobility, titles handed down through the bloodline, and think Europeans are silly practicing that, yet we fervently believe in hereditary wealth, money handed down generation to generation through the bloodline or arbitrary decision. We believe in the restraints of political power; we oppose any forms of restraint on economic power. Worst of all, we do not see any contradiction in this at all. On the subconscious level, where truth often lies, American society and money have become one and the same. Money can do no wrong in America. It has acquired the status of divinity, for the status of money is matched by the traditionally exalted status of God. After all arguments have been heard, money has the last word and often the last laugh.

Why is politics restrained but economics liberated? As all our political acts are elaborately structured and balanced apparently for the good of all, would similar elaborate structure and balance in economic acts also be for the good of all? Historically it is understandable why the Founding Fathers wanted all political exercises of power to be strictly governed by rules. After all, they had just come out of a thousand-year rule of political control in the Middle Ages. Although somewhat restrained by community and religious practices, political powers in feudal Europe were far from being just. Witnessing the fall of the feudal era, it was utmost on everyone's mind—especially the leading philosophers'—that political powers should be severely limited once and for all. The West, in the aftermath of this political triumph, however, never saw the dangers of *economic powers*. Nobody had had much experience—historical or otherwise—with the dangers of economic tyranny up to that time, and there was so little accumulated personal wealth. So they chained one beast and set free another. Burdened by the weight of past history, the political beast was thoroughly chastised and condemned to an eternal deprivation of power while the economic beast, having no such deadweight to carry, was set free to do as he wished. The Profit Ethic, which had been severely restrained in the Middle Ages, was thus set free of its restraint. The idea that both beasts—political *and* economic—might have the same beastly elements in them when translated into actual power almost never occurred to anyone. So much so that today no officials can get by without public watchdogs, while their counterparts in corporations enjoy virtually unchecked powers of economic privileges. By

habit and self-interest, everyone wants politics controlled. But hardly anyone wants economics controlled in America.

No political power in America is allowed to become "private." That is,
the power must remain in the "office." An official—elected or appointed—
cannot transfer his power of office to someone of his choice without public
approval. George Bush cannot give his power to his son Neil Bush, yet he
can leave all his wealth to his son. Translated into power, both political
power and economic power are exactly the same: political power compels
people to do things against their will; so does economic power, only more
thoroughly and absolutely than does political power. While political power
is not private, the same power in economics is allowed to be private in the
way one can do anything one wishes with money. One can give it to
someone of his choice, one can climb up a tall building and throw all his
wealth down on the street, or one can decide to do nothing with it or bury
it somewhere where no one can find it. We say political power is *public* and
must be guarded carefully against its arbitrary and presumably unjust uses.
But we say wealth is *private*, so that it's nobody's business what one does
with one's money.

It bothers no one that political power comes from the public (through
voting, etc.) and economic power comes also from the public (through the
marketplace, etc.). Free enterprise, like any other, is a *system of society*, which
cannot be maintained unless the society's whole structure—military, police,
law, in short, *government*—sustains it. There is no such thing as "free
enterprise" unless the government *makes* it and *keeps* it free. It is simply
incomprehensible that we allow such discrepancies in our logic with such
steadfastness and assurance. If public control of political power is a necessity,
then so is public control of economic power. If excessive, both are just as
cruel. If monopolized, both are just as dangerous. If privatized, each is just
as effective as means of control as the other. Perhaps more so for economic
power.

If the free-market philosophy is the defense of America's economics, why
not apply the same rule of freedom to America's politics? If freed from all
constraints, politics would indeed be "free politics" in the same way economics is "free economics." In free politics, one's political success would
depend on one's hard work, ingenuity, and energy, among other things.
All the power one earns one keeps for himself for life and bequeaths to
one's children when one dies. Since there is no limit placed on how long
one can keep one's wealth or how much, the same practice in politics would
give anyone unlimited access to power as long as it is acquired in the free
market of power, not by illegal force or fraud. The qualities that create
economic empires and dynasties would also help create political empires
and dynasties, from husband to wife, from father to son, and beyond.
George Bush would bequeath the presidency to Barbara Bush, then to Neil
Bush. George Bush's reason for doing just that: he worked hard for it and

he *earned* every bit of it; he deserves to do anything he wishes to do with the presidency.

If the above paragraph does not seem right, even as a parody of our contradiction, then the parody must be pursued further. The Constitution of the United States is a statement of political control. It establishes three branches of government, each of which balances the others so that no exercise of political power can be arbitrary or undemocratic. But notice that we do not have an "economic constitution"; nor do we have a branch of government that oversees our economic checks and balances so that no one exercises undue economic control over another. A sort of "economic judiciary" would be in order to ensure the same kind of justice in economic power that now exists in the political sphere. While American society is elaborately protected from the tyranny of political power, thanks to the Constitution of the United States, it is totally vulnerable to the tyranny of economic power. There is nothing in the Constitution or anywhere in America that can protect anyone from anyone else's economic tyranny. There are no economic courts of law, no economic police, no economic administration of justice whatsoever. As far as economic tyranny is concerned, the United States is back in the Middle Ages or, worse, in the Stone Age. Before the tyranny of wealth we all stand naked. Because the Constitution only prevents political tyranny, economic tyranny is left to the workings of the marketplace, unfettered, unrestrained, and free to devour anything in its path and within its range. Political power cannot be perpetuated, yet economic power can. No one will agree that young Bush should become the next president when his father dies, but no one objects to a Getty Jr. inheriting all his father's wealth and, therefore, power when the father dies. One form of inheritance is opposed; another form of inheritance is eagerly upheld. This irony did not escape Bertrand Russell decades ago:

It is curious that the rejection of the hereditary principle in politics has had almost no effect in the economic sphere in democratic countries. We still think it natural that a man should leave his property to his children; that is to say, we accept the hereditary principle as regards economic power while rejecting it as regards political power. Political dynasties have disappeared, but economic dynasties survive.[4]

It might not be altogether too unrealistic to wish to limit economic power in the way we limit political power. We control political power simply because we believe no one should become *too powerful* or hold power *too long*; we limit the presidency to two terms, and when the terms are up the president must leave. At this writing, limiting congressional terms is also a hot topic. We do not allow anyone to *multiply* his power in absenteeism: no one can exercise power dead or physically absent (not permanently or long-term anyway); no one can *own, organize,* or *control someone else's votes* legally and add them to his *own*; political power never grows with rents and interests in absenteeism. All political power is limited to the person who holds it for specific terms of tenure under specific terms of administrative arrangements. Could we apply similar rules to economic power? If not, why not? If we believe that no one should be too powerful or hold power too long, couldn't the *same rule* apply to economic power as well?

The idea of controlling the limits of economic power is not as farfetched as it seems at first blush. The principle of the minimum wage is really one-half of that principle. The rule of the minimum wage implies that no one should be *too poor*, which can be logically extended to the next step: that is, no one should be *too wealthy*. If the principle of minimum wage can be established, a principle for *maximum* wages could certainly be established by simple logical extension. If there is a limit to how poor one can be allowed to be, then by the same token there should be a limit to how wealthy one can be allowed to be. The existence of the minimum wage—economic equivalent of one man, one vote—certainly justifies the existence of a maximum wage. But then, at least in American society, money is a difficult subject in which to find logic or reason.

Economic power is represented in wealth; political power in equality, as in checks and balances, elections, one man, one vote. We do not give a person with a Ph.D. in political science or a political columnist any more political power—in spite of their obviously superior talent and skill in things political—than a kindergarten dropout who cannot spell *politics*. In matters economic, only the sky is the limit to one's reward for his superior talent and skill in amassing his fortunes and therefore power. No concentration of political power is allowed; no limit on economic power exists. While we are allowed only one vote each regardless of our individual talent or skill, we are allowed virtually unlimited economic power equivalent perhaps to 100 votes, 1000 votes, or even a million votes. No matter what logic or philosophical argument is used in justifying this inconsistency, some difficulty remains.

In spite of the contradictory reward systems in politics and economics in America, the two are remarkably similar in many ways. The way political power is gained runs a course almost parallel to the way economic power is accumulated. First, an idea that is acceptable to the public is conceived ("better life" for politics and "a new, improved mousetrap" for economics). Second, the idea needs supporters and backers both in political support and financial backing of the idea. Third, a working organization is established once supporters and backers are secured. Fourth, the workers are hired and trained and production begins. Fifth, the product is marketed and the public is persuaded that the new idea for better life is better than the old and the new, improved mousetrap better than the old mousetrap. Sixth, the public agrees and a public acceptance of the new product takes place and both ventures are pronounced a success. Seventh, the politician of new "better life" triumphantly enters his elected office, the businessman of the new, improved mousetrap his bank account.

However, this is where all the similarities end and contradictions begin. Both are success stories in the best American tradition of ingenuity, creativity, and dynamic drive to success as far as the process—as seen in the above scenario—is concerned. But these American success stories diverge sharply from here: The successful politician soon finds himself strapped down with all sorts of rules and regulations that govern his behavior in office. His counterpart, the successful businessman, on the other hand, faces no such strappings, being totally free to enjoy the fruits of his labor, and that of others, exactly as he pleases. For the businessman, there are no rules and regulations governing the result of his success: wealth. He uses it in any way that pleases his fancy. But his politician counterpart cannot even use his office telephone to order flowers for his wife's birthday without fear of those watchful eyes all around him. Both are success stories to be sure, at least on the surface of things. But the rewards for success are so inconsistently applied that one wonders at the fact that they both exist in the same society without much public awareness of this contradiction.

Of course, there is always the possibility that the success in politics, as an investment of sorts, can be enormously profitable in the marketplace later. The temporary hardship in politics is then a necessary measure of investment for greater rewards or what is called delayed gratification. In the meantime, however, we presume no such ulterior motive for the sake of argument. One might argue that there are fringe benefits in politics— free housing, good food, transportation, and other daily amenities at public expenses and many intangible rewards of public office. But such things can be gained and enjoyed many times better in economic success. On the other hand, it can be argued that the businessman is equally susceptible to government regulations and filling out all the bureaucratic forms necessary in complying with government rules. But these chores can simply be delegated to a hired hand, such as a secretary, a lawyer, or an accountant. We must agree, after all, the contradiction and inconsistency between political power and economic power are real and insoluble with argument.

So let's give in to the temptation of reason. What if we applied to economic power the rules of political power in America? The basis for strapping political power with all sorts of restraints is the idea—quite fundamental in modern democracy—that political leaders are "public servants," to "serve" the public. Public welfare being the purpose of democracy, we cannot allow the political leaders to abuse the powers inherent in their offices so that they are kept from the opportunities for a political abuse of power. The elaborate rules and regulations governing the exercise of their political power attest to our recognition of the dangers of power. A principle behind this awareness of power, also essential to modern democracy, is the idea that in an open, democratic, egalitarian society no one should be regarded as better than another.

This notion of equality among persons is at the core of political theory in the West since Thomas Hobbes bequeathed it to us through John Locke, Thomas Jefferson, and the Declaration of Independence. The political leader—even Hobbes's sovereign, the Leviathan, who is an absolute ruler— is no better than the commoner who casts his vote for him. The West is nothing if it has not upheld this belief with blood and bullets. Nowhere is this theory that all men are created equal more strongly held than in the United States. The simple fact that American society has never been threatened with political tyranny even when a president was elected to four successive terms in office proves the point. Both in political theory and in daily consciousness we do not tolerate the idea that our elected leaders are in some ways superior to the electors. It is indeed difficult to form respect for these leaders, unlike the European leaders, when our so-called leaders kiss our babies, shake our hands, and in many cases literally *beg* us to give them votes. The comments made by the irate constituents considered earlier may be recalled here. The idea is clear: political leaders exist for the public, because in politics no one, even the high elected officials, is superior to anyone.

But this notion central to political equality is totally dismissed in economic practice, if not in theory. We are constantly told that "customers are the king," "we do it all for you," and so on. There may even be some salutary evidence sometimes that we are indeed the king and they do it all for us in certain specific instances. But the idea that the corporate seller and individual consumer or the corporate employer and the individual employee—not unlike the elected and the elector—are essentially equal is quite alien to our conception of reality. It is almost alien as the idea that President Bush's son should be the next president by right. We do not view business leaders in the same way we view political leaders, while their enormous power to affect public welfare is certainly similar. If we fear the abuse of political power and therefore strap the political leader with all sorts of precautionary measures, rarely allowing him to enjoy anything the ordinary citizen is not entitled to, the same fear can be expected also in the abuse of economic power.

If a man gets elected with 2,000 votes cast for him, he does not control the 2,000 people. In fact, the effect is exactly the opposite: he feels and acts profoundly indebted to the voters as the source of his political office. But when a man starts a factory with 2,000 hired hands, his control over these employees is virtually absolute, exceeded only by that of the worst of dictators and tyrants. Not only does the factory owner not feel grateful to his employees for their service, without which he could not possibly produce the mousetrap, but he also feels absolutely superior to his employees in every way. Not the least is the impressive way he rewards himself financially, limited only by the fact of profit margins. The kind of superiority and arrogance wealth brings to these economic leaders is nowhere hinted in the political arena, no matter how exalted the office may be. (Can we imagine a TV program showing the "Lifestyles of the Rich and Famous Politicians"?) No mousetrap can be produced or consumed without the workers producing it and the public consuming it. Yet this simple functional relationship is completely dismissed in economic psychology. The owner of the factory feels justified in acting as if the employees and the public owe *him*, rather than the other way around, like his political counterpart.

The simple fact of economic life is that no product can be produced or sold unless it is conceived as a *social* activity. The absence of one single part makes the whole enterprise collapse. America's philosophy of economic life consists of solitary individuals prowling the land for business opportunities. But this philosophy traces straight back to the "state of nature," not to any human community. The aim of the theories of politics and economics in the last three centuries has been singularly clear: to prove that we are still in the state of nature and, therefore, the solitary image of man prowling in search of his next victim is entirely justified. But simple common sense tells us that the one who conceives of the mousetrap, the one who produces it with his labor, and the one who buys it should all be *equal partners*— because they all are *necessary*—in that social enterprise of mousetrapping. All three main elements are joined together by their respective functions— the idea, the product, the use—and, as such, there is no earthly reason why all three parts cannot be entitled to equal rewards and status in society. Such equality in partnership would have no negative effect on either productivity or beneficence of the product. It is a simple principle derived from simple facts of economic life, in the same way political leadership is impossible without the electors and the social structure that provides all that is necessary for political life. But while in politics we allow no dictatorship, we freely concede dictatorships in economics as a matter of principle or even of expediency and practicality.

The only reason—or perhaps the main reason—that we cannot accept the equality among various economic elements (the owner, the worker, the consumer) is because in the market system of society *we must assume the worst about human beings*. The very principle of self-interest assumes that human beings cannot be motivated by anything other than their own selfish motives. Utopians, socialists, and Marxists have tried altruistic motives to compel human action. The historical jury is not in yet with the verdict on this alternative approach, because a society of selfless altruism is still a future world. In the meantime, our market society must assume that no man will work unless he is threatened with starvation, no man will excel unless motivated by selfishness, no man will extend good deeds to another unless they bring concrete rewards. We tend to dismiss, especially in our era of the Profit Ethic, contrary examples of extraordinary human generosity as exceptions to the rules of human nature. "People are selfish," money man Andrew Tobias has flatly declared. "Give them an incentive to work, they will. Give them a low-risk way to cheat on their taxes, and they will. We do, most of the time, what's in our selfish best interest." In the last two hundred years Western societies have worked incessantly to mold men and women into selfish but good economic agents of profit and simply say: "Look at them, isn't human nature selfish?" The question is *not* whether man is selfish, because he *is*. It is what to do about it: to exploit it or to discourage it.

We are now in a position to construct economic equality on the basis of political equality, perhaps against our own tendency toward the Profit Ethic and its assumptions about human nature. To put it in a nutshell: *economic equality must be based on the person, not to be conceived or materialized outside the person.* To emphasize the "person" is simply to follow our political principle. After a certain age and regardless of size, intelligence, education, sex, race, social class, whatever, each person gets the right of one vote, which cannot be taken away. The person is a living human being: he sees, hears, eats, works, plays, lives, dies. He is born with one body and dies with one body; no one in the world can have two bodies or more than one lifetime. Emperors and beggars, saints and sinners, heroes and cowards, all have one reference point: the *person*. It is the beginning and ending of all things. In democratic politics, no political control of one by another is allowed so as to restrict the extension of one person into a multiperson. Only a political dictator can privatize other people into himself. In a market economy, however, wealth can extend one's control of others many times over as far as the amount of wealth would allow. This is economic dictatorship at its starkest. In this sense, any economic power that extends one's person beyond one's own individual necessities of life is in direct contradiction with the principle of political equality. This contradiction may be manifest in many forms: a person may extend economic power *beyond* himself in the form of hiring contracts, speculation with stocks and bonds, rents and interests in absentee ownership.

We assume that in politics one's own talent and skill are rewarded, but never beyond the person himself. We have seen that democratic power cannot multiply, be inherited, or be exercised in absenteeism. Even the president of the United States is but one citizen who casts one vote; the reward for his political talent and skill is strictly limited to himself, his person, nothing beyond him either in time (inheritance of power) or space (multiplied power). Regardless of one's prodigious talent and skill in politics, political rewards are essentially a one-shot existence: one electoral triumph is good for one term; one landslide is just one landslide; the powers of office are limited to that office only. How can we apply this political principle to economic power? For one thing, we can limit the rewards of one's economic talent and skill to that person only, both in time and in space, so that the rewards extend neither into a multiple person nor into another generation. Like all political rewards, economic rewards then also become a one-shot existence, beginning and ending with that person alone. Since in a free, happy society one must be allowed to be rewarded for his personal talent and skill, this principle of limiting rewards to the person's own time and space must be exercised with caution so that all human talent and skill are fully encouraged and developed. So the question naturally arises: what if one's own talent and skill lead to extraordinary economic achievements and therefore extraordinary economic rewards?

Since this is a common, almost subconscious, reaction from most Americans when confronted with the question, we need to take it seriously. To do so, it is necessary for us to introduce a theoretical model to counter this deep-seated misconception. Let me, therefore, introduce a pair of concepts that I would call *arithmetic* and *geometric differences*. Through these concepts I aim to establish that by virtue of human nature *no one is many times better* than the next person, either in intelligence, weight, height, speed, strength, or whatever other ways human differences may be measured. At best, the difference between the "best" and the "average" person is merely one-half. This is how I would proceed with my argument.

Individuals in society, while fairly similar in the state of nature and in their own physically defined needs and imperatives, are nevertheless *not* identical. Differences among them do exist. Some are smarter than others; some are faster than others; some are stronger than others; some are taller than others. Variations are endless. But one thing is certain: *no variation among individuals can DOUBLE the average.* No one is twice as fast, as tall, as strong, as smart, and so forth, as the average person. The fastest man in the world, who runs a hundred-yard dash in under ten seconds, is still not twice as fast as the average man who can run the same distance in fifteen seconds easily—less than a 50 percent difference. The tallest man in the world is still less than one-half as tall as the average man. Aside from the few pathological exceptions, the heaviest man is still less than twice the average weight. Even the "genius category" of IQ (150) is still less than twice that of an average person (100). Technically, IQ scores and "how many times smarter" cannot be compared because they involve different "scales," comparing two different things. What is numerically twice as much (say, an IQ score of 200) does not necessarily mean that 200 is twice as smart as 100. Besides, IQ scores measure potential, not achievement. We may certainly agree that someone is more talented than someone else, but find it difficult to prove the former is *many times* more talented than the latter. No reasonable logic or experience has ever been able to prove that point. In reality, we get tired of the issue and simply point to the after-the-fact income differences in wealth already in existence. To borrow Thomas Malthus's famous formula for the difference between food production and population growth, we can now say that *the differences among individuals are arithmetic, not geometric (much less exponential)*.

To apply the theory to reality, let's say that the average worker in a corporation makes $20,000 a year and the president $2,000,000 a year. The difference between the average worker and the president is an astonishing 100, which puts the value of the president at 100 times that of the average worker. It is indeed a gigantic, geometric, or even exponential leap between two individuals who should be only arithmetically different, if at all. Considered on the basis of true (arithmetic) differences among human beings, the income should vary only in the manner of 20,000, 21,000, 22,000, 23,000 and so on, not 20,000, 40,000, 80,000, 160,000, and so on. Even conceding that the president is smarter or more important than the average worker, even twice as smart, saying that he is *100 times* smarter or more important requires a new logic yet unknown to mankind.

For the sake of clear thinking, let's reverse the two roles: the president and the average worker switching their jobs. (Which decent average worker doesn't believe he can do a better job than the president?) The new president's job performance may not be quite as good, granted. But would the difference between the two presidents be 100:1 or the new president's performance just *not as good*, perhaps falling by 50 percent? Even not having a president at all would change no more than 50 percent. With the exception of catastrophic times, any large organizations move on their own predetermined inertia. The larger the organization, in fact, the less important is who is in charge. Conversely, the smaller the organization, the more important is the role of the one in charge. The *smallest* organization of all— one's marriage—is the most difficult "organization" to manage. In it, every decision one makes is crucial. In fact, one-half of all decisions in a marriage come from each individual, and that's a lot of room for catastrophic mistakes. As the organization increases in size, however, its decision-making becomes diffused among many hands.

Is it possible that a person could work, by his sheer determination and physical superiority, 100 times as fast or as much as another? Can a shoeshiner shine 100 times as many pairs of shoes as his competitor? Of course, it is not possible. The difference he can create with this best effort is still snail-paced, creating only arithmetic differences: 1, 2, 3, 4, 5, and so forth, not 2, 4, 8, 16, 32 and much less 10, 100, 1,000, and so on. Even the fastest shoeshiner cannot be more than twice as fast as the average shoeshiner. All material logic proves that point. (Citing the fact that in 1990 the average CEO earned 85 times the average worker, even the normally pro-business *USA Today* was upset: "Are CEOs worth 85 times the average worker?" it asked. April 26, 1991.)

What about the "extraordinary" personalities whose talents and skills are simply beyond our standards of measurement, such as the Einsteins, the Beethovens, and the Shakespeares of the world? Should they deserve the

differences of 100 times or possibly so? No. These extraordinary personalities define their own needs and satisfaction unaffected by their society's
average standards. They think, work, and live in a world of their own
totally unrelated to our mundane economic thinking, working, and living.

Arithmetic rewards are based on one's own industry in the form of
particular goods and services deemed necessary in the society's survival and
life's comfort. The costs of production and values of products are fairly
well defined, and no exaggerated profit can be added. Increase in arithmetic
rewards can be accomplished only by stretching one's capacity to its very
limit, and even at that, it does not go very far. Stretched to its limit, the
arithmetic principle gives one the advantage of a small percentage difference
over his fellow men. Arithmetic rewards are based on concrete factors of
work, industry, labor, function, rationality, and so on, all according to the
principles of social needs and resources. Arithmetic differences result in
higher productivity and better community cooperation, for the rules and
outcomes are clearly articulated in arithmetic rewards. They cannot be
multiplied by manipulation. Arithmetic differences, above all, assume a
material industry and culture in which *things* are produced and consumed
according to the rules of social function.

Geometric rewards, on the other hand, are based on the principle of profit.
There is neither a clear idea of cost and value in the goods and services produced nor a definite process of demand and need in them. The very idea of
multiplied profit, geometrically and exponentially leaping from 1 to 100,
presupposes a form of irrational, wild, speculative fantasy, not unlike Veblen's pecuniary class's, whose main ingredients are mostly luck and chance.
The mind-set that expects this multiplied reward based on a miniscule investment is hardly one that believes in hard work, industry, rationality, or
functional necessity in society. It is not the material world of production and
industry, but a "psychological" world of manipulation and speculation. All
geometric rewards are based on this fantasylike quality. The geometric
world is characterized by entertainment products, control of minds, exploitation of images and fears, management and organization of others' talents
and skills, advertised demand in goods and services. Its objective tends to be
fantastic, its method ruthless, and its mind-set irrational.

In the last several decades since World War II, the American economic
system has gradually moved from the arithmetic stage to a new geometric
phase. In this world of geometric rewards, economic behavior is a misnomer. There is nothing "economic" about it. Those who thrive in it—
businessmen, advertisers, producers, planners, designers, market researchers—might as well be psychoanalysts, counselors, astrologers, mystic gurus,
stargazers, and anyone who tries to "read" the consumer's mind. It has
nothing to do with "economics" and much less with "science."

In a "political society," like the prereform Soviet Union, economics is
subordinated to the political process, often in the name of equality. In a

political society, there is at least a theoretical stalemate in economics, no one having any economic advantage over another. This fact makes the "political" struggle for power all the more grim and fierce. Economic equality having thus been achieved through nullified economics, the Soviets used to wage their battle of dominance over each other on the political front. While money was being effectively eliminated from competition, no more or less to be made, politics was still a place where a wild, free-for-all, every-man-for-himself chase was possible. While the winner of all this achieved little in the way of economic advantages, his political power was virtually unlimited.

In an "economic society" like the United States and the liberal West, on the other hand, politics is effectively subordinated to economics in the name of freedom and free enterprise. In an economic society everyone has one vote and political exercises of power are so restricted as to be meaningless as a source of power. With this political stalemate, the war of economic advantages still to be gotten rages, because economics is where all the differences, real and possible, remain. There is little to be made in politics as politics, but only the sky is the limit in economics. The president makes $200,000 a year, a good sum for most Americans. But most corporate presidents make many times more; even an average professional football player or baseball player makes more than that. But upon leaving the office, the ex-president can easily command multimillion-dollar deals for his service on a corporate board or on a speaking circuit.

In a strange but poignant way, both the United States and the prereform Soviet Union emerge with only one-half each of what we might regard as social justice: we with political justice, the Soviets with economic justice, if we do not quibble over some exceptions in either case. It is not without irony that both societies have claimed total justice for themselves. The Soviets ignored the terror of midnight visits by KGB agents; we ignore the terror of a "pink slip" being visited upon us. Which is more terrifying is a pointless argument; both *are* terrifying.

The Soviets have had "political" prisoners who were sent to mental institutions and labor camps in Siberia. We do not have political prisoners in America, at least not in the Soviet fashion, but we have "economic prisoners." Our economic prisoners—the wretched underclass of America—are permanently kept in their own economic Siberia. Few of the underclass—the unemployed, the uneducated, the homeless, and the minorities who may combine all of the above attributes—ever escape or expect to escape their prison, not unlike their counterparts in the Soviet Union. Not unlike average Soviet citizens about their political prisoners, most Americans manage to avoid consciously thinking about their economic prisoners, because the prisoners are generally kept out of sight from the sunny side of an affluent society. It is indeed irrelevant to ask which of the two types of prisoners—political or economic—is having a tougher time. What is relevant is that neither side can claim justice and that our traditional claim of social justice superior to the Soviets requires some enlightenment.

Another way of looking at politics and economics in American society—their respective decline and rise relative to each other—is to see what punitive damages each can inflict upon its critics. Recall the irate citizens once again. For ordinary citizens, criticizing one's mayor or governor or even the president of the United States brings back no apparent punishment. In fact, criticizing one's elected officials is one of the pastime activities in America; it is fun and there is no danger in it. But no American citizens with a reasonable presence of logic and sanity would *dare* criticize their bosses at work of any rank, not even the foreman. While we are absolutely free from the tyranny of our political leaders and their power, we are absolutely unfree from the tyranny of our economic bosses and their power, from the lowly foreman to the more lofty president of the company.

Just about every American who has been employed at one time or another has a speech rehearsed—with no expletives deleted—to hurl at his boss at the moment of his glorious, long-awaited exit from the slavery and the bondage of the workplace. Nothing gives an American greater pleasure than the ability and opportunity to say to his boss, "Take this job and..." But, alas, the spirit is there, but the opportunity is not. By the time one retires, all is normally forgotten and forgiven as well. All this talk about "open society," "free society," or "individual freedom" goes out the window when the boss or the employer walks in. Economic bondage in America is absolute and total and final; there are no ifs and buts in economic relations. Hence our loud and often boisterous demonstration of contempt for *political* leaders, as if to make up for all the humiliation and slavery we suffer at the hands of our *economic* overlords.

Both the United States (an economic society) and the Soviet Union (a political society) have claimed at one time or another that their own system is the best. But as we have seen, both have had only one-half justice: the United States with political justice and the Soviet Union with economic justice, if the reader would forgive my necessary over simplification. In American society, political powerlessness is shared equally. The Soviets have shared their economic powerlessness equally. We have defended our system as a system of justice; the Soviets did theirs. But both have defended their one-half as if it were whole. Societies must be just *both* politically *and* economically. Since American society has made politics meaningless, it has given economics a carte blanche to control, amass, exploit, or do whatever else in the name of the marketplace. The prereform Soviets, on the other hand, have been given little or no economic freedom—in job preference, basic necessities, and so on—leaving political control as the sole arbiter of all human relations in the land.

This contrast between the two societies makes up one-third of a typology of social justice: first, there are societies where at least one-half of justice is achieved; second, there are societies where neither of the two is achieved; third, there are societies where both of them are achieved. We can give the United States and the pre-Gorbachev Soviet Union as examples of the first type. We may give present Liberia and black South Africa as examples of the second type, where neither political nor economic justice is available. When we think about the third type, where both economic and political justice are reasonably present, Scandinavia comes to mind.

Much has changed since 1989. Communism is no longer on the world's center stage. Whatever historical role it might have performed—including the role of "the instrument of development" from feudalism to the threshold of modernity, as Ralf Dahrendorf has suggested in his book *Reflections on the Revolution in Europe*—its collapse has given us historical pause. What was our Cold War against communism all about? Why was the West so *afraid* of communism? Ironically, its collapse has given us greater insight into the mind of the West than might have been had it continued its world role. At any rate, time and changed circumstances give us a better perspective.

The communists were afraid of the corrupting influence of our "freedom"; we were afraid of the same corrupting influence of their "liberation." It was a tug-of-war of influencing history and the human mind. They believed that we, if unchecked, would dominate the world through the marketplace; we believed that they, if unchecked, would dominate the world through ideology. Neither side was sympathetic in this war of attribution; we called the Soviet Union an Evil Empire, and others called us the Great Satan. The two forces were equally determined; one derived its strength from the theory of nature, the other from the force of history. The First World influenced the Second World (and the Third World) with the possibility of affluence; the Second World of communism influenced others with the promise of justice. Their deadly opposition—although locked into a fairly sophisticated set of theoretical articulations—could be summed up in this: one is inspired by the love of money (money to be "free"), the other by the vision of power (power to do "justice"). Who won the war?

On the basis of recent historical development, it is safe to assume that the world of money has won. There is much reason for celebration: the West is affluent, the other side struggling even with its daily necessities; they defected to us many times more than we to them; American jeans and rock music are more popular in Russia than Russian ballet and vodka in America; and so on. To be sure, capitalism has the upper hand with the offers of money and promises of prosperity. But each offering of money saps humanity from the individual, both the offerer and the offeree, and each demonstration of affluence severs the invisible links of humanity to its community. The dollar sign kills the human spirit in the individual and turns his predatory instinct loose; each instance of affluent consumption destroys the basic foundations of its own society. There are many more dollar signs and many more instances of consumption to go, giving the impression that capitalism as a system of human thought and action is strong, as it has won its mortal battle with communism. But each instance of its strength and its winning score over communism is also the pernicious acid drop that corrodes its own community and humanity, slowly but surely. The reservoir of dollar signs and affluent consumption is enormous and could resist the corrosion much longer than our ordinary powers of observation could tell at a glance. But the process of our own internal corrosion is ceaseless and becomes only stronger as our own economic machine itself becomes more thriving. Thus the ultimate irony is that while having won its battle against communism in the short run, capitalism is losing its war *against itself* in the long run. It is this maddening contradiction of ourselves—at once thriving yet collapsing, prosperous yet doomed—that gives our time its most historically tragic poignancy.

Why were we in America afraid of communism? In certain quarters of America there has been inordinate fear of communism, greater than in any other developed Western nations. The fear could not have been military, for our military might was always equal or superior to theirs. Nor could it be economic, for our economic strength easily surpassed theirs. There was little evidence that the communists would ever catch up with the West economically anytime soon. Nor could it be historical, for we have never been under communist rule to know or feel its terror. Then what was the cause of this fear, which drove even a reasonable man in America to wholly unreasonable reactions? There can be only one reason: the *moral* one.

Even while we boasted our superiority over the Soviets in military, economic, and historical terms, there was the undercurrent of uncertainty in whether we were indeed morally superior to them, however the term may be defined. In insensitive and often "imperialist" expansions of foreign markets, in displays of material overconsumption and economic disparity, in supporting corrupt dictators the world over, in the mindlessness of illusion-making entertainment, in the intermittent bursts of scandal in high society, and in other such actions and inactions we somehow felt that we were internally decaying and hence vulnerable to moral criticism. This moral vulnerability has often led to still greater material overconsumption at home and increasing reliance on the almighty dollar and military might abroad to settle the score. Once puritanical and productive but now mere consumers of often useless products, we sensed and still sense in our bones that our own affluence has become the very symbolic demonstration of our own moral corruption.

The Soviets had their own inordinate fear of the West, however. But their reasons were exactly the opposite of our reasons for our fear of them. Militarily, they felt they were encircled by the West; economically, their material standards were vastly inferior to ours; and historically, the memory of foreign invasions was etched in their collective remembrance. But it was in *moral* terms that they felt smugly superior to us. Morally, they were absolutely certain that their community had greater human substance than ours, that their interpersonal relations were more authentic, their emotions more honest, and their views of life less burdened by self-interest and irrational passions for accumulation, and that their economic life was much more productive and prudent and their cultural pursuits less wicked.

It is this sense of moral superiority among the hardworking and puritanical communists that was the main source of *our* fear. We are now neither hardworking nor puritanical, both in production and consumption. Our hard work has no concrete objective, nor can our puritanical heritage stand up to the "distressing flaw in the social fabric of America." Naturally, we feared that the communist foothold in the Western Hemisphere would spread by way of Cubas and Nicaraguas. In rare moments of honest reflection we recognized the potency of communism in a wholly moral sense. In spite of our proven superiority in material and military terms, we were afraid of communism because we felt vulnerable to it, we were vulnerable to it because its moral tenet was deemed superior to our own, and we felt it superior to our own because our side is basically without friends, without community, and in the final analysis without humanity to define and defend its own moral commitment together. It is the fear of those who stand alone and naked; it is the fear of those who are afraid of themselves. The end result of all this was alternately doubting, self-loathing, and overreacting in personal as well as national moods and actions.

In short, it was the embodiment of our Profit Ethic and Substitute Society in their most revealing and fearful emptiness.

NOTES

1. Robert Heilbroner, *The Worldly Philosophers: The Lives, Times, and Ideas of the Great Economic Thinkers* (New York: Simon and Schuster, 1961), 280–81.

2. "Donald Regan: 'When I Say Jump...,' " *U.S. News & World Report*, 21 January 1985.

3. Bonnie Angelo, "Fingerspitzengefühl," *Time*, 17 February 1986.

4. Bertrand Russell, *A History of Western Philosophy* (New York: Simon and Schuster, 1945), 622. I am somewhat surprised that, to my knowledge, no other discussion on this issue exists in the literature on inheritance or political power.

Chapter 10

Democracy for Sale

In American society politics has acquired the characteristics of sports. Both sports and politics, as games, follow the rules of the game. There are clearly defined objectives for both: Both want to score the winning points. They both have referees to determine winners and losers. They are played out as appropriate human drama, with their respective legends and myths. Sports exhort heroic exploits, victory and defeat, emotional crisis, courage and excellence. Politics proclaims democracy, leadership, equality, freedom, justice, rights. Both are played in front of a crowd and *for* a crowd, and as such, both are also means of entertainment. What seriousness and significance we may attach to them are the creation of our imagination, for both have little significance to real life. With or without them, real life goes on. These games are played with their perfunctory regularity, with their heroes and villains, with their themes of victory and defeat, and with their exhausting emotional anticipation–climax–resolution cycles of crowd amusement. Both events are half-serious, half in jest, appearing to be real yet having little or no substance. They take place as rituals in American life in their specifically appointed season. Not surprisingly, political leaders of the United States mostly take on the characteristics of entertainers, their "political" activity a form of low-rated entertainment.

Politics, while having become basically useless in and of itself, serves a fairly important function in America. Not unlike sports, it *pacifies* people as their democratic ritual. It gives them something to do, to vent their energy unspent in their economic struggle. Even as a spectacle of no serious consequences the game of politics still attracts contestants, supporters and detractors, ideas and slogans—all with serious intentions. In a society where nothing—other than one's own conscious desires and actions for self-interest—can be taken seriously, it is difficult to make an exception for politics. At best, we follow politics with no more interest than our interest in the rise and fall of our favorite sports teams. And perhaps that's where politics should be in the American context of things.

American "politics" is no longer a political process; it is a cultural spectacle. And as such, it conforms to the rules of American cultural fulfillment: politics can be counted on with a regular supply of events, characters, and stories. Presidential primaries are squeezed in between the Super Bowl and the real baseball season. Like the two sporting events, politics creates an atmosphere of anticipation. Bets are made and scores kept. The anticipation of the king's coronation whets the crowd's appetite by the suspense of *who* shall be the king, not unlike the Roman crowd wanting to know which gladiators would survive. The event is scheduled, the characters line up, and the story unfolds, graphically and blow by blow, for the expectant crowd. On lesser levels of politics, lesser events, characters, and stories are staged to a lesser crowd and its anticipation. The political game is played by the classic scenario of all games: first, the game must be played by the rules; second, there will be winners and losers. The first premise makes the game possible to play; the second premise makes the anticipation possible to sustain. They all point to that climactic scene where the outcome is finally unveiled.

This gamelike playing out of politics is made possible by the comforting thought that the outcome offers no major national significance no matter who wins or loses. If the outcome were so catastrophically important, the decision would not have been put to this gamelike contest in the first place. All major historical events have taken place *outside* the game arena, often in elite chambers, on the streets, with titanic intellectual struggles, or in bloody battles. No major historical event has ever occurred through the niceties and comforts of political gamesmanship. Having been made *politically* meaningless and irrelevant, politics in America has been transformed into a cultural event. But as a cultural event, it is no different from other cultural events that delight the crowd. All truly historic events are unanticipated and unexpected from the routine runs of daily life. But no cultural events ever created such major changes. American political routines have settled into this cultural anticipation and expectation with comforting regularity and uneventfulness. But as a cultural event, politics must survive the ratings and the attention spans of the ever-scatterbrained crowd.

Since no reality is at stake in each political game, traditional political ideas and slogans must be replaced by more culturally appealing shortcuts. Political gossip thus emerges as the stuff of political news and analysis. The so-called political reporters are often little more than political gossipmongers and analysts of games. Their "analysis" or "report" has almost wholly to do with which politician is going to do or not going to do what and what significance it would have on the fortunes of such and such politicians. When Congress is debating an issue under heavy pressure from the president, it is not reported as a political debate of opposing ideas. But it is thought of as a game for the president, his party, and whatever else that stands to "win" or "lose." They say it is a "tremendous" victory or defeat for the president or such and such persons, not the idea itself that wins or loses. All political decisions are held in suspense, or are built to a climax, until the score is settled. It is the stuff of which entertainment is made. In America everything, including politics, must become Great American Entertainment.

As if we are trying to make up for what we cannot accomplish at the marketplace, politics is tackled with all the determination of economic competition and ingenuity. In a democratic society like ours, the idea that sustains politics is the same as the idea that sustains the market economy: there is something to be gained out there, and players are contesting to get it. Our liberal democratic system—the political half of the Profit Ethic— assumes that everything in politics is up for grabs, in the same way our market economy assumes that everything in the marketplace is anyone's game. Hence the meanness of political struggle in America is matched only by the meanness that exists in the marketplace. While fairly insignificant compared to corporate executives', American political rewards are nothing to laugh at compared to the salary scale of secretaries and teachers. Starting at the top with $200,000 for the president, the salary ranges of most political positions are certainly many times larger than those of the ordinary citizen. Some examples, as of January 1991*:

Chief justice	$163,600
Associate justices	$153,600
Vice president	$160,600
House speaker	$160,600
Cabinet members	$138,900
Deputy secretaries	$125,100
Majority, minority leaders	
of House	$138,900
of Senate	$113,400
President pro tem of Senate	$113,400
Appeals court judges	$132,700
District court judges	$125,100
Tax court judges	$125,100
Members of House	$125,100

Members of Senate	$101,900
Agency heads	$101,300
Bankruptcy judges	$68,400

*Information provided by the Office of Congressman Charlie Rose, December 1990.

Spoils go to the victors, and American society has never made bones about who gets what after each political battle. Large or small, American political rewards have become economic rewards. The process of getting them is a cultural spectacle, not a political contest. No longer a contest of ideas and slogans among political groups, classes, and generations, if it ever was, American politics is a predetermined gamut of open-field running. In it, everything is fair game. There are main players, game plans, and campaign strategies, but there are no grand designs and plans for the millennium or beacon on the hill. As winning and losing each game goes, so goes the rise and fall in the size of one's paycheck. As a rule, millions of dollars were spent once on political campaigns that, on the surface, promise rather minor returns. For example, $20 million is spent on a $75,000 congressional job. But many times more than the $10 million rides on congressional votes in trade policies, welfare and warfare decisions, tax laws, business and commerce regulations, and so on. They are, in the end, the ultimate economic gains for the winner's circle. Normally candidates are chosen by the party, not the party by candidates, for the party has to put up someone who will give it the maximum possible returns. Sooner or later, as in all democracies, American politics must settle its score in the pocketbook.

While the fortunes of American politics shift almost regularly between Republicans and Democrats and between conservatism and liberalism, American society itself has shifted steadily toward the "economic" pole. Whether Republican or Democratic, whether conservative or liberal, one's politics is one's pocketbook. When the issue concerns money, Republicans and Democrats are indistinguishable. Even the die-hard Democrats talk like Republicans, simply because they must. When the pocketbook is the issue, there is no real difference between the two political parties. When money speaks, both parties listen, when money demands, both parties accede, and when money votes, both parties become conservative. This lesson is learned time and again, especially through the 1990 elections.

In this the very idea of democracy—the heart and soul of the modern world—has been transformed in America. While every American believes in democracy and has faith in it, no one wants to die for it, not any more than they will die for "free enterprise." One dies for God, mother, or love, but not for democracy. In America democracy is regarded as a means to an end, a servant that serves its master. Americans do not serve democracy or die for it. We believe in it and have faith in it simply because *democracy is the best means of getting what we want*. In the West, where the idea has been most extensively tried, democracy was never meant to be an end in and of itself, the shining city of our millennium. It was never meant to be anything but a means to an end. No man in modern political philosophy—since the fall of the Middle Ages—has ever defined what we should do with democracy, not any more than what we should do with the wealth that is supposedly produced in the marketplace. Be democratic, we have been told, you will prosper; be wealthy, it has been assumed, you will be happy. Democracy makes *anything possible* because the crowd can change its tune anytime for any reason. It is this *possibility* that excites the crowd in a democratic society. In an absolutist monarchy where the crown is handed down father to son, there is little or no possibility of power's changing hands unexpectedly. In such societies politics was never popular as pastime. The kind of exciting frenzy and suspense possible in today's liberal democracy would be so rare in a traditionally predictable monarchy (like Saudi Arabia) that hardly anyone would rely on it for amusement.

What is democracy supposed to *do*? Surprisingly, this question has almost never been raised. Once we achieved democracy, it was assumed, everything would fall into place and all of us would prosper. But no one in the West has been made prosperous by having democracy itself, for democracy itself is nothing unless it can *do* something for *oneself*. Democracy, as we understand it today, is not something to be produced and placed on the mantle, to be admired for generations. Rather, it is a specific tool with which we wish to accomplish something. But what is it that we wish to accomplish by using democracy as a means? The traditional answer is: *whatever our self-interest desires*. It was in this original identification of democracy with self-interest that economics and politics, good and evil, and whatever else were united and their differences resolved. Democracy was chosen as the servant, the tool, the means to the end, of self-interest because, under the old kings and popes, this self-interest had been severely repressed. Democracy, or what we call liberal democracy, gave us political freedom; the marketplace gave us economic freedom. Liberal democracy and the marketplace have thus become the twin pillars of modern Western civilization.

Liberal democracy, like its cousin the marketplace, assumes self-interest as central to modern man's view of himself and his fellowmen. The assumption of self-interest therefore accepts the checks and balances of political equality and the marketplace outcome of economic inequality. But political equality in a democratic society is not a state of being, not any more than marketplace inequality is a state of being. For both situations can and do change unpredictably. It is this possibility of change that gives both democracy and the market economy their unpredictable dynamics as political and economic systems. Power in someone else's hand can be taken away in the same way wealth in someone else's hand can be repossessed.

All one has to do is follow the rules of the game in the political arena and the marketplace. All things are fair in politics as they are in the marketplace, and some play the game better than the others. One simply plays the game against all others who have similar designs of self-interest at heart.

Every man (and woman) is a calculating machine, according to liberal democracy, rationally weighing pros and cons of his (her) thought and action. It assumes that every man is after everyone else's power and fortune and all is fair as long as it is done *democratically*. Thus democracy assumes the worst about mankind and absolves the worst by giving it a means, a tool, an excuse that justifies it. Since no one knows what one is supposed to do in a democratic society, other than pursuing his self-interest, democracy itself can never serve any good purpose in and of itself. It is a modern system of thought about mankind, yet it assumes the most primitive instinct of man as his "nature." It is a social system devised to maintain peace in a human community, yet it causes fiercely contested battles of self-interests. The Profit Ethic is simply the most openly economic emphasis of this liberal democratic doctrine.

Democracy assumes a perennial redistribution of power, but it says nothing about who should get how much. Since no government in the world can distribute power to everyone's satisfaction, employment of human ingenuity and imagination is most wildly displayed in a liberal democratic society by everyone striving to gain the biggest share. No battle is more fierce than that among those whose standings are equal or close to it, no battle is bloodier than one in which there is no limit to the spoils, and no battle is more never-ending than one inspired by self-interests. Democracy provides the rules of this determined battle of wits against wits, every man against every man. Politics provides the arena in which the battle is fought out among the contestants. It is a forum for debate and vote-taking, not a moral definition of what is right and wrong or what man's actions should be to define and achieve happiness and justice. Thus what is democratically debated and voted on has little or nothing to do with its moral validity. That an issue has been duly debated and voted on according to the rules of democratic politics does not mean that such public decisions are necessarily right or just.

But the democratic *process* itself makes anything done democratically right by virtue of its being done democratically. Democracy itself—in majority votes, most commonly—is the ultimate judge of all moral rights and wrongs, although as a forum and arena for self-interest it has nothing to do with moral rights and wrongs. On the contrary, the very assumption of self-interest in the democratic processes makes any result suspect as to its moral quality. Democracy has no obligation to be right or just. It is under no obligation to do the right thing. Its only obligation is to be "democratic." We can lynch the innocent, confiscate private property and rights, legislate unfair laws, and do any number of things against one another as long as they are carried out democratically. Some thinkers—notably Plato and Alexis De Tocqueville—feared democracy precisely because of its private passions without its public virtues. De Tocqueville formed this opinion about a popular liberal democracy after touring nineteenth-century America.

Like all other systems of social relations, democracy is neither absolute nor final as a way of regulating social relations. Democracy simply says that people can decide what they want and do not want. Democracy in and of itself does not sanctify the people's choice, nor does it make the people's choice any wiser *because* it is democratic. As has been shown time and again in history, decisions coming out of a democratic process can be just as foolish or evil as those out of any other political process. The democratic system is neither a magic wand nor a panacea for ignorance, self-interest, or unhappiness. It is the purpose of democracy—what people choose to do or choose not to do—that determines the nobility or folly of the system. But democracy blithely assumes the worst about mankind, encourages the worst from them, and blesses any outcome in the name of democratic principle.

The way the term *political* has changed its meaning in recent years is illuminating. Whatever it might have meant in a bygone era, the term nowadays means anything that has to do with one's self-interest. "Political" is whatever one decides for one's self-interest. Many nowadays complain that "people are *so* political!" or "he is *so* politically oriented," and so on. Such expressions of course do not mean that people have become more politically conscious, rushing to join the Democratic or Republican party or form their own political organizations or begin grassroots campaigns for public issues. What they mean, needless to say, is that people have become so *opportunistic* that every "political" action is one that is calculated to maximize one's self-interest. Political and selfish thus become synonymous in the idioms of contemporary American human relations. When Jeff Kemp debuted as the Rams' quarterback in Los Angeles, his father, Congressman Jack Kemp, known to have White House ambitions, observed, "For political reasons, I wish he was playing in Buffalo." Everyone knew what he meant by "political": what was good for Jack Kemp's political fortunes in his home base, Buffalo. The corruption of the term *political* to mean a purely psychological and personal jockeying for advantage, so naturally fitting in today's American culture, says much about our democratic politics and its undemocratic meaning.

The perils of democracy increase when we consider the means by which we elect our leaders in a democratic society. The perils can be put as a question: if a man is selfish and knows nothing else as guide to his action, why would he think and act any differently when he chooses his political representatives from when he chooses his sales representatives? It is unlikely that a majority of electors would rise to a higher level of public virtues when they elect their political leaders than when they go about their daily business, where self-interest is supreme. If they are self-interested in private, could they be expected to rise above it in public matters, such as electing their leaders? It is highly unlikely, and here is one of our persistent problems of democracy. The statement that people in a democracy deserve the government they have is attributed to Winston Churchill, who, incidentally, had a rather low opinion of democracy. The gist of Churchill's remark is that the level of leadership quality cannot be expected to be appreciatively higher than the level of those who do the electing. This makes perfect logical and historical sense. Few ever rise higher voluntarily, and voluntarily one must rise to a higher level of public virtues in a democratic society. When a federal judge nominee was heavily opposed in the Senate for being "mediocre," then president Richard Nixon countered the opposition by saying that mediocre judges were also necessary to balance judicial wisdom. Perhaps he had a point. If federal judges were to be *elected*, I am certain there would be many more "mediocre" judges on the bench.

It is quite puzzling to some observers that the presidential elections create such stirs of interest in the national media when so little is at stake in their outcome. The presidency and congressional leaderships are positions of relatively inconsequential power. When was the last time a president of the United States did anything against a fiercely unified public outcry? We recall the comment made by Donald Regan about the difference between being a company chief executive at Merrill Lynch and being a U.S. president's chief money man. Political power in America—aside from its nice paychecks and the frills of the office—is hardly power at all. Compared with that in the Soviet Union until recently or even in some two-bit republics, political power in the United States is really much ado about nothing. The crushing burden of checks and balances—not only from other branches of the government but also from the public, the media, lobbyists, law—makes any exercise of political power worth the name virtually impossible. There is no American Siberia at the disposal of any leader. In fact, as the level of formal authority increases, the level of real authority declines, and vice versa. A sheriff's deputy in a small town can and does have more actual power than the state governor or even the U.S. president. People fear what the sheriff's deputy can do to their well-being much more than what their president or governor can do.

The most convincing proof for the political leaders' powerlessness is the very fact that they are *elected*. This is the supreme irony of democracy. Positions of any consequence—from bank tellers to corporate executives—are never elected. Corporate chiefs, athletic coaches, military generals, and others whose action produces immediate results and who are directly accountable for results are never elected. No democrat ever cries foul only because these positions are not elective. It is safe to assume that any position that can afford all the waste and foolishness of election *must* be inconse-

quential. A position that can withstand the inherently unstable and whimsical process of democratic election is either all-powerful or all-powerless.
A dictator who is so sure of himself regardless of the election outcome may
allow a certain amount of ceremonial foolishness and waste to pacify his
people, but then few all-powerful dictators would see any need to mess
with elections in the first place. A position of governance that is subject to
approval by the governed cannot be a position of power by simple logic.
If this is difficult to comprehend, just imagine something closer to home:
imagine being a father or a mother who is subject to the children's election,
recall, impeachment, ouster, or what have you; then imagine how strong
the position of being a parent might be. If the power of your right hand
depends on the approval of your left hand, there is no way the right hand
can exercise any semblance of power over the left hand. Dictators, kings,
emperors, and queens are never elected, but the presidents of the United
States and of student body governments *are* elected.

It is little wonder that the American public by and large is uninterested
in politics. As entertainment, it is not amusing enough, with few exceptions
and for the wrong reasons. As an issue of power, it is not significant enough.
Americans generally rank at the bottom of political participation among
industrialized nations measured by their voting. This neglect finally caught
up with them in a cruel joke when the Democratic party members nomi-
nated two "LaRouche candidates"—a combination of KKK and the Nazi
party in philosophy and paranoia—to posts of secretary of state and lieutenant governor for the state of Illinois in early 1986. But not to worry.
Even if they *were* actually elected to their respective posts, what could they
possibly *do* as state secretary and lieutenant governor? Little or nothing. At
about the same time a Milwaukee newspaper poll showed that nearly one-
half of those polled could not name their U.S. senator (William Proximire),
who had been in the Senate since 1957 and who had "shaken the hands of
more citizens than has any other politician in Wisconsin history." Perhaps
the Wisconsin citizens could name the Green Bay Packers' starting quarterback, memorize the Brewers' stats, or recite the Milwaukee Bucks' records
more proficiently.

Dictators, kings, emperors, and queens have their images etched in the
daily consciousness of their subjects; they cast a long shadow—often terrifying—because their power is real. The question of who becomes the next
dictator or king is a truly bloody struggle because the stakes are enormous.
None of this is true with American political leaders and their political power.
In one of Gregory McDonald's gritty, hard-boiled "Fletch" novels an old
hand is breaking in a new press representative in a presidential campaign,
and no reality can be truer than this fictional character's statement about
political campaigns in America:

Something ol' Vic taught me, and it's always proved to be true: statesmanship has
no place on a political campaign. A campaign is punch and duck, punch and duck.

Fast footwork, you know? Always smiling. The voters want to see fast action. Their attention won't hold for anything anymore. From day to day, give 'em happy film, and short, reassuring statements. If you really try to say anything, really ask them to stop and think, they'll hate you for it. They can't think, you know? Being asked makes us feel inferior. We don't like to feel inferior to our candidates. Against the democratic ideal, you know? The candidate's just got to keep giving the impression he's a man of the people—no better than they are, just doin' a different job. No one is ever elected in this country on the basis of what he really thinks. The candidate is elected on the basis of thousands of different comfortable small impressions, not one of which really asks the voters to think.[1]

The American political leader is much like a tour guide: He takes the majority where the majority wants to go. If he refuses, the majority simply dismisses him and gets itself a new tour guide who will take the majority wherever *it* wants to go. It has been said time and again that a good leader in American politics is one who can lead the public where it might not want to go but "ought" to go. He accomplishes this with his dazzling charm and rhetorical inspiration, while maintaining his popularity with the public. In other words, a good leader can lead the multitude on a path of righteousness—always a rough one to walk on—and is still loved and liked by the suffering multitude. Not that we have not had those leaders, but they had help from depressions, wars, and other events of grave consequences. Pundits say that this leadership quality is what separates politicians from statesmen, the latter being those leaders who make unpopular causes popular. But in a democratic society, especially in America today, the burden of election is real and constant on any politician's mind. Recall that John F. Kennedy's famous "ask-not" speech was made *after* he was elected. Democratic electors do not vote for anyone in particular out of respect; they must "like" the politician. Since respect is earned with time and reputation (therefore not given frivolously or overnight), it is reserved for someone historically special. Liking someone takes neither time nor reputation, and liking is therefore given frivolously or overnight. Anyone likes or dislikes anyone else for no reason or for any reason. But one does not show respect unless there is established reason for it.

Political leaders are not the respected lot. The electoral burden allows no respect to be formed between the elector and the elected. This fact of leadership has a significant influence on the general character of those who seek electoral positions in America. One who is popular with people is not always the best leader or the person with the best character. But that sort of person tends to seek and get political success. The following remark by James Reston could equally apply to any election: "Looking around, it's fairly obvious that the people who are running for president in 1988 are not really as qualified as the people who are not running." There has always been a long list of leaders who would make a "good" president. But, alas, they are not "electable." The following observation made by Walter Lippmann is also relevant:

With exceptions so rare that they are regarded as miracles and freaks of nature, successful democratic politicians are insecure and intimidated men. They advance politically only as they placate, appease, bribe, seduce, bamboozle, or otherwise manage to manipulate the demanding and threatening elements in their constituencies. The decisive consideration is not whether the proposition is good but whether it is popular—not whether it will work well and prove itself but whether the active talking constituents like it immediately. Politicians rationalize this servitude by saying that in a *democracy, public men are the servants of the people.*[2]

Being servants of the people is one thing; being *servile* to the people is quite another. What is perhaps more remarkable is the fact that this observation was made almost a half-century ago.

Statesmen may emerge with time and reputation, but politicians cannot wait for that to happen. They must advertise themselves into overnight recognition and popularity ratings. What we call "political campaign" is really nothing but advertisement. Those goods and services that are advertised are those goods and services that *need* to be advertised simply because their worth has not been established by either time or reputation. There is no public knowledge accumulated around the product that must be advertised. In other words, people know little about or have little need for the product. A politician *campaigns* because people know little or nothing about him established through time and reputation. George Rodrique reports Germany's reaction to U.S. elections in 1990: "Actors and peanut farmers, no matter how charismatic or brilliant, would have almost no chance of winning top jobs in Germany unless they had paid a career's worth of party dues." Political writer Roger Simon subtitled his book on 1988 elections, *Road Show*, "In America Anyone Can Become President: It's One of the Risks We Take." He might as well have underlined "Anyone."

Does advertisement help the public know about the candidate better? Not necessarily, because advertisement—mostly twenty- or thirty-second spots or short speeches—is not geared to establish knowledge. It is geared to creating impressions or images in short and repeated bursts of exposure. Political campaigns, which are really a series of advertising spots, add excitement to politics because it is through the campaigns that the public can expect the interplay of events, character, and story. Impressions and images are staged; front-runners slip and dark horses gallop forward; blunders and faults begin to magnify. To avoid or minimize such mistakes, campaign managers carefully package their candidates in the best light possible and show the public what is essentially a packaged reality. Less than two decades ago, such packaging of candidates was considered scandalous. Today it is not only publicly acknowledged, but also made available to the public so that every move made by the candidate and his manager can be anticipated and assessed in advance.

The media experts, the new specialists in image-making, compile their own records of achievements and failures. It is of little or no consequence that they manage the campaigns of one candidate as opposed to another. Their portfolio is that of a businessman, not a political ideologue or believer. Mostly independent of political labels and party affiliations, these experts do their job in selling their candidates. Linda Hasler, the image-maker for a political neophyte, Fob James, in his successful campaign for governor in Alabama, was openly proud of how she accomplished that feat. It is a classic in its genre. In an interview for the *Birmingham News*, this is how she described her triumphant image-making campaign for Fob James.

MONTGOMERY—The problem, Linda Hasler recalled, was finding a house with burglar bars on it. A house that would photograph well, too.

As it turned out, one that fitted the bill belonged to a relative of Fob James in Opelika. And Opelika was where the camera crew was shooting.

"So, we tore down a bunch of wasp nests and started shooting. It came out perfect," Miss Hasler remembered.

"Fob walked up to the door and said something about there being 12 burglaries in that neighborhood during the last three weeks. He knocked on the door. This tiny voice comes back: 'Who is it? '

"He answers, 'It's Fob James.'

Then she opens the door and says louder, 'Fob James! '

"See, we got his name in there twice very early in the spot. I thought it went off very well. He ended it—I thought this was almost too much—looking out of the house through the window, holding on the burglar bars and saying how people shouldn't have to be prisoners in their own home.

"It was good. It went over very good.

"*Of course, we had to shoot it several times to get it right. And Fob had to learn his lines.*"

Miss Hasler is a copywriter for Walker and Associates, the Memphis-based political wiz group which has just added the name of Fob James to their list of victories.

Walker is an old hand at putting unknowns into office. Two years ago, few people in Alabama had heard of Fob James. Most who had thought his name was misspelling "Bob." Walker's mission was to make Fob James a household word in Alabama.

He did just that. And he did it *mostly through the tube* that sits in just about everybody's home.[3]

Some political scientists and pundits have questioned the real "effectiveness" of political ads, especially those on television. But whether political ads work or not is a silly question, for they *do* work. The real question should be *which* ad works and which doesn't. It is answered in the nitty-gritty technicalities of the quality of ads, specific changes in public perception, competition among ads. The effect of campaign ads therefore is best determined if we compare ads with nonads, and it is no contest. Ads *are* effective. Comparing effects *among* various competing ads is irrelevant because they tend to cancel each other out and much of the effect of ads is to "respond" to the other side, leaving only one ad campaign as a "successful" one. All political ads compete against each other, and obviously only *one* series of ads (the winner's) would be considered effective. Of course this is an incorrect way of judging whether campaign ads are effective or not. They all are effective. It just happens that *some are more effective than others, thus determining winners and losers.* Yet there is no doubt that no one can win without ads and their image-manufacturing. In a column only too comically titled "My Media Man Can Beat Your Media Man," Alan Ehrenhalt of *Congressional Quarterly* observes:

Nobody seems to have uncovered a theme in the elections, but everyone seems to agree on how they are going to be won. They are going to be won with television.

To read about any of the nation's dozen or so high-visibility Senate campaigns is to read about media consultants, filming techniques and methods of buying time on the air. In California and Florida, the past few weeks have brought more stories about the candidates' TV strategies than about all other aspects of the campaigns put together.

The preoccupation with the airwaves is understandable. Over the past two decades the role of the media in Senate contests has increased with each election cycle.[4]

"But," laments columnist Tom Wicker, "30-second spots—which make up virtually the whole of many campaigns—convey no more useful or reliable information than, say, one of those commercials in which male-bonded yuppies or superannuated jocks extol the virtues of beer guzzling." In America, of course, all campaigns are designed by the same adman: religious campaigns, don't-drink-and-drive campaigns, political campaigns, campus-visits-during ball-games campaigns, be-honest-and-don't-lie campaigns, read-*Penthouse* campaigns, give-to-the-poor campaigns. God, safety, politics, higher learning, honesty, pornography, charity, and what have you are all the brainchild of the same advertising principle. The electronic evangelist may speak of God and Dr. Ruth of sexual raptures. But when their programs are advertised, God and sexual raptures are promoted exactly in the same way, one campaign being more or less attractive than another. Both God and sexual raptures have to go Madison Avenue and employ the techniques of Advertising 101.

To say that television has altered the very nature of American politics is to say that it has become as important or as *un*important as television itself. People change channels frequently, but they seldom turn the TV off. TV itself, although different channels compete for market shares, is supreme in its position. As such, television no longer follows political action. Political action, rather, is *staged* for the benefit of television. TV is a supreme selling instrument because all things in America happen on TV and virtually nowhere else. It is only natural that politics also takes place on TV. "If TV ads could sell M&Ms," dryly observes Roger Simon in his book about media strategies in the 1988 campaign, "they could also sell a President." It is no exaggeration to say that now everything political is everything about television. But what changes the very character of American politics on television is that it is a medium very different from printed media. Needless to say, television is about pictures, especially pretty pictures. "TV producers are like nymphomaniacs when it comes to visuals," Albert Hunt of the *Wall Street Journal* says. "Television's insatiable need for pretty pictures has cheapened the campaign." Cheapened? Perhaps. But one thing is certain: television has "televisionized" politics, as it has everything else in America. Why not politics? So what *is* televisionized politics? Roger Ails, who was instrumental in George Bush's 1988 TV-inspired victory, defines it as three things: "visuals, attacks, and mistakes." These words describe it in its barest essence. In fact, television presentation had become so essential, especially in Bush's campaign against Dukakis, Roger Ails, Bush's television adviser, was heard *screaming* at the candidate's media rehearsals, "There you go with your fucking hand again. You look like a fucking *pansy!*" Notice that the candidate was still the *vice president* of the United States. But media people are vital. When President Bush visited the U.S. troops in the Gulf at Thanksgiving in 1990, "the network anchors [who accompanied him] created as much stir among the troops as the President himself."

These media experts have naturally become precious commodities both in the United States and now increasingly abroad. The new democracies in Central and Eastern European countries are being flooded with the newest import from America: the campaign consultants. This is how Walter Shapiro described the phenomenon:

America is aggressively exporting political technology and campaign expertise. Whether it is bringing exit polls to the Soviet Union or the first negative spots to Argentine TV, Americans are there—on the ramparts of freedom—trying to turn the world into one vast Super Tuesday primary.

This is one high-tech arena where the Japanese and the West Europeans still cannot compete: America leads the world in the sophisticated techniques of manipulating voters in free elections.[5]

"Should Americans feel elated," asks Shapiro, "if election campaigns from Manila to Moscow become as vacuous as the contest between George Bush and Michael Dukakis? . . . Perhaps the U.S. can survive irrelevant politics and low-turnout elections. But fledgling democracies cannot afford such decadent luxuries." Can even the United States survive such irrelevance and decadence? It is instructive also that Shapiro rates America's ability above Japan's in this all-important field of illusion-making.

Televisionized politics has radically altered the way television covers political news. Kiku Adatto, a Fellow at Harvard, compared the television coverage of two presidential campaigns, 1968 and 1988. Not surprisingly, the 1988 coverage—the most sophisticated state-of-the-art television campaign—was quite different from the 1960 coverage, in the infancy of televisionized politics. In 1968 the networks ran an average footage of over forty-two seconds, showing candidates *speaking* uninterrupted. This fell to less than ten seconds in 1988. By 1988, the "visuals" of the candidates, with no speech accompaniment, had increased by more than 300 percent. In 1968 there was rarely any comment on *how* the campaign was being *staged*, merely 6 percent. In 1988 comments on the background—"the setting and the stagecraft"—constituted 52 percent of coverage. Between 1968 and 1988, television changed politics from political ideas to theater stages, researched and designed by experts like Roger Ails, who was impeccable in his diagnosis: by 1988, politics virtually consisted of visuals, attacks, and mistakes.[6] Dianne Feinstein, who lost the 1990 gubernatorial campaign in California, understood it, too. "Ninety percent of leadership," she said, "is the ability to communicate something that people *want*." Feinstein herself was described thus: "she is *telegenic*, speaks extremely well and *conveys warmth*."

But televisionized politics must compete with other "regular" television programs that are geared to entertain. In this, politics is no competition. No political speech, no political blunder, could match the entertainment value of the regularly scheduled programs. People who watch politics on television see no reason to watch political events unless they are entertaining. It is what people have come to *expect* from television. What is not entertaining is normally kept out of television. It is the Age of the Zapper. "If you couldn't say it in less than 10 seconds," Dukakis, the very victim of that televisionized politics, lamented in retrospect in 1990, "it wasn't heard because it *wasn't aired*." Television is important to most Americans because it amuses them, not because something *important* happens on it. One cannot possibly take seriously what one can zap in an instant with a remote control. Politicians know it; evangelists know it. If God Himself descended upon us with His Second Coming, it is doubtful that it could be announced other than as a media event.

Naturally people lose interest when politics gets boring. True politics is fairly boring. There are only so many visuals, attacks, and mistakes in it. They tune it out and turn to Cosby and Roseanne Barr and football. Michael Oreskes, writing for the N.Y. Times News Service, observes:

American democracy is being undermined by citizens who are so indifferent to national elections that an "astonishing" number of them did not even know who the candidates for vice president were in 1988.

Polls for [a commission studying presidential politics] showed that half the voting-

age public did not know in September 1988 that Sen. Lloyd Bensten of Texas was
the Democratic running mate of Gov. Michael Dukakis of Massachusetts.[7]

"We've got a kind of politics of irrelevance, of obscurantism," said Walter
F. Mondale, unhappily observing the 1990 elections, "that is more prevalent
than in any time I can recall." A cartoon shows the Congress of the United
States standing up, pledging their "allegiance to television." Television has
trivialized, atomized, and paralyzed American politics, concludes Oreskes.
(The perceived role of television is crucial in election outcomes. One reason
the Democrats keep losing presidential elections is that they see television
primarily as a political forum to debate and disseminate political ideas. Their
Republican counterparts simply take it as a means for "selling" a product;
to them, selling a president is no different from selling a product. The
Democrats criticize the Republicans for playing dirty; but the Republicans
simply play *Realpolitik* and win.)
   Politics made irrelevant, the national concern easily shifts to economics.
Oddly calling upon Hegelianism to support this theory, Francis Fukuyama,
a hitherto obscure official at the State Department, even declared, that world
history—which to him meant political history—had ended. Capitalism and
materialism had won. And there was no more politics left to be undertaken.
The remainder of our history would be devoted to fulfilling our material
consumption. Charles Krauthammer, writing for *Time* magazine, agrees.
"The great political debates are over," says Krauthammer. "The romance
with isms, with the secular religions of socialism, egalitarianism and total-
itarianism, is dead . . . Remember that indifference to politics leaves all the
more room for the things that really count: science, art, religion, family
and play." We already know science, art, religion, and family have already
given way to play.

   Essential to political campaigns is, of course, the poll taking. The science
of poll taking, a peculiarly American artifact, has developed to such a level
of sophistication in recent decades that accurate predictions are possible with
little or no error. This art of poll taking, in the words of Jimmy Carter's
former pollster Pat Caddel, is "the driving engine of the campaign." Polls
are taken with the sole aim of manipulating public opinion. Since American
society has lacked both a historical past and an elitist tradition, everything
must be "persuaded" to generate any consensus. The art of persuasion is
nothing but the art of manipulation. One is persuaded only if one "sees"
the point, and there is no point in American politics to see aside from
individual self-interest. Polls help the experts establish strategies for persuasion or, put in another way, find the weakest spot for the voter's self-
interest. It is a matter of strategic contests, neither theoretical nor ideological. Congressman Les Aspin once gloated after a "win" over then defense

secretary Caspar Weinberger, "My strategy worked. We put pressure on Weinberger, and he caved."

But what is this thing called the poll? Simply described, it is a measurement of public opinion on a particular issue at a particular time. Well selected and calculated, the results can project a long-term trend and anticipated outcome with fair accuracy. But we know all that. Yet it is through correct management of poll results that many election campaigns are won or lost. The election outcome itself may not make much difference in the way people go about their daily business. But polls have significant roles in the campaign itself and are interesting in themselves. Several basic assumptions behind them require our careful examination.

The central assumption about poll taking is that people *change* their opinions on issues and things. If such changes did not occur, of course, there would be no need to take polls. We would know exactly what people think about a particular issue without asking. The polls measure how people change their opinions. But people change their opinions only on matters that are *unpredictably changeable*. People do not change their opinion about God, mother, or whatever else remains constant. One's opinion about God tends to remain relatively constant; it is unlikely that one changes one's opinion about Him before one brushes his teeth, after lunch, or during sleep. Such trivial matters as brushing the teeth, eating lunch, or sleeping would have no ramification on how one thinks about God because the matter is too important to change unpredictably.

However, as people think politics *un*important, they also think politicians *insignificant*. Only about insignificant things in life do we change unpredictably. Michael Dukakis, who was the second-most popular man in America behind George Bush at one time, dropped to a nobody within a year. George Bush himself suffered a radical drop in popularity once the Gulf crisis deepened. In February 1990, Bush's approval rating was in the 80s. By the end of 1990, it dropped below 50. What happened? In both Dukakis and Bush, they were exactly *the same* people they had always been. Nothing in them changed appreciatively between their "high" and "low" periods in popularity. *What* or *who* changed, then? Why, of course, the people, the voters, the consumers, the television viewers themselves, who are *expected* to change unpredictably. That's why we take polls. It is the very nature of American society that one rises in popularity for no apparent reason, then one's popularity declines for equally fuzzy reasons. Easy come, easy go. That's the way the game is played in America. The trick is to stay one step ahead of these changes or anticipate them in the nick of time.

But polls work only on things about which people change their minds often and unpredictably and for the strangest of reasons. Political campaigns are some of those things about which people change their minds often, unpredictably, and for the strangest of reasons. This keeps the pollster busy and puzzled. People change their minds about political campaigns only because they care little or nothing about the campaigns. Only because the campaigns are insignificant, little things like an utterance, an expression, a slip of tongue, an image, and so on can make millions of people change their minds. The very fact that polls are valuable in political campaigns shows precisely how unimportant those campaigns are, at least to the public exposed to such poll-taking operations. The polls are no more or no less important than the market research polls that show how many people prefer New Coke to Classic Coke. People switch between political opinions as precariously and unpredictably as they do between New Coke and Classic Coke. The results are just as important or unimportant, depending on one's involvement in the choice. Given this unpredictable fluctuation in election campaigns, calculating how one's political decision would affect the voter's mind is a nerve-wrecking process. When the Senate was considering the controversial William Rehnquist appointment as Chief Justice of the U.S. Supreme Court, David Broder wrote, for example, that many senators *facing reelection* "agonized over the vote and discussed it up to the last minute with their campaign consultants." A principled man would not have done so.

Political campaigns, or political advertisements, are rather similar to those goods and services advertised in an Inverted Economy. A candidate or a product is advertised precisely because no one feels the need for the candidate or the product. The candidate must sell himself as much as the product must sell itself. This selling analogy is fairly common in politics when strategies are discussed. "Marketing Pros Were Key to Bush's Win," the title of a column by Jim Fain says. The pros elected Bush, in Fain's analysis, which is almost universally, even by Bush himself, agreed upon, "on the shoulders of convicted murderer Willie Horton and media adviser Roger Ails." A candidate who is well established through time and reputation needs neither campaign nor advertisement. A candidate with no such establishment may succeed in selling himself to voters through good campaigns. But it is not because the public has realized his qualities, but because his advertising strategy has succeeded. In American society, no one really cares how one gets elected. All candidates must be packaged "commercially," and it is impossible to tell who is and is not a product of successful selling. As we must suspect the real usefulness of a product when it has to be advertised, we must of course immediately be suspicious of a candidate who has to advertise himself.

But, then, that would make politics in America virtually impossible. People know generally next to nothing about their political leaders and would know much less were it not for the media gossips and tidbits that come to their knowledge. Good leaders with strong moral and intellectual character—where they exist at all in America—do not appear in the news or gossip columns, so we know little about them; those about whom we know a great deal through the news media and gossip columns are not those truly deserving of our leadership. Nor is our knowledge about them a true reflection of what they really are. So we come to this agonizing conclusion: without advertising no politics is possible, but with advertising no truth about candidates is possible. Advertising has perhaps made American politics possible in the grand tradition of entertainment, but it is also what has made politics irrelevant in American life.

As the burden of moral judgment in a market system rests on the individual citizen, in a liberal-democratic society the burden also rests on the citizen who controls his own destiny. For if anything is wrong with his government or society, it is essentially his own fault, with no dictator or dictatorial system to blame. This burden is a great one, for the whole validity of liberal democracy is determined by that of the voluntary action of the voter as a citizen. The cornerstone of Western democracy has assumed that the will of the voter is infallible, absolute, and final. But can the voter be *wrong*? If so, what would make him wrong, and wrong in what sense? Whether or not the consensus of a democratic society, spoken through the medium of voting, is a valid decision is indeed a difficult question. It presumes a certain measure of morality imputed into liberal democracy. For, as we have seen, the very idea of democracy itself precludes all argument as to whether the majority can ever be wrong. If the majority can be wrong and is found to be wrong in certain specific instances, what can anyone do about it? Of course, there is nothing anyone can do about it; nor is there any force greater than the majority vote as an actual instrument of policy change just short of revolution. Once the majority has spoken, the will of the people has been expressed. In a democratic society where the "people" govern, we cannot invalidate the will of the people without invalidating the very democratic system itself. Both in theory and in practice, there is no way we can say the majority can be wrong.

But this question can be approached in a different way. We can ask ourselves what sort of circumstances under which democratic decisions are made *can* be considered *wrong*. The "campaign" tactics—the packaging of candidates—can be considered one of these circumstances. We can say the majority consensus achieved under those "market" circumstances cannot possibly be valid, although that's what the majority wants. For democracy cannot be for sale. If the leaders are chosen in any manner other than one considered democratic—through debate and analysis, not packaging—we might say that the result of such processes could be invalid.

There is a concrete way of looking at the issue: that is, by posing a hypothetical question of children being able to vote. Under this hypothesis, let's assume that children could vote and electioneering is in full swing. Political candidates of all stripes would try to persuade the children in the best way they can. The most obvious tactic would be to offer them what they would *like* to be offered. Let's say that one candidate offers them, as incentives, unlimited credit to candy stores, unlimited television watching, easy schoolwork, little or no homework, little or no house chores, and so on, as he articulates things that would appeal to children. No doubt, these offers in exchange for votes would have considerable voter appeal.

Let's say that there is the opposing candidate who, in contrast to the first candidate, proposes a severe limit to candy eating because it's bad for health, equally limited television watching for reasons of poor cultural influence, enlarged and toughened up school curricula and homework, strengthened work programs, and so on. The second candidate would propose these on grounds that his proposals would have profoundly more beneficial consequences in the long run than what his opponent offers, although the latter's would have a more immediate appeal. The election result is already obvious from this simplified contrast. The candidate who promises sweet things—more candy, less schoolwork, and so on—would win by a landslide against the one who only makes things more difficult now, although they may have greater benefits later. The reason for this supposition is simple: children can't think very well. For this simple reason alone no society allows children to vote. Children are children, and you cannot treat them like adults.

But the problem of this hypothesis is that it is *not* altogether hypothetical. It is *real* in American society today. At every election time *we treat adults as if they were children*. So-called campaign strategies naturally assume that all voters are as infantile as children. Candidates promise all sorts of things that have immediate appeals to voters (candy, more television, less school-work, or "Read my lips—no new taxes!") knowing well that they are bad, if kept as promised, in the long run. Voters on their part, knowing full well that what is immediately appealing hurts them in the long run, still accept such ingratiating promises. In other words, candidates in American politics promise childish things and voters accept them *as if* they *were* children. Overestimating voter intelligence is one of the most hazardous practices of American politics; one can never overestimate voter intelligence, even to the point of treating them as children. It was the lesson Michael Dukakis learned—painfully, in defeat. Under these circumstances, we might argue, a majority consensus derived from liberal democracy cannot be valid although the result follows all the requirements of an open democracy. Only those election results derived from *adult* votes—not from children in adults' clothing—should be considered valid.

It is difficult not to conclude that our current democratic system—by virtue of its premises that are invalid—is corrupt and therefore its consequences, however "democratic" in their practices, are also corrupt. If one thinks the term *corruption* is too strong a word to describe our system, one can simply imagine a society where children's votes are solicited by all kinds of unsavory promises to get elected. The election results, regardless of their democratic processes and substance, would be regarded as corrupt by any judgment. The very system of market economy reduces—rather than enhances—our intelligence to the level of primitive responses, as in most commercials on television. The very system of liberal democracy likewise reduces our political instinct to the level of immediate gratification so that no candidate can offer long-term solutions and immediate sacrifice as a way to power. The marketplace and democracy—the twin towers that symbolize our civilization—are thus at the very heart of our stupefying and infantilizing economic and political decision-making. We cannot act or think adult in them.

To say that the voter can be wrong or that the leadership so elected can be corrupt by virtue of the method is actually to say that there is something fundamentally wrong with our prized democratic system. It is in reality a democracy for sale. This is indeed a difficult realization to accept and uphold. It may be as difficult for us to realize our errors about our own system today as it was for the ancients to realize that the earth was not the center of the universe. For us, democracy—and the marketplace—is the only way of social order we know. Geocentrism was the only way of universal order the ancients knew and accepted. In the face of unsettling logic and experience, however, we may yet have to change our minds about democracy, as the ancients had to about geocentrism in their own time. Today in our political practice, candidates promise anything to get elected; in our marketplace, promoters resort to anything to sell their products. Common to both is their essential assumption that we—as voters and consumers—are stupid children. The rules of political games and the marketplace assume simply that there are no rules.

Equality is one of the central concepts in American politics and culture. Americans by and large believe in equality and practice the idea in their actual social relations to a degree that is a source of marvel to foreigners. But upon reflection, we soon realize that the idea of equality in America means, and its practice results in, something quite different. For, in reality, we say equality when we mean *in*equality. When we say we believe in equality, we really mean to say that we believe in equality only if it makes us become *superior*. In a strange way, the form of equality in America rests on the substance of *in*equality. To *believe* in equality is to *practice in*equality. Everyone in America professes to believe in equality, but hardly anyone wants to *stay* equal to everyone else for the rest of his life. "Equality" is, at most, a stepping-stone, from which one passes into a more superior social station and become unequal to everyone. We claim equality so that we can become superior to others and make others inferior to us. Equality in a utopian or socialist sense means—by way of contrast—a state of social relations, perhaps an end in their politically desirable state where everyone can stay equal. But in America this static conception of equality contradicts the very notion of American democracy and marketplace. This is to say

226 WEALTH & POWER

that equality in America is upheld for a wrong reason and pursued for an end contrary to its professed aim.

There is nothing quite like the burden of equality as a source of tension and neurotic anxiety. For no decent American believes in *being* equal in a state of permanent equality with fellow Americans. This means that equality prevents one from *becoming* successful, powerful, or wealthy and consequently superior to all the others. This is so repugnant that this definition of equality itself seems outright un-American. We normally do not show respect for other Americans because of the principle of equality; we do because we must, in view of the power differentials between us. No company president believes in and practices equality toward his subordinates as long as he is president; no subordinate insists on equality with his company president. In spite of what we say in public, first-name-calling included, no one expects to be treated equally when power differences make their relations unequal. In a society with no historical or feudal background, equality in America simply means that *everyone deserves to be what he is and what he is is determined by how much power he has relative to another.*

Since everyone is "created equal," the American mind goes, no one is better than anyone else. This much is all clear. But since everyone is created equal and no one is better (or worse) than another, we all have the same value on each of us. The social value we are all born with—since it is the same for everyone regardless of his social station—nullifies everyone else's value and makes everyone's social value a zero, nothing better, nothing worse. This only leaves, by simple logic, what we have gained through the political and economic struggle as our true value. It is for this simple reason alone that a society notable for social equality—at least rhetorically—is also a place where the fiercest struggle goes on for political dominance and economic superiority. For that is the only difference we can create for ourselves. All men may be created equal, but they certainly do not *stay* equal. Anything one gains makes one superior; anything one loses makes one inferior. Hence the death struggle to become superior in a land where everyone is equal. Every advantage is crucial in one's attempt to escape from equality.

In a land of supposed equality where no one is superior, the only thing that makes one superior to another is what one can demonstrate as one's "difference." One of the ways to achieve that distinction—the bureaucratic version of "conspicuous consumption"—is our curious cultural phenomenon we could call title mania. Since the largely ceremonial and perfunctory raise means very little real difference in one's status symbols, we insist on new titles as a way of political and economic distinction from our fellow-men. "Don't bother with the raise," we say. "Give me a new title." It is the phenomenon of title mania that has transformed everyone into a "director" of something or a "coordinator" of something, street-sweepers into "sanitation engineers," salesmen to "sales representatives," and other such demonstrations of official superiority. As our belief in equality is strong, so is our struggle to *escape* equality. We claim equality until we become equal. After that we struggle to shed the status of average equality. In a society where one would expect paramount satisfaction in being equal to everyone, we find deepest dissatisfaction in the state of being equal.

In America, being condemned to eternal equality would be tantamount to being on social death row. Once on the death row of equality, there is no hope of becoming superior someday with one's ingenuity and dynamic selling job. The psychic tension created by equality is strongest where equality is most evident: in a middle-class neighborhood where every house and lawn looks about like everyone else's house and lawn. This puts tremendous pressure on everyone to best one's neighbors in *some* ways, in some appearance or symbolism, to escape the condemnation of equality. One may drop a hint that one is expecting a big promotion, a big business deal, or a possibility of moving out of the neighborhood and into a better one, and so on. All this has to be done subtly, for, after all, one is surrounded by one's equals where one has no distinct visual advantages that can be demonstrated. Here one's success obviously consists of escaping that indistinction. In a free society, no one deserves to suffer the ignominy of being average. This tension in a typically middle-class neighborhood is made more obvious if we can contrast it with the more relaxed, laid-back, devil-may-care atmosphere of a ghetto or a lower-class neighborhood. There it is assumed that everyone is equal—they all have plenty of nothing—and no one particularly cares to escape that equality.

We sometimes modify our stance on equality by saying that it is the equality of "opportunity." But what is this opportunity? An opportunity to do *what*? Of course, it is one's opportunity to become successful, powerful, and wealthy to escape that dreadful condition known as equality. This is a land of opportunity, we say, which simply means that this is a land where everyone *deserves* to be unequal or superior by his own ingenuity and dynamic business spirit. People who have come to America might have done so with the idea of equality in mind, but as soon as they get here they are easily seized by the peculiarly American fever of inequality. Every immigrant and his sons dream of one day escaping that condemnation of equality. One is not an American if one is equal to other Americans or is condemned to stay equal to other Americans. Being a true American means one has proven to be superior by making it in politics or in business. The kind of humble frame of mind and humility that may be associated with a Jesus or a Lincoln is not the image we now associate with the "equality of opportunity." "Give me an opportunity," we declare, "and I will show you how superior I can be." We want to monopolize the opportunity, not distribute it equally to all. There is nothing more American than this pursuit of inequality.

The frantic struggle to *escape* equality—a condition to which most Americans are unfortunately condemned by the simple fact of political and economic averageness—has given the time-honored tradition of America's majority a new twist. The charming insolence and the spirit of independence that gave the nineteenth-century Americans their peculiar brand of equality are no longer possible in our new economic era. Today we live in a cultural milieu in which our desires and activities have neither shape nor substance. Our thoughts and acts have no definite objective, as they are swayed and influenced by the persuasive voices of the political arena and the marketplace. We are told that we need this and that, we ought to do this and that, and we have the time and money to think and do this and that. But the satisfaction we receive from our material affluence is still uncertain; the satisfaction we receive from our social relations is often unfulfilling. In this cultural landscape of material and social seduction, equality is the final blow that adds to our fanciful flight from reality. Equality makes us a frightened majority even as we flex our muscle in sheer number, for there is little comfort in number. Equal strangers are united by the most fragile thread of accident and chance in a land where that very equality makes any human connections impossible. We can only maintain the most superficial kind of relations with our equals. As a whole, there is nothing that unites the equal majority. Equality thus creates an insecure majority: there is neither a political punch in its number nor economic security in its unity. Equality, in short, has no substance in American society. It is neither public philosophy that rallies people nor a personal belief in human relations. The very theory of liberal democracy and the marketplace—"everybody can make it"—makes the idea of equality impossible to cherish or practice. In substance, it amounts to nothing.

In political practice this equality is expressed through the concept of one man, one vote, or "universal franchise." Not unlike the rhetoric of equality itself, not much is accomplished by this once-noble idea of one man, one vote. For one man, one vote works only if all those who vote are *actually equal in power*. If not, one man, one vote merely maintains the status quo or business as usual, accomplishing little or nothing in the way of substantive political changes. Since every man's equality is nullified by every other man's equality, American society is by logic a society of unequal individuals. This inequality may be corrected by a political measure, giving extra power to a segment of the population where such extra power may make up for its lack of real power. But in an allegedly equal society where everyone is equal to everyone, nothing can ever change. Things in an equal, one man, one vote society remain exactly the same as before no matter how often elections are held and new political leaders elected. Saying that all are equal before the law—the ultimate expression of equality—simply means that poor people and wealthy people would be treated exactly *as they are*: the poor *as* poor and the wealthy *as* wealthy. Since the law refuses to recognize the built-in inequality between poor and wealthy, thereby giving extra consideration to the poor so that genuine equality may be achieved, no real justice is ever attained through this method of equality. As a result, the poor always get arrested, tried, and convicted more often than the wealthy even in the same category of crime.

Equality is thus a double-edged sword: it could help bring about equality in society as easily as it could perpetuate inequality, which already exists. In American society, our claim and practice of equality just about guarantee inequality, for the simple reason that equality is upheld in America so that everyone can be unequal. One man, one vote is upheld so that politics— in which the voting right is exercised—can remain irrelevant as an agent of social change. Equality before the law is upheld so that the wealthy can enjoy the utmost of legal justice while the poor only get legal equality, which means they get what they cannot use wealth to avoid: namely, injustice.

By giving the poor and the wealthy one vote each and the powerful and the powerless one vote each, the whole political exercise is made absolutely meaningless, especially where there is a large middle class that tends to side with the wealthy and powerful. As a rule, in a profit society, the middle class almost always sides with the upper class. In a just society, the middle class almost always sides with the lower class. In American society, "Republicans should not fear class warfare," observed columnist William Safire, himself a Republican, upon the occasion of the 1990 elections, "[because] most of the people in the middle tend to identify with the almost rich, whom they want to become." Like the poor and wealthy before the law, the equal voter comes to his ballot box exactly as he is: the poor on foot, the wealthy in his limousine. The poor goes back to his poverty, the wealthy back to his wealth. The ballot box of equal votes does not change one bit before or after the ballot.

While one man, one vote may not have any appreciable impact on political relations, however, the idea has its own appeal. It is a gift certificate from one's society for which certain value is promised. But there is no intrinsic value in the voting right: it cannot be cashed; it cannot be exchanged for the concrete object; it must be given away to somebody for its value to be realized. This act of giving away one's vote is 100 percent certain, for once given away it is lost for good. But what one receives in exchange is never certain; it is not even certain whether one will receive anything at all. History is against any high expectations of return from votes: no revolution has ever occurred by voting; no power has ever toppled by voting; no dictator or tyrant has ever been ousted by voting; no wealth has ever been given up by voting.

But in a market society nothing is ever given away for nothing. A vote is a commodity that has specific value assigned to it. Its value goes up as the value of the electoral office goes up. Unlike in "banana republics," where votes can be purchased outright for a price, we do not allow any

direct cash value on votes in American society. But judged from the desperate appeals made by political candidates, the voter is certain that his vote
has some significant value in some way. Although there is no cash value
in each vote, there is some value in each vote in other ways, or the candidate
would not be so desperately asking for it. Here comes the good old American way of bargain hunting: every American voter asks the candidate,
"What can you do for *me* in exchange for my vote?" Of course, the candidate
already has a list of things he would do for the voter in exchange for his
vote. All sorts of political and economic promises would be made by the
candidate, and all sorts of promises would be extracted by the voter as the
price of his vote. As long as the vote is wanted by someone, the political
marketplace raises the value of each vote and each voter demands that the
full value of his vote be realized in some form of future returns for his
investment. American politics—a complex series of vote bargain hunting
by both candidate and voter—is therefore determined by the process in
which the candidate can promise anything without actually having to deliver
and the voter can extract the maximum market price for his vote without
actually selling it. Every electoral process becomes a complex crisscross of
promises and extractions, for a promise to one takes away an extraction
from another.

One final, perhaps most important, issue remains among the events,
characters, and stories of the political game. That is the issue of freedom.
What is freedom? What do we make of our insistence on freedom in America? There are basically two kinds of freedom: freedom to inflict injustice
on others and freedom to escape injustice.

The first kind of freedom—unrestrained, individually defined—exists in
a state of nature where one is free to do anything one wishes according to
one's own definition of "wishes." It is unrestrained because natural freedom
cannot be controlled, either by the freedom process itself or by the free
person in dictators and tyrants; it is individually defined because the idea
that others might have the same freedom does not enter into one's own
definition and exercise of freedom. The only way this type of "natural"
freedom can be stopped is if another force equal to or greater than it physically restrains it. The dictator or tyrant must die or be overthrown. He
himself cannot restrain his own power of freedom as long as it remains
free.

The second kind of freedom is what galvanizes revolutions and revolts
and stirs the heartstrings for generations and is the stuff the human spirit
of liberty is made of. In short, it is a freedom to resist the dictator's and
tyrant's freedom. If we call the first kind natural freedom, we might call
this second kind social freedom. This kind of freedom has a specific *social*
objective to achieve, and it is collectively organized to achieve the objective.
Each individual takes part in the undertaking because such collective pulling

of resources is absolutely necessary; one must subordinate one's own interest
to the benefit of the whole in order to achieve it.

What kind of freedom does American society believe in and prefer as its
national commitment and as historical fact? Of course the first kind, the
"natural" kind in which freedom is defined as "everyone doing his thing."
But what is this "thing" that everyone wants to do with his freedom? In
the American society of democracy and the marketplace, *one's freedom is
possible only when someone else's freedom is negated*. It is the freedom of a
dictator or tyrant, not the kind that is shared by all. In any society, one's
freedom is limited by someone else's freedom. Depending on the society's
own ethos, how much freedom one enjoys is defined by how much freedom
for another is constricted. Obviously, not everyone can enjoy 100 percent
freedom, because that leaves zero freedom for everyone else. Very much
like equality, freedom in America is expressed as one's desire to take away
someone else's freedom and add it to one's own. In a democratic and market
society, freedom is like anything else: some have more or less of it than
others. Like equality, our claim that everyone is free in America simply
means that some are freer than others. If everyone is free to do his thing,
then only those who can *afford* to do their "things"—through fair democratic
and market competition—can be free by doing their things.

Doing *one's* thing in society means that someone else is *not* doing *his*
thing. Because everyone in America is free to do his thing, one who has
more freedom—in power, wealth, whatever—can enjoy his freedom more
than another who has less. All freedom has to be expressed in *some* ways—
walking in the park when one wants it, going to Florida on vacation if one
wants it, joining the country club if one wants it, and so on—but that
expression must always contend with the expressions of other freedoms.
Some might want to monopolize the park by buying it up for land development; one might not have enough money to go to Florida because of
one's meager income; the country club leadership might make it difficult
for some citizens to join it. Freedom, unlike its connotation, is not free at
all. Every bit of it has to be fought for and paid for.

So freedom *as* freedom means nothing unless one has the means to enjoy
it. But, alas, the means of freedom—power, wealth—is always in someone
else's hands, at least in the quantity that one wants. As equality in America
results in inequality, freedom for all in America necessarily results in freedom for some and little or none at all for others. The democratic and market
free-for-all society distributes freedom (like equality) rather unevenly
among people who want it. The company president has many times more
freedom than the secretary. Claiming that all are free in America would
not do the secretary one bit of good, because the claim has to be substantiated
in some concrete way. So both the president and the secretary declare that
they are free human beings, in the same way they are created equal. Their
similarity ends right after their declaration of freedom: immediately, the

president goes to his office, the secretary to hers. There, their freedoms differ sharply. In their mutual definition of freedom, the president's is close to 100 percent, the secretary's to zero. Their claim—and America's honoring that claim—that they are free means absolutely nothing. The claim must be honored in reality. It is in this agonizing reality of freedom that as one's freedom increases, someone else's freedom must decline in correct proportion. If one is free, to that very extent someone else is unfree, for we cannot all be free in the "natural" sense of its definition. In a "natural" definition of freedom, freedom for one is none for others. In its "social" definition, on the other hand, freedom for one is freedom for all. It is for this reason that one who believes in freedom in America is often the greatest menace to freedom for all—unless his belief is in freedom for *others*. But that is not normally the objective of a fierce "freedom fighter" in America; one's fight for freedom means fighting the others' freedom.

In America freedom is defined and exercised with one central assumption: that it is possible to *enlarge* one's freedom through the fair politics of liberal democracy and fair competition in the marketplace. Since freedom in America is defined strictly from one's own point of view, one's enlargement of freedom—however fairly obtained—cannot be possible unless one assumes to *take* someone else's freedom. In practice, it is what always happens. One's enlarged freedom means one's enlarged political advantages and economic means. But one cannot have enlarged advantages and means unless someone else's advantages and means shrink in correct proportion. To enjoy freedom in America, all one has to do is go out and get it and in the process take away someone else's freedom. As *enlarging* one's own freedom is an all-American thing to do, so is *taking away* someone else's freedom. One cannot exist without the other. America gives one his freedom by allowing him the freedom to take away someone else's freedom. For one's freedom in America *consists* of the freedom to take away someone else's freedom, which normally takes place in the marketplace. In a society where freedom appears to be more prized than anything else, it is indeed strange to know that freedom, like anything else, is up for grabs, too. Out of all this, some triumph with much freedom and others lose much of it. Thus the supposedly freest society in the world is also one where there is so little sense of security with one's freedom. One pink slip, and freedom crashes.

As an adjunct to freedom we tend to make much of the fact that American society is "open" to social mobility. As it is an open society, no inherent barrier to anyone's making it in America is recognized. Because it is open, all are free to challenge anyone in society. But strangely enough, this open-society concept assures that political and economic rewards will always be denied to some and that some will always get more than others. Open competition, although we prize it highly, does not mean much unless all the contestants are equal in power and means to compete. Here at the starting line we have a person with a motorcycle, a person with one leg, a person with arthritis, a person with small lung capacity, and we tell them they are all free to compete out in the open. It would never occur to anyone that those with handicaps should be spotted some artificial advantages and means so that the contest itself would be fair because then everyone has a chance to win the race. In nature's jungle this handicapping may not be necessary—for, after all, it is a jungle out there. But in society it is necessary because this compensation is what makes humans human and society social. What we presume in America is that because the contest is held fairly—which it is, after a fashion—the *results* are also fair. In this way we expect, when we throw a hundred one-dollar bills randomly at a crowd of a hundred people, that all will end up with a *dollar each*. The fact that the contest is "open" only ensures that the result will always be "closed" according to some predetermined principles of advantages and means. The simple premise that the rewards are held out in the open for all to see and to compete for signifies that they can never be distributed fairly or justly. Never is a thing to be fairly or justly distributed thrown to "open" and "free" contests; it is carefully parceled out.

In an open society everyone has the freedom to climb up to the top floor. Social mobility aimed upward is one of America's entitlements that it allows its citizens. But every upwardly mobile person must be accompanied by someone going down. Everyone's success story is someone's sob story. Doing one's best is always to bring out someone's worst, for "best" and "worst" are always defined relative to someone else's performance. Upward mobility presupposes downward mobility, and this fate of musical chairs creates a chain of human misery in its wake. Avoiding that encounter with Fate or holding it off as long as possible is one of the most agonizing life sagas in American society. What we pride as the most noble feature of life in America is really a chain of human misery visiting all of us sooner or later. The noble intention of open mobility is nothing but the sound of someone crashing downward and the triumphant howl of someone who just pushed him out the window. Closed societies—the Middle Ages, the pre-Gorbachev Soviet Union, the Amish community—may or may not be just, depending on their reasons for being "closed." But an open society—notably the United States, for no other society is as "open" or as "free"—necessarily creates injustice by virtue of its open rewards and rules of competition. To a pack of hungry wolves American society says: here is your meat; just compete according to our rules of democracy and the marketplace. For miraculous reasons of faith and wishful thinking we expect to achieve equality, justice, and freedom with all the hungry wolves and hope to find them in a state of communal sharing with the crippled, the weak, and the young in the pack.

One cannot, of course, discuss freedom without discussing freedom of "choice," an idea so dear to America's traditional heart. But like equality or freedom, freedom of choice is no virtue by itself; it all depends on what the choice exists for. In an age of increasing affluence and varieties of goods in the market we now define this freedom of choice essentially in the range of available choices. But what kind of freedom of choice is there when all the choices are essentially the same? We believe that our range of freedom enlarges when the range of choices is enlarged. But as our choice increases, all that is enlarged is our uncertainty. No matter what we choose, in the end there is still what we *did not* choose. The larger one's choice, the larger one's frustration in one's inability to make a sensible decision. When equally delicious ice creams are presented in thirty-one different flavors and one can choose only one of them, one's inability (hence frustration) increases in corresponding ratio. Often all we want is one good kind we grew up with or are used to. What we have in the marketplace is not freedom of choice but a waste of precious choice-making freedom.

Choice implies that one can think between two or more equally plausible alternatives. The alternatives must be mutually exclusive or contradictory, in the sense that they involve a choice between two or more irreconcilably different alternatives. Thus one's true freedom of choice involves choosing between freedom and slavery, between profit and community, between good and evil, between ice cream and no ice cream, between buying a car and not buying a car, between watching television and not watching television. But we have nicely twisted freedom of choice into a series of trivia involving one flavor of ice cream over another, one kind of car over another, one channel on television over another. These "choices" *seem* to involve freedom of choice, and the exercises are carried out in the ritual of freedom of choice. But in reality, like the rats in a maze, we merely run the predetermined course to the prerecorded music of freedom of choice in the background.

Freedom in the American context begets more freedom, which means those who have the means of freedom only become freer. Those without the means of freedom lose theirs as a result. The enlargement of freedom for the strong always results in the decrease of freedom for the weak. American society—through liberal democracy and the marketplace—protests freedom exactly as it exists. It protects large freedom as well as small. But since it protects all freedoms equally, it always protects the large ones *better*: the powerful institutions and wealthy individuals get their freedom protected much better than the powerless and poor. It is not that American society has a definite design to deprive some people of their freedom. Quite the contrary, it wants to protect everyone's freedom equally, because it is part of America's creed. But because it protects everyone's freedom equally and because freedom is already distributed *un*equally through the political and economic differentials among individuals, it eventually ends up *protecting unequal freedoms equally*. What begins as a noble intention of freedom for all—the president's (freedom) as well as the secretary's (freedom)—ends up protecting the president's freedom 100 times better than the secretary's. What they each have is so unequal to begin with that their equal protection of freedom almost always ends up as protection of the president's freedom over the secretary's. America's defense of freedom therefore *always helps those who are already free against those who are not.*

In American society today the struggle for freedom is really a struggle to dominate, not to escape domination by another. To that extent it is a solitary struggle. The struggle to escape domination is a collective endeavor, binding men and women with a common goal and vision. The struggle to dominate others is nothing short of being, in Hobbes's immortal words, "solitary, poor, nasty, brutish." By expanding one's freedom through power one merely *expands* oneself, rather than *transcending* oneself into the larger community and humanity. By virtue of its freedom through democratic and market practices, which gives a free rein to our self-expanding impulses, American society does its most terrible injustice to the very freedom it cherishes. It is our freedom that enlarges itself *over* others' that our society so cherishes and protects, not our freedom *from* someone else's freedom that is many times larger than our own. It is nature's freedom in a tyrant's hand that is at the heart of America's concept of freedom. It is not society's, which aims at freedom from tyranny. In a real, and certainly ironic, sense, the most freedom-loving society in the world defends the tyranny of democracy and of the marketplace, all in the name of freedom itself. And its defense of freedom ends up being a defense of freedom to do injustice to others. More disturbing still, just ask anyone in pursuit of freedom what he *would do* if he were given *absolute freedom* to do anything he liked. Would he ever list anything that is good for others? Not very likely. In the meantime, he is fiercely pursuing all the freedom he can get. To do exactly *what* with it?

Good or bad, it is the end result of the logic and premise of a democratic market society, which it cannot avoid. For American society upholds nature's (and profit's) right over society's right, creating terrible consequences for its own society.

But what kind of consequences?

NOTES

1. Gregory McDonald, *Fletch and the Man Who* (New York: Warner, 1983), 111.
2. Walter Lippmann, *The Public Philosophy* (New York: New American Library, 1955), 28.
3. Francine Cooper, "How Expert Help Elected Fob James," *Birmingham News*, 23 June 1978.
4. Allan Ehrenhalt, "My Media Man Can Beat Your Media Man," *Congressional Quarterly*, 21 September 1986.
5. Walter Shapiro, "America's Dubious Export," *Time*, 4 September 1989.
6. Kiku Adatto, "The Incredible Shrinking Sound Bite," *New Republic*, 28 May 1990.
7. Michael Oreskes, "Americans Indifferent to Elections, Study Finds," *N.Y. Times*, 15 July 1990.

Part V

The Wages of Sin

Chapter 11

The Pound of Flesh

In taking one final stock of ourselves, let's bypass all the academic history of American society and go straight to George Will, a former political scientist, whose description of America's foundation is accurate and to the point:

The Founders, like [John] Locke before them, wished to tame and domesticate religious passions of the sort that convulsed Europe. They aimed to do so not by establishing religion, but by *establishing a commercial republic—capitalism. They aimed to submerge people's turbulent energies in self-interested pursuit of material comforts.*[1]

America has done well in its pursuit of happiness, as we have seen, beyond the wildest imagination of the Founding Fathers. So well, in fact, that Will himself, normally the most articulate apologist for American materialism, called contemporary America "the sclerotic, its arteries clogged by dumb consumption." During the height of this development in the last decade, Will observed in another context:

For the mass of Americans, a suitable symbol of the decade was the remote control wand for VCRs and cable-equipped television. The American grazed in private in a vast field of frivolous choices, actively choosing which pictorial stimuli passively to absorb.[2]

However, in spite or perhaps *because* of our enormous social and technological development and the kind of material affluence we now enjoy, we find ourselves unkind to each other and unhappy within ourselves. Our psyche seems unable to escape the dark fears that surely must have possessed the long-ago cavemen. In our social relations, we still feel we are in nature's grip, endlessly locked into mortal combat with all. In economics, we act as if we still fear starvation or, more commonly, the inability to provide our basic necessities for ourselves and our children. Would millionaires feel any better? Steven Spielberg, the producer-director of many hit movies, when asked what he thought of his wealth, said that his wealth now meant "security for my family and the certainty that I'll be able to send Max [his 6-month-old son] to a good school." This humble remark about family security and decent education came from a man who was reportedly making as much as *$1 million a day*! In America, where the pursuit of materialism is endless, the wealthy and the not-so-wealthy alike are all fearful. *What* or *whom* are we afraid of? Who are our enemies? *Why* are we still afraid?

In the contemporary United States, the very idea of economic survival has no legitimate basis in reality. No one actually starves to death in America as a matter of economic fact—nobody ought to, at any rate. Yet the fears exist and their existence is as real in our subconscious as their existence is unreal in our economics. The reality of material affluence intersects the unreality of economic fears at every step of our daily lives. We are exhausted by this contradiction, and it affects our social relations with one another in a profound way. We are told that ours is the most affluent society mankind has ever known, yet the fears of economic survival are felt in the deepest veins of our social life. We see the symbols of our affluent civilization all around us in America, yet we are still very much the captives of our cavemen's haunting legacy.

As a metaphor for life, nature's beast is still what describes our individual conduct with one another and our society's character in America. The animal skin-clad barbarian is now roaming Wall Street and Madison Avenue and the marketplace, armed not with spears and stone chips, but with the latest in computers and marketing science and telecommunication networks. Throughout the seeming evolution of mankind, self-interest has remained intact as the vital link between the Western man and his atavistic passions and impulses. Ironically, we have evolved only to become more barbaric and savage with ourselves and with one another.

The most singularly important cause of this morbid irrationality as individuals and as a culture is, in a strange way, deeply rooted in the Western conception of "society." We have viewed society in the West primarily *as an extension, not as a replacement, of nature.* This idea of nature versus society is so central to understanding our present predicament that it would be well for us to pause here to examine the idea in a summary fashion.

We are the only species in the entire animal kingdom that can and has made the transition from nature to society. We have thus attained and maintained around us a world of our own creation—rules, institutions, language, art, love. It is this transition from nature to society that is responsible for our civilization. It is also to this transition that we as individuals owe our capacity for "social" and civil conduct with one another. Often, for individuals as well as nations, this remains only a capacity, not reality. In a market society like ours, what passes for "society" is little more than an elaborate version of "nature." Consequently, the rules, institutions, language, art, love, and what have you as symbols of that nature-to-society transition end up being nature's rules, nature's institutions, and so on, having nothing to do with society and civilization.

This fundamental flaw in Western philosophy can be gleaned in our time-honored definition of human beings as "free and rational persons concerned to further their own interests." These words are from Professor John Rawls's well-known book on justice. They also summarize the classic notion of human nature in society as expressed by most Western thinkers from Locke to Kant, from Rousseau to Jefferson. The image of (Western) man, solitary and self-centered in fortune and power hunting, is not terribly difficult to visualize, nor does it require much historical examination to validate. *We* are the "free and rational persons" trying to "further their own interests." This definition forms the very essence of Western culture, its basic thesis of human nature, and its practical scheme of life. It is also the core of American society in its political philosophy as well as its economic strategy. The idea is simple. Individuals have formed their society so that they can *better* advance their self-interests. Neither deliberate economic callousness nor a devastating destruction of social relations is intended in this assumption. The catastrophic consequences we experience today as a result of the assumption, however, stem from our forefathers' inability to separate society from nature decisively and radically. Under ideal circumstances this is how it has happened.

Let us assume that 100 free and rational individuals concerned with self-interests, but tired and fearful of the lawlessness of nature in which no one is safe from one another, decide to form a society. For their collective existence they agree on a certain format: democratic form, representative principle, majority rule, and so on. Notice that these rules of governance would be scrupulously observed: elections would be regularly held; the state would administer justice according to the rules; violators would be punished. But also notice that depending on who has a louder voice, displays stronger or more intimidating muscles, or commands a more sophisticated argument and so on, the rules of society in this free and rational community of men are established of necessity *in favor of* those who would benefit from them most. Remember, they are all interested in the same thing, necessarily against one another. Their freedom and rationality—so dear to the Western heart—are thus their freedom and rationality to pursue their self-interests, not those of their collective agreement. By definition, a society of men is collective, as an alternative to solitary existence in nature. But since all members are free and rational *only* as regards their self-interests they simply fail to realize this fundamental flaw in their collective community known as society. Their freedom and rationality only serve *them*, not their society.

Consequently the society's two most important assets in economic wealth and political power, often in the same person, become subject to fierce competition among the free and rational individuals. Few win; many lose. Others in between facilitate and philosophize the difference. In this way, although the 100 free and rational men freely and rationally decide and devise to establish a society—presumably to get away from their former state of savage nature—*their "society" remains nothing but an extension of their previous state of natural war*. Form has changed, but not substance. The celebrated freedom and rationality of the West, when subordinated to the pursuit of self-interest, cannot possibly avoid a return to the state of savage nature. Hard as they may try, the 100 men cannot escape the circle of violence common in nature, which they claim to have replaced with a "human" community.

Such has been the state of human society in the West in the last two centuries or so of its cultural and technological development. Thanks to our increasing arsenal, a perfectly free and rational society is only more savage now than before. Elaborately facilitated and philosophized, this is the image of what Professor Rawls and others before him have blithely called a *just society*.

These first 100 men are not exactly a hypothetical case, however. They are the Founding Fathers of the United States. As a rare historical case, American "society" was formed after due deliberation by the "first 100 men." (Their deliberation is recorded in *The Federalist Papers*.) What we now have is what these men assumed to be the very idea of society, of human nature, and of the role of freedom and rationality in the pursuit of happiness. Their formula for society was by no means unusual, given the philosophical and intellectual climate of the time. As a reaction to the Middle Ages, which they had just destroyed, it was only natural. Much chest-beating self-congratulation was followed by the inevitable conclusion that it was about time for all good men to come to their self-interests, for a change. No more self-denial or ascetic godliness; no more suppression of sensory pleasure; no more glorification of poverty and chastity and salvation. The reward of life had to be here and now. Man was by nature selfish, and American society would symbolize that very essence in freedom and rationality as its first real historical experiment or, in Seymour Martin Lipset's term, as "The First New Nation." Self-interest—now under "free enterprise," "marketplace," "the invisible hand of demand and supply," "individualism," what have you—would become its national creed. The American pioneer "left political civilization," observed Hans Morgenthau on the origin of American social character in his book, *The Purpose of American Politics*, "and restored that state of nature" in the New World.[3]

Ironically, however, the New World was not really new. It was the *oldest*—and consequently crudest and cruelest—of all worlds. Thus the crucial decision was made, and this conception of man and society determined our way of life with one another then, now, and beyond.

Our historical association with "nature," "natural society," "natural man," "nature's God," and so on is expressed essentially in two contradictory terms. In one view nature is nasty and cruel (Hobbes, Kant); in the other, benign and innocent (Rousseau, Jefferson). Which is the truer nature of nature? Can both aspects of nature be true at the same time? The answer to the second question is yes, which also answers the first. The seemingly contradictory observations we hold of nature (Rousseau saw it both ways) really refer to two different *levels* of nature: one beneath the surface and the other on the surface. Any natural setting would do to verify this. On the surface everything is idyllic. Birds and insects, lizards and mammals, flowers and vines, all live in perfect harmony. Beneath this surface, however, a savage struggle goes on. Because the savage struggle goes on beneath the surface, the surface itself maintains its orderly and peaceful appearance. But the savage struggle knows of no mercy: a lion attacks and kills a baby zebra; a predatory bird devours the innards of an infant turtle sea-bound in its desperate struggle for survival; a golden mole burrows in the sand to catch and feast on a lizard; a coyote hunts down a gopher in the snow and tears into it.

It takes no great imagination to superimpose this "true state of nature" beneath the surface upon our market society. The characteristics of our marketplace and the actions of our market men are fairly close to the descriptions of savage struggle given above. When a man is contemplating the takeover of a vulnerable company and is planning strategies appropriate to the task, is he any different in his thought and action from the predators of nature? When a market man is in fierce competition against another market man for survival, can he possibly think and act in any way outside the state of nature? Would his savage struggle be any less savage? When an employee is given a pink slip from his employer, is his desperate fear any different from that of a cornered animal in nature's savagery?

The true state of nature and that of market society are remarkably similar, and their similarities are not coincidental. Our Founding Fathers in their infinite wisdom in freedom and rationality designed our society in the image of nature. Let us retrace the similarities so that our stock taking completes its accurate though painful self-portrayal, if not self-atonement. The similarities converge on these concepts: power, deception, violence, and solitary existence.

Both nature and the marketplace operate on the assumption of "natural power." Any means of self-defense is justified in the name of survival—or profit—and the powerful do all the justifying. In both places, power relations are beyond dispute: the frog cannot argue against the lion any more than the poor against the wealthy or the powerless against the powerful. Neither the lion nor the wealthy and powerful feel the compulsion to explain their action. Their being wealthy and powerful *is* all the explanation necessary. In nature, size, strength, and cunning naturally endowed is the final word; in the marketplace, it is the size of one's wealth, the strength of one's drive, and the cunning of one's strategy. In both, neither the need nor the capacity for sympathy toward their victims is appropriate.

Deception is a cardinal virtue of exploit both in nature and at the marketplace. Both the beasts in nature and the market men are efficient with their tactics of deception—a chameleon, an adman—to lure, in the immortal words of Lincoln Savings & Loan's instruction to salesmen, "the weak, meek, and ignorant." No trickery is too tricky and no deception too deceptive. In this battle of deception, an animal would make itself colorful and attractive to lure its prey; a market man would deploy all the charms, all the advanced research techniques, to persuade his victim-consumer. To be successful with the art of deception, one must appear to be harmless, trustworthy, and concerned. Genetic selections help the beasts; colleges and experts help the market men.

Both nature and the marketplace are the worlds of violence, one literal and the other metaphorical. Neither makes concession to what might be called civility, the ability for sympathy toward fellow creatures. Civility is essentially a learned, human attribute, which is found neither in nature nor in the marketplace. Every move, every act, every plan, every ounce of energy must be enlisted in annihilating one's adversary. As always, it is victory or death. It is the ultimate game of survival, where winning and losing can be a matter of slightest chance. There can be no rest in their soul, neither the beast nor the market man. They must sleep with their eyes open, arms at the ready for the unseen enemy.

It is a solitary existence for both, the beast in nature and the market man in his market. The beast frolicking with its offspring and the market man enjoying an afternoon with his family are just the surface appearance of peace, taking place only between savage episodes of warfare. Their lives are those of hunter and hunted, one minute the hunter and the next the hunted. Both creatures stand essentially alone both in time and in space, the beast by nature and the market man by socialization. In time, neither recognizes forefathers or children; in space, neither is aware of others around them as a form of community and society. Alone, they are in a permanent state of war against one another. Alone, they see nothing but prey and predators, an opportunity to exploit and a danger to avoid. It is ultimate, solitary life at its starkest.

As if to sum up the similarities between the true state of nature and our own marketplace, I have a real picture before me. It is a photograph taken at the New York Mercantile Exchange. The photograph shows a state of great agitation at the stock exchange. Oil prices had just nose-dived. A dozen or so men are raising their hands, frantically calling out their buy-and-sell orders. The faces are contorted with the menace of their tasks and the terror of their decisions. They are human faces for sure, for they have the appearance of human faces, with eyes, noses, and mouths. But upon closer inspection, after the photo has been enlarged on a copy machine, their expressions magnify the anguish, desperation, kill-or-be-killed frenzy. The whole fearful symbolism at the stock exchange reveals little or nothing that I could consider "human" or "civil." Are these men human beings like the rest of us, or are they back with their cavemen ancestors who killed or survived, but only in our modern garb and with our modern technological metamorphosis? Do they have families, friends, lovers? Do they manage to regain a semblance of humanity after the stock exchange closes? How do they act when they go home? Do they turn into human beings and act "normal" with their loved ones? That is, until the stock exchange opens again the next day?

In a metaphorical sense, this photograph can be preserved for posterity as the frozen-moment representation of the marketplace in America. It can also be preserved as a pathetic reminder of how little progress we have made from the cave in the last twenty thousand years or so of our evolution. Or it can simply be the triumphant, victorious display of conquest by the Profit Ethic over the vanquished Social Ethic. Or, still, it can be a reminder that we have reversed our civilization and returned to our hunting-and-gathering means of survival: hunting for our victims and gathering our profits.

The development of technology tends to confuse us more often simply because of its more obvious sophistication in appearance. The level of sophistication involved in an intercontinental missile or a video-game machine is obviously more captivating than the spear killing and marble games that our cave ancestors possessed. But this appearance is highly deceiving, for the purposes for which we have developed the intercontinental missile (killing) and the video game (amusement) have not evolved to any higher level since the spear and the marble. As our ancestors spent their days killing their foes and amusing themselves, we still spend our days today doing the same thing with the uses of technology. However, now the killing and amusement have nicely been dovetailed with profit-making. Technology has made us more effective with our killing techniques and more efficient with our amusing acts.

Civilization develops through society and is manifest in two concrete ways. It first establishes an elaborate system of social institutions. What used to be a simple one-man or one-group centered mode of operation becomes a complex social system in which many different institutions are assigned different functions. Ordinarily, one measure of civilization in a given society can be seen in the elaboration of such institutional arrangements. The more complex the arrangements, generally, the higher the evolution of civilization in that society. American society qualifies to be a higher civilized system on this point, for its institutional complexity is unsurpassed.

The civilized society also develops—and this is where American society badly flunks—"social behavior" appropriate to the level of its civilization. By social behavior we obviously mean certain behavior traits we would normally call civilized. We would expect the civilized man to act according to some predictable, not arbitrary, standards; we would expect him to act with a view to benefit the whole, not self-interest; we would expect him to display a healthy respect for the spiritual, artistic, and profound in meaning, not the physical, sensuous, and immediate; and finally, we would expect him to be prudent with the uses of natural as well as social resources and bounties, not capricious with their uses. These social behavior traits—if they sound familiar—are the standards of the Social Ethic with which we began our analysis in this book. Those were the traits with which we separated the Social Ethic from the Profit Ethic. It is on this second point of civilization that contemporary American society reveals its essentially "uncivilized" or even "regressive" state of existence. It is in the absence of those behavior traits that define civilized man and civil society that we can clearly describe America's market society and its enormous troubles.

Self-interest is one single most important trait that separates the beast in nature and the market man on one side and civilized human beings on the other. Emphasis or rejection of self-interest as a standard of behavior divides the Profit Ethic from the Social Ethic and individual warfare from collective welfare. Historically in any given society or era, the "good" citizens, the "decent" human beings, or whoever deserved such accolades from their community were those who gave part of themselves to others, those who sacrificed their self-interest for the benefit of the whole, and those who risked their lives and fortunes to help others. Even in American society, where money success has been a fairly accurate measure of public esteem, such good and decent individuals have always been recognized and their deeds appreciated. Even to the time of World War II selflessness was a quintessential ingredient in American social ethics. Governments of various levels could rely on at least a modicum of public display of selflessness. The idea of civic obligations—though never overshadowing the great American pursuit of rights—was never too far from the core of America's social character.

What has surprised many observers of America society in the last several decades has been the robust and assertive emergence of self-interest as the almost sole representative America value. In our daily subconscious as well as in national political themes, in cultural anecdotes as well as refined legal structures, in the images of heroes and villains as well as children's tales and moral lessons, self-interest has overshadowed all other values in our market society. Self-interest has become so dominant in our Inverted Economy that now to say anything uncomplimentary about it may be taken as positively un-American or as a sore loser's complaint. We just *assume* everyone is selfish. What was in the beginning an explanation for the economic exchange at the marketplace by Adam Smith is now the driving force of the biggest economic machine the world has ever seen. It is also the cultural obsession of the whole society, whose intensity and magnitude easily surpass even the hitherto fanatically committed religious or political demagoguery. A moralist or a social critic may dispute all that is dear to America's heart, but he dare not dispute self-interest. It is where all diverse religious conflicts, all political differences, and all intellectual theories of human behavior converge in perfect unity. It is where all subcultures, all ethic diversities, all social classes come into perfect harmony. It is one single notion on which virtually all Americans can agree. It is the battle cry with which we go about our daily hunting and gathering in the marketplace. And it is Darwin's progress to the drumbeat of Adam Smith. Yes, we are all selfish and we are proud of it. Those who lament it for one reason or another must now pick up the pieces at the marketplace. But what pieces?

Casualties of self-interest litter the great expanse of American society. It destroys families; it unbinds human bonds; it makes interpersonal relations difficult to maintain; it makes personal loyalty meaningless; it makes friendships rare and transient; it makes religion and all that it implies irrelevant; it fulfills our lives with emptiness; it is responsible for our public corruption in high places; it makes everyone distrust everyone. The list is endless. How does self-interest create all these social and human malaises in American society? How exactly does self-interest manage to undo the basic fabric of society, undermining the furthest corners of personal as well as public well-being? For the sake of simplicity, I give my preliminary statement here: *self-interest makes a just and truthful life impossible in America.* Once this conclusion has been stated, we can now go about finding out just how such a conclusion is possible.

What is justice? What is truth? Let's define the two concepts in a way that is more manageable so that we can avoid all the metaphysical pitfalls that such concepts normally invite. Let me put it this way: *justice is selflessness in action and truth is selflessness in thought.* Justice results in human action and truth in human thought, to the extent that we are free from self-interest. People who are thoroughly selfless are never too far from achieving justice in their action and truth in their thought no matter what they do or say. Who are they? They are in three main groups: (1) those who are altruistic: saints, artists, martyrs; (2) those who have nothing to lose: death row inmates, the terminally ill, the hopelessly impoverished; and (3) those who are incapable of formulating self-interest: children, the insane, the "primitive." If self-interest unites us in the marketplace, selflessness also unites us in justice and truth. Justice is what we *think* without our self-interest; truth is what we *say* without our self-interest. Conversely, a person with much to lose—meaning much self-interest—can rarely attain justice in his action and truth in his thought. The ability thus for a just and truthful life in individuals and in society as a whole is inversely related to the presence of self-interest. The powerful and the wealthy, therefore, find it almost impossible to do justice and speak the truth, no matter how hard they try. Where there is no self-interest, justice and truth naturally prevail. Where self-interest prevails, on the other hand, only injustice and untruth are produced by individuals and society. Self-interest destroys American society by destroying our very ability to act just and speak truthfully with one another.

What is a "just man"? One whose thought is free of his self-interest as he speaks his mind. Since selflessness is possible only in a human society— for there is no such thing as conscious self-sacrifice in nature—the very idea of justice and truth is made possible also only in a *human society*. The distance between self-interest and selflessness is the simplest measure of the individual's and the society's capacity for a just and truthful life.

Self-interest, in spite of its economic function in our culture, is a heavy burden. As a force of individual motive, it never sleeps, rests, or diverts; it is always there, to overwhelm our action and thought with its relentless force. As a mechanism of social relations, it constantly comes into conflict with others' self-interests; as a result, it creates nerve-wrecking tension in our human relationships and demands a bone-wearying struggle for dominance and manipulation. As a social guideline for individual conduct, it causes an endless war in each soul between selfishness and his sense of moral decency; no human being is without some notion of right and wrong, and in his struggle to define right and wrong he finds it irresistible and overpowering.

From a purely theoretical point of view, self-interest also proves to be a bad idea. In nature, one's survival does not necessarily depend on another person. But in society, no one can survive alone without others who make up the whole of his community. Even in the most primitive and simple social system, a society survives because everyone does something to make the survival and comfort of the whole possible. In countless ways, everyone's social life is involved in a tangled web of interdependency with everyone else's. In nature, one's space is unconnected with another's. In society, however, one's space is connected to everyone else's to form a cultural and psychological whole as well as a territorial boundary of community and nation-state. In nature, one's failure to survive does not affect the ability of another to survive. In society, one's success and failure are intimately tied in ever-widening ripples of falling dominoes. In society, no man is an island.

Intellectually, self-interest shrinks one's world into the narrowest sphere of the here and now. One cannot think of anything outside his bodily occupation; there are no other societies, no cultures and human beings but himself. He shows no interest in events anywhere in the world unless they are somehow related to him directly or amusing enough. It is impossible for him to grasp the very meaning of "other worlds" outside his own. At the same time, his attention span shrinks as well. He becomes a "one-minute thinker." There is only one minute for eating (junk food, microwave dishes), one minute for love (sex), one minute for God (salvation without pain, TV religion), one-minute persuasion (images, commercials), one-minute patriotism (Olympics, "Rambo," flag-waving), one-minute communication ("reach out and touch someone," Hallmark verses), one-minute parenting (experts, "quality time"), and so on into an infinite variety of American ingenuity for illusion and substitution.

Self-interest also destroys interpersonal, communal, and international peace. Disputes and conflicts occur when two unyielding sets of self-interests collide, neither side, by the weight of its self-interested commitment, willing to give. All disputes and conflicts that we have ever known, it might be said, are caused by self-interest. Conversely, there can be no disputes or conflicts that cannot be resolved once the parties involved can overcome their self-interests. On the interpersonal level, self-interest is responsible for individual stress and marital breakups; on the community level, it causes group prejudice and regionalism; on the international level, unbridled nationalism and ideological interests lead to global tension and war. More felt than seen, self-interest causes social distress on the job, at home, and in random encounters. Our response to the self-interest of others is also in kind: mutual suspicion, distrust, and alienation. Self-interest may be the fuel that fires our economic machines and pumps our individual adrenaline in the economic battle, as it is believed in America. But it may also be that most human ills today have their singular genesis in that powerful force in all of us called self-interest.

Wealth and power naturally corrupt because of their inherent tendency to defend their self-interest against their foes. Because of this tendency justice is always impossible in any self-defensible power. Self-interest makes truth impossible in a similar way. A person facing the possibility of gaining or losing something dear to him must weigh his thought according to the calculus of gaining and losing. This "rational thinking" is what modern economists count on as their "economic model." So, from a rational, economic point of view, he weighs his gains and losses as possible consequences of his decision. But, obviously, no rational, economic person who is thinking about his self-interest can think about truth, disregarding his possible gains and losses. Thus economic gains make truth absolutely impossible.

The inability to pursue truth because of self-interest does not end with the simple absence of truth. As inevitably as the two sides of a coin, the absence of truth is always accompanied by the abundance of lies. A culture of self-interest is also a culture of liars, for self-interest makes a liar out of any otherwise decent human being. Deliberately or subconsciously, our inability to speak truth makes us habitual liars. In the face of self-interest people find it impossible to tell the truth, for telling the truth may result in the loss of a promotion, a raise, a job, a profit, a favor, a vote, a power base, self-esteem, or whatever. In a culture of self-interest, everyone learns quickly that truth hurts. Thus lying increases as one's self-interest increases and self-interest increases as one's economic success increases. A man who is in a position of importance—therefore greater self-interest at stake—lies much more than a man whose station in society is negligible. The company president tends to lie big, while his secretary may lie small, all according to their proportional self-interest to protect.

As one climbs up the ladder of success, as one's self-interest increases in economic dimension and social significance, his need to lie increases correspondingly. By the time he reaches the pinnacle of success—say, becoming a corporate president, a high government official, or an elected politician—lying has become his way of life as a habitual defense of his self-interest. We, by cultural prejudice and ignorance, tend to view lying as basically a lower-class phenomenon in which the poor and wretched would do anything for a buck. But their lying, where that exists, is kid stuff in contrast to the big-time lies that the more successful of our society commit without thinking twice. Between these two classes, just about everyone lies in America for no other reason than there is something to protect by lying. We lie as workers, as taxpayers, as neighbors, as lovers, and even as strangers, as long as there is self-interest to protect.

The very nemesis of lying—the act of "whistle-blowing"—sometimes materializes in America. Whatever his motive for blowing the whistle on his employer or his institution may be, the whistle-blower's life is not likely to be a happy one. Sooner or later, the whistle-blower gets the ax for violating one of the most sacred trusts in American life: lying for the company. Everyone hates a smart aleck, but everyone hates the morally superior more. How much self-interest is actually involved, or how much real reward there is for lying matters little, because it is the mind-set that has become an American ritual.

Not surprisingly, then, lying has become not only a respectable but a highly lucrative profession in American society. Those who specialize in lying for the company—"public-relations" specialists—now go to college and study the subject with utter seriousness and in great depth. Every institution—large and small—has a person in charge of lying for the organization. He is generally a good-looking man with all the physical attributes for a quick impression that favors him; he speaks smoothly and dresses appropriately for the purpose of the lying business; he has mastered all the necessary techniques of lying for his institution that are in his college curriculum and also gathered from his practical experience and expert consultation. Normally the public-relations man is a type—one who is believable by virtue of his image and style more than anything else—whose personal virtues are in no way in abundant evidence. His trade is to lie convincingly so that the public believes him. In this sense, the public-relations man always lies twice whenever his lies for his company: once for himself because he must survive in his job capacity and for his other more immediate self-interests and once for his company because lying for the company is his job. Someone said a diplomat is an honest man who lies for his country. We might say that a public-relations man is a *dis*honest man who lies for himself and his company. Of course, all this should apply equally to public-relations women.

As a cultural by-product, self-interest is also responsible for creating and maintaining huge quantities of "stupidity" in America. The more involved we become with our self-interest, the more we tend to become stupid. Stupidity has its vital function in the American economy, in its chain of demand and supply and consumption. But what are its functions in American "society"? Let's first define what stupidity is and then understand why stupidity increases in correct proportion to the increase in self-interest.

We have seen that advertisers by habit rely heavily on one of our consistent public qualities: that is, stupidity. Anyone who watches any commercial on television would have to agree that the underlying assumption has to be that the public is stupid or else that sort of commercial couldn't possibly enter the adman's mind. But let's understand stupidity first by contrasting it with ignorance, with which it is often confused, for ignorance and stupidity are by no means the same thing.

Ignorance is a state of lacking knowledge about certain things; it is specific, to the point. If a man falls through a manhole because he didn't know about its existence, that is ignorance. You can fool an ignorant person but once, because once fooled, the person is then equipped with the necessary knowledge. The cure for ignorance is simply an adequate supply of knowledge. Realizing the existence of the manhole, of course, one will not fall through the same manhole again. It is one mistake at a time, proportional to the amount of knowledge that is lacking. To varying extents we are all ignorant of certain facts, but that does not necessarily render us helpless to those who wish to take advantage of our ignorance. In most issues of life we can get by with what we already know. Life may be viewed as a series of mistakes, but with the new knowledge gained through each mistake we become wiser for each mistake we make. Ignorance may not exactly be bliss, but it is not as catastrophic as many people tend to think.

Stupidity is different from ignorance. In fact, there is no causal relation between the two at all—that is, ignorance causing stupidity or vice versa. For while ignorance is caused by lack of knowledge, stupidity is caused by self-interest. It is therefore largely a matter of attitude, quite unrelated to knowledge or ignorance. Self-interest makes one so blind that he cannot see anything clearly. He may have an abundance of facts at his disposal; he may even possess a Ph.D. in some sophisticated field. But he is stupid, for stupidity has nothing to do with knowledge or lack of it. Stupidity is caused by self-interest. Because of this self-interest at the core of stupidity, a stupid person basically never learns from his mistakes and, consequently, he remains vulnerable to the same process. It is mainly for this reason that you can't fool an honest man, at least not twice. One is subject to repetitious stupid decisions and thoughts as long as self-interest is his motive for being. Obviously there is no cure for stupidity as there is basically no cure for self-interest, either for the individual or for his society as a whole. You can send a man to college and give him the highest academic honor there is to give; he will still be bound by self-interest and continue to display his stupidity. The whole of a self-interest-oriented society contributes to his perpetuation of stupidity.

As a company liar always lies twice, once for himself and once for his company, a stupid person cannot display his stupidity in one single episode at a time. In this sense ignorance has its decisive virtues over stupidity. Stupidity is always compounded in its effects because of its unique constitution. *When one is stupid or motivated by self-interest, he is stupid in everything he does.* No part of his life is immune from such self-interested, stupid premises. If he is stupid in economic actions, he is also stupid in interpersonal relations, in political decisions, in intellectual judgments, in aesthetic appraisals, in daily human responses. If he is stupid at his office, he is also stupid at home, among friends, neighbors, and coworkers, to strangers, and as a citizen. In stupidity and self-interest there is no such thing as stupid just once or selfish just once. Once conditioned to be stupid and selfish, one is always stupid and always selfish. One's action and thought in self-interest multiply human errors in everything one does. Thus the market man of self-interest is the stupidest lot among all and his society the stupidest of all societies.

Notice also that ignorance has to do with *material* facts. It relates to something concrete in our day-to-day material life. If a man learns the existence of a manhole where he did not expect it, the experience teaches him once and for all that there *is* a manhole there. Or if he learns that one particular store tends to overcharge him for the same goods and services, he will stop patronizing that store. To ignorant adults and even children, given the innate capacity for a modicum of learning, factual lessons can easily be taught. Such is the very nature of ignorance.

But stupidity applies mostly to *social* situations—that is, human relations. It is therefore faulty reasoning in regard to social ethics, moral values, political ideas, truth and justice, good and evil, pleasure and happiness. Normally, an excellent market man may be a stupid husband, neighbor, friend, or citizen. Once stupid, it is difficult to teach him anything different. The reason for the difficulty of teaching a stupid person, in contrast to an ignorant one, is in the simple fact that it is not material knowledge. The stupid person cannot learn anything that cannot be spelled out or demonstrated in material terms. But social situations and human relations consist of *ideas*, not things, and therefore cannot be spelled out or demonstrated so that a child can learn. Virtually anyone can learn material facts; not everyone can easily learn moral lessons, which normally requires a totally concerted effort by the whole social system.

Naturally, there is an important psychological distinction between ignorance and stupidity as well. Ignorance makes one feel intensely uncomfortable, proportionally to the amount of his ignorance. This discomfort compels one to seek appropriate knowledge to overcome one's ignorance. Ignorance, in other words, is often the springboard of action in pursuit of knowledge. It reaches for solutions and new awarenesses. Stupidity, on the other hand, has exactly the opposite psychological quality: *it makes the stupid person feel immensely comfortable with his own stupidity*. The stupid man is fairly proud of his state of stupidity, and hence he makes no move to correct it. (It is for this reason that teachers much prefer the ignorant to the stupid.) Being stupid is quite similar to mental depression or the state of stupor in alcohol or drugs. Like depression, alcohol, or drugs, and unlike ignorance, stupidity creates a sense of euphoria, a state of contentment with one's whole being. For stupidity—or its origin in self-interest—itself makes any objective judgment about oneself impossible. Being stupid, one feels no compulsion to improve oneself, examine one's beliefs, or consider other alternative actions and thoughts. If ignorance compels one to action, stupidity compels one to *inaction*. In stupidity, one is totally happy with his state of stupidity, not unlike the depressed with their depression. It is because of this self-comfort that a stupid person cannot stand criticisms; he is just too proud of his stupidity. This inability to open itself to self-criticism is also true with a stupid society—except on a much larger scale of course.

Since stupidity is unrelated to knowledge or lack of it, it is found in everyone who is driven by self-interest: from presidents of the United States, college professors, judges, doctors, and lawyers to bricklayers, secretaries, bakers, and ditchdiggers. As we have seen in the case of lying above, however, the extent of stupidity tends to decrease as we move down the ladder of success. Stupidity decreases as we move down the social scale and increases as we reverse back up the classes in correct proportion to the amount of self-interest embodied in different social classes and successes.

But self-interest and its stupidity have their cardinal virtues in a market society that needs its stupid consumers. As the consumer insists upon his self-indulgence, the marketplace insists upon the consumer as king. But it is largely a king who, in his mighty ability to consume, cares little about the consequences of his own consumption. With the marketplace willing and able to furnish him with all the objects of his largely childish—not to say stupid—demand and beyond, the king eventually succumbs to the intentions of the market mechanism. The marketplace is satisfied only when the consumer-king goes through the cycles of convulsive overstuffing as predicted by his stupid nature. Among its more impressive accomplishments, this very ability of market society to goad a stupid human weakness into the meanest kind of self-destruction may stand above all else.

What our final stock-taking gives us is not a pretty sight to see. In the absence of justice and truth on the most fundamental level, distrust among Americans has steadily increased. Not just those specialized in high finances and politics, but virtually everyone suspects everyone else of undercutting and treachery; everyone sues everyone for the slightest of personal inconveniences and economic advantages; every adult is assumed to be a menace to a nearby child; every male is a potential rapist for every female; every employee must pass a urine test for possible drug abuse and its consequent moral compromise. Corruption of the mind is natural to all this. Self-interest isolates the individual in his solitude, solitude creates demand for self-pleasure, and self-pleasure is the inevitable first step toward corruption. Money, title, fame, tangible and intangible rewards, whatever, will do the job as long as the price is right. Everyone has his price and, after this principle is agreed on, all we have to do is find the right price to buy and to be bought.

The oft heard comment that America is turning into an "urban jungle" is especially poignant to us now that we know whence that "jungle" comes. Home security is a multibillion-dollar business, protecting everyone from one another on our own home front. Consider the following description of American *society*:

In Phoenix, metal lawn signs in front of homes warn burglars that gun-wielding guards will greet them if they enter. In Cleveland, a school for canines turns tail-wagging family pooches into snarling guard dogs. In Los Angeles, uniformed attendants at a bunker-like command post study screens and consoles day and night, watching for signs of home break-ins. When an alarm goes off, they lift a red telephone to summon police, or bark out a microphone command that dispatches members of their own gun toting security force.[4]

The fear and anxiety one can feel from the scene above could have come straight from a Cro-Magnon cave, from an Orwellian nightmare, or from a concentration camp of the worst kind. In fact, "fear" and "anxiety" are used in bold letters in a local newspaper's description of the "coming recession." Fear and anxiety naturally compel human beings to savage reactions. The mind-set and the language of the marketplace are nothing short of war metaphor. It is once again kill or be killed. As the new owners of an apartment complex in Milwaukee forced some elderly old-timers out, battle cries were heard. "This is America," one of the three new owners shrugged and said. "It's capitalism." What is surprising is that we are surprised at all with such displays of callousness among our market men.

Notice the following as "maneuvers" taken by corporations to "defend themselves" against corporate raiders and as strategies of battle:

One example is the so-called poison pill, in which a company makes an acquisition so expensive that the predator usually responds by abandoning his quest. Rohatyn would also act to eliminate some "shark repellents," whereby companies take measures, such as changing their bylaws, to ward off potential acquirers.[5]

Notice the language of war: "maneuvers," "defend themselves," "poison pill," "the predator," "abandoning his quest," "shark repellents," "take measures," "ward off." Top to bottom, the fierce battle goes on as a way of life. Back in nature, it is finally war of all against all that is the heart and soul of modern America.

What kind of battle-tested children would be waiting in the wings to continue our savagery? Listen to some middle-school teachers:

"Teaching in a middle school is like being a zookeeper in charge of the health, well-being, comfort and productivity of the animals." "Teaching in a middle school is like working with thirty hand grenades with their pins half-pulled." "It's like trying to teach a gland." "It's like being in the middle of a battle zone and you've lost your red cross." "It's like being fairy godmother to Godzilla." "It's a combination of R-rated movies and Smurf stories . . ."[6]

The nation's school teachers, like everyone else, are worn out with their struggle against nature. Never before in human history has a society so totally, so absolutely committed itself to a destruction of its own community and humanity, calling the destruction a dream—the American Dream. But we now know that with each dream dreamed, corruption must be its price; with each dream realized, a part of our social life is destroyed; and with each dream broken must be laid the trail of human sorrows in its wake. This self-destruction is the ultimate wages of our economic sin.

We asked in the beginning of this book whether a purely economic society could survive without community and humanity as its binding social fabric. There is no doubt that the economic rewards in America's marketplace are enormous. The material affluence the marketplace has created is unsurpassed in history. However, along came the belief that materialism increases human happiness, that two cars make us twice as happy as one car, that a 5 percent increase in our GNP improves our civilization by 5 percent, that our meaning of life increases with the increasing space of our house, that when we get a 5 percent raise it makes us 5 percent more fulfilled. How else are we to explain our national obsession with the daily percentage rise and fall in income averages, Dow Jones indexes, and GNP figures, as well as our own paychecks and job titles?

As the spectacle of America's material indulgence has been great, as we have seen, so is the price America must pay for its sins. We have lived by money; we may yet die by it.

In 1980 *Time*'s Lance Morrow wrote, paraphrasing my book, *The Dead*

End, that America's obsession with material consumption "amounts almost to a *national death wish*."[7] (These are not the words I used in the book, however.) Ten years later, another writer for *Time*, Charles Krauthammer, upon the occasion of President Bush's inauguration, found reason to be optimistic about America. "The continuing fluidity of [American] society," he wrote, "is its greatest asset and its primary defense against the doleful prophecies of American declinists." How did America's fortune change from "a national death wish" to its "greatest asset" within a decade? Did it really happen? If it did, *how* did America do it? Krauthammer's answer: "The American blessing is to have invented a system that . . . allows us to *re-imagine the world—every four years*." So that's how we do it. Reimagine things. All we need to do to feel good is simply switch the channel that allows us to imagine another world. Like Maria in *Sound of Music*, we just think about our "favorite things," then we feel good again.

But the real world—the world that demands a pound of our flesh for all our sins—refuses to go away. It is still with us. We cannot simply imagine it to go away. It does not go away with a new president, a new job. Only months after Krauthammer's optimistic forecast, Lance Morrow wrote in the same space about "shortsighted, vicious, stupid" American politics; about "fathers, mothers, bankers, Senators, solid citizens" whose "soul begins to die," which "passes over into realms of the surreal and savage, into moral blackout and passivity"; about ignorance "becoming an American addiction—part of a quest for painless life"; about Americans who are "addicted to television, a true enslavement, a dreary mania . . . to credit and debt, to mobility and high speed . . . to a hope of painlessness." Alternating between rosy optimism and painful escapism—or between the world of illusion and the world of reality—is a full-time job for most Americans. In one sense, their lives are full of excitement and playfulness; in another, nothing but anxieties and fears. How do we explain this?

American society today is intertwined with two philosophies that are mutually reinforcing the worst in the other: *fascism* and *hedonism*. As fascists, Americans are fearful of loss, uncertain of values, and brutal in economic conception. As hedonists, they are euphoric in self-fulfillment, assertive in entitlements, and individualistic in cultural demand. In the nation's *public* self, America is fascist: it is intolerable with smaller countries, hostile toward the unorthodox, and unsympathetic to the poor and powerless. As a fascist nation, it mistakes brute force for strength. In America's *private* life, everyone is a hedonist: one is a relativist with lifestyles, minimalist in work ethic and public obligations, and sensitive only to the here and now. As a hedonistic person, one mistakes pleasure for happiness.

Active America is hedonistic, "liberal" in its action; *reactive* America is fascist, "conservative" in its reaction. Liberal America wants more hedonistic pleasure in individual life; conservative America wants more fascist regimentation. Most Americans alternate between the two poles, depending on their immediate interests. In personal life (lifestyles and entitlements) they are liberal; in public life (taxation and militarism) they are conservative. These two Americas are not permanently fixed along personal or class lines; they shift according to the mood and calculus. In the world of illusion and Substitute Society, America is hedonistic; in the world of brute reality as America tries to escape it, it becomes reactionary and fascist.

In neither world does America control itself. As the sources of hedonism (entertainment, happiness, materialism) are false and flimsy, so are the sources of fascism (fear, force, reaction). Both sources are manipulated, the first by the profiteering economic overloads and the second by the power-seeking political ideologues. More often than not, the economic overloards, and political ideologues find themselves rubbing shoulders with one another; they find a coincidence of interest in keeping America permanently hedon-istic and fascist. As hedonists and fascists, Americans are easy to manipulate and control. Commercial appeals and political slogans can easily dominate their minds. Those who seek happiness and those who seek dominance—the hedonists and fascists—are forever like children in their mind-set. As children, people unpredictably fluctuate between the two philosophies.

The most popular president in recent history, Ronald Reagan, was a master tactician in recognizing this fact—also true to some extent of his minor version in George Bush. He alternately and skillfully appealed to American hedonism in the materialist middle class ("The world is your oyster"), to American fascism in its attitude toward the domestic poor and minorities ("Government, get off the back of the people!"), and toward the smaller nations (attacks on Grenada, Libya, and Nicaragua). He played up to the strong and was hostile to the weak. He encouraged hedonism in individualists, and he appeased their fascist tendencies in foreign affairs and domestic policies.

America *wallows* in hedonism, but it *repents* in fascism. The world's trash-iest culture is also one that is most stern in its moral commandments. In its hedonistic self, America is hell-bent for pleasure; in its fascist self, Amer-ica is also the hotbed of fundamentalist moralism and reactionary myopia. It either overindulges or overreacts. In either, it is most extreme. In cultural, political matters, anything goes. In economic, military matters, the mind-set is unforgiving, reactionary, and stupid. In the reality of daylight, Amer-icans are fascist at workplaces and as money changers. In the illusion of private life at night, Americans are hedonists in bed, with television, and at mealtime. There is no escape from either extreme, and the violent clashes between the two worlds leave virtually everyone exhausted and confused. The friendly, smiling, first-name calling hedonist could instantly turn into a vicious, schizopherenic, calculating moneymonger and militarist.

Few Americans are consistently one variety or the other in belief and personality. Virtually all hedonists are profiteers in their "real" life; virtually all fascists are capable of disarming smiles and dazzling personal charm.

Even George Bush, who has been possessed by the "marketplace" in his entire adulthood, can sincerely talk about a "kinder and gentler nation" and act grandfatherly. Hedonists want abortion legalized in the name of freedom of the pregnant; fascists want abortion illegalized in the name of life for the unborn. But both are quite capable of maintaining a double life: the hedonists ruthlessly trampling the "freedom" of others to compete and succeed in the marketplace, the fascists remorselessly and blithely advocating life-killing death penalty and military actions. Hence there is no genuine belief in freedom among hedonists and no authentic belief in life among fascists.

In the world of hedonistic illusion, Americans are pampered with false courtesy, commercial appeals, and political praise. In it, all Americans who can consume are kings, aristocrats, and royalty. Their individual worth ("feeling good about oneself") is constantly overvalued and their individuality overemphasized. In the world of fascist reality, Americans are domineered, threatened, degraded, and humiliated. If the hedonistic American is a consumer, the one in fascist reality is a delinquent customer who is late on payment. For the latter, the red carpet is abruptly withdrawn from under his feet, leaving him dizzy and confused as to what his true status is. A customer may be the king, but the delinquent account is a common thief. The overdue notice quickly settles the status question. In the fascist economic and power play, the American is cut down to size with proper distinctions among the underclasses—thieves, servants, prostitutes, footmen, bodyguards, peasants, workers, slaves, pimps, mercenaries—to which he rightly belongs. In this world, the individual is chronically undervalued, ignored, and manipulated. Prompt payment, however, delays this status revolution and keeps one a bit longer in his world of illusion. For this very reason, every American is determined to stay employed, for as long as he stays employed and makes the payments, he can maintain the illusion of a hedonist.

In America staying sane between the extremes requires one's whole concentration and determination, "as though Americans live in two separate worlds," as columnist Flora Lewis has commented, "that have nothing to do with each other." But illusion's progress is powerful and relentless. It makes inroads into our intellectual, religious, psychological—in short, private and subconscious—self and occupies it for good. Given the choice between pleasant illusion and painful reality, all things being equal, Americans will always choose the former. It is the very American way of life. In it, we willingly bear false witness about ourselves and others. Both hedonism and fascism encourage bloated and often self-serving images of ourselves. "We" are always better than "they." Compare the following comments:

In the Soviet Union informing on one's fellow man was taken so far that Pavilk Morozov became a national hero for ratting on his father.

—Richard Hornik, *Time*, May 1989

Drug Czar Encourages Students to Tell on Peers Who Use Drugs. William J. Bennett [then director of the Drug Enforcement Agency] instructed students here Thursday to do something that is virtually unthinkable among teen-agers: tell on their friends. "It's an act of true loyalty—of true friendship"

—N.Y. *Times* News Service, August 1989]

During the McCarthy Era informing on other Americans was a national pastime. Today there is a special government number for whistle-blowers to call to tell on the wrongdoings of their companies and institutions. Stores often remind their customers to report on shoplifters. Why do we think it is a peculiarly Soviet phenomenon and such a disgusting one, too? Compare another one:

[In the Soviet Union] their education and everything they have heard from the media have led them to expect that they could enjoy economic benefits equal to those of capitalism with none of the risks or pain.

—from the same article by Hornik above

[An old-timer talking about "today's high school students"] They were lazy, he said. They wanted their money quick and easy; they didn't want to have to work hard for it. The only things that held their attention were the things that were fast and fun. They wouldn't do anything boring, even if it was important. "How did they get this way?" he asked me. I didn't answer.

—*"Shall We Gather at the Game?," John Krull, Indianapolis News,*
2 March 1990

No comment is necessary for the one above. The 1990 Nobel Peace Prize was awarded to Gorbachev, which prompted a cartoon in America showing two hungry Soviets asking him, "Congratulations. . . . Is it edible?" Now an American would have asked a different question: "Congratulations. . . . How much is it worth?" Would the American reaction necessarily reflect a better society? Our false self-image would obviously think so.

The more our society produces, the more we must consume. The more we consume, the *more* we must *work*. Oddly, as more machines have taken over our physical chores through the glorious Industrial Revolution, the more we must toil now. It is "I owe, I owe, so off to work I go." To pay for the things that we no longer want or need, we work today longer than at any time in this century. According to the 1989 Harris survey, America's leisure time has declined by 37 percent in the last two decades. Modern technology was created mainly to save time and toil. But modern Americans have less time and more toil. If leisure is defined as a domain in which one truly becomes oneself, then more and more of American life is occupied essentially by forces alien to the individual. The wealthiest nation and the "freest" society in the world are also the place where little humanity or true self exists.

In pursuing hedonism and in repenting in fascism and in work and play, Americans are essentially alone. It is in the very nature of hedonism and fascism. Neither hedonistic action nor fascist reaction creates true community or human spirits. All hedonists live and die alone. Their "relationships"—love, family, friendship—are ultimately hollow and transient; thousands of cheering fans do not make a common humanity. Hedonists want to take, not give, and no lasting or true relationships are possible among hedonists. All fascists may act united as long as there are victims— the poor, the weak—for their brute strength in number, in wealth, or in power. But their unity is likewise untrue and temporary. During the Gulf crisis, James Webb, former assistant secretary of defense, observed, "While most Americans are laboring very hard to support [the president], a mood of cynicism is just beneath their veneer of respect." All hedonists and fascists are victims of their own folly.

No one perhaps personifies our age of hedonism and fascism better than Donald Trump, and no one perhaps is more *alone* than Donald Trump. As a hedonist, he wants the pleasure of his new acquisitions; one of his associates foresees him, according to Otto Friedrich and Jeanne McDowell for *Time*, as "finally ending, like Howard Hughes, a multibillionaire living all alone in one room." As a fascist, he is fearful and distrusting. Guy Martin, writing for *Esquire*, describes a dinner given by Trump: "The unusual thing was that throughout the evening, even in the dining room, Trump was surrounded by his personal bodyguards, big ugly guys with Uzis sticking out of their jackets. Can you believe it? I mean, even in his own house, while entertaining *friends*" (emphasis original). Yes, we can believe it. But can you believe that all hedonists and fascists are frustrated, closet Donald Trumps?

In what is described as "Darwin's proving ground" of competition and battle for survival we now have a society, in David Broder's words, "that has lost its moral bearing." Even James J. Kilpatrick, the normally staunch conservative defender of capitalism, things "the love of money" is "the root of all evil." The love of money, he laments, "is corrupting our political system." And this is from a man who breathes and sleeps capitalism. Why is the American public so blasé about the savings-and-loan scandal? Don Shoemaker, writing for the *Miami Herald*, is exasperated. His answer: "Perhaps other competing crises are sexier." This leads him to some global philosophizing. "Communism collapsed from within because it couldn't work," he observes. "What are we doing to capitalism?" What he obviously understands is that in a society of illusion, truth causes a great deal of inconvenience.

We know what happens to a capitalist *society*, as we have seen. But what happens to *capitalism*, the Darwinian proving ground where hard work makes one wealthy and happy? If old capitalism rewarded hard work, new capitalism rewards incompetence, or so it seems. As capitalism's *society* collapses within, its own work habits also collapse. Everyone wants to *enjoy* the fruit of labor without the labor. Everywhere we hear cries of incompetence. "Whatever Happened to Service?" irate columnist Marilyn Geewax, writing for the *Atlanta Constitution*, inquires. Should we blame the individual workers? Not really, Geewax says. "When a problem is so widespread," she correctly guesses, "there must be some larger issues involved." After some exasperating personal experiences of incompetence among American employees, she comes to the final conclusion: "This is it—the United States is going to collapse because clerks have gotten so bad they no longer can tell the difference between hot and cold." Harold A. "Red" Poling, CEO of the Ford Motor Company, relates his decades of experience with American workers, as reported by Andrew J. Glass for the Cox Newspapers: "These days [Poling says], 70 percent of the work force cannot write a decent letter seeking employment. Three-fifths of his hourly workers cannot add up their tabs in the company cafeteria."

As consumers and business leaders lament the lack of proper training among American workers, two columns in the morning paper are striking. David Broder, the dean among American columnists and often one of the voices in the wilderness, wrote a column about the poor educational preparations of American youths in high schools. Right below it is the one by Joan Beck, who writes for the *Chicago Tribune*, opposing the now-increasing distribution of condoms at America's high school campuses. (Against this backdrop, listen to Secretary of Defense Dick Cheney's praise of the weapons and equipment used in the Gulf War, as told to David Broder: "It's American. It works. It works damn well." In case my point is too subtle, notice *what* works, and how *desperately* proud the secretary is about something that really works in America.)

If these commentaries have succeeded in giving the impression of a society falling apart, the reader and I may be understanding the situation correctly. But to make sure that we are not too easily persuaded, let us eavesdrop at some length below on an internal memo from the manager at a car dealership intended for his fellow workers. I quote it verbatim:

Dear Associates,

It is with a certain feeling of failure and disappointment that I find it necessary to publish this communication to our staff. . .

I want to relate to you want I mean, in the past 10 working days alone what has happened.

A. 6 PM a service writer goes home and leaves a customer, who we had not repaired his vehicle properly, standing in the parking lot. When I arrived the sales dept. has already spent about 20 minutes listening and not knowing or believing what they heard. The service advisor did not offer a car or offer to see that the customer got home or anything. I spent about 1 hour with the customer that night and by noon the next day the problem was solved with only a loaner car provided and no good will dollars spent from [name of dealership deleted]. As of this writing no service personnel has come and mentioned that problem.

B. A service advisor gets into a discussion with a customer concerning a broken door lock. We know the linkage was off the door when we wrote the RO because the door wouldn't open when he went to check the mileage. The customer has ESP Total. We didn't offer to repair the door, we argued with the customer as to who broke the linkage, us or the wrecker driver. I do not see the significance of who did it but I do see the problem of not fixing it and arguing with the customer. It was finally fixed under ESP with no additional charge to the customer.

C. Card from customer exactly as written: "I had an 8 AM appointment. At 11:55 I asked foreman if my vehicle was ready. Yes, it was. It only took an hour but no one came and told me." The vehicle was ready by 10 AM according to the work order. We didn't even notify the customer.

D. Customer card dated Nov. 8, as written: "After multiple phone calls was unable to find status of repair or its nature. Was in shop from 11 AM to 4 PM the next day to replace a battery. Service poor." No contact from us. (We have 9 people to answer phones).

E. Friday evening, 4:30, I walked into the service office—no employee inside. Four customers are waiting, 2 phones are ringing—1 service writer is outside talking with a friend, one service writer is working on his own car in the shop, no dispatcher or anyone else, in the office.

As I started this communique I stated that I had a feeling of failure and disappointment and from the above which I used to think were the exceptions are not really that abnormal. I have not impressed on us that customer service excellence is not just a saying but an actual experience. The only one who apparently understood that was myself. I never convinced the rest.[8]

Are the sorrows and lamentations of the unhappy manager unique to that car dealership and not others? They are not. All other dealerships—for that matter, all firms in America that are engaged in service—suffer this malaise of incompetence, sloth, and listlessness. Workers find little meaning in their work and much less in the pleasures that their wages bring. Their morale is low and their spirit sagging. They see nothing happy with their present and expect nothing brighter in the future. They are mad at themselves and grumpy with the customers. Simple exhortation brings no improvement either in their workmanship or in their spirit. American workers are more dissatisfied than lazy or frightened. All the pleasures that their wages promise are not worth their appalling daily grind at work. What the poor manager, caught between complaining customers and the profit imperative, has to deal with is the grown-up version of middle-school children. Unlike with the children, neither the carrot nor the stick is enough to motivate the grown-ups. We can manipulate the worker's mind only so long and only so much. Life is long and manipulative effects short. Whenever there is *real* work to be done, American workers long accustomed to illusion cannot be counted on. All things considered in America, we cannot possibly avoid the final payment on our wages of sin: a pound of flesh is being cut out from our community and humanity.

All is not lost, however, We can explore ways to restore some sense in our senseless economic irrationality and to retain a measure of humanity lost in our market struggle. The last leg in our journey through American society is an attempt to argue—perhaps against logic and experience—that such irrationality and dehumanization are not really necessary in American life any longer and that human happiness can be achieved without such savagery.

We shall attempt this in the chapter to follow.

NOTES

1. George Will, "Court Affirms Founders' Intent: Religion Is Free, but Subordinate," 22 April 1990.

2. George Will, "In the 1980s, Socialism Committed Suicide," 1 January 1990.

3. Hans J. Morgenthau, *The Purpose of American Politics* (New York: Vintage Books, 1960), 27.

4. John Greenwald, "The New Fortress America," *Time*, 12 September 1983.

5. John Greenwald, "Today Things Are Badly Getting Out of Hand," *Time* 23 December 1985.

6. Julia T. Thomason and Walt Grebing, *We Who Laugh Last* (Columbus, OH: National Middle School Association, 1990), 3.

7. Jon Huer, *The Dead End: The Psychology and Survival of the American Creed* (Dubuque, IA: Kendall/Hunt, 1977). Mr. Morrow's essay, "On Being Citizens and Soldiers," appeared in the 9 June 1980 issue of *Time*.

8. I have used this memo without the author's permission on the account that its source will remain anonymous and that its content itself is nondescript. My thanks go to the unnamed author of the memo at the dealership, which is an outlet in a medium-sized city for one of the three major automakers.

Chapter 12

Back to Humanity

Has the "American experiment with democracy . . . run its course?" *Harper's* editor, Louis Lapham, exasperated at America's civic decline, recently asked.[1] Indeed, has it? To be sure, no society has ever survived as a purely economic or profit-calculating mechanism of self-interest. No human society before our time, perhaps, ever existed purely as a market society. The idea is as audacious as it is unprecedented. Undoubtedly, the prize of America's audacity to experiment with the idea has been our affluence; the price of our audacity has been the loss of our community in the roar of the economic machine and the jangle of the cash register. Between the prize and the price of market society, America has become profoundly bewildered with its own traps.

In the last decade, those Americans who expect "things to get worse" in the near future rose from 20 to 40 percent. And this is in a society that has known little else but security and prosperity in its history. What is causing this gloomy prospect in their minds? Has the "American experiment" with self-interest finally run its course? If it has, what now? What could replace or modify the system we have known and loved for centuries?

In this last chapter, as the reader has been persuaded enough to come this far, we need to pull ourselves together into some sort of new thinking. Indeed, radical times require radical thinking.

Let's cast our glance forward and think history for a moment. What if, just now, we discovered *another* New World where a wholly new society can be built? When the Founding Fathers first contemplated the future of the United States, they only had *their* own historical knowledge, mainly from the memories of the Middle Ages, to draw upon. And they debated and designed the new society according to what they knew. What would *we*—the new Founding Fathers in the hypothetical newer New World—debate and design as *our* new world? Would we want a carbon copy of the old New World? Or would we want a *different* society altogether, now that we have more knowledge about society and human behavior? If the latter, as our common sense might compel us, what would be the changes in the new society that are different from the old? What would we consider destructive to community, society, and humanity that we see in the old society and that we would not want to see in the new one we are about to build?

Of course, there is no new continent to be discovered, no new utopia to be designed, no new nation to be built, no new life to be born. The American society we have with us now is the only one there is. Good and bad, it is the only material we have that we must work with. But our hypothetical exercise serves two important purposes, one of imagination and the other of sociology. It frees our imagination to pursue whatever social changes we feel are necessary to have a better community, society, and humanity. By following this hypothetical case of sociological history construction, we can also see what needs to be changed in our current society that we have.

Indeed, if we had to change all we could, what would we *want* to change? On reflection, a few obvious things come to mind. If the reader can recall the components of the Social Ethic discussed in the beginning of this book, it also helps.

First, the most important change would be in the way political leaders are chosen. Remembering how irrelevant and corrupt America's election had become, the new Founding Fathers would particularly want to avoid the old mistakes: mainly, use of television in political campaigns, the system of money contribution, the effect of special-interest lobbying, even the universal voting model itself. Since America's experiment with old democracy had run its course—to dismaying records of corruption, indifference, and irrelevance—the new leaders might want to establish a different but better system of democratic politics. Lessons from the old New World would be recalled again and again in debating and designing the newer New World. It is likely that the new Constitution would be different from the old, especially in some of the following aspects.

Second, before deciding on the crucial "economic system," they would want to conduct a massive environmental inventory to see what kind of economic system would be most beneficial to us, to the nation, and to posterity. The new Founding Fathers, we would hope, would not want to repeat the hitherto steady destruction of our environment. Would they also want to limit our conspicuous and prodigious urges to consume? Would they also want to moderate our hell-bent credit spending in all its forms—government, business, private? Would they make sure that a few wealthy individuals or corporations do not monopolize all economic bounties of the new society and that there would continue to be a healthy, real, and fair economic competition?

Third, the new Founding Fathers might, we hope again, want to change the very philosophy of the profit system as detrimental to civilization. They might want to curve the destructive national energies spent on money-making. To do so, it might not be altogether unthinkable to put a cap on the total size of wealth a person or a corporation can accumulate. It might also be plausible to think that the new society would install a mechanism whereby the poor would gradually be absorbed into the mainstream of social life.

Fourth, the new Founding Fathers, in view of the nation's wealth, might want to initiate a nationalized system of welfare on important issues—health, education, housing, food.

Fifth, the new society might want to limit television in some ways. Since they are aware of the potential influence that commercial television can have on the masses, they would want to pay particular attention to the ways television is used in affecting the nation's intellectual, political, and cultural well-being. It would be fairly unthinkable that the new Founding Fathers—the leading intellectuals of their time—would ignore television and leave it to commercialism.

Sixth, very likely the new Founding Fathers would want to build a mass transit system as a way of cheaper transportation and of coping with wastefulness. America's historical and cultural obsession with automobiles would teach the new leaders that the obsession must be avoided in the new society.

Seventh, equally likely, the new founders would want to radically alter the system of justice. Lessons learned from the "American experiment" would not be lost on them when they contemplate justice in the new society. Above all, the role of lawyers would be drastically reduced and the adversary system of justice between two mercenary lawyers would also be modified. What the new Founding Fathers want would be a system that is more efficient, more just and substantive, and less dependent on the procedural trickeries and theatrics of lawyers.

Eighth, child-rearing would be the new society's primary commitment, remembering how the old New World botched it up—to everyone's lasting sorrow. . . .

The changes would be endless. In setting up the newer New World, all the mistakes, indulgences, and corrupt practices of the old New World would be constantly reminded and recalled. The new Founding Fathers would vow never to repeat them in their new society. But alas, this is only a hypothesis, a dream. We must carry on with our reality. Can our present American society be *changed* to its own Newer World? I believe it can. How? But the real question is, Why?

Every society consists of *bodies* to feed, protect, and propagate as purely biological and physical *things* as its first obligation. The society's economy must be efficient and rationally run; demand and supply must be reasonably balanced so that neither is wasted on the other; all resources must be explored to the fullest for the society's continuing survival and life's reasonable comfort. But, obviously, this is not all there is to a society, although this part of social function has been more or less the central theme of world history since time immemorial. Mankind by and large has always had the misfortune of lacking in even the most basic of amenities for survival and comfort. This fact of material scarcity has been so predominant in our historical past that it has understandably dominated the better part of our philosophical speculations and scientific inquiries. As John Kenneth Galbraith has put it, "We are guided, in part, by ideas that are relevant to another world; and as a further result we do many things that are unnecessary, some that are unwise, and a few that are insane." To some extent, preoccupation with feeding, protecting, and propagating in the most basic sense is still the highest priority in many parts of the world.

While this primary function of society is in operation—in its own unceasing fashion—yet another social obligation or function is also in operation with its own dynamics and creativity. Each body to feed, protect, and propagate is also a *soul*—in a wholly secular sense—to reflect, imagine, and moralize. This second role of society is directly responsible for our civilization; it is the stuff with which our art, history, virtues, justice, and truth are defined and maintained. If the first function is a "necessary" ingredient of society, then this second part is what makes it "sufficient" as a human community. Animal packs and insect colonies exist, but they do not form "community." When the first and second functions are combined in an ideal proportion to each other, say 50:50, then we can say we have a happy human society. These two dimensions may be thought of as two separate *functions* of society going on at the same time. Or they may be thought of as two historical *stages*, normally the second stage of civilization following the fulfillment of the first basic requirement. But as a historical fact, up to our own century, no society has had the ideal development of both requirements for the whole population. Perhaps enough food to go around for all, but not enough civilization for all. Perhaps aristocratic indulgences in fragmented episodes of high mental development, but not for the whole population. One thing or the other has always been lacking in the past.

In our contemporary American society, we may conclude that the first function has been *overdeveloped* to the extent that (1) it has gone beyond the level of sufficiency and (2) it has in the process destroyed the second function within its own society. As the first purely "economic society," America's basic functional capacity has overshot its mark to become an Inverted Economy. In the process, its human civilization has been rendered largely meaningless, empty, and irrelevant, existing only in the shadow of its original form as a Substitute Society. Once these facts are so recognized and understood, our task can now be more easily defined: we must reorient our social existence and consciousness so that (1) *the market economy is brought to a measure of social control and (2) the human community, now nearly extinct, may be revived to regain that control over the economic machine.*

We must restore the balance between economics and society, which has been critically listing in favor of economics. We must revive the balance between economics and society, because the marketplace is an institution *of* society, not society itself. The struggle for feeding, protecting, and propagating is only *one* of society's obligations and *one* of human capacities, not the whole purpose of existence. There must be a force in society, as Professor C. B. MacPherson says, "sufficient to offset the centrifugal forces of a possessive market society." In short, our society must become happier by becoming *less* economic.

What can do the job of restoring the balance between economics and society by restraining the rampant economics? The answer lies in that very mechanism that has been made irrelevant and impotent in America by the very forces of economics: namely, politics. *Politics must control economics to the point of a reasonable balance between the two forces of society.* Only political forces can counterbalance the "centrifugal forces" of economics. Politics must not only be revived as a social force, but also *strengthened* to do the job. The business-as-usual model of liberal democracy, as we have seen, would not do; economics would simply continue to dominate its counterpart politics.

In this new thinking, we need a new theory of justification. Why do we *want* the change, and why do we *think* it is justifiable? To answer these questions, I would call upon an intellectual model I would term the Theory of Obligation, whose ancestry may be traced to the model of checks and balances. The gist of it can be stated thus: *for any power to be justifiable, it must be balanced by its obligation to society to the extent of its power.* In other words, power must be rendered powerless by its obligation. For political power, we have seen that through the historical quirks of modern democracy, the political powerholder in America has been rendered more or less powerless. Even the president operates under the rules that stipulate that his power cannot exceed his obligations to society. Although one may disagree with his particular decisions, no one *fears* his power. Thus, in our day-to-day life, the president has been made an insignificant person. For economic power (that is, wealth) to be justifiable in America, it must carry its similar obligation to society to the precise extent of its power in wealth. How does the Theory of Obligation justify this formula?

In American society today, the idea of balancing different forces—power versus obligation—so that no *one* institution can dominate the rest is not new. To call our attention to a contemporary example, I will use the military institution to make my case.

Historically, American society has always insisted on and prevailed even in wartimes with "civilian supremacy." The idea is that the military is too

strong a force if not controlled by civilian authority. If left to itself in some
vague notion of "free enterprise," what the military could do in defense of
its institutional self-interest would be simply mind-boggling. Hence the
justification for civilian supremacy. The justification of civil authority over
the military is based on the simple recognition of the military's awesome
power, both destructive and controlling. But the importance of the military
in America as an actual instrument of power is close to *zero*. No American
is consciously aware of the dangers of a military takeover; no one in America
expects his city hall, state government, or federal authority to come under
the jurisdiction of military power. With the exception of fiction—such as
in *Seven Days in May*—no military coup d'état has ever entered anyone's
subconscious mind. It has never played, in behalf of itself as power, any
"political" role in America. The military, as awesome as it is, might as well
be *nonexistent* as a source of power in society. The military, in other words,
has been completely *neutralized*. But why is the military institution rendered
powerless and thereby justifiable in a democracy? Why is it awesome destructive power totally harmless in American life?

The answer is in the Theory of Obligation. In the wisdom of civilian
supremacy, in the structure of an elected commander in chief, the *military's
power has been rendered exactly equal to its obligation*. In other words, what
society giveth it, society also taketh away from it. All power is made
harmless only if it is weighed by the equal weight of obligation. It is Inverse
Politics at its simplest. Obviously, then, the extent of obligation corresponds
to the extent of power: the more powerful a person or an institution, the
more extensive his or its obligation to society; conversely, the smaller one's
power in society, the smaller one's obligation in it. Through its constitutional legacy American society has rendered the military so obligated to
society that the military *as military* is less powerful than a local teenage gang
in exerting influence. The powerless, on the other hand, need no obligation
to society because they *are* already overobligated. The powerless enjoy few
or no privileges in America in correct reflection of their powerlessness.
Obligation thus applies only to the powerful—powerful enough to endanger
society.

The military institution, accordingly, is one institution upon which the
American public retains a tight rein. In American society, where political
interest is rather lethargic and unreliable, the only sure issue that stirs the
public to political debate is one that involves the uses of the military—
namely, war. No commander in chief has been able to deploy the military
casually. The Constitution mandates a congressional declaration of war,
thus effectively putting the military under the elector's control. The public
actively participates in protests and debates when the issue is military. The
Theory of Obligation in the case of the military thus comes full circle. The
military's power is negated under a civilian commander; its actual use is
under the mandates of Congress; the existence of Congress depends on the

elector. Thus the Theory of Obligation completes its cycle with the military
ending up powerless.

The military as an "obligation institution" is indeed organized in a way
that is the model of social compliance. Its pay scale top to bottom—from
a four-star general to a private, reminiscent of the U.S. president–average
worker pay ratio—is less than 10:1. It is a small difference in contrast to
the business world's. Top to bottom, all military personnel wear the same
clothes, eat the same food, and are, with minor variations in ranks, subject
to similar living conditions. The differences in special privileges accorded
various ranks are small in nature, especially compared to the business
world's, and are rather severely circumscribed. It is also a fairly integrated
institution: its top man—chairman of the Joint Chiefs of Staff—at this writing is black; of the 450 or so general grade officers, close to 10 percent are
black. This is a remarkable fact when we consider the presence of no black
chief executive officer among Fortune 500 corporations in America. Likewise, the military is much more democratic than its larger society: no senior
in rank is allowed to engage his subordinates in any duty other than that
which is so functionally prescribed by the institution. One can also transfer
fairly easily from one unit to another if conditions require it.

Can we control the economic marketplace as too powerful left unto itself
in the same way we control the military? Are there enough similarities
between the two powerful institutions in America to justify the application
of the Theory of Obligation to the economic institution as well? Would it
be necessary, in view of the power of the economic, to put a civilian
"economic" commander in chief in charge of the business world? I believe
there are strong similarities between economic and military institutions,
enough to justify social control of the economic institution in the fashion
of the military's obligation to society. Economics needs *its* obligation to
society to nullify its power over society. (We should remember that politics
used to dominate economics before our market epoch reversed the politics-
economics order. It is still true today in many other societies.) How specifically we should go about applying the Theory of Obligation to economics will be discussed shortly. But in the meantime we must be convinced
that military and economic are similar. Let's, therefore, see what those
similarities are.

First, the most obvious point is their *power* to control those under their
domination. The economic institution directly controls its employees and
indirectly its consuming public in general. The consumer-king is one of
those myths in America. The consumer, as Andrew Hacker has convincingly shown in his still-relevant book, *The End of the American Era*,[2] has to
consume what the corporations produce and pay whatever price they demand. Simply, there is no other way. The consumer-king is no more real
than coronation with a paper crown from a Burger King. Against the very

best and brightest in America who engage in the most sophisticated mind-bending advertisement, every consumer is fair game. There is no power—intellectual or otherwise—to stand up to the power of the economically powerful. The military's power—not necessarily its better known "military-industrial complex" type of power—is raw and absolute. As the ultimate solution for national defense and maintenance of civil order, the military has the capacity to control all civilians and their institutions totally, utterly, and finally. The military's sheer power over the nation could be frightening if it were not for the tight control we exert over it through our elected officials. Time and time again we witness in the Third World nations what an uncontrollable military can do: it simply takes over the government almost at will. If we can justify controlling the military, why not the economic institution?

Second, the way they operate their basic institutional machineries is almost identical. Both institutions maintain an iron-fisted chain of command. The flow of hierarchy leaves no doubt as to who is in charge at every moment and on every level. In both institutions, by necessity, decisions made in the top echelon are carried out with near perfect efficiency and imperative. They maintain a mode of operation that is basically top–down: some give orders and others carry them out; few command and many obey. Both institutions generally follow the pyramid model of organizational structure characteristic of all modern bureaucratic organizations, which is designed to be efficient and rational.

Third, both institutions are also similar in another way. They are singularly dedicated to amazingly simple premises: economics to making money, the military to destroying the enemy. The economic institution cannot and does not tolerate, other than as cosmetics and image gimmicks, "secondary" objectives—social consciousness, employee morale, nationalism—in the purpose of its primary existence; all roads, sooner or later, must lead to one destination—that is, profit. After all the public-relations props have been played out, after all the charitable donations have been displayed, after all the concessions have been made to the welfare of the consuming public, the bottom line must show a profit for the company. The singularity of profit-making for the economic institution is matched only by the singularity of the military. As far as the purpose of the military goes, war is the normal state of things, peace only a recovery period between warring episodes. The military exists for one thing only, as it should, to make war and to destroy the enemy. In it, defense is offense, offense defense. All other considerations are simply irrelevant to its existence. Left unto itself, the military would be in perpetual war.

Fourth, it is also in the psychological profile of those men and women who make up the employees, warriors, and cannon fodder for both institutions. They are both striking in the simplicity of their definition of purpose. Both market men and soldiers are in many ways like children, utterly incapable of reflection and self-examination and wholly dedicated to the games they play. It is as if both are driven by some primeval force of self-interest and survival, by accumulating and destroying. The faces of the men at any stock market are remarkably similar to those of the soldiers under fire: grim, menacing, and possessed by the primitive instinct for self and survival. There is no such thing as a thinking businessman, as there is no such thing as a thinking soldier. Both institutions severely discourage as contrary to their vested interests the reflective, "human" types who tend to ask questions, critically analyze the premises, and examine their own roles and motives.

Fifth, both organizations command state-of-the-art technology. Indeed, they almost monopolize all technological and scientific marvels that are top of the line. It is instructive that these two institutions are the two top users of modern computers. The economic institution's assets in technology, equipment, and capital are astronomical; the military's possession of arsenal, organizational structure, manpower, and material is equally staggering. The society's other remaining assets and resources pale by comparison. Anything that is highly valued in American society today is likely to be owned, managed, or organized by either of the two institutions. All other institutions carry on as secondary backup functions for the two.

Then, finally, there are the "ideological" similarities. Both institutions maintain their absolute hold on American psychology with something vaguely defined as "survival." Economic activity is seen as central to individual survival; the military establishment, to collective survival. Not only do they require the material and structural resources from their society—the best and the brightest that their society can provide—they also demand habitual psychological obedience from the public. Anyone who is less than enthusiastic about American business is anti-American and possibly "socialist," whatever is good for the General Motors is also good for America, business is what has made America great, and so on. The same reason is also applied to the critics of the military: national security cannot be questioned either in terms of material support or on the grounds of ideological loyalty, anyone who is too critical of the military gives aid to the enemy, and so on. (Upon receiving a House bill reducing arms budgets, then president Reagan urged the American public to "retaliate" against legislators who "trifle with our national security.") Both business and military eventually get what they want from their society, be it a tax break or a weapons budget. More absolute than the public necessity of acquiescence is the loyalty they demand from their own employees and soldiers. By the means of economic rewards and of military necessity for obedience, these institutions maintain a tight stronghold over their men and women. Both in their specific functions and in their more subconscious private moments, they have to become "company men" (and women) in the true sense of the term.

Why do we attach such importance to them? If we recall the two outstanding psychological traits in America today—hedonism and fascism—it is not difficult to understand their essential hold on our minds. The economic institution supplies goods and services for our hedonistic pursuits; the military is our primary weapon of fascistic reactions. Individually we pursue our hedonistic pleasures as one of our predominant drives. Collectively we flex our muscles on the less fortunate and for the smallest of provocations, for the powerful always justify their action de facto. As these institutions subordinate all things in America to their existence, we allow all our inner necessities to depend on their existence as well. In material necessity as well as in psychological longings, our "materialistic-economic" and "militaristic" model indispensably and imperatively dominates our whole perspective.

There may now be little doubt that the idea of controlling the economic institution by a political means is thus justifiable in the Theory of Obligation and desirable in practical necessity. In view of such similarities and their disturbing potential and proven consequences, we cannot justify our tight rein on one while leaving the other virtually untouched in the name of "free enterprise" or marketplace philosophy. If the principle of political control is justifiable for one, then it should certainly be justifiable for the other.

The "why" thus answered, now, *how* do we actually go about it? How do we actually restore politics to a position in which it is at least in parity with the influence and power of economics, as it is with the military? How do we impose on the dollar the same obligation we impose on the bullet? I can suggest a way. Its principle can be stated here in simple terms: In order to control an Inverted Economy with a now-powerless political mechanism and to apply the Theory of Obligation to the economic, we must make our politics also inverted. The idea is to give those who have less power their compensating power (or "reverse obligation") in order to balance the already-powerful. We take power away from the military by assigning it an equal value of obligation to society. In economics, we follow the same principle until power and obligation are equalized. The following is offered as a practical how-to formula for this Inverted Politics.

Inverted Politics can be stated in the following principle: *beginning with the average income, one's vote is weighed in inverse ratio to his income level, so that the lower one's income, the higher his vote value, and vice versa.*

Let's assume that the national average income is $20,000 a year. A person who makes $20,000 a year would keep his one man, one vote normal political weight. But as the income decreases below that line, the person's vote is inversely weighed so that as his income decreases his voting power— hence his political power—increases proportionally. By the same token, the person whose income is above the national average of $20,000 a year would lose his voting power proportionally to his higher income. This way, we increase the political power of those who have little economic power and reduce the economic power of the wealthy to smaller political power to offset the imbalance. As we have seen earlier, one man, one vote might have been a good idea initially in establishing the basic human rights. But its subsequent "stalemate" among all those who have one vote made politics virtually meaningless. "Political" actions through voting could not change anything substantial. No wonder politics has lost its relevance as a means of social change and the public has largely lost interest in it. That left, by default, economics or the marketplace as the only arena where meaningful differences are created and maintained. Now this inverted way of politics is to correct that inequality without revolution or bloodshed, slowly and imperceptibly, with justice and fairness in view, and in the American way of democracy with its checks-and-balances principle. Ideally and in a highly simplified version, the following would represent the new distribution of political power as measured in inverted votes:

CLASS	NUMBER OF VOTES
Upper	0
Middle	1
Lower	2

The idea of giving the "weaker" among us a break so that a certain balance may be restored is already very much a part of our contemporary social practices in America. We concede easy physical access to the handicapped, reserving choice parking spots for them, making ramps available for their use, and creating other special considerations for them not normally available to others. Busing school children and giving special considerations to minority job applicants, the "affirmative action" policy, follow the same principle. While certainly controversial on the question of its effectiveness, the philosophy has been with us as an important recognition of the need to restore social balance.

But the best example of this give-the-weaker-among-us-a-break philosophy in America is demonstrated by one of America's most popular and most economically successful corporate bodies: the National Football League. The NFL maintains a perpetual Theory of Obligation to the happiness of all participants: the owners are happy, the players are happy, and the fans are happy. How do they do it? By "inversing" their order of power. The last-place finisher gets the best compensation the next time around. The drafting of new college players is assigned in "inverse" order of each team's record; that is, the worse the won-lost record, the better the drafting order, so that the best new players go to the weaker team; the schedule of the following season is made up so that the weaker among them play an "easier" schedule; there are also elaborate measures of compensation within the league so that no one team becomes thoroughly dominant or thoroughly dominated by others. Both Major League Baseball and the National Basketball Association also practice similar policies in order to maintain a model of perpetual parity—their own versions of the Theory of Obligation— among the teams.

While unbridled competitiveness may be presented to the public for the purpose of excitement, beneath it is the obligation-principle that the teams hang *together*: one for all and all for one. Can this principle also work in our *real* world? Of course, what we are willing to concede in "games" we may not be so willing to concede in real life. But the principle is the same even in these "economically" competitive organizations. And they all prosper together. Why can we not extend this practice to the whole of economic activity in America? No one ever calls the NFL, NBA, or Major League Baseball socialist systems, which they are, any more than the military is called a communist organization, which it is.

The main idea of Inverted Politics is to have our political power gravitate toward the middle eventually and hence toward the point of parity. Lower-income persons could add strength to their votes and truly elect those political spokesmen who would represent their interests. As the number of those lower-income representatives increase, America's political balance of power would also change, however gradually. Election after election, power would gradually shift from the wealthy to the poor, while the "middle class" would try to hold the center for stability and continuity. I foresee the passing of at least a whole generation before any visible change in America's fundamental social structure can take place. But still, it is better than the status quo. The changing composition of the legislative branch on all levels of government can then pass new laws according to the composition of those who represent various groups. As it stands now, the powerful and wealthy normally stand alongside other powerful and wealthy by virtue of their self-interests. Our inverted legislative changes would be so slow and gradual that by the time the "poor man's legislature" is substantially in command, everyone in society would have been accustomed to the changes already. Such major historical changes are never without pain. But the alternative to this—that is, continuing our present self-destructive course—is too catastrophic to contemplate.

What then would be the actual goal of Inverted Politics, as its inversely weighed power pushes the center of power toward the middle, away from the top? What would actually be at the core of its legislative agenda? As its single most important task, the legislature of Inverted Politics would restore the Social Ethic in place of the Profit Ethic and emphasize human happiness instead of economic prosperity. The following section presents my final argument as to why such changes in America are not only desirable as a matter of moral justification, but also *possible* as a matter of indisputable material fact. Few other societies and certainly in no other historical time than American society today could contemplate such a possibility, a possibility of building a social system that is at once just, rational, and happy in all aspects of its existence. It would balance "direct" costs and "indirect" costs so that their utility ratio is maintained at a perfectly balanced 50:50 (as discussed in Chapter 8). How is all this to be made possible? This final— and I should think most crucial—section of this book may also be considered a summary reflection of all that has been discussed previously, now essentially in light of this new possibility. It is the possibility of a wholly rational and civil society and its equally rational and civil economy.

The ultimate aim of all economic activity organized within a social system that ever existed in human history is to achieve and maintain society's survival and life's comfort. This aim can be said to have been achieved when all basic needs arising from life's necessity and comfort are met. Using the more traditional terms of *demand* and *supply*, but in a nonmarket sense, we can also define this state of full self-sufficiency as a point where *demand and supply are in perfect balance*.

How, then, do we define demand and supply themselves? What would be the state of perfect balance between the two? These are questions central to our task, for all things hinge on how we define them. What we demand and supply must follow some human reason and logic, not how much demand and how much supply we can *afford* individually and as a society. To remind ourselves: to say that we demand what we can afford to demand and we supply what profits would motivate is to succumb once again to our worst instinct. We need a different approach to the notions of demand and supply.

Let us imagine, in order to formulate answers to the questions raised above, a "perfect state of economy," which is the aim of all societies in history. In it, everything economic operates perfectly and ideally. That perfect and ideal state would pivot on two central concepts: demand and supply, or what people *need* and *ways* to satisfy the needs. First, in this state of balance between the two, *no one would demand more than one needs*. Second, *all that one needs would be supplied*. Third, *no one would supply more than what is demanded*. And finally, with demand and supply in perfect balance, *everything in this state of balance would cost nothing*. (The last point would be further discussed later, since it is the theoretical underpinning upon which demand and supply depend.) In this ideal state of economy desired by all but achieved only by few, demand is determined by necessity and supply by (1) the extent of demand and (2) whether the society has enough resources to meet the demand.

But for most societies and for much of our historical time, however, this state of perfect balance between demand (necessity) and supply (availability) has not been attainable because of the simple fact that *demand almost always remains larger than supply*. The sheer lack of physical resources—land, capital, technology, material, organization—keeps supply from ever adequately catching up with demand. Population growth often outstrips what few gains are made on the supply end. But the effort to overcome this state of imbalance is also just as doggedly determined as is the gap between necessity and availability itself. Because of this gap, every use of energy and resource available in society is channeled, by simple necessity, into overcoming that difference between demand and supply. Thus we can say that in a society where demand is larger than supply *every unit of energy and resource is used for the "positive" purpose of overcoming that deficiency.* In spite of this generally miserable condition where basic needs lag behind their satisfaction, we are moved to recognize that it is after all a "positive economy." It is positive in the sense that everything possible is being done to overcome that gap—of course, not always with positive *results.* Hence we would term this economic stage where demand is larger than supply a *positive economy*, in spite of its less than positive reality. Still, the idea is that all its effort will bear fruit sooner or later.

It can be said that all societies in the process move toward that historical point where demand and supply are in perfect balance. We may call it utopia, paradise, or affluence or by any other name, but the idea is just the same. Arriving at this point is every society's scheme and dream. Depending on where a society may be in this progress, people suffer through their poverty because their basic needs are not met adequately. Poverty hurts, and people suffer. In a sense, a positive economy is defined by the very fact that human suffering exists. It is this suffering, ironically, that gives their economic effort its "positive" quality: human suffering must be reduced by all means.

In order to give substance to the meaning of this suffering as a historical process, I would like to introduce the idea of *value*, a central concept in all of modern economic history. Therefore, we will detour briefly from our historical journey around the point of value. First we will confront it as a problem of theory, and then we will give it a new definition for our purpose. Then, the detour over, we would be back on our original journey better equipped for clarity.

"Value" has been a thorny issue in political economy since Adam Smith. Everyone since then has been trying to come up with a universally valid, scientifically exact, and mathematically simple formula that would be a satisfactory definition of value. Attempts at the solution span the whole history of political economy. Witness "cost of production," "price," "labor value," "labor time," "labor power," "exchange value," "use value," "natural value," "Just Price," "equilibrium price," "relative price," "marginal utility," "market price," "utility," "demand and supply," "desire," "want," "commodity value," "toil and trouble," "auctioning (prix crie)," and so on, which have been offered to define and explain value. These definitions and explanations may have been satisfactory purely as economic concepts.

To be satisfactory for us, value cannot simply be explained by something that is mathematically identical to it. We understand nothing if we define the value of one dollar as equal to what the dollar can buy. By trying to define value by assigning it another mathematical value equivalent to the value, the economist only creates a tautology. Even when the attempt is successful so that something manages to define value precisely, that very precision is what makes the endeavor pointless for us. All the concepts and explanations offered for value tried by everyone—even if they *are* equal to value—define value only as a circular definition. They may define value, but they do not explain anything about value.

Obviously, anyone can see that the value of X must be defined by its equivalent in some other form—for example, as labor, as price, as cost, and so on. Or to put it more simply, what comes out of the muzzle of a gun is equivalent to what goes into its chamber: what is loaded and what is fired are defined by each other for their mutual value. After all such mental acrobatics, however, we still have nothing outside that tautology. For those of us who are not professional economists and who have no patience for academic concept games, such circular mental acrobatics have no real usefulness for understanding. We want something about value that has specific meaning in our real life, not an academic plaything. This requirement leads us to a couple of further unhappy observations on value.

There is something called "marginal utility" as a definition of price popular among economists. Marginal utility says that the value of a good is equal to the consumer's levels of desire for the good and its price is determined at the precise point of the consumer's take-it-or-leave-it attitude toward the product. As such, the concept assumes that the marketplace determines value. To make their work easier, most economists go no further than this in explaining value and price. Whatever people are willing to pay, the concept says, is the precise value of a product. But as we have seen, the marketplace has no rationality or logic in its behavior. There are goods for which a wealthy man would pay any sum, while a poor man would not spend a penny for them. Thus the wealthy man's marginal utility is very different from the poor man's. In fact, the difference is so great that the economist normally leaves the wealthy out of his calculation of market norms. When money is no object, economics becomes irrelevant. "Desire" as the only thing that counts in a money-free society would ruin everything for the economist. The concept of marginal utility could work only if wealthy man and poor man had equal access to money with which to buy the item, thus making their desires identical. This, of course, may make the concept useful, but is only hypothetical because, in that case, we would have no economics and would need no economists. (In a way, the economist's existence also hangs in balance in the land of marginal utility. There would be no use for him where everything is abundantly provided for, such as on a South Pacific island, and where life is so harsh that surviving is everything, such as in the remote corners of Alaska.)

Value is difficult to define yet in another way. The idea of value as a
precise reference point in market behavior assumes some definite "parity"
between demand and supply. The unit of demand and the unit of supply
must be roughly equal in some measurable way. Price then becomes the
Value Index of this parity. When one loaf of bread is demanded and supplied
and its price is one dollar, the assumption is that one loaf of bread demanded,
one loaf of bread supplied, and one dollar are all equal. But this assumption
is valid in an economic era where "things" are demanded and supplied. In
our present Inverted Economy neither demand nor supply, hence nor value,
can be clearly identified. Demand is mostly created by advertisement, supply
is pushed mostly without demand, and their unifying index (price) is consequently made irrelevant. The difficulty can be demonstrated simply by
comparing how the price of bread and the price of a movie videotape are
determined. In bread it is reasonable to assume equality between consumer
satisfaction and the cost of that satisfaction as expressed in the price, but in
videotape this assumption does not operate. (The manufacturer may arbitrarily decide to price it at $99 or $19, depending on nothing but speculation.) Thus our solution must be found somewhere outside traditional
economic thinking.

Let's therefore tackle the problem noneconomically—that is, without the
analytic obsession that muddles our thinking. Article X is said to have
value. But why does it have value? Because it is "valuable." To *what* is it
valuable? The traditional economist would say "to another value equal to
it or to another article of equal value." To whom is it valuable? The economist would say "to the person who owns article X so that he can exchange
article X for article Y, which is equal in value to article X." This way we
still run around the circle, chanting that two equal values equal each other.
For us, the key concept in value is in "valuable." *Why* is it valuable? If we
watch our step here and do not repeat the economist's mistake, we answer
that "because article X *means* something to our life." Then how does that
article X create meaning for our life in society? The answer to this question
is crucial to our definition of value: because it makes the difference in our
life by being there or not being there when we need it. Now we are in a
position to state the definition of value clearly: *A thing is said to have "value"*
if it can cause human suffering by its underpresence or overpresence. This definition
has two obvious advantages over any traditional attempt: first, it avoids
the problem of tautology and rescues the concept of value stranded forever
between two equal values or as a mere after-the-fact abstraction ("people
tend to do what they do because that's what they are observed doing").
Second, and more significantly, our definition gives the concept some "human" substance. As a human concept, it explains what "value" means to
an actual human being in his real social life. This way it becomes a real,
live component of the demand-supply equation in our economic life.

Once we have defined value this way—as a thing's ability to cause human suffering—we can now see that the size of value is *proportional* to the difference between demand and supply in society. In other words, value increases or decreases its size as the difference between demand and supply increases or decreases as a whole. In measuring the society's total size of value, we simply measure the difference between what is demanded and what is supplied. The difference between demand and supply, then, becomes the society's size of value. Depending on what stage of development the society's economic state is in, the size of value in society varies accordingly. Some advanced, affluent societies have a small difference between demand and supply, hence a small size of value and vice versa. A society with a "positive economy"—most societies presently in existence—has its own corresponding size of value depending on its own demand-supply discrepancy. But as we have seen, the size of value in society has direct human meaning in suffering. The size of value always equals the size of human suffering. In a positive economy, it is the size of underpresence in goods and services that is directly responsible for the size of human suffering proportional to the underpresence. Overpresence is also a problem but in a different way, but that issue will be discussed shortly. Here our brief detour is over, and we can get back to our original historic journey toward a perfect economy.

While the society is still struggling to narrow the difference between demand and supply, its human suffering is measured in two ways. Objectively, it is manifest in the mathematical difference between demand and supply—or how much is wanted and how much of that is satisfied—as the objective quantity of human suffering. Subjectively, it is felt in individual hunger, wants, discomfort, discontent, domination-subordination social relations between haves and have-nots, and other similar miseries and injustices. Naturally and imperatively, pressure to narrow the difference and alleviate its corresponding human suffering bears intensely upon the social system. Historically, societies have responded in one of the two ways: some have chosen the "market" system or the "free enterprise" model, best represented by the United States; some others have taken the "socialist" road, most dramatically represented by the Soviet Union until recently. (There has also been the so-called third approach, combining the two.) With a positive economy, that is, demand being larger than supply, the purpose of both economic systems is the same—to equalize supply with demand. In the "positive" phase of development where demand is higher than supply, the aim of any poor society—be it capitalist or socialist—tends to be identical, that is, reducing the human suffering inherent in the demand-supply difference. To do that, the society might adopt one form or the other of the two economic models. It sometimes alternates between the two as it experiments with each.

By logic and human nature, however, it is easy to see that every human ingenuity and every unit of energy and resource are concentrated on overcoming the source of that suffering. And, however slowly, progress is made. Rarely does a society ever continuously go backward in its economic history. Things eventually get better. Hence our name for that stage— positive economy—because all human as well as nonhuman resources are aimed at creating positive results. Given this human factor and technological evolution, the economy improves and the gap between demand and supply narrows. At the same time, as a result of this improvement, value—and its corresponding human suffering—declines in all positive economies. That all poor societies will eventually reach a state of balance between demand and supply is warranted by neither history nor logic. However, it is an assumption—perhaps necessary out of faith and hope more than reason— that is central to human existence.

Either by luck or by dint of hard work, some societies arrive at that point of history where all reasonable demand is met by reasonable supply. What is deemed reasonable has been discussed earlier, but to remind ourselves: demand is defined by needs, supply determined by demand, and no one demanding more than one needs and no one supplying more than is de- manded. This balanced state of affairs also assumes a total absence of *artificial reasons* to demand more than one needs or supplying more than is demanded. Here is where history and utopia intersect, demand and supply are in perfect balance for the first time, and human suffering, dependent on the size of value proportional to the size of demand-supply difference, vanishes as a result. This is the proverbial paradise where one's needs are perfectly met by one's ability to satisfy them. No one has to suffer because of unmet demand. Because value is now zero, human suffering in this happy state of being is also zero. The United States and perhaps few other advanced societies in the West might be said to have reached this point in their economic history. For the American economy, the Point of Inversion in the 1950s, as we discussed in Chapter 8, may be recalled here. Perhaps most important of all, all goods and services at this point of economy become *free, without value, costing nothing,* when demand and supply are in perfect balance. How is this possible?

The air we breathe may be used as an example of zero value where demand equals supply. Air has no value because it cannot be exchanged for anything else of equal value. The reason for its inability to have any *economic* value whatsoever, although "valuable" and "precious" in every way, is simply because it is *independent* of the market mechanism in determining its demand and supply. It is one life-sustaining item over which neither a sovereign power nor a wealthy individual can claim ownership. Its demand and supply cannot increase or decrease by underpresence (where demand is larger than supply) or overpresence (where supply is larger than demand.) Its demand and supply must always remain exactly in balance. When a thing is incapable of artificial manipulation for its demand and supply—typically in the mar- ketplace and through the form of ownership—it is also incapable of acquiring value by being exchanged for other goods and services of equal value. When it is incapable of acquiring value because it cannot change its own level of demand and supply, it is also incapable of causing human suffering. Why? Because it is permanently in balance between demand and supply, being able neither to increase nor decrease artificially in the marketplace or by any means.

Because of this permanent balance, air's value is always zero. No one can make other people suffer with air. As such, it is economically incapable of causing human suffering by its underpresence or overpresence. It is always free, without value, and costing nothing. It is neither demanded through the marketplace nor supplied through the marketplace. No one, hard as he may try, can demand more than he needs, and no one, hard as he may desire, can supply more than is demanded. And no one—a human agent or a market mechanism or a state—can cause human suffering by manipulating its level of demand and supply. In fact, use of air is so perfectly balanced and ideally managed that air demand and air supply can be thought of as the most unequivocal—and perhaps rarest—example of human rationality. Neither greed nor profit nor folly nor irrationality can upset the level of demand and supply with air. We only take what we need and no more, and no one tries to increase supply for profit. Likewise, when a society's economy reaches a state of balance between demand and supply—where no artificial mechanism interferes to cause fluctuations in demand and supply, for profit, power, control, or whatever—all goods and services demanded and supplied in that economy have the precise value of zero. At this point, positive (poor) economy finally comes to an end and a state of "perfect economy" begins. In it, all wants have been satisfied and human suffering from wants—supply being smaller than demand—has disappeared.

When the society reaches the state of economy where demand equals supply, neither the state (as in socialist economy) nor the marketplace (as in capitalist economy) is now necessary to regulate the demand-supply factors, since there is no deficiency between the two anymore. The original, primary aims of all societies and of all human activity in history have now been achieved. The society's basic obligation thus fulfilled, it enters what we might call a posteconomic era of high civilization and lofty humanity. For all human activity hitherto defined in the "economic" equation of demand and supply is no longer relevant. In the new state of balance, all the problems of classical economy have come to an end. The conflict between work and leisure has been dissolved into "intrinsic value" of free choice in occupations determined only by the extent of necessity in society. And the balance between "necessary" goods and "luxury" goods or between utility and comfort or between direct and indirect costs in our productive system has been achieved. The yoke of mankind from time immemorial—the suffering and fear of scarcity, always not having enough to eat, not enough to live in reasonable comfort—has been finally removed from our fate. Shouts of joy and triumph are heard everywhere; congratulations pour in from everyone, friend and foe. The society becomes a focus of envy, admiration, and emulation. And the era of true freedom—freedom for art, science, love, and whatever else was under the fetters of economic tyranny, now freed—begins for all.

But, alas, the celebration is short-lived and paradise gained is soon paradise lost. Why? What happens here? Because of the built-in profit motive in the economic system, the market mechanism continues its manipulation and control of demand and supply in spite of the fact that it is no longer necessary, judged from a purely rational point of economic life. Because of this profit structure, the market society is unable to maintain the perfect balance between demand and supply that it has worked so hard and long to achieve. The market society continues to operate its productive system, which was expanded into enormous production capacity during its "positive" stage. Therefore, *supply now necessarily exceeds demand*. For the first time in history, supply is larger than demand for the whole society and its entire population. People who have everything must now consume more of everything, in spite of the fact that "more die in the United States of too much food than of too little," as Professor John Kenneth Galbraith put it.

As the capacity of supply exceeds the size of demand, every unit of the society's energy and resource multiplied by technological advancement must now be used in production, promotion, and consumption of goods and services that nobody needs and in excess of collective demand. This surplus use of energy and resource cannot produce any "positive" results. It no longer reduces human suffering. No positive result ever comes out of this economic system once the balance of demand-supply passes in favor of supply. From this point on, everything that this surplus economy does is to compound its material waste, economic irrationality, and human misery. Everything demanded and everything supplied beyond the point of balance add waste and irrationality. Hence we would term this economic system where supply is larger than demand a *negative economy* because of its certifiably negative uses of economic resources. While the positive (poor) economy has a positive end in view for its economic progress, our negative economy, itself a new historical phenomenon, can *never* have a positive end in view. Nothing good can ever be made out of waste and irrationality. Only greater and greater irrationality and waste await the negative economic system as it progresses further. Placed in a concrete instance of American society today we might also term this economy *Inverted Economy* because of the supply-demand inversion. What is a "demanded" economy virtually worldwide is a "supplied" economy in the United States, the most advanced form of surplus society. In it, consumption is the whole economic purpose.

Why is it inevitable that the negative-surplus economy cannot produce any positive results with its increasingly larger supply capacity? Isn't "more" and "larger" always better and more desirable?

The answer is no. The explanation for the negative answer lies, once again, in the essentially *finite* capacity of the human body and its sensory system. As always, the human body has its definite amount of requirements for sustenance and comfort. And the requirements do not increase over time, nor over increasing supply. No matter what the level of supply is, the demand of the body remains constant over time and across different cultures. The human body cannot consume more than required by its finite physical self. In the same way, the human senses—seeing, hearing, tasting, and so on—have their finite level of tolerance. They cannot accept more than the maximum level of stimulation that the senses can handle. Like the body, no amount of increasing supply can alter that fact. Any more than that is simple insanity.

Let's try, then, to comprehend our current economic insanity, however. In the West, and especially in the United States, central to the explanation has been the concept of economic "growth" that is equated with increasing happiness. The size of one's paycheck, the power of one's car, the square footage of one's house, among other things, have been assumed to be the yardstick of one's happiness. The bigger, the stronger, and the larger, ultimately the better and the happier. But given the limits of the body and its senses, further growth in size, power, or volume becomes *meaningless*. Food becomes meaningless at the precise point at which the stomach becomes full; the senses cannot take any more than the maximum stimulation they can meaningfully recognize and respond to; money becomes irrelevant beyond living expenses. Economic waste and human irrationality are inevitable when one tries to stuff more food into his stomach or tickle his funny bone when it can no longer accommodate or respond. A society and its population likewise require only so much for their survival and comfort and no more. Beyond a point of optimal economic development, any increase in the supply capacity of that system becomes meaningless, because neither the human body nor the human senses have any use for it.

In this Inverted Economy, obviously, the effort to produce, promote, and consume excessive supply is much more frantic and sinister than the effort in a positive economy to simply produce more. The effort to increase food production in a positive economy is not the same kind as the effort to sell cosmetics or VCRs. The Inverted Economy must now create a phony reality in which phony demand can be manufactured. Advertisement, manipulation, and deception are necessarily its essential mode of operation. The traditional model of demand and supply, or of need and satisfaction, that is the logic of economic behavior no longer applies. The gap between demand and supply in a positive economy is normally the result of insufficient natural resources. There is just not enough to go around for everyone.

But in a negative-inverted-surplus economy, the defeat is artificially created and manipulated. It is a demand-supply gap that is both unnecessary and illusory. We simply overproduce and frantically overstuff ourselves. Why? Because we have always believed that more is better.

The effort to feed someone is very different in human quality from the effort to sell someone something he absolutely has no need for. The former effort is made by a producer, the latter by a salesman. The former effort is clearly defined in physical terms of need, utility, requirements of life; the latter is undefinable and present only in strictly psychological terms of vague urgency and conformity. The former effort produces positive results, however slight; the latter wears one out with aimless consumption. The defects in the positive-poor economy are clearly seen, felt, factual, and observed; the waste and irrationality in the negative-surplus economy, on the other hand, are difficult to see, analyze, or observe, for they exist in the unreality of Substitute Society and its phantom desire for happiness. The former arises from the physical terms of necessity; the latter, from the adman's manipulation, the market man's drive, and the consumer's stupidity.

As supply becomes larger than demand in our negative economy, more significantly, all goods and services produced and consumed in excess of demand *now reacquire their "value" once again*. What this means is obvious. Human suffering exists when demand is larger than supply, which disappears when supply finally catches up with demand in that happy state of balance. But as supply becomes larger than demand in our society, value now reappears. With this reappearance of value in goods and services, human suffering proportional to the value also reappears in the negative-surplus economy. But unlike in the positive-poor economy, this time it is by *overpresence* of things. In multiplying the productive capacity, thanks to technology, the negative economy thus overproduces and overconsumes. Every bit of this new economic activity now contributes to the increase in value and also in human suffering. Value in a poor, negative economy necessarily declines with time and human suffering along with it. But value in an overproductive negative economy *never* declines or reaches a point where waste and irrationality may eventually end.

The demand-supply equality is the end of the journey for a positive economy; it is not a happy journey by all means, but the end result is a happy one. For the negative economy, however, the demand-supply gap widens proportional to its technological capacity for overproduction and widens forever. Supply—the combined effect of technology and profit-making—now becomes infinitely larger than demand. In other words, there is no end to its economic madness in irrationality and waste. It must produce and consume, produce and consume without an end. With each cycle of production and consumption, individuals and their society go through a wretched convulsion in illusion-making and overstuffing. But pressure from the culture of overproduction and overconsumption is relentless, the most relentless pressure the history of mankind has ever experienced. Everyone lives and works just to consume, consume, and consume still more. It is like a locomotive, a primeval force in human nature, that cannot stop or slow down once set in motion with its self-destructive logic. Thus human suffering in the negative economy knows no relief, either now or later. Unlike its poorer counterpart in a positive economy, human suffering in the overstuffed economy only becomes infinitely greater over time. The negative economy's driven capacity for overproduction knows not when to quit. It only multiplies by the factors of technology and profit.

Once the economic system enters into this period of overproduction and overconsumption—creating huge value and huge human suffering along with it—demand and supply would never meet again as equals. As a result, in a negative economy (1) *the gap between demand and supply*, (2) *value as a measure of human suffering*, and (3) *economic waste and human irrationality, all increase proportionally to the economy's overall progress*. In our inverted American society, as things get "better" in the economy, things get only worse in the community. Or to put it in another way, as the economy of the Profit Ethic thrives, the humanity of the Social Ethic suffers. And there is no end in sight. What was once possible and desirable—high civilization and lofty humanity in a posteconomic era—has been crudely destroyed. We are once again gravitated into the era of a demand-supply war.

One final irony in all this is the role of the marketplace, the stalwart of our negative economic system. What was once an asset, as the manager of the then-struggling positive economy, now becomes a liability in the negative economy. In a society of surplus, it is now an idea whose time has passed and whose service is no longer required. It is still there, however. Even though the economic capacity is way past the point where all our needs are more than satisfied, it is still there, demanding our obsession and stupidity. No longer a contributing agent to a positive cause because its basic function has been fulfilled, the marketplace now contributes to increasing human misery and economic chaos with its oversupply. Currently American society has become a hostage to its own dynamic economic past. What "made America great" once is now dragging American society through the swamps of economic senselessness, human suffering, and cultural illusion. Once an asset, the marketplace in America's economic life has become its sinister liability, making our freedom *from* the marketplace most imperative. For it would continue to stuff food down our throats and tickle our funny bones long after we stopped eating and laughing.

In a just and truthful society where demand and supply are in perfect balance, our occupational work is defined by the extent of our demand and the extent of our demand determined by the extent of our necessity. In an Inverted Economy, where supply is larger than demand, however, any "work" we do in order to consume the difference is necessarily "surplus" work. Any amount of labor we must now perform in the Inverted Economy is essentially to consume goods and services we no longer need. Since we can never consume all that is produced for us to consume, our surplus work—expenditure of unnecessary energy—is limited only by the extent of surplus time we possess.

It so transpires that we are "forced" to work to fulfill the requirements of a surplus economy. A surplus economy requires surplus consumption. But surplus consumption requires a surplus income to be earned only through "surplus work." Thus all surplus work is time deprived that could be better spent with one another, in our family, with friends, and in human company. Our surplus work in an Inverted Economy only puts more children in daycare centers than necessary; its necessary mobility makes us move to another city, uprooting our social bond, at the slightest provocation from economic advantages; and it alienates us from one another in general in the senseless race of who can consume more. Translated into economic activity, all surplus work represents the amount of wasted human energy and social resources. We spend much more time at work than necessary or beneficial. Why? For the simple purpose of maintaining an Inverted Economy in which neither social happiness nor human comfort is the issue. Whatever material or physical pleasure our surplus work may bring, it adds nothing to our happiness or comfort. What it demands in human price is simply too great.

What begins as the rational quest for social survival and human comfort thus becomes, in the strange twist of an economic nightmare, a cause of immense suffering and madness. What mankind has always dreamed of—simple satisfaction of basic needs—now turns into an obsession that overpowers our better judgment. In the process of marshaling the most awesome productive force the world has ever seen, we have forgotten our humble and reasonable purpose of life. What should end in a happy state of abundance and enjoyment instead enslaves us to the beast of our own creation.

Let us recapitulate. The Social Ethic assumes that if not manipulated artificially, demand should arise only from natural necessity, not from supply. Left alone, supply is likewise determined by demand and its own ability to supply, which is always equal to the level of demand. In this happy state, we can pursue our individual activity in high art, science, love, and creative and personal uses of leisure. At the precise moment at which all our basic needs are met, the primary obligation of our society ends and our individual life begins. No society is under the obligation to "entertain" its population and "fulfill" their private yearnings. It is for the individual human beings to live their own lives in pursuit of true happiness. Freedom from the wants of basic necessities of life leads to a great release of energy the likes of which only the most privileged in past history have experienced. Now that freedom is for all Americans in the Social Ethic to claim and enjoy and explore.

The problems of American society today with its Inverted Economy—

the decline of the Social Ethic and its consequent destruction of community—are not insurmountable. They are simply problems of bad social practices. We have allowed ourselves to be dominated by the Profit Ethic and its destructive self-interest. There are no inherent moral weaknesses in us or evil instincts we cannot escape. *We* caused them, and now *we* must solve them. Human happiness cannot be added, subtracted, divided, or multiplied by any known economic calculus. It is absolutely, logically, and practically independent of economic considerations. We must transform ourselves from "economic man" to "social man." It is absurd, indeed stupid, to make economics—essentially a bread-and-butter issue of survival and comfort and nothing more—the total preoccupation and commitment of our existence. We have made "economics" irrelevant through progress. Predicting a resolution of the "economic" problem a half-century ago, Lord Keynes declared that "the economic problem is not—if we look into the future—the permanent problem of the human race." And he proved correct much sooner than expected—at least for American society.

The Profit Ethic, as articulated among its economists, has always assumed that (1) there are those who desire things, (2) there are things to be gotten, but (2) being always smaller than (1), therefore, (3) economic life is almost predetermined to be nasty for mankind and only the most beastly can survive and prosper. This is Economics 101, pure and simple. We have inherited this miserable scarcity economic thought from our past and have become enslaved by it. Even in an era of overabundance we cannot manage to escape from that fear of scarcity without an enormous mental struggle. Our economic reality has changed from scarcity to abundance, yet our economic model is still with scarcity. The Profit Ethic's preoccupation with economic "efficiency" was also the product of this scarcity mentality. In the era of scarcity, an efficient distribution of resources was always utmost in everyone's mind. It is still in the minds of our own misguided economic men. But what these men have forgotten is that overproduction is just as painful and evil as, or perhaps more than, underproduction or scarcity. Today the Profit Ethic as we know it has become an uninvited middleman between demand and supply at the marketplace. When the marketplace is no longer necessary because demand and supply meet each other directly in our self-sufficient economy, the need for the Profit Ethic—and economics—should disappear. In our posteconomic era, economic considerations should fade from individual consciousness as well as from social structure. The point now is to be happy with one another in a human community and enjoy our freedom from want.

In the Social Ethic, our society should be one unit of production and consumption, an extended family of sorts, since there is no reason for one to make a profit off another within the same social unit. Trade should exist only *between* different societies, possibly with profits in view, but not among members of the same community. That the Social Ethic is predicated on demand and supply being equal does not mean, of course, that it should be a "static" or "stagnant" system. For demand and supply can improve at the same time to a *higher level* of demand and supply, as long as one does not try to catch up with the other. All employers and employees would become equal *partners* in the true sense of the term; so would demanders and suppliers; so would scientists and humanists, artists and inventors, and presidents and secretaries.

Such is the essence of the Social Ethic possible only in a very different American society from what we now have—possibly in the newer New World of our longings. The realists and idealists among us would argue over what is possible and what is necessary, over self-interests and collective welfare, over concerns for now and those of posterity. In a land of illusion and consumption, even immorality is profitable to too many. When all share in the trough of corruption, change is naturally shunned. They say things are bad and will only get worse, but they are addicted to their present course. It is infinitely more attractive. It is wrong to assume that the road to Hell is necessarily paved with torture and pain. It is also wrong to assume that only because people recognized that their lives are miserable they would be susceptible to suggestions for change.

Whatever one's philosophy on life and living, however, it is our intellectual and human privilege to think about and hope for a better world, often against our more practical and weary judgment. We can do no other. To close this book with a reference to essential human nobility, I will quote Max Weber: "It is the stigma of our human dignity," the eminent German social observer said many years ago, "that the peace of our souls cannot be as great as the peace of one who dreams of such a paradise."

NOTES

1. Lewis H. Lapham, "Democracy in America?" *Harper's*, November 1990, 48.
2. Andrew Hacker, *The End of the American Era* (New York: Atheneum, 1970), especially the chapter titled "Corporate America." Although dated, it is still one of the most accurate and readable accounts of the corporate economy in America.

Bibliography

CHAPTER 1

"ABC Studies Suit to Keep Irish on TV," from wire service reports. Wilmington, NC, *Star-News*, 7 February 1990.

Brunner, Steve. "Wheels of Fortune," on Greg LeMond. *USAir*, March 1990.

Engelberg, Stephen. "Warrant Officer Says Greed Led to Spying." *New York Times*, 19 July 1989.

Farnsworth, Clyde H. "Former U.S. Officials Lobby Japan's Causes." *New York Times*, 17 December 1989.

Fiske, Edward B. "Parents, Students Want Money's Worth for Tuition." *Star-News*, Wilmington, NC, 22 August 1989.

Greenwald, John. "The Wizard Bows Out," on Peter Lynch. *Time*, 9 April 1990.

"Hero to Endorse Apparel," on Joe Montana. Associated Press, 14 February 1990.

Kome, Hunter. "Maybe Greed Is out of Fashion." Wilmington, NC, *Star-News*, 17 December 1990.

"Last-Minute Money Grab, The," on Drexel. *Time*, 5 March 1990.

Lewis, Anthony. "In South Africa, at Long Last, There's Hope," *Washington Post*, 14 February 1990.

Littwin, Mike. "Notre Dame Just Doing Business." *Baltimore Sun*, 8 February 1990.

Nocera, Joseph. "How to Get Rich in the Iraq War." *New York Times*, 28 October 1990.

Ostling, Richard N. "Heresy on the Airwaves." *Time*, 5 March 1990.

———. "Those Mainline Blues," on religion. *Time*, 22 May 1989.

"Rivals Denounce Irish's Move," from wire service reports. Wilmington, NC, *Star-News*, 8 February 1990.

Rosenthal, David. "You Can Still Make a Million Dollars." *Parade*, 26 January 1986.

"Salaries Top $1M at Bankrupt Drexel." *USA Today*, 26 December 1990.

"Sports Woes Begin at Home." Wilmington, NC, *Star-News*, 7 February 1990.
"Teenage Pregnancy Is Rending the Country's Social Fabric." *Time*, 9 December 1985.

CHAPTER 2

"Brandon Tartikoff's Ten Commandments of Network Programming." *Time*, 16 September 1985.
"Now, the Hangover," on Vaclav Havel's speech. *Time*, 15 January 1990.
Will, George. "Society Should Be Allowed to Control Beggars." 6 February 1990.

CHAPTER 3

"Fortune to the Brave and Canny," on Murdoch and TV. *Time*, 19 November 1990.
"Star Wars at the Networks," on TV journalists. *Time*, 3 April 1989.

CHAPTER 4

Bouchier, David. "The Affluent Elderly Too Often Ignore Young People." Atlanta *Constitution*, 21 October 1990.
Broder, David. "Trivialities Distracting Us from Real Problems." 17 June 1990.
Daniel, Clifton. "Not Alone: Groups Finds Emotional Healing through Sharing of Experience." Wilmington, NC, *Star-News*, 23 October 1990.
"Democrats Vow to Catch Up, Win." Associated Press, 17 October 1988.
"Diane Sawyer's 'Terrific.'" Wilmington, NC, *Star-News*, 9 August 1989.
Ditka, Mike. "Ditka: An Autobiography." *Chicago Tribune*, 24 July 1986.
"Faces of the Decade." *Time*, 1 January 1990.
Greve, Frank. "N.C. Guardsman Sues to Avoid Deployment." Knight-Ridder-Tribune News Service, 14 November 1990.
Henry, William A. III. "Psst . . . Did You Hear About," on gossip and celebrities. *Time*, 5 March 1990.
"In the Driver's Seat," on Morgan Freeman. *Time*, 8 January 1990.
"Last Days of Jesus, The" *U.S. News & World Report*, 16 April 1990.
Marriage & Family—a Complete Course, on make-believe marriage. Buffalo Grove, IL: Patio Publications, 1986.
"NPR Morning Edition," on Nintendo among adults. National Public Radio, 26 October 1990.
Quindlen, Anna. "Mr. Bush Needs to Listen to His Consumers." *New York Times*, 27 November 1990.
"Raiders Will Return Home." *Star-News*, Wilmington, NC.
Raspberry, William. "Jackson's Right: Blacks Must Save Themselves." 3 February 1990.
"Return of a Curmudgeon, The," on Andy Rooney. *Time*, 12 March 1990.
"Southern Populism Doesn't Always Exploit Racial Fears, The", Wilmington, NC, *Star-News*, 18 November 1990.

"This Star's Search Nets His Own Fame," on Ed McMahon. *USA Today*, 31 December 1985.

Truly, Pat. "Our Mideast Force Defends Right to Get Goofy." Fort Worth *Star-Telegram*, 3 September 1990.

"U.S. Navy Lies Dead in the Water," on sports metaphor. *Star-News*, 16 November 1989.

Wilbon, Michael. "CBS to Get Breath of Fresh Air," on Brent Musberger. *Washington Post*, 8 April 1990.

Will, George. "Celebrity Cult Hunts Idols, Then Topples Them." 12 July 1990.

———. "Reporting Means More Than a 'Moment,' " column on "60 Minutes." 3 November 1982.

Williams, Lena. "Decisions, Decisions: Freedom of Choice Takes Toll," *New York Times*, 8 May 1990.

Zoglin, Richard. "Star Power," on TV journalists. *Time*, 7 August 1989.

CHAPTER 5

"Craxi Begins to Rebuild Coalition: Reagan's 'Dear Bettino' Letter Boosts Italian's Stock." *Chicago Tribune*, 22 October 1985.

"Moscow's Big Mac Attack." *Time*, 5 February 1990.

"Reagan Happy to Be Part of 'Story of a People.' " Associated Press, 15 January 1989.

Reagan, Ronald. "An American Life: The Memoirs of Ronald Reagan," excerpts in *Time*, 5 November 1990.

CHAPTER 6

Chapman, Stephen. "Sullivan's War on Tobacco Puts Us All in a Yoke." *Chicago Tribune*, 4 March 1990.

Fatsis, Stefan. "Milken's Road to Disgrace Paved with Early Successes." *Fayetteville Courier*, Fayetteville, NC, 22 November 1990.

Flanigan, James. "As Honda Bettered Its Line, Iacocca Lined His Pockets." *Los Angeles Times*, 27 May 1990.

Haney, Daniel Q. "Doctors Who See Profit from X-rays Have Them Taken 4 Times as Often." *Star-News*, Wilmington, NC, 6 December 1990.

———. "Study: Some Doctors Benefit from Extra Care." Associated Press, 12 April 1990.

McCartney, Scott. "S & L Memo Said Weak, Ignorant Good Targets." *Star-News*, Wilmington, NC, 9 September 1990.

Pytte, Alyson. "Besieged Tobacco Still Has Clout in Congress." *Congressional Quarterly*, 27 May 1990.

Shapiro, Walter. "Is Washington in Japan's Pocket?" on Japan lobby. *Time*, 1 October 1990.

Sidey, Hugh. "Say a Prayer for Gorbachev," on Bush's Soviet account comment. *Time*, 7 August 1989.

Tobias, Andrew. "I Was a Teenage Communist." *Time*, 31 July 1989.

"Today's Bright Teens More Conservative than Those Two Decades Ago." Associated Press, 14 October 1990.

Tudor, Martha Anne. "Hospitals, Physicians Adopt Business Practices." *New York Times*, 5 September 1989.

Kadlec, Daniel, "Wall Street Sees Good News in War." *USA Today*, 12 November 1990.

"What Rimes with Citrus?" on citrus freeze. *Time*, 8 January 1990.

CHAPTER 7

Nelson, John. "NBC Stuck with Arizona Protest Bowls." *Observer*, Charlotte, NC, 13 November 1990.

Palosky, Craig S. "Personal Ads Popular, but They Must be Sincere." *Star-News*, Wilmington, NC, 25 November 1990.

CHAPTER 8

Boyd, Brendan. "Bad Plastic," on credit card spending. *Universal Press Syndicate, Observer*, Charlotte, NC, 19 February 1990.

Cour, Jim. "Seattle Fans Send Largent Off in Style," on "getting a real job." *Star-News*, Wilmington, NC, 25 December 1989.

Daniel, Clifton. "Divorce's Financial Changes Can Jolt Unprepared Spouse." Wilmington, NC, *Star-News*, 3 April 1990.

Tobias, Andrew. "Give Greed Another Chance." *Time*, 26 November 1990.

CHAPTER 9

Dahrendorf, Ralf. *Reflections on the Revolution in Europe*. New York: Random House, 1990.

Dowd, Maureen. "Public Responds to Shut Down: 'We'll Remember at the Polls.' " *New York Times*, 7 October 1990.

Grady, Sandy. "Who's Deserving Blame? Ask Pogo Possum." *Philadelphia Daily News*, 11 October 1990.

Green, Charles. "Public Gets Mean about Lean Budget; Reps Seek to Justify It." Knight-Ridder-Tribune News Service, 5 October 1990.

CHAPTER 10

Bonfante, Jordan. "Charm Is Only Half Her Story," on Feinstein. *Time*, 18 June 1990.

Broder, David. "Mudball Politics Still Thriving," on negative political ads. *Washington Post*, 5 November 1990.

"Bush's Media Wizard," on Ailes's role. *Newsweek*, 26 September 1988.

Butterfield, Fox. "Dukakis: TV Threat in Politics." *New York Times*, 22 April 1990.

Fukuyama, Francis. "The End of History?" *National Interest*, Summer 1989.

Oreskes, Michael, "Shallow Politics: American Way Falters As Its Vision Changes World." *New York Times*, 18 March 1990.

Rodrique, George. "U.S. Elections Puzzle Germans." *Dallas Morning News*, 9 November 1990.

Zuckerman, Laurence. "The Made-for-TV Campaign," on Ailes. *Time*, 14 No-
    vember 1988.

CHAPTER 11

Beck, Joan. "A Case Against School Condoms." *Chicago Tribune*, 12 December
    1990.
Broder, David. "Can We Learn like the Germans?" *Washington Post*, 12 December
    1990.
———. "We Lack the Moral Fiber to Shun Big Crooks," on moral bearing. 29
    April 1990.
Friedrich, Otto, and Jeanne McDowell, "Donald Trump: Flashy Symbol of an
    Acquisitive Age." *Time*, 11 January 1989.
Geewax, Marilyn. "Whatever Happened to Service?" *Atlanta Constitution*, 1 De-
    cember 1990.
Gibbs, Nancy. "How America Has Run out of Time," on leisure. *Time*, 24 April
    1989.
Glass, Andre J. "Car Maker Steers in New Terrain," on Poling's view of workers.
    Cox Newspapers, 13 December 1990.
Hornik, Richard. "Communism Confronts Its Children." *Time*, 22 May 1989.
Kilpatrick, James J. "We've the Sleaziest Congress Money Can Buy," on evil of
    money. *Washington Post*, 8 November 1989.
Kleinberg, Howard. "Sucking Turtle Brains Could Lead to Trouble," on degenerate
    society. Cox News Service, 10 May 1990.
Krauthammer, Charles. "The Secret of Our Success." *Time*, 30 January 1989.
Lewis, Flora. "America Needs to Quit Whining," on two Americas. *New York
    Times*, 7 December 1990.
Martin, Guy. "Worst Millionaire News," on Trump. *Parade*, 1 January 1989.
Morrow, Lance. "In the Land of Barry and the Pilots." *Time*, 23 November 1990.
Rawls, John. *A Theory of Justice*. Cambridge, MA: Harvard University Press, 1971.
Shoemaker, Don. "The S & L Disaster: Public Robbed of Billions; Few Seem to
    Care." *Miami Herald*, 11 November 1990.
Webb, James. "Gulf Strategy: We Can't Say What We're Doing," on thin support
    for Bush. Wilmington, NC, *Star-News*, 30 September 1990.
Will, George. "Is America Aging Gracelessly?" on America as sclerotic. *New York
    Times*, 29 October 1990.

CHAPTER 12

Galbraith, John Kenneth. *The Affluent Society*. New York: New American Library,
    1963.

Index

Adatto, Kiku, 219, 235

Advertisement, 101, 139, 217; American vulnerability to, 133–34, 139, 140–41, 142, 143–45; appeals to emotion, 137, 140–41, 149–50; arousal in, 169; and class, 148–49, 150–51; compared to India, 134; Constitution and, 137; decline of power and, 138; effects of, 133–34; facts about, 130; and false freedom, 138; false power through, 150–51; and freedom of choice, 135–37, 138; graphic display, 135; happiness and, 139; as idea, 138–39; interchangeability of, 139–40; irrationality in, 168–70; manners of, 130–33; and manufactured sincerity, 130–31, 135, 144; negative, 131–32; new exploitation, 148–50; and patriotism, 142–44, 145; planned spontaneity in, 135; in politics, 141–42, 215–20, 223; simplicity in, 140; social conditions for, 133–35; socialization and, 146–48; stupidity necessary for, 145; targeting for, 149–50; in United States and Finland compared, 129–30

Affluent Generation, 21, 39

Agassi, André (ad), 135

Ailes, Roger, 218, 219

Aldrin, Buzz, 100

Alger, Horatio, 150

Alienation, 33–34

Alka Seltzer, 144

American culture: advertisement in, 129–51; Age of Television, 111; bestsellers in, 161; comfortable make-believe, 84–85, 92, 103–4; as commercial success, 7; consumer choice, 138, 165–68; contrasts in, 4–5; falsehood in advertised reality, 150–51; fear and anxiety in, 5–6, 137, 226, 240, 254–55; feel-good society, 79–80, 256; first-name informality in, 91–104; freedom of choice in, 79; Good Life in, 176–77; Good Things in, 157, 159, 161; graphics in, 63–65; and marketplace, 107–8; as market society, 28; money worship in, 115, 126; in the 1950s, 175–78; politics and, 211; as pure capitalism, 26; as schedule of events, 65–66; smiling in, 63, 92; sports in, 82–83,

ABOUT THE AUTHOR

JON HUER is Associate Professor in the Department of Sociology at the University of North Carolina at Wilmington, and is the author of a dozen books critical of American society and its many institutions. Among these are *Tenure for Socrates* (Bergin & Garvey, 1991), *The Dead End* (1977), *The Great Art Hoax* (1990), and *Art, Beauty, and Pornography* (1987).